IN MY HUMBLE OPINION

In My Humble Opinion
Musings of a Sports Columnist

Additional copies may be ordered from the publisher for educational, business, promotional or premium use.
For information, contact ALIVE Book Publishing at:
alivebookpublishing.com

Cover photo:
The author (standing, far right) on the day he interviewed Joe Dimaggio (seated, far left) in August 1974.

Book Design By Alex P. Johnson

ISBN 13
978-1-63132-280-8

Library of Congress Control Number: 2026905420
Library of Congress Cataloging-in-Publication Data
is available upon request.

First Edition

Published in the United States of America by ALIVE Book Publishing
an imprint of Advanced Publishing LLC
3200 A Danville Blvd., Suite 204, Alamo, California 94507
alivebookpublishing.com

PRINTED IN THE UNITED STATES OF AMERICA

10 9 8 7 6 5 4 3 2 1

IN MY HUMBLE OPINION

MUSINGS OF A SPORTS COLUMNIST

MATT SIEGER

ABOOKS

Alive Book Publishing

This book is dedicated to my wife,

Leigh,

who has always supported me in

every way, including in my writing.

CONTENTS

Introduction

I cut my teeth on sportswriting at the *Cornell Daily Sun* as a student in the early 1970s. I then completed the master's program in magazine journalism at Syracuse University's Newhouse School of Public Communications.

My first professional sportswriting job was with *The Cortland Standard* in Cortland, New York, where I was mentored by sports editor Jere Dexter.

My life's journey pulled me away from sportswriting, which I detail in my column "Once a Sportswriter " in these pages. However, no matter what career I found myself in, I continued to interview athletes and write freelance articles for magazines.

I bookended my sportswriting career as a sports reporter and columnist for *The Vacaville Reporter* in Vacaville, California. Many of the columns in this volume are from that time.

After retiring, I wrote a book, The *God Squad: The Born-Again San Francisco Giants of 1978*, which you can read excerpts from in a number of the chapters of *In My Humble Opinion*. After publishing *The God Squad,* I still had the writing bug and stumbled on a great platform for anyone who likes to write about sports. Run by retired Michigan State sociology professor Frank Fear, *The Sports Column* is an open-access website that publishes columns on any and all sports. Frank serves as editor and does a wonderful job of formatting the articles, often adding photos and videos.

All columns in this volume without attribution have been published in *The Sports Column.*

PART 1

My Experiences, Race, Ethics, and the Craft of Sportswriting

"Lessons from Little League"

I have photos of me holding a bat when I was three years old. While that doesn't compare with Mickey Mantle's dad putting baseballs in his crib, my dad loved baseball and, at a very young age, so did I.

My first foray into organized baseball in my home town of Hackensack, New Jersey, was in the Pee Wee League for eight- and nine-year-olds. I remember the tryouts in the gymnasium, where the Pee Wee League coaches watched us perform and made their selections. I handled every grounder they hit. I loved fielding.

I moved on to Little League, for ten-, eleven-, and twelve-year olds. At our first practice for our team, sponsored by the local 7-Up factory, I missed the ball swing after swing in batting practice. I thought I was doomed, but Coach Anthony Bassano kept throwing until I started to hit. He retained that faith in me and made me the starting shortstop. I hit a respectable .390 for the season.

Our team boasted an excellent pitching staff, led by Butch Bassano, the coach's son. Having finished first in the National League, we faced the American League champs for the title in a best-of-three series.

We lost the first game. A couple of speedy runners on the opposing team hit routine grounders to me at shortstop but beat my throws to first.

Before our next game, Coach Bassano showed me I was taking a couple of hop steps before releasing the ball. He hit me a bunch of grounders and showed me how to anchor my right foot and release the ball without additional steps.

That paid off in games two and three, when I was able to

throw out every runner who hit a ground ball to me. We won both games to become the champs.

So much of getting an edge in baseball is mental. In my final year of Little League, I noticed one game that when the opposing pitcher threw ball four and it escaped the catcher and rolled to the backstop, the catcher walked lazily to retrieve the ball.

After the game, I asked my dad if, in that situation, it is legal for the batter to keep running to second base. He told me it was.

Hackensack had two Little League fields. Field No. 1 had a long distance from home plate to the backstop. Field No. 2 had very little distance.

The next time we played on Field No. 1, I executed my plan. I took ball four, which was way off the plate and skidded toward the backstop. As I headed toward first, I looked back over my shoulder and saw that the catcher was lollygagging in retrieving the ball. So I went into a full sprint, turned the corner at first base, and sped into second. By the time the catcher noticed, I was standing on second base.

These lessons on how to use my head in baseball came in handy as I advanced to play varsity high school baseball my senior year and Connie Mack baseball the summer after my senior year.

In a high school game against Englewood, a team in our league, I was on second base with less than two out. The batter lofted a soft fly not very far back of first in foul territory. The first baseman pursued it with his back to home plate. I tagged up at second, figuring that his main focus would be on catching the ball. I lit out as soon as he caught it. Perhaps he forgot that it is just as legal to tag up and advance on a foul ball as with a fair ball, but I easily cruised into third base.

In the North Atlantic Regional Connie Mack tournament that summer, I was on second base with no outs. Coach Howard Shaw called on the batter to lay down a sacrifice bunt to move me to third, As he squared to bunt, I started toward third, but not too far, as I wanted to make sure the bunt was down. As the batter lunged at the ball, I took several more steps toward third. But he missed the bunt. There I was in no man's land, closer to second than third, but still ripe for the picking. In that situation, the catcher should have run at me to force me to go one way or the other. Had he done so, I would have been a dead duck. But he made the mistake of throwing all the way from home plate. Since I was closer to second than third, he threw toward second base. But as he uncorked his throw, I lit out to third base and made it easily.

During that tournament, I played mostly third base but also had a few games at shortstop. My lesson from Coach Bassano had stuck, and I had a very quick release on one grounder that just beat their fastest runner to first.

Speaking of picking someone off base, I played second base for my high school team. We had an All-County catcher named Art Sarro. We were playing the first of two games against the team we would eventually defeat for the league championship, Wayne Valley. We were leading 5-2 as they batted in the bottom of the last inning. They had a man on second base with two outs. Art and I had a signal. If I saw the man leading too much off second base, I would gently tap my glove on my left thigh a couple of times. Trailing by three runs, there was no need for the runner to take a big lead, but he did. I flashed the sign to Art, and on the next pitch he rifled a perfect strike to me and we nailed the runner as he tried to dive back into second base, ending the game.

To me, baseball has always been a thinking person's game. That's one of the many reasons I love it.

* * *

"Monterey Little League Memories"

I grew up in Hackensack, New Jersey, a suburb of New York City. I played organized baseball in Hackensack. Beginning at age eight, I played Pee Wee League (ages 8-9), Little League (10-12), Babe Ruth League (13-15), Connie Mack and American Legion ball (16-18), and high school varsity ball.

In 1961 when I was eight, our family began vacationing every summer in the Berkshires in western Massachusetts. My father, who worked in Manhattan, portioned out his vacation days through the summer. He would take Friday off every week, sometimes both Thursday and Friday. While my mother, older sister, and I stayed in the Berkshires all summer, my dad would drive up from New York City, either on Wednesday night or Thursday night, to spend the long weekends with us.

We stayed in a cottage in Monterey, which had a population of 500 the rest of the year but 5,000 in the summer due to vacationers enjoying Garfield and Buel lakes.

Monterey had a Little League team that played against teams from neighboring towns. When my Hackensack Little League season ended, our family left for the Berkshires, and I joined the Monterey team. Even though the town had a huge summer population, I was the only non-native on the team.

The Monterey Little League schedule started and ended later than the Hackensack schedule. So when we arrived in

Monterey each summer, the local team had already played several games, but many more remained.

Monterey did not have a Pee Wee League team as we did in Hackensack for eight and nine year olds. Instead, kids from eight to twelve years of age formed the Monterey team. The talent level was higher in Hackensack, a city of some 50,000 people, than in Monterey. Fortunately, I was skilled enough at eight years old to earn a starting spot on the squad.

My Monterey teammates had some colorful names—"Thumper" Messer, nicknamed after the *Bambi* rabbit, and Lanny Lanew.

Mr. Greene lived in a big house near Monterey's Little League field. An elderly gentleman who was still spry, he was not only the caretaker of the field but the coach of our team. The field was eventually named Greene Field.

Mr. Greene was a great guy, but his baseball knowledge was suspect. I was a good bunter, but Mr. Greene chose the oddest times to have me bunt. On at least two occasions, he had me bunt with the bases loaded. That is not a good idea in Little League baseball because the runners cannot leave the base until the ball reaches the plate. That means the runner on third cannot get a jump, making it easy for the pitcher to field the bunt and throw home. This also eliminates the suicide squeeze play, where the runner on third takes off for home plate as soon as the pitcher releases the ball.

The second reason a bunt with the bases loaded is not a good idea is that it is a force play at home. The catcher does not have to tag the runner coming in from third base. All the catcher has to do is step on home plate for the force out.

So, even at age eight, I thought it odd when Mr. Greene twice gave me the bunt sign with the bases loaded. True, I was not very big and maybe he liked my chances of getting on base from a bunt more than my swinging away. In any case, both times I complied and laid down a bunt and lit out for first base. For some reason, both times the bunt was successful. The runner scored from third and I was safe at first. I have no idea what took place behind me, as my back was to home plate while I was running to first base. Maybe the pitcher bobbled the ball, who knows? In any case, it made Mr. Greene look like a genius.

The other oddity with Mr. Greene was how he instructed us infielders (I was a shortstop) to throw the ball to first base. Have you ever seen a submarine ball? A submarine is a pitch in which the ball is released just above the ground, but not underhanded, with the torso bent at a right angle and shoulders tilted so severely that they rotate around a nearly horizontal axis. Did you ever try to throw to first base that way? I was one of the few who was able to do it in practice. We abandoned any effort to do it in the games.

Mr. Greene made another unorthodox move. Whenever I pitched, Timothy Daggett, the son of the local minister, played shortstop. He was a fine fielder, but he was left-handed. There are no left-handed shortstops in the major leagues for good reason. It is impossible for a left-handed player to make the pivot for a double play when receiving the throw from the second baseman.

Prior to my last two Little League years, Mr. Greene retired from coaching and was replaced by Mr. Amidon, whose son Phil played on the team. Mr. Amidon never called for a bases-loaded bunt or had us throw submarine style to first base. I welcomed the change.

One highlight of my final year in Monterey Little League was being selected to play in the All-Star game. Prior to the game, the league held a few fun contests. One featured a wooden oval in the shape of a catcher's mitt suspended by a metal arm over home plate. Each contestant got three tries from the pitcher's mound to hit the mitt, which would then swing around on the metal arm. I hit the mitt all three tries and won the contest. To top the day off, I hit the only home run of my Little League career, including my years playing in Hackensack. There was no fence, but I hit the ball to deep right-center field and circled the bases before the fielders could throw home.

* * *

"The Summer of Steve"

My mother, who lived to 100, was one of eleven children, raised almost single-handedly by my Grandma Bessie, as her husband was either not around or not much help and they eventually separated.

After World War II, about half of her children moved from Brooklyn to the Los Angeles area and convinced Bessie to come along. The other children remained back east, including my mom. They raised their families on their respective coasts. I grew up in Hackensack, New Jersey, a suburb of New York City, about eight miles from the George Washington Bridge.

So I had a bunch of cousins in California whom I had never met. In the summer of 1963, when I was ten, my mother, sister, and I flew to Los Angeles to visit the West Coast relatives. We were there for six weeks, and my dad joined us about halfway through.

That's when I first met the Bezdekas, my Aunt Phyllis's family—her husband, Tommy, and boys Steve, Ken, and

Jeff. I also met the Tlumaks, my Aunt Florrie's family—her husband, Irv, daughter Judy, and sons Rich and Rob.

I was closest in age to Steve, Rich, and Rob, and we got along great—playing baseball, swimming, wrestling, all that stuff. I also remember having my first taco. The highlight of the trip was Irv and Tommy leading us in their campers on a trip up Highway 1, the Coast Highway, to San Francisco, then across California to Yosemite National Park, where we floated down the Merced River on inflatable rafts and gazed up at El Capitan and Half Dome.

The next summer, 1964, the Tlumaks returned the favor, visiting us.

From 1961, when I was eight years old, through 1968, our family vacationed in Monterey, Massachusetts, for the summer. My father, who worked in Manhattan, portioned out his vacation days through the summer. He would take Friday off every week, sometimes Thursday and Friday. While my mother, my sister and I stayed in the Berkshires all summer, my dad would drive up from New York City, sometimes on Wednesday nights, sometimes on Thursday nights, to spend the long weekends with us.

We stayed in a cottage in Monterey, which had a population of 500 the rest of the year but 5,000 in the summer due to vacationers enjoying Garfield and Buel lakes.

When the Tlumaks arrived in Monterey, we had a great time and were so sad when their camper pulled out to leave us. But to our amazement and joy, about an hour later Rich and Rob popped their heads up, looking at us through the windows of our cottage. Their camper had broken down and they had to stay another day.

The next summer, 1965, the Bezdekas arrived.

There was a Sunday late afternoon tradition in Monterey,

one the Tlumaks had missed out on because they hadn't been with us on a Sunday. At 5 p.m. every summer Sunday, locals and summer residents met at the town's lone Little League field for an impromptu softball game that lasted till dusk. Kids and adults were welcome to play. I don't remember if anyone kept score, as it really didn't matter. We just played and played till the sun went down.

On this particular Sunday, with the Bezdekas in town, we went to the game. Steve was the oldest, a year or two older than me, while Ken and Jeff were still too young to participate. At one point in the game, I was stationed in left field and Steve in right field. A bruiser, an adult named Ray Tryon, came to bat. I instinctively retreated way back in left field, so that I was actually standing in marshland. Ray pounded a long fly ball coming straight my way, but I could see it would be over my head. I retreated as fast as I could, and, as I fell backward into the marsh, the ball plunked hard into my mitt and I held on. I was filthy and wet, but Ray was out.

That same inning, another adult hit a laser shot to right field. It looked for sure like it would go over Steve's head for an easy trot around the bases. But at the last minute, Steve somehow leaped up and made an incredible backhand catch. The cousins had done it.

Years later, when I was a young man, I drove through Monterey one summer, intentionally arriving at the ball field with my baseball glove at 5 p.m., hoping the softball tradition had lasted. But at least that Sunday, no one was there.

As the title of Thomas Wolfe's novel says, you can't go home again. But I will always have my Monterey memories of my cousins, the summers of Steve and Rich and Rob.

***

"My Favorite Ballpark Moments"

Unless you were still in a stroller, you probably remember your first time going to a major league baseball game. I couldn't have been more than five, but that memory is still clear.

My dad took me to the old Yankee Stadium for my first game. I remember walking up the ramp between the stands on the second deck and suddenly seeing this immense pasture of beautiful green grass set against the clear blue sky, cumulus clouds, and the grand upper facade of the third deck (Mickey Mantle once belted a ball off the right-field facade, just missing hitting it out of the stadium, a feat never accomplished in the big leagues, although many claim that Josh Gibson hit one out when playing in the Negro Leagues).

Perhaps because we are more impressionable as children, the baseball games I most fondly remember are those I attended. Here are my favorites.

Yankee Stadium, June 14, 1959, Yankees-Tigers doubleheader

I was only six years old, but I was already used to the Yankees winning almost all the time (they won the American League pennant from 1955 to 1958). So, with my Dad and I comfortably nestled in the second deck alongside one of the many columns that blocked the spectators' views (fortunately not ours that day), I settled in for what I was sure would be another Yankees victory, especially as the Yankees took a 2-0 lead, one of those runs scoring on a solo home run by Bill "Moose" Skowron.

Whitey Ford took that 2-0 shutout into the eighth inning. I was certain nothing could go wrong with the Yankee southpaw ace on the mound. However, the Tigers put a couple of men on base and noted Yankee killer Charlie Maxwell came up. Right on cue, the left-handed-hitting outfielder drilled a ball over the wall in right-center for a three-run homer.

I couldn't believe it and burst into tears. An old man sitting behind us touched my shoulder to comfort me. The Tigers held on to win 3-2. Detroit went on to win the second game 8-2. But I had been inoculated into the possibility of the Yankees losing a game and took the second loss pretty well.

Polo Grounds, May 30, 1962, Mets-Dodgers doubleheader

To fully appreciate what the Mets meant to New York fans in their inaugural season of 1962 (when they went 40-120), one has to remember that the fans hadn't had National League baseball since the Dodgers and Giants moved west after the 1957 season. The Mets' caps were Dodger blue with the orange "NY" monogram of the Giants.

On Memorial Day 1962, the Dodgers made their first visit to New York since playing in Ebbets Field to face the Mets in a doubleheader. A remarkable 55,704 attended, the largest crowd in the major leagues that season.

Sandy Koufax pitched the opener for the Dodgers against Jay Hook, and it was like Jesse James squaring off against Wilbur from Mr. Ed. Hook was given the hook after two innings, trailing 5-0, and the relievers didn't fare much better. Amazingly, the Mets put together thirteen hits and six runs against Koufax, but it didn't matter much, as they lost 13-6. Koufax struck out ten. I remember my father wincing when the great lefthander struck out Mets catcher Harry Chiti the third time in a row.

For the second game, my dad maneuvered us from well back in the stands on the third-base side to a couple of seats in the second deck right above home plate. The Mets lost again, 6-5, but we had a great view of an incredible play.

With Maury Wills on second and Jim Gilliam on first with no out for the Dodgers, Willie Davis hit a liner that appeared destined to be a single to left field. But Mets shortstop Elio Chacon leaped skyward, pulled down the line drive in the web of his glove, and flipped to second base to nail Wills. Second baseman Charlie Neal fired to Gil Hodges at first, who appeared to stretch toward second too far and pull off the base. But the ball arrived before Gilliam, and the umpire gave the thumbs-up for the triple play. My dad said the ump had to overlook Hodges' questionable footwork with 55,000-plus fans in the stands rooting for the Mets.

Polo Grounds, June 7, 1963, Mets-Cardinals

With a lineup that included legendary players Jimmy Piersall and Duke Snider, the Mets faced off against the Red Birds on a Friday night.

I remember the Cards' great third baseman, Ken Boyer, launching a massive solo home run to left field that carried clear out of the park to give St. Louis a 2-0 lead in the sixth. Starter Ron Taylor carried that lead into the bottom of the ninth, but the Mets managed to get runners on second (Ron Hunt) and third ("Hot Rod" Kanehl) with one out. As Snider, the now-beloved Met who used to play in Ebbets

Field for the Dodgers, strode to the plate, it looked like a redo of "Casey at the Bat."

The Duke did what Casey could not, jumping on a pitch from left-handed reliever Diomedes Olivo and smacking it into the upper deck in right field for a three-run walk-off homer and a 3-2 Mets victory. But when the ball struck the bat, all the fans in front of me—much taller than I—stood up, and I never saw Duke's shot land in the seats.

This column first appeared in The Vacaville Reporter *on August 29, 2020.*

* * *

"Hackensack Baseball Memories"

I grew up in Hackensack, New Jersey, a suburb of New York City. I played organized baseball in Hackensack from age eight until I graduated high school in 1971. I played Pee Wee League (ages 8-9), Little League (10-12), Babe Ruth League (13-15), Connie Mack and American Legion ball (16-18), and high school varsity ball.

When you are playing Little League baseball, you don't imagine that the kids you are playing with will grow into teenagers with whom you will share more baseball experiences. But that's exactly what happened.

I was a pitcher and shortstop in Little League. I had developed into a pretty good pitcher by my final year. My record was 7-2 for 7-Up, sponsored by the local soda factory. But there were two players that I could never seem to get out—Rich Toscano of the Optimists and Mitch Harley of the Vitamins. Both were left-handed batters. I tried to pitch Rich outside, but he had the annoying habit of reaching across the plate with his bat and plunking a hit over the shortstop's head into left field. Mitch, on the other hand, hit for power, so I was just glad if I could keep his hits from going over the fence.

The Vitamins were the strongest team in the league. One game I was pitching in the last inning, holding onto a one-run lead. With two outs, Mitch singled and Kenny MacDonald, another good hitter, stroked a double to put men on second and third. We were playing on Field No. 2 in Foschini Park, which had a short distance between home plate and the backstop. But I knew if a pitch got by our catcher, Bruce Chase, Mitch would try to score. Sure enough, a pitch scooted by Bruce (could have been a wild pitch or passed ball, I don't remember). I ran toward home as Bruce turned to retrieve the ball. I yelled for him to toss it to me. Here came Mitch, barreling down on me. Just as I received the ball from Bruce, Mitch ran me over and knocked me down. But I held onto the ball. He was out and we had beaten the Vitamins.

Mitch, in addition to later becoming my high school baseball teammate, became a bruising running back for the high school football team. So knocking people over was in his athletic DNA.

In Babe Ruth League, ages 13-15, Mitch and I were again on different teams. Mitch had blazing speed. I was playing shortstop and Mitch was on second base. The pitcher uncorked a wild pitch and Mitch lit out for third base. I went over to back up third base in case the catcher's throw got past the third baseman. Sure enough, it rolled past him. As I went to retrieve the ball, I saw Mitch look back at me. Surely he wouldn't try to run home? But there he went, and, even though I had a pretty good arm, he outran my throw home and scored.

Another great hitter in Little League was Artie Sarro, a catcher who played for the Elks. Artie was also my neighbor. I lived on Essex Street, and Artie lived on Thompson Street, one block over. We used to play stickball in his backyard. When Artie got hold of one in stickball, the ball traveled high and far—really far. He was the premier power hitter in our National League in Little League.

Fast forward to our 1971 Hackensack High School baseball team. Mitch, Rich, Artie, and I are all now senior teammates. In an important early season league game, we trailed Garfield High by a run on our home field in our last at bat. Simon Parker got a hit, bringing Mitch to the plate. Mitch, as I had seen him do so often in Babe Ruth League, blasted a shot way over the right fielder's head. It rolled all the way to our clubhouse, by which time Mitch had easily circled the bases for a game-winning home run.

The title came down to the last league game against our rival, Wayne Valley. Wayne had a record of 14-3, while we were 15-2. If we lost, we would have to settle for a tie for the crown.

Wayne had a very fast leadoff hitter. When he reached base, we all knew he would try to steal second. I was the second baseman, and Artie was the catcher. The runner lit out for second as I ran over to cover the bag. Artie unleashed a perfect throw, right to my glove inches above the ground, and I applied the tag. Out!

In the second inning, with the score 0-0, Artie, who batted sixth, hit a monster drive over the left fielder's head for a home run and we led 1-0. I batted next. I jumped on a low fastball and drilled it into left-center field, where it rolled for another round tripper. Back-to-back home runs. We went on to win 4-1 to claim the title.

That summer, Rich, Artie, and I played for the Hackensack Connie Mack League team. We won our league title, state title, and the North Atlantic Regional tournament, qualifying us to travel to Albuquerque, New Mexico, for the Connie Mack World Series.

In our first game, we faced the host team, Farmington, New Mexico. By the luck of the draw, we were the home team, so we batted last. Trailing 7-2 going into the last inning, we rallied. I had one of the hits, and we tied the game at 7-7. Up came Rich. Just as he had all those years before against me in Little League, he reached across the plate for an outside pitch and poked it into left field to score the winning run.

Although we lost the next two games in the double-elimination tournament, it was a great experience. I was happy to share it with my Little League opponents who had now become my teammates.

* * *

"Listen to Your Coach"

Teenagers generally think they know best, which explains why they are often at odds with their parents. This generally applies to their view of coaches in sports—at least, it did for me.

As a high school baseball player with Hackensack High in northern New Jersey, my coach, Dave Seddon wanted to overhaul my batting stance completely. Looking back, I don't know why I fought him so hard, considering my previous batting stance had not done any wonders for me. I was in the lineup for my defense at shortstop on my freshman team and my sophomore and junior years on junior varsity. I hit in the low .200s as a JV player.

Between my junior and senior years in American Legion ball, Seddon advised me to aim to hit .250 on varsity the following year. To achieve that, he suggested I alter my stance. Until then, I had used a thick-handled bat, choked up on it, and held the bat vertically while I crouched with my feet together and took a long stride toward the ball. It wasn't a pretty stance or very effective, but pigs grow accustomed to their pigsty and don't want to be cleaned up.

In practice, Seddon broadened my stance so that my feet were wide apart, and I took a very short stride. He had me hold the bat back, parallel to my body. You will get the idea if you watch YouTube videos of Joe DiMaggio's stance. (I may have stood like DiMaggio, but I'm not saying I hit like him. The longest hitting streak I had my senior year was four games.) I also switched to a thin-handled bat, a Vada Pinson model.

After a couple of unsuccessful at-bats in an American Legion game, I approached the plate for at-bat No. 3. Seddon, coaching at third, told me to assume the new stance. I shook my head vigorously, but he insisted. I faced a flame thrower, Rex Peters, who had overpowered me in my first two plate appearances. As I waited in my new stance, he reared back and fired. I swung, missed, and looked down the third-base line pleadingly at my coach. He wouldn't relent. I stepped back into the box in my new stance. Peters threw another laser, and again, I swung and missed. I looked down at Seddon again, but he wasn't changing the game plan. I stepped in again, and Peters threw another heater. To my great surprise, I connected solidly this time and smacked a hard line drive into right-center for a single.

From that day on, I was sold. Being on the thin side, neither terribly strong nor fast, I spent that fall and winter working out. I consulted our track coach on how to gain speed and did what he said. I asked a P.E. teacher how best to utilize our new weight room to my advantage, and I went into school early three times a week to do as he suggested. I swung a bat with a heavy doughnut 100 times a night in my bedroom.

When spring came around, I was amazed when, in an early-season game, I slammed a curveball over the left fielder's head for a double. I hadn't hit a ball over an outfielder's head since Little League. I did it again in a league game and then again in a scrimmage against the Lafayette College (Pennsylvania) junior varsity college team.

The culmination of my new stance and hard work came in the final league game of the season. We were 15-2 and hosting Wayne Valley, the second-place team with a record of 14-3. We had to win the game to win the title outright. In the second inning, our All-County catcher, Art Sarro, hit a tremendous home run over the left fielder's head that rolled a mile (we didn't have fences) for a home run. I batted after Sarro in the seventh slot. I picked out a knee-high fastball and drove it between the left and center fielders. It also rolled a long way as I circled the bases for a home run (my first since Little League) to give us a 2-0 lead.

We went on to win the game 4-1 and clinch the league title with a 16-2 mark. I hit .294 on the year and was named the All-League second baseman (I shifted there from shortstop my senior year).

That summer of 1971, what was essentially our high school team played in the Connie Mack League and went on to play in the Connie Mack World Series in Albuquerque, New Mexico. Coach Seddon accompanied us as an assistant coach. I had not hit well during the Connie Mack regular season. While in New Mexico, Seddon noticed that I had reverted in some ways to my old stance and had me make the necessary corrections. Immediately in batting practice, I started hitting the ball with authority again. That carried over into the World Series. We were eliminated after three games in the double-elimination tournament featuring the best eight teams in the country, but I went 5-for-10 at the plate.

It's hard to see this when you are young, but high school coaches are in that position because (a) they probably played the sport; (b) they have been teaching the sport for years and have helped countless players before you; (c) they are not in it for the money (coaches are laughing at that one) and (d) they want you to improve and genuinely have your best interests at heart.

So when you return to the field or the court, whenever that may be . . . ***listen up!***

This column first appeared in The Vacaville Reporter *on April 7, 2020, when local high school sports were shut down because of the COVID-19 pandemic.*

* * *

"A Tribute to My Coach"

I grew up in Hackensack, a northern New Jersey suburb of New York City.

My dad loved baseball and I caught the bug early. My first organized baseball experience was in the local Pee Wee League for eight- and nine-year-olds. In my second season, we were coached by Howard Shaw Sr., whose son Mickey was eight years old and in his first year on the team.

I was a pitcher and shortstop. I wasn't a bad hitter, but excelled at defense. I loved playing shortstop.

When I advanced to Little League for ten-, eleven-, and twelve-year-olds, Mickey joined my team my second year and Howard again became my coach. I was still a pitcher and shortstop and hit fairly well but was better known for my defense. I remember overhearing an opposing coach saying, "That kid gets everything."

I also remember during practice Coach Shaw hitting me ground ball after ground ball when I was getting some work in at third base. He kept hitting them harder and harder and I kept fielding them. Finally he whizzed one that got by me, and he yelled with a laugh, "That one moved you!"

I progressed to play junior high and high school baseball, as well as American Legion and Connie Mack baseball in the summers. In the latter league I reunited with Coach Shaw. Mickey was on the team and his dad coached the squad. I was still the shortstop.

In high school, I didn't make the varsity until my senior year. Mickey made it as a junior, so he and I were teammates once again. Mickey played third base and I was at short. Our coach was Dave Seddon, one of our high school history teachers, and a great baseball man.

I have always been high strung, and I was nervous assuming the role of the starting varsity shortstop. Early in the season, my nerves resulted in a couple of costly errors. Sensing my discomfort, Coach Seddon made a bold move. He moved our junior second baseman, Tommy D'Arminio, a tremendous hitter who had been on the varsity since his freshman year, to shortstop, and me to second base.

I had a stronger arm than Tommy, but he was extremely steady as a fielder. And playing second base took the pressure off me, so I performed well there. Tommy was named first team All-County shortstop that year, and I was selected as the first team All-League second baseman. Our team won our league and finished with an overall record of 26-6.

Tommy, Mickey, and I all played on Howard Shaw's Connie Mack team the summer after my senior year. The team was pretty much our varsity squad. Coach Shaw put me at third so another fine second baseman and solid hitter, Michael Gnerre, could play second base. Mickey played first base and Tommy was at short.

We were a very solid infield, and after winning our league, our team went on to compete in the North Atlantic Regionals.

In the first game of the Regionals, Tommy pulled a muscle. The injury limited his range, so without hesitation, Coach Shaw put me at shortstop for the next game and Tommy at third.

I don't know if Coach Shaw knew about my early struggles at shortstop my senior year, but he had seen me play that position since I was nine years old. Whether it was the confidence he showed in me, the beautiful manicured field in Ridgewood, New Jersey, for the Regionals, or the great weather, for the next three games, which we won, I played the best shortstop of my life.

I felt totally at peace out there. On a soft ground ball that rolled past the pitcher to his right by the fastest man on the opposing team, I charged the ball and knew that I had to get rid of it in a huge hurry. I still don't know how I unloaded it so fast, but I got him out by a whisker, keeping a big threat off the basepaths.

Later in the tournament, a runner on second, with nobody on first and less than two outs, committed the cardinal sin of trying to get to third base on a ground ball in front of him. I fielded it cleanly, Tommy wisely retreated to the third base bag, and we threw him out, ending another threat.

Coach Seddon attended all those games and I'm sure he was pleased to see me back to my better self at shortstop.

By the fifth and final game of the tournament (we won them all in the double elimination setup), Tommy was well enough to return to shortstop and I went back to third base. That win earned us a trip to the Connie Mack World Series in Albuquerque, New Mexico that summer.

That was a thrill for us, especially as we won the first game in the bottom of the last inning. We trailed 7-2 and came back with six runs after we had two outs. I had one of the hits in the rally. We lost the next two games in the double-elimination tourney, but our second loss was a 5-4 defeat at the hands of the eventual National Champion from Dallas, so we acquitted ourselves well.

But the thing I remember most from that summer is the trust that Howard Shaw placed in me, a trust born of his coaching me since I was a Pee Wee Leaguer.

Trust builds confidence, and it sure worked for me.

* * *

"A Simple Twist of Fate"

Good memories linger in your heart and mind even in old age. Every time I read or hear the name "Jim Bouton," I am drawn back to the summer of 1971 after my graduation from high school.

I played baseball for Hackensack High School in northern New Jersey. I finally made it to the varsity my senior year through great advice from my coach Dave Seddon and much hard work.

I played second base and was selected as the All-League second basemen. We played in the Northern New Jersey Interscholastic League (NNJIL) and won the championship by defeating Wayne Valley High on the final day of the season. We finished with a league record of 16-2, while Wayne Valley fell to 14-4. Our overall record was 26-6.

We kept much of that team together in the summer of 1971 as our Connie Mack League team. We won the North Atlantic Regional tournament and then traveled to Albuquerque, New Mexico, to play in the Connie Mack World Series agains the other seven regional winners. We won our first game but were eliminated via two consecutive losses in the double-elimination tournament.

That summer I also played in the Metropolitan Baseball League, a semi-pro organization in northern New Jersey. I use the word "played" loosely. The team, coached by former major league catcher John Orsino, largely consisted of the Fairleigh Dickinson University team that he coached. So most of the starters were from that college team, and they pretty much played every inning.

I understood that arrangement when I was asked to join the team, but I thought it would be a good experience for me to mix with more accomplished players in the league.

One of these was Jim Bouton, known for his controversial 1970 tell-all book, *Ball Four* and as a fireball pitcher for the New York Yankees, posting two outstanding seasons in 1963 and 1964. He pitched in the World Series both seasons, including two wins against the Cardinals in the 1964 Fall Classic. He went 21-7 in 1963 with a 2.53 ERA.

An arm injury in 1965 derailed his signature fastball, so he turned to a knuckleball until his retirement midway through the 1970 season. Bouton grew up in Ridgewood,

New Jersey, near my hometown of Hackensack. After retiring and writing his book, he became a local celebrity as a sports anchor for New York City station WABC-TV.

He also joined the Ridgewood team in the Met League. Bouton never lost his competitive fire, plowing his way through the minor leagues in 1975 until he was called up in September 1978 to pitch for the Atlanta Braves, for whom he went 1-3 with a 4.97 ERA in five starts in his major league swan song.

One evening that summer of 1971 we were playing Ridgewood on their beautifully manicured field, one I had played on in my high school and Connie Mack leagues. As game time approached, Rick Murray, our starting second basemen, an All-County selection in high school and a starter for Orsino at Fairleigh Dickinson, had not shown up.

So Orsino penciled me in the starting lineup to play second base. And guess who was pitching for Ridgewood that day? That's right—Jim Bouton.

Here I need to commend Coach Orsino. When Murray, who had experienced car trouble, finally showed up around mid-game, Orsino left me in the lineup for the entire game. Murray was the better ballplayer, but on principle Orsino left me in, not necessarily punishing Murray for being tardy, but sending a message to the team that players need to be on time.

The first time I faced Bouton, he absolutely froze me with two off-speed pitches that may have been knuckleballs, but acted like big breaking curveballs, both for strikes. So he threw it again. This time I managed to top the ball, sending a perfectly place swinging bunt down the third base line.

I was not the fastest guy in the world. I ran as hard as I could, but Bouton got to the ball and his throw to first beat me by an eyelash. The ump made the right call—out! All I could think about was that I almost got a hit off Jim Bouton.

The next time up, early in the count Bouton threw a fastball. The funny thing was that as he threw, his cap fell off, which was his trademark when he used to uncork his heater for the Yankees. At the same time he let the pitch go, he groaned because he knew he had left the pitch up in the strike zone.

I took advantage and lined the ball back up the middle over his now bare head. As the ball continued its flight over second base, I was just beseeching it to drop, drop, drop before it could reach the center fielder. The ball obliged and there I was, standing on first base, with a hit against Jim Bouton.

The next time up I grounded one of his knuckle curves to the shortstop, who booted it, and I reached first base again. But on neither occasion did I score. Bouton beat us that day, I think 2-1. I only had one play in the field, a popup that I handled.

When I got home, my parents, who were on a business/vacation trip in Europe, phoned. My dad, who had seen almost all my games since Pee Wee League, was thrilled when I described my hit against Bouton.

Bouton passed away at age 80 in 2019. Most will remember him for *Ball Four*. But I will remember the day Rick Murray didn't show up.

***

"Hackensack Basketball Memories"

Besides being the most name-dropped city in New Jersey, Hackensack is where I grew up.

You may have heard its name in the first Superman movie (it was the target of Lex Luthor's second missile), in Billy Joel's "Movin' Out," and in Arthur Miller's play, *Death of a Salesman*. But to us who grew up in this suburb of New York City, eight miles from the George Washington Bridge, it was our ethnically homogenous hometown.

I played organized baseball in Hackensack from age eight on, but I didn't touch a basketball until sixth grade. I did not play organized basketball until Hackensack Junior High, where I made the eighth grade team.

It was a blessing and a curse competing with classmates for a spot on our basketball teams. Hackensack has a great history of basketball, and our school at that time (1968-1971 were my high school years) had a student body of about 2,200. So there were a lot of good basketball players.

I was the starting point guard for our eighth grade team, but as the years progressed, I never made it past junior varsity and didn't play regularly there. I was too small (not short, but skinny) and too slow to protect the basketball well from pesky defenders, a necessity for a point guard.

But I still have some good basketball memories.

Our eighth grade team was playing an excellent team, St. Mary's, on our home court. The game was close throughout. In the closing seconds of the first half, I had the ball a good 25 feet from the basket, but nobody was open. With time about to expire, I heaved up a shot, which would have been good for three points today (no three-pointers back then) and swished it through.

That would be important because in the closing seconds of the game, we were down by one point with just a few seconds left. We were inbounding the ball under our own basket. We usually ran a play where one of our players would start at the top of the key and curl to the basket to receive the inbound pass for a possible layup. But our coach realized the other team would be packing the paint, so he had Gary Myles, an outstanding athlete who would go on to star for our varsity, curl further out, about twelve feet from the basket, to the baseline. He received the inbound pass and nailed a jump shot to win the game as time expired. I realized then how important my basket at the end of the first half had been.

One thing I learned to do was shoot free throws. We always shot twenty-five free throws at the end of practice, and I remember once making twenty-three.

That helped me in a game against Westwood, another talented team. The game was close throughout. I scored fifteen points, seven of them on the nine free throws I attempted, and we won the nail-biter 39-37. Yes, I still remember the score.

My free throws helped our junior varsity team in another way. Mike Fratello, who went on to coach the Atlanta Hawks, Cleveland Cavaliers, and Memphis Grizzlies in the NBA, is a Hackensack alum who helped coach our team at that time. After every practice, we ran a drill known as "suicides," where players set up on the baseline and then sprint to the following lines, returning to the baseline after each touch: nearest free throw line, half-way line, furthest free throw line, opposite baseline. We would run as many suicides as the coach deemed fit.

After one practice, Coach Fratello issued a challenge. He would shoot five free throws. We needed to select a player to also shoot five free throws. If that player sank more free throws than the coach, we would not have to run suicides that day. The team selected me. Coach Fratello made four out of five free throws. I sank all five. No suicides.

We had a sophomore team as well as a junior varsity team, and I was the starting point guard on the sophomore squad. One game we played Englewood, a predominantly Black high school. Hackensack also had a large Black student population. My dad attended the game, and, afterwards, he said, "Did you realize you were the only white guy on the court?" I hadn't even noticed, which is a tribute to how my parents raised me. My mom and dad were color blind and accepting of everyone. But my dad couldn't help but notice that day. I am glad I grew up among students of many different ethnicities in Hackensack.

As I said, there were not too many more happy basketball memories for me, as the competition seemed to grow bigger and faster and I didn't.

But I did have one more memorable basketball moment at Hackensack High. My senior year I formed an intramural team. We played at 7 a.m., before school started. It was a challenge to get my guys to show up that early. There were six teams in the league. The top four would make the playoffs. We lost our first two games but won the next three to qualify for the playoffs. We won our first-round game, then in the championship game faced the team that had beaten us badly the first game of the season.

Fortunately, we had five guys show up—a junior named Lou and seniors Danny Peragine, Bob Sedlack, Isaiah Keeling, and myself. We won 24-10. Danny started us off with a bomb of a jump shot. I put my basketball knowledge to use, drawing a charge to negate a layup and running two fast breaks where, as I had been taught, I stopped at the foul line, looked for an open cutter, and, seeing none, canned both jump shots. I was especially pleased that our varsity coach, Jim Kay, was in attendance.

The next time you see Hackensack in popular culture, think of us.

***

"A Tribute to Coach Jim Kay"

The other day I was surprised to receive a Facebook message from the wife of the son of my high school's varsity basketball coach.

Jim Kay coached when I was a student-athlete at Hackensack High School in northern New Jersey. I graduated in 1971. Tragically, Coach Kay, who coached the varsity team for eleven years, died of a heart attack in 1974 at age forty-four.

Kay's teams had a winning percentage above .700 during his tenure, and in 1966–67 compiled a 22-0 won-lost record during the regular season. That team lost by one point to Dickinson of Jersey City in a state tournament game.

Twice Kay was named county coach-of-the-year by the Bergen Coaches Association, first in 1966–67 and again in 1970–71.

His daughter-in-law, Debra, explained that her husband was very young when Coach Kay passed away, so he doesn't have many memories of him. She found a Sports Column article online in which I mentioned Coach Kay. She asked if I would share my memories of Coach Kay with her and her husband.

Here's what I wrote:

Debra,

I never got to play on the varsity for Coach Kay. However, I did have some positive interaction with him.

I was painfully shy in high school (except when I was on the baseball field or basketball court), also nervous and high-strung. One day during a junior varsity practice, Coach Kay was watching and called me over. He had a slip of paper and showed me what was written on it. The problem was I was so nervous I glazed over and just pretended to read it. Coach Kay then said something like, "Pretty good, huh?" And I just agreed. To this day I wish I had read it because I'm dying to know what was on it. I'm sure that he was trying to share a bit of wisdom with me.

One day Coach Kay asked me to practice with the varsity to utilize me in a defensive scheme. He wanted his point guard to experience the type of extreme ball pressure he would be facing in the next game. So he put me on the court with five of the varsity guys on defense and had me and one of those guys double team the point guard. At one point we trapped him along the sideline, and the point guard, who had a temper, shoved me with his forearm. Coach Kay firmly but mildly corrected him, telling him that's the kind of pressure he would be facing next game.

On another occasion, our junior varsity team was practicing with the varsity and afterwards a few of us were working on our shooting. I had a basket to myself, and Coach Kay happened to be standing close to my basket looking on. Conscious of his presence, I concentrated extra hard on my shooting and made something like seven jump shots in a row. "Don't you ever miss?" asked Coach Kay with a smile.

After my junior year, when I didn't start on the junior varsity, it became obvious to me I would never play for the varsity. Even if I made the team, I would be relegated (not unfairly) to the bench. So I decided not to try out for the team my senior year, and instead to spend those winter months working out to improve in baseball, which was my real love. I thought I should tell Coach Kay, as he had been a mentor to me in the basketball program, even indirectly, as our freshman and junior varsity teams ran the same offensive and defensive schemes as the varsity.

Coach Kay was also one of our physical education teachers. So I went into the P.E. office one day and told him my plan.

All winter I came into school early and lifted weights and ran around the track. Every night at home I put a heavy doughnut on my baseball bat and swung it 100 times. When baseball season came around my senior year, I made the varsity and became the first-team All-League second baseman. All my hard work had paid off.

One day I was in the locker room after P.E. class and Coach Kay stopped to ask how I was hitting. The day before I had gone three-for-three in a victory over our arch rival, Wayne Valley, and told him so. He was pleased and said, "Can't do much better than that!"

The last game of the league season we faced Wayne Valley for the second time. They had a record of 14-3, while we were 15-2. We had to win to claim the title outright. Coach Kay was in the bleachers to watch the game. In the second inning, with no score as yet, our catcher Art Sarro hit a tremendous home run to left field to give us a 1-0 lead. I followed Art in the order, and I also smashed a home run, my first and only one that season. We went on to win 4-1 and claim the league championship. I was so pleased that Coach Kay got to see that my baseball plan had paid off.

In my Sports Column article you read how I was equally pleased when he saw my team win the intramural basketball championship, as I was implementing the basics I learned in his basketball program.

Coach Kay produced highly disciplined basketball teams. Some fans wanted to see a run-and-gun offense, but that often leads to turnovers, and Coach Kay valued every possession. His 1-2-2 zone defense was also very effective. His demeanor and basketball knowledge reminded me of UCLA Coach John Wooden.

I was in college in 1974 when my parents told me Coach Kay had passed away. I wrote a letter of condolence to his wife, and she wrote a very nice note back to me. I don't remember what I said, but I'm sure it would have conveyed the same appreciation I hope you sense in this email.
Matt

* * *

"Memories from an Aging Softball Player"

Like many baseball players who never played beyond high school, I gravitated towards slow-pitch softball.

My first team was Owego Street IGA (a supermarket chain) in Cortland, New York, when I was twenty-three years old. I was an infielder in high school, so I loved that I got to play shortstop. I have always enjoyed defense more than offense, although I became a pretty decent slow-pitch hitter.

In my first year on the team, my manager selected me and a teammate to represent IGA in the All-Star game. I was surrounded by older players, most of whom had been in the league a long time and were seasoned slow-pitch guys.

In my first at-bat, I lined a pitch down the left-field line that just kept on going on the fenceless field as I easily circled the bases for a home run. My next time up, I laced a long fly between the left and center fielders that went for a triple. In my final at bat, I drilled a single between short and third. I played shortstop and my IGA teammate played second, and we turned a 6-4-3 double play. I was named the MVP of the All-Star game.

Fast forward fifteen years when I was living in South San Francisco, California. I played third base for my brother-in-law's slow-pitch team in the city's league. The most memorable game was against a team called the Raiders, which had the personality of the Oakland Raiders football team. They were a bunch of pirates—swearing, unsmiling, shouting at the umps and everyone else. They oozed evil.

If you know slow-pitch softball, you understand that it is usually a high-scoring affair. Hitting the high-arcing pitch takes practice, but it's a lot easier than batting in fast-pitch softball. Most batters get the hang of it and place their hits where the fielders aren't (remember Wee Willie Keeler who "hit 'em where they ain't"?). So generally a lot of runs are scored.

But this game turned out to be a low-scoring affair. In fact, we defeated the Raiders 2-0. They couldn't believe it. The play I remember best is when I was stationed at third base and a Raider hit a vicious line drive to my right, so fast I barely saw it. But I instinctively reached across my body and backhanded it. I can still hear the whoosh of the ball and the sound of it as it stuck in my web for the out.

Let's move forward twenty-plus years when I was sixty years old. Still living in South San Francisco, I played third base for our church's team, which was in a league in the neighboring town of Brisbane. It was not a church league (sometimes church leagues conjure the image of not-very-good softball, though I have found that is not always the case). In any case, it was a pretty competitive league. My wife and I had been on vacation in England, so I had missed the last few league games. But our team progressed in the playoffs, and I got back just in time to play in the championship game.

At a crucial moment in the game when we were staging a rally, there were two outs and a man on third base. I hit a groundball in the hole at shortstop. I ran as fast as I could, knowing that if I could reach first base safely, the run would count. I crossed the base and half a second later heard the ball plunk into the first baseman's mitt. "Safe," the umpire correctly called. The run scored and we went on to win the game and the championship.

I later asked my teammates, "What happened? Did the shortstop bobble the ball?" They said no, he fielded it cleanly, and I just beat it out. I am not very fast. It was my hustle out of the batter's box and all the way down the line that had beaten the throw.

Now let's move ahead another ten years, when I turned seventy. Now living in Martinez, California, our church fielded a team to play in the local church league. This league belied the stereotype of church league slow-pitch softball. These teams were very competitive and very good. We were not so great, but we had a lot of fun. In my first year on the team, I was playing first base with a runner on first. The batter bounced a ground ball far to my right. I knew if I could cut it off instead of letting it reach the second baseman I could throw out the runner on a force play at second base. I caught up to the ball and backhanded it, but my lunge caused me to start falling to the ground. As I fell, I transferred the ball to my right hand and managed to toss it on a bounce to the shortstop covering second base as I crashed to the ground. Out at second! My teammates, not accustomed to seeing seventy-year-olds diving on the ground, gave me a huge ovation.

I played one more year. We were better the second year and managed to make the playoffs and win one game before being eliminated. I was playing first base in one of those games. The batter hit a blistering one-hopper right at me. I had learned when playing third base that you just need to keep the ball in front of you, even if you don't make a clean catch. So I got down on one knee and the ball caromed off my wrist, a few feet in front of me. I picked it up and stepped on first for the out. Our manager commended me in the dugout.

I hung up my spikes after that season. It's challenging playing against players who are the age I was when I first started. But I still have my memories.

***

"Race, Sports, and Childhood Memories"

I grew up in Hackensack, New Jersey, a suburb of New York City eight miles from the George Washington Bridge.

Hackensack had a diverse population—many Italian-Americans, African Americans, and Latinos. And a small Jewish contingent, of which I was a part.

My parents, both Jewish, were color blind and imparted that attitude to me at an early age. When I was five years old and my sister eight, my mom and dad took us to Washington Square Park in Greenwich Village in Manhattan. My dad frequently drove us into New York City, as he and my mom were born in Brooklyn, and my dad worked in Manhattan. He liked to show us the city.

On this occasion, the four of us engaged in an impromptu baseball session. My mom was the catcher, my dad pitched, and my sister and I took turns batting, with the one not batting playing in the field. We were using a rubber ball which went pretty far if you hit it squarely. We were soon approached by an African-American boy about my age who asked if he could play with us. He joined right in and was invaluable because when we hit the ball out on the street, he was great at dodging cars and retrieving the ball, one time scaling a little gate and going down steps which led to a basement apartment to get the ball. We had so much fun playing together.

I also remember my mom and dad taking us to visit Al and Rae Davis, an African-American couple, in their brownstone home in Brooklyn for several Christmas gatherings. My sister Jamie remembers them better than I. She says, "There were others there too, the Davis's friends and family. I remember how warm and welcoming they were to us. And all the good food!" That made an impression on me and my sister, that my parents were completely comfortable having friends of a different race.

Growing up in Hackensack, I attended Fanny Hillers elementary school, grades kindergarten through sixth. All the students were white. But in sixth grade, the school system decided to deliberately integrate and we imported two African-American boys from Beech Street elementary school, Billy and George. They were both fun to have around, and that was my introduction to Black classmates.

A couple of years before that, I had begun to play Little League baseball. Our team was sponsored by the local 7-Up factory. I had a couple of African-American teammates, including a boy named Jeffrey Johnikin, who lived in what we would now call the projects, housing for lower income families. It was a very long walk from his home to Foschini Park, where we played baseball. So every game my mom and dad would pick him up in our car and drive us to the park and back to his home after the game. That helped form a bond between Jeffrey and me.

When I entered Hackensack Junior High in seventh grade, the populations of all the elementary schools came together. In gym class and when I played baseball and basketball in eighth grade, I mixed with many Black classmates.

That continued during my high school years playing those two sports. We had a sophomore and junior varsity basketball team, and I was the starting point guard on the sophomore squad. One game we played was at Englewood, a predominantly Black high school. My dad attended the game, and, afterwards, he said, "Did you realize you were the only white guy on the court?" I hadn't even noticed, which is a tribute to how my parents raised me. My mom and dad were accepting of everyone. But my dad couldn't help but notice that day. I am glad I grew up among students of many ethnicities in Hackensack.

I know it's a cliché for a white person to say, "Some of my best friends are Black," but one of mine was—Isaiah Keeling, who played on my championship intramural basketball team my senior year. Ike passed away in 2022. Both of us were shy, but he had a lovely spirit and was someone I could talk to, even after high school.

When I went off to Cornell University, I met many students from upstate New York who came from lily-white towns. I have noticed that people who grow up in towns like that often bring their negative stereotypes of Black people or other races with them. I am thankful for my parents and for Hackensack for giving me the opportunity to mix with people of other ethnicities, to see that we are all just people, regardless of our background or the color of our skin.

This has helped me throughout life, working and interacting with people of diverse ethnicities, especially here in the San Francisco Bay Area, a great melting pot. As a journalist, it has also helped me to be accepting of everyone I have interviewed or interacted with.

Sports are a great way to break down racial barriers. As a now-retired sportswriter who covered high school sports, it has been wonderful to see the acceptance by athletes of teammates of all ethnicities and the camaraderie they have developed.

Martin Luther King, Jr. said, "I have a dream that my four little children will one day live in a nation where they will not be judged by the color of their skin but by the content of their character . . . [where] little Black boys and Black girls will be able to join hands with little white boys and white girls as sisters and brothers."

Perhaps there still is hope.

* * *

"Remembering the Syracuse 8"

In 1970, nine members of the Syracuse football team, erroneously remembered as the "Syracuse 8," took a stand for racial equality. When their demands were denied, they boycotted their team's season. They sacrificed their athletic careers, and it took the university over three decades to formally apologize.

Despite what happened, the sacrifices of **Gregory Allen, Richard Bulls, John Godbolt, Dana Harrell, John Lobon,**

Clarence "Bucky" McGill, A. Alif Muhammad, Duane Walker, and **Ron Womack**—all working-class kids from inner cities—led to fundamental changes in the school's football program.

–There was a lack of playing time, especially against other schools that weren't integrated.

–They were told they couldn't date white women.

–They were not allowed to take advanced courses while on the team, while white athletes allegedly had no such policy.

–They asked that the program hire a Black assistant coach.

The players first met at Syracuse in the late 1960s, after the assassinations of Martin Luther King Jr., Malcolm X, and Robert Kennedy. Syracuse was a nationally prominent football program—national champion in 1959—with the proud legacy of Jim Brown, one of the greatest football players of all time, and Ernie Davis, who, in 1961, became the first African American to win the Heisman Trophy.

When Allen first arrived at Syracuse, the coach who had recruited him picked him up at the airport. Allen told WBUR radio about his ride to the university.

Gregory Allen: "We get in the car, and we begin, you know, the small talk. You know, 'Greg, Gee, I'm glad you're here. We want you to have a good time while you're at Syracuse. We want you to get a good education. We want you to grow. We want you to have a great career as a football player. But the one thing we're gonna ask you to do is not date any white girls while you're here.' It was a little bit of a shock for me because I knew that I had traveled north of the Mason-Dixon Line, not below it."

Later, Allen was told he couldn't be a biology major

because he wouldn't have time to participate in labs, a policy that didn't apply to white players. He also said the team doctor was hesitant to touch Black bodies. "You know, there were two sets of latex gloves. And anything that could be avoided was avoided," he said.

Harrell told WBUR that Syracuse and other northern schools followed unofficial rules about how many Black players could be on the field simultaneously, even at home games. "You could have three outstanding halfbacks, but you wouldn't play them all together because you didn't want the 'big money boosters'—that's what I call them—the big money boosters to accuse the program of going Black," he said.

Allen attended a meeting where students and university leaders discussed starting a Black studies program at Syracuse. A few days later, he got a call to meet with head football coach Ben Schwartzwalder. "So I walked into the coach's office, and I sat down, and he peered at me over his glasses," Allen said, "and he looked at me, and he said, 'What's this I hear about you and this Black crap?'"

Allen started to explain his position, but he said the coach wasn't paying much attention. "So he looked me in the eye and said, 'Well then, you have a decision to make. You can't be Black and be a football player.' Of course, I was a little taken aback. I said, 'Well, coach, you know, I'm going to be Black all my life. I'm only going to be a football player for a short time, but I don't see how one would interfere with the other.'"

The players had been asking for a Black assistant coach for a year without results. Former SU great Floyd Little, then of the Denver Broncos, was brought to Syracuse for two days of practice in April 1970, but players soon learned that this was a common occurrence. "The misrepresentation of Mr. Little as the Black coach," the players wrote in a statement, "was a breach of promise made to us. Thus, we initiated a boycott of spring practice."

They boycotted in May 1970. All nine were suspended from the team. Some of their white teammates threatened to boycott if the Black players were allowed back. The nine went home for the summer, not knowing what would come of their protest.

In July, SU Chancellor John Corbally ordered Schwartzwalder to hire a Black assistant. However, Corbally also sent a statement to the suspended athletes that he required them to sign before they could return to the team. The players thought the document was demeaning and rejected reinstatement. Only Allen and Lobon would ever play for SU again.

However, SU created a committee to investigate its athletic department. After a ten-week study, the committee concluded in December that "racism in the Syracuse University Athletic Department is real, chronic, largely unintentional, and sustained and complicated unwittingly by many modes of behavior common in American athletics and longstanding at Syracuse University." The committee went on to say that the "Athletic department showed an unwarranted insensitivity to attempts by Black players to question [offensive] treatment" and criticized the "long-standing authoritarian role of Head Coach Schwartzwalder."

The nine celebrated the decision. Eight went on to graduate from SU, four earned master's degrees, and Harrell went to law school.

They received further vindication in 2006 when they were invited back to SU to receive the Chancellor's Medal—

the university's highest honor—and their letterman jackets, which were handed out during halftime of a home game against Louisville.

Let's hope it doesn't take another three decades for the demands of today's Black athletes for racial equality in our nation to become a reality.

This column first appeared in The Vacaville Reporter *on August 27, 2020.*

* * *

"Remembering Tony King and Other Good People in Sports"

The ugly virus of hate is something our country has yet to eradicate. So, it's always good to hear positive examples of people stepping up to the plate in sports to counter racism.

In 1934, Tony King was the captain of his American Legion Post 21 baseball team from Springfield, Massachusetts, when the team traveled to Gastonia, North Carolina, to play in the Eastern Sectionals of the Legion World Series. Officials told his team that their African-American friend and teammate, Ernest "Bunny" Taliaferro, could not play. King told the officials that he and his teammates would unanimously back Taliaferro. That didn't move the officials, so instead of playing the next day, the team got on the train and returned to Springfield, where they received a hero's welcome.

The story is being retold now because King, who was 102, died of COVID-19 on June 22, 2020. King's niece, Ann Haskell, told WSOC in Charlotte, North Carolina, that he never mentioned what he did back in 1934. When asked why King never talked about it, she responded, "He said 'cause it was just the right thing to do.'"

The story didn't come to light until 1994 when Springfield constructed a monument to honor King's team. Ten years ago, Gastonia reconciled for forcing the Springfield team to leave. The city's American Legion squad traveled to Springfield for a game, and King threw out the first pitch.

Two books written by Richard Andersen and a documentary film produced by Rich McGrath tell the team's story. The documentary is archived in the National Baseball Hall of Fame in Cooperstown, New York.

Kareem Abdul-Jabbar wrote a book in 2017 titled *Coach Wooden and Me,* chronicling his lifelong relationship with the legendary UCLA basketball coach. In the book, Abdul-Jabbar discusses times when he and Wooden encountered racism during the years Abdul-Jabbar played for him in college. Wooden remained Abdul-Jabbar's teacher and emotional guide until the former coach's death at 99 in 2010.

Abdul-Jabbar enrolled at UCLA during intense racial strife in the United States. Malcolm X had just been assassinated, the Watts riots in Southern California erupted, and police had attacked and beaten civil rights marchers in Selma, Alabama. Abdul-Jabbar was often the subject of racial epithets from crowds while at UCLA and writes of several incidents in which he and Wooden faced racism. On at least a couple of occasions, Wooden was there when autograph seekers and others who approached Abdul-Jabbar used a racial epithet to his face.

Abdul-Jabbar's book quotes an interview with Wooden in which the coach questioned his philosophy of the goodness of his fellow men. "I had no idea how tough it was for him at times," Wooden said. "I learned more from Kareem about man's inhumanity to man than I ever learned anywhere else. I had never imagined that people could feel or talk like that." Abdul-Jabbar was greatly affected when he saw that statement. "I felt a deep sadness after reading that," he writes, "knowing my presence had caused him to doubt his fundamental beliefs."

Abdul-Jabbar decided not to play on the 1968 Olympic basketball team because of racial inequality in America. He received much backlash for that decision, and one woman criticized him in a letter to Wooden. It was not until after Wooden's death that Abdul-Jabbar saw a copy of the letter Wooden had written in response defending his player's position. The coach had never mentioned the letter.

Wooden told Abdul-Jabbar about his first coaching job at what is now Indiana State University. The team was invited to the NAIA national tournament but told Wooden that the team's one African American player, Clarence Walker, was not welcome. Wooden rejected the invitation. The NAIA changed its policy the following year and allowed Walker to play. He became the first African American to play in a postseason college basketball tournament. Wooden also said the team went elsewhere when restaurants refused to serve Walker.

"I couldn't have been more surprised," Abdul-Jabbar wrote. "Coach had been an early civil rights pioneer, risking his career, and he'd never told me about it. Any other coach would have used that to gain my loyalty and respect. What made Coach's stance all the more admirable, I found out later, was that Clarence Walker wasn't even a starter."

If you have seen the movie *42*, you are familiar with how Jackie Robinson's white teammates, Pee Wee Reese and Eddie Stanky, stood up for him during Robinson's inaugural year in the big leagues, when he faced an unbelievable amount of racist venom from players and fans alike, including some from his teammates.

Tony King, Wooden, Reese, and Stanky are just a few examples of what should be the norm in how we treat our fellow man. **Let there be many more as we move forward.** *This column first appeared in* The Vacaville Reporter *on July 2, 2020.*

***

"How the Negro Leagues Gained Major League Status"

In December 2020, MLB Commissioner Rob Manfred bestowed Major League status upon seven professional Negro Leagues that operated between 1920 and 1948. The decision means that the approximately 3,400 players of the Negro Leagues during that period are officially considered Major Leaguers, with their stats and records becoming a part of Major League history.

NOTE: This column first appeared in *The Vacaville Reporter* on September 15, 2020, several months before Manfred's ruling.

In August 2020, Major League Baseball celebrated the centennial of the founding of the Negro National League, the first of the seven segregation-era circuits formed during the 1920s or 1930s that have collectively come to be known as the "Negro Leagues." While a wonderful gesture, it also highlights one way that the Negro Leagues are still segregated and snubbed.

Due to a prejudiced decision of a committee that met

more than fifty years ago, the Negro Leagues are still excluded from the official list of major leagues, which includes not only the National and American Leagues but also the American Association (1882-1891), Union Association (1884), Players' League (1890), and Federal League (1914-1915).

So, according to Major League Baseball's current records and classifications, the players major leaguers are honoring this year were not big leaguers themselves. The good news is that MLB is considering elevating the Negro Leagues to the Big League level.

In 1968, Baseball Commissioner William Eckart convened MLB's Special Baseball Records Committee as part of an arrangement with publisher Macmillan to produce *The Baseball Encyclopedia.* The task of the SBRC, an all-white, five-person body that consisted of American and National Leagues officials, the commissioner's office, the Baseball Hall of Fame, and the Baseball Writers' Association of America, was to determine which leagues were considered major.

But the committee never even considered the Negro Leagues. David Neft, who oversaw the assembly of the *Encyclopedia,* told *The Ringer,* "The one thing that I am absolutely certain about is that there never was any SBRC discussion about treating the Negro Leagues as major leagues."

According to author John Holway, in 1971 Joe Reichler of the commissioner's office, one of the SBRC members, told Satchel Paige, the first player inducted into the Hall of Fame as a Negro Leaguer, to "sit down" when Paige started talking to the press about the many other Negro Leaguers who deserved induction. That made Paige so angry that he never returned to Cooperstown.

John Thorn, the official historian for Major League Baseball, told *The Ringer* that the league has never considered the Negro League's candidacy in any official capacity until now. He added, "If Negro Leaguers' statistics were to be integrated into the MLB historical record, one might anticipate an objection that most players never competed against their MLB contemporaries. But that was not their doing."

Author Todd Peterson noted that every one of the sixteen MLB teams in operation between 1901 and 1960 played a Black club at some point in its history, and the Black players more than held their own. From 1900 through 1948, Black teams went 315-282-20 against MLB teams. In comparison, from 1900 to 1950, MLB teams went 1690-677 against minor league teams.

Sabermetric guru Bill James, when asked by *The Ringer* whether he supports the Negro Leagues' case for inclusion: "Oh, absolutely! My argument has always been that it is impossible for a league to produce that many players of that quality in that period unless the quality of play in that league was not only equal to the white leagues but probably superior to it. You can't reach that level of excellence while playing against minor-league competition. So designate it as major league."

In terms of accuracy of statistics, Gary Gillette, co-editor of *The ESPN Baseball Encyclopedia,* told *The Ringer* that the Negro League stats "are as good or better than some of the nineteenth-century data which has gotten the official imprimatur of Major League Baseball." Thorn asked, " . . . if we can accept as official Ross Barnes's .429 in 1876 (70-game schedule), why not Oscar Charleston's .433 over 77 games in 1921, or Josh Gibson's .466 over 69 games in 1943?"

That argument is strengthened by this year's pandemic-shortened sixty-game season. "If there ever were a season more erratic than 2020, I'd like to see it," Gillette said. "There's no moral justification for excluding the Negro Leagues, and the last rational arguments you could even advance have been destroyed."

As Dan McLaughlin wrote in the *National Review*, "'Majoring' the Negro Leagues would be a further step—following the enshrinement of Negro Leaguers in the Hall of Fame—to remedy a true historic injustice and increase the recognition of players who were long denied their proper due."

Dan McLaughlin: "It remains somewhat awkward to reclassify men as major leaguers when such a large part of their life story and struggle was precisely their exclusion from the majors. Still, doing historical justice sometimes requires acting imperfectly and unevenly. As far back as Paige's induction in Cooperstown in 1971, baseball has fumbled its way toward giving proper due to men who would and could have been major-league stars if not for the color of their skin. It's appropriate to make that recognition official: they were big leaguers."

* * *

"Breaking the Stigma of Mental Illness in Sports"

Sarah Fielding, writing in *Talkspace:* "The normalization of mental illness won't happen overnight, but major platforms—like the NFL—can help push progress forward. The sooner the stigma around mental illness is broken down, the better—for professional athletes and all of us."

Several years ago, Skip Bayless, perhaps the most hated media personality in sports, made remarks about Dallas

Cowboys quarterback Dak Prescott that most people considered over-the-top insensitive—even for Bayless. In an interview with Graham Bensinger, Prescott revealed that he had sought help in the offseason for anxiety and depression brought on by the death of his older brother, Jace, and the COVID-19 pandemic.

Dak Prescott to Graham Bensinger: "When you have thoughts you've never had, I think that's more than anything a chance to realize and recognize them, to be vulnerable about them. Being open about it and not holding those feelings in was one of the better things for me."

Bayless responded: "I don't have sympathy for him going public with, 'I got depressed. I suffered depression early in COVID to the point where I couldn't even go work out,'" Bayless said. "Look, he's the quarterback of 'America's Team.' If you publicly reveal any weakness, it can affect your team's ability to believe in you in the toughest spots, and it could encourage others on the other side to come after you."

Prescott, who shouldn't have had to defend himself, responded to Bayless' remarks, telling reporters, "Before I can lead, I got to make sure my mind's in the right place to do that and lead people to where they want to be. I think it's important to be vulnerable, genuine, and transparent. I think that goes a long way when you're a leader; your voice is heard by so many, and you can inspire."

Even Bayless' network, FOX Sports, chastised him, saying, "We disagree with Skip Bayless' opinion on *Undisputed* this morning. We have addressed the significance of this matter with Skip and how his insensitive comments were received by people internally at FOX Sports and our audience."

Some NFL players jumped to Prescott's defense, including then Green Bay Packers quarterback Aaron Rodgers, who told reporters, "I think it's great. I saw what Dak said, and I applauded him. I think it's phenomenal that he is speaking out because that's true courage and strength. It's not a weakness at all."

Immediately after Dallas defeated Atlanta, Falcons tight end Hayden Hurst caught up with Prescott on the field and commended him for his remarks. The exchange was captured on the Falcons' mic'd-up video from the game. "I've got a lot of respect for what you did," Hurst told him. "Came out and talked about—me and my mom have a foundation about suicide prevention. Respect the hell outta you for talking about it, man."

What do academics who study athletes and mental health have to say about the issue? UNLV professor Brad Donohue says that "football players are less likely to pursue mental health programs than athletes in other sports, and one of the greatest reasons for this is perceived stigma."

Former NFL wide receiver Brandon Marshall told USA Today, "If you would have asked me eight years ago what mental health means to me, I would have said mental toughness. Football players are taught never to show weakness or give an opponent an edge. To open up when something hurts, in our culture, is deviant. But when you think about it, connecting with those emotions is the real strength."

That said, consider Hershel Walker's situation. The Heisman Trophy winner and NFL star running back was diagnosed with Dissociative Identity Disorder (DID), also known as multiple personality disorder. Walker told Jim Thompson of the *Athens* (Georgia) *Banner-Herald* that he was particularly surprised by his NFL friends, some of whom he'd helped through their crises, who didn't want to have anything to do with him after he started talking about his illness. "DID is not *Sybil* or *Three Faces of Eve,*" Walker told ESPN then. "DID is just an illness that people are dealing with."

Legendary Pittsburgh Steelers quarterback Terry Bradshaw, who won four Super Bowls, has been open about his Attention Deficit Disorder (ADD) and his struggles with depression. "I thought maybe I could help people with awareness, help men get the strength and courage," Bradshaw told the *Chicago Tribune*. "I have run into some colleagues who have made fun of me. I've had people try to make light of it. Depression is not something you make light of. It's serious."

In an interview with psychiatrist Alan Axelson, Bradshaw said, "I just didn't want anybody to know all of the things about me that I didn't want you to know. I didn't want to be your hero; suddenly, your hero has flaws. That had something to do with it. I didn't want to tell anybody the bad things about me."

In a study on NFL players and mental health published in the *Journal of Clinical Sports Psychology,* one player said, "The reason it's so lonely is we put those walls up . . . and nobody can know that I'm feeling concerned about my performance, that I'm insecure about this or that because football, in a sense, is ultimate meritocracy and such a manly thing that you just you always feel like you gotta be on, you know?"

Kudos to Prescott, Walker, Bradshaw, and others who are breaking down the stigma of mental illness in sports.

This column first appeared in The Vacaville Reporter *on September 26, 2020.*

* * *

"A Sea Change in College Baseball Recruiting"

Etzio is a senior at an excellent baseball academy. An outstanding defensive catcher, he can also rake.

During his sophomore year in high school, Etzio entered into a verbal agreement to play baseball for a New England university. For the next two years, Etzio spoke to no other colleges nor would coaches from other colleges approach him because of the agreement.

Then, in fall 2024, the NCAA settled landmark class action lawsuits totaling $2.8 billion. The lawsuits were initiated by college athletes who claimed they were denied opportunities to earn income from endorsements and media appearances, alleging violations of antitrust laws.

One ripple effect of the settlement was that in July 2024 the NCAA, in anticipation of the settlement, reduced roster sizes for baseball from forty to thirty-four. The immediate impact on Etzio—the university's coach phoned him to tell him he had revoked his scholarship.

Etzio and his dad, Carl, went into a mad scramble to obtain another college baseball scholarship. The problem was compounded by the fact that catchers, shortstops, and pitchers are the first targets of college baseball coaches. As a result many of the scholarships for catchers were already awarded.

"We crammed two years worth of recruiting into two weeks," said Carl. "We sent 115 emails to head coaches and one text. Etzio got a dozen replies ranging from, 'We are no longer recruiting in your class given the NCAA roster limits,' to 'We'll come watch you,' to 'Come to our camp.' We went to two camps after he spoke with the coaches to make sure it wasn't a money grab. The one text he sent was to a college coach who responded by saying 'Let's have a chat.'

"That chat happened on a Friday and it was to invite Etzio to tour the school and meet in person that Monday. At the meeting the coach told Etzio, 'I know how you are and I've seen you play. Here's your scholarship offer.' Etzio accepted."

Not all these stories have a happy ending. In fact, 96 percent of high school athletes never play in college.

Many college baseball coaches use fall ball to pare down their rosters. Etzio's university could have as many as forty-one athletes competing for the thirty-four slots in the baseball roster. That includes eight seniors who were seemingly finished with their college careers but have an extra year of eligibility under the class action settlement. And that's before transfers and eleven preferred walk-ons.

The fifth year of eligibility issue is a thorny one. In a lawsuit against the NCAA, a judge granted Vanderbilt quarterback Diego Pavia a fifth year of eligibility. Pavia played one year at a junior college, which the NCAA considered a year of eligibility, but the courts overruled the NCAA.

The settlement allows colleges to offer baseball scholarships to all thirty-four players on their roster. Previously, Division I schools could distribute 11.7 scholarships across a baseball roster of thirty-two players. But not all colleges will be able to afford scholarships for every player. Instead, colleges might look for athletes who may not need the help because they have lucrative name, image, or likeness (NIL) deals which are a key component of the settlement.

Are there any remedies for this sea change in college baseball recruiting?

Etzio's dad Carl agrees that reducing roster sizes, enlarged during COVID, is the right move, though he feels the timing of the decision—July, so late in the recruiting window—was awful. But he believes the transfer portal problem has to be addressed.

"The court's decision to give the junior college kids an extra year is fascinating," he says. "You've just committed money to a set of incoming freshman and now you have some kids currently on a scholarship who may stay. Etzio's university has eight of those junior college transfers who may get to play another season."

As a result, some athletes will not make the thirty-four-man squad. The coach might not keep all eight of the transfers, or not renew the scholarship of a player who didn't perform well, or cut an incoming freshman while still giving him the scholarship money. The problem could be solved by reverting to the maximum of four years of time spread out over five years rather than allowing a full five years of service. That may entail an uphill battle through the courts, however.

Most D1 scholarships are renewable on an annual basis. This brings much uncertainty to student-athletes who may not be able to afford to continue at the college without the scholarship. The problem could be solved by awarding four-year scholarships, though colleges will probably balk at the idea.

But they shouldn't, given how much money they rake in from their student-athletes. Pre-COVID, in 2019, of the $15.8 billion in revenues from athletics at Division I schools, only $2.9 billion went to athletes as athletic scholarships and one percent was spent on medical treatment and insurance. Even with the NIL agreement, about 80 percent of the money comes from donor collectives and the other 20 percent from business endorsements. So the universities are not paying.

Etzio has a binding one-year contract that cannot be rescinded unless he is ineligible to play, which includes injury. According to Carl, the two best players on the team are catchers who are seniors. One will be moving on, while the other gets an extra year because he played one year at a junior college. In any case, if Etzio continues to perform as he has, he could be the future backstop for the team.

But renewal of his scholarship each year is not guaranteed.

"It's a total guessing game," says his dad. "Especially because you don't know what kids will be disgruntled at their current school and decide to enter the transfer portal and want to come to Etzio's school. So a good coach is keeping my scholarship money in their pocket for those kids."

* * *

"Another Gambling Scandal Hits Major League Baseball"

Gambling has once again reared its ugly head in Major League Baseball.

Cleveland Guardians pitcher Luis Ortiz has been placed on "non-disciplinary paid leave" as MLB launches a probe relating to gambling. According to ESPN, at issue are two pitches and the unusual gambling activity tied to those pitches, bets placed on whether the pitches would be balls or hit-by-pitches, which were flagged by a betting-integrity firm and referred to sportsbook operators.

The first instance came in the second inning of a June 15, 2025, game against the Seattle Mariners. Ortiz started Randy Arozarena, the first batter of the inning, with an 87 mph slider far outside the zone.

The second instance came in the third inning of a June 27, 2025, game against the St. Louis Cardinals. Ortiz spiked a first-pitch slider way wide of the strike zone to Pedro Páges, the first batter of the inning.

If those pitches were intentional and related to betting, Ortiz experienced some seriously bad karma. He walked Arozarena and the Mariners ended up scoring five runs that inning. Páges hit a home run two pitches later and the Cards scored three times that inning.

No one in MLB can claim ignorance. The rules from the MLB handbook are posted in every clubhouse in both English and Spanish.

Rule 21d(2) in the MLB handbook states: "Any player, umpire or club or league official or employee who shall bet any sum whatsoever upon any baseball game in connection with which the bettor has a duty to perform, shall be declared permanently ineligible." Rule 21d(3) states: "Any player, umpire or club or league official or employee who places bets with illegal book makers or agents for illegal book makers, shall be subject to such penalty as the Commissioner deems appropriate in light of the facts and circumstances of the conduct."

A year ago, MLB punished five players for gambling. The league banned San Diego Padres infielder Tucupita Marcano for life for betting on his own team, even though Marcano did not play in any of the games on which he placed bets. The league also suspended four other players for one year for betting on baseball.

MLB fired umpire Pat Hoberg earlier this year after it was determined that he shared sports betting accounts with a friend who bet on baseball games.

Of course, any mention of betting on baseball brings up the issue of Pete Rose and the Hall of Fame.

In May 2025, MLB Commissioner Rob Manfred, acting on a petition from Pete Rose's family, reinstated Rose, along with the infamous 1919 Black Sox, making them eligible for election to the National Baseball Hall of Fame.

In other words, Manfred overrode Rule 21(d)(2). Manfred decided that Rule 21 was meant to keep people away from baseball who were considered a threat to the integrity of the game and to be a deterrent. He decided the "threat" portion no longer applied once a person is deceased.

To me, this is mere sophistry. "Permanently ineligible" means permanently. Permanently includes after death.

Some argue that Rose, who took fifteen years to finally admit he bet on baseball, only bet on the Cincinnati Reds to win when he was manager. Therefore, it really didn't affect the outcomes. This is short-sighted. Rose may have been tempted to make certain decisions to win the games he bet on which he would not have made had he not bet on those games. For example, would he leave a starting pitcher who was doing well in the game beyond his usual pitch count? Would he call on an injured player to perform when he should be resting? And those decisions would impact availability of those players for future games, a chain reaction.

Let's look at this another way. Let's say, for the sake of argument, that Guardians pitcher Ortiz was not caught concerning those two questionable pitches. Let's imagine he went on to an incredible major league career, winning 300 games and establishing Hall of Fame credentials. Then, just when he was about to retire, the scandal involving those two pitches years ago was revealed and Ortiz was found to be guilty. He would then be declared "permanently ineligible" from baseball. At his death, however, he would be removed from the permanently ineligible list and be eligible for Hall of Fame election. Knowing his involvement in the betting scandal, would you vote for him to enter the Hall of Fame?

I wouldn't. And I wouldn't vote for Rose, either.

A number of sportswriters have said that Rose's reinstatement does not change their opinion that he doesn't belong in the Hall of Fame. Consider steroid-era players like Barry Bonds, Mark McGwire, Sammy Sosa, Roger Clemens, and Rafael Palmeiro. None of those players were declared ineligible, because steroids were not banned from baseball when they played. But none of them are in Cooperstown because writers take their position as gatekeepers seriously.

Rose is no longer eligible for consideration by the writers, who can vote on players for a ten-year period that starts five years after their last game. His candidacy would pass to the Classic Baseball committee that next meets in December 2027.

The Black Sox Scandal of 1919, when several players on the White Sox conspired to throw the World Series, resulted in the appointment of Judge Kenesaw Mountain Landis as the first commissioner of baseball. Despite the fact that the eight accused players were acquitted in a public trial in 1921, Landis permanently banned all eight players from professional baseball.

Landis set the standard. Any hint of gambling by players in baseball needs to be quashed. It tarnishes the integrity of the game.

I still have a soft spot for Shoeless Joe Jackson. Years later, all the other seven implicated players said that Jackson was never present at their meetings with the gamblers. Claude "Lefty" Williams, one of the eight and Jackson's roommate, later said they only mentioned Jackson in hopes of giving them more credibility with the gamblers.

* * *

"Do Nice Guys Finish Last in Sports?"

Leo Durocher is credited with the now-famous phrase, "Nice guys finish last."

Leo "The Lip" made that remark when managing the Brooklyn Dodgers in 1946 before a game against the New York Giants at the Polo Grounds. During batting practice, he talked to reporters about Eddie Stanky, Durocher's pesky little infielder known as "The Brat," whom the manager admired because of his combative ways.

When the Giants, led by manager Mel Ott, emerged from the dugout to take their warm-ups, Durocher remarked: "Take a look at that No. 4, a nicer guy never drew breath than that man there." He then called out the Giants' names as they came out: "'Walker Cooper, Mize, Marshall, Kerr, Gordon, Thomson.' Take a look at them; all nice guys, and they'll finish last. Nice guys finish last."

I speculate that some readers might find this column more interesting if I had written about the rotten apples among the professional athletes I have interviewed. Instead, this piece is about some of the "nice guys."

Marquise Goodwin. Goodwin, who played with seven NFL teams during his career, was one of the fastest players in the league and one of the most generous with his time. He loves organizing summer youth football camps, and his wife, Morgan, helps. They are a genuine and lovely couple who have experienced some hard times and are very open about it. **Quote** (when asked if he and 49er quarterback at the time, Jimmy Garoppolo, were in a good rhythm in training camp): *"I'm in a rhythm with anybody. I just run fast and catch the ball."*

Joe DiMaggio. "The Yankee Clipper" is considered one of MLB's all-time greats. Even though biographers have revealed some not-so-nice aspects of DiMaggio's personal life, when I interviewed him at the Yankees AA minor-league franchise in Oneonta, New York, in 1974. I was impressed by how unassuming, approachable, and congenial he was. **Quote** (when asked how the talent in the major leagues in 1974 compared to that of DiMaggio's playing days): *"They're bringing along young ballplayers a little too quickly so that they come out of the minor leagues unrefined. I remember when I was coaching for Oakland and Reggie Jackson first arrived. He couldn't catch a fly ball We'd hit it to him, he'd pound the glove a few times, and the ball would drop twenty feet behind him I'm not kidding."*

Gary Carter. This Hall of Fame catcher may be one of the nicest guys ever. Carter was sincere, friendly, and forthcoming in my interviews with him. Nicknamed "The Kid" for his enthusiasm for baseball, he was rarely too busy to sign an autograph or talk with a young fan. **Quote:** *"I don't ever try to underachieve I always try to overachieve."*

Brett Butler. Butler played for six MLB franchises and coached two more. I found him to be very open about his life and career, more on the serious side than Carter. Giants fans would probably really like this guy if they could forgive him for jumping ship to the Dodgers in 1991 (bad enough) and then hugging manager Tommy Lasorda in front of 55,000 at Candlestick during pre-game introductions at San Francisco's home opener (a mortal sin). **Quote:** *"I've always tried to give it my very best in baseball, but as I've discovered, even your best is not guaranteed job security."*

Steve Alford. An Indiana University basketball star under Bobby Knight, this now-college coach is another frequent flyer, having served as head coach at six colleges, most recently at Nevada Reno. He also played in the NBA for four seasons, and I interviewed him when he played for the Warriors. A polite and honest young man who was twenty-two then, I was most impressed with what he didn't say—not a single bad thing about Knight, who many considered a tyrant. **Quote:** *"He (Knight) brought out more abilities than I thought I had. He made me a better player and person, and he made sure I graduated on time."*

Brent Jones. This former 49er tight end has the credentials (many feel) to be in the NFL Hall of Fame. At the very least, Jones should be in "The Nice Guy Hall of Fame." When I interviewed him in 1992, he invited me into the Niners' locker room at their Santa Clara training facility. Someone walked by, and Jones greeted him with "Hey, Flash." I looked up, and there was the legendary Jerry Rice, not three feet from me, quite a thrill for a young reporter. Jones gave me all the time and made me feel at ease. **Quote** (on retiring from football): *"The toughest thing about playing football is that all my friends have ten years of experience in their jobs, and I'll be starting back at stage one."*

Sparky Anderson. The Hall of Fame manager (Cincinnati Reds and Detroit Tigers) made his mark with "The Big Red Machine," a club some believe is the greatest baseball team ever. Anderson was more than a manager; he was an ambassador for baseball. I interviewed him after the 1976 season and found him to be affable, straightforward, and approachable. **Quote** (when asked about his comment after the 1976 World Series, which the Reds swept 4-0 from the Yankees, that New York's catcher Thurman Munson was not in the same league as Johnny Bench): *"I do think Thurman had a right to be upset. But again, nobody is Johnny Bench Not him or anyone else."*

So, back to Durocher. Durocher's comment is ironic: in 1951, he managed the New York Giants when Bobby Thomson hit the "Shot Heard 'Round the World" to beat the Dodgers and win the pennant. Stanky, then the Giants' second baseman, and Durocher danced in the third-base coach's box and grabbed Thomson as he reached the base during his home-run trot. That's the same Thomson that Durocher had derisively referred to years before as "one of the nice guys."

Sometimes nice guys finish first.

This column, which has been contemporized, first appeared in The Vacaville Reporter *on June 21, 2019.*

***

"Is it Ever Okay to Lose on Purpose in Sports?"

We've all heard of sore losers. How about intentional losers?

Let's start with Australian tennis player Bernard Tomic, who was fined $56,100 for not trying hard enough in his first-round Wimbledon loss to Frenchman Jo-Wilfried Tsonga in 2019.

Tomic lost in straight sets in just fifty-eight minutes, the shortest Wimbledon match since 2004, according to BBC.

Prior to a rule change in 2018, professional tennis players who qualified for one of the four Grand Slam tournaments could start play in a first-round match, retire (quit) during the match and still collect the full loser's share of the prize money.

A lot of players were cashing in.

Under the new rule, an injured player who withdraws before a Grand Slam tournament receives 50 percent of the prize money normally given to first-round losers. Their replacement player receives the other 50 percent (if they lose).

This helps players who did not qualify but would have had a slot if an injured player had chosen not to accept the invitation to the tournament.

Also, a player who competes in a first-round singles match and retires or performs below professional standards may be fined up to all of the player's first-round prize money.

This is not the first time the rule was applied. American Anna Tatishvili was fined $50,000 at the 2019 French Open after losing 6-0, 6-1 to Maria Sakkari of Greece. Mischa

Zverev was fined $45,000 at the 2018 Australian Open after retiring in the second set of his first-round match.

It's instructive to hear what Tsonga said about being handed the win over Tomic.

"For me, it's like what I did was not win," he said in a press conference. "It's like I was just here and I just won because they said he didn't play enough."

That's just one of the effects when someone tanks a match.

As long as we're handing out fines for not trying, why not fine the entire Philadelphia 76ers organization and former general manager and president of basketball operations Sam Hinkie?

Their now infamous "Trust the Process" method of losing for years to stockpile the best draft picks paid off. They selected Joel Embiid, the 2017 NBA Rookie of the Year, in the 2014 draft and made it to the conference semifinals the following season.

Strangely, many 76ers fans idolize Hinkie. During the 2018 playoffs, they sometimes chanted TRUST-THE-PROCESS instead of DE-FENSE or LET'S-GO-SIX-ERS. Embiid loves Hinkie and totally embraces "the process."

Although no NBA general manager would publicly admit it, teams are racing to the bottom of the standings toward the end of the season to get the best draft picks.

It's hard to argue with the 76ers' results. But is there still a thing called ethics in sports? Is it ever okay to lose on purpose?

Rudy Gobert of the Minnesota Timberwolves says no.

"I don't believe in tanking, all that stuff," he told Sports USA. "I believe you learn how to win by winning. You don't learn how to win by losing on purpose to get a nineteen-year-old who you've never seen."

If you want to see a real travesty, look on YouTube for the badminton doubles matches in the 2012 Olympics in London. Teams from China, South Korea, and Indonesia were disqualified for "not using one's best efforts to win a match."

There's an understatement for you. They hit fault after fault, bashing the ball into the net so they could face an easier opponent in the next stage of the round-robin tournament.

One ugly incentive for losing on purpose has always been money. The Black Sox scandal of 1919 is the classic example. If you don't know much about it, watch the movie *Eight Men Out.*

Match fixing has been all too common in many sports including cricket, football (soccer), tennis, and even college basketball (point-shaving).

There may be some shades of grey in the "losing on purpose" discussion. For example, a runner in a preliminary track meet may not go all out in order to conserve energy for the final. I don't think anyone could make a credible argument that that is morally wrong.

Similarly, baseball managers commonly rest their best players after clinching the league title so that they will be fresh for the playoffs. Nothing wrong with that either.

Losing on purpose is a different animal, and I think people generally know when they've crossed the line.

And what is the impact on young people who see this behavior in the athletes or coaches they admire?

"Once you instruct a child, 'Don't be your best,' or even 'Be your worst,' you've greatly diminished the opportunity for that individual's character growth," wrote Jack Bowen in an article for the Santa Clara University School of Law on intentional losing. "There should be no doubt that one characteristic we value in individuals is the drive to be one's best. And once we accept this as our foundation, evaluating actions within sport such as intentionally losing becomes much easier."

Trust the process? How about trust your instincts. Do your best.

This column, which has been contemporized, first appeared in The Vacaville Reporter *on July 15 2019.*

* * *

"No Place for Selfishness in Sports"

A professional athlete may have all the talent in the world, but if they have a me-first instead of a team-first attitude, fans and teammates quickly lose respect for them.

In the 1994 NBA Eastern Conference semi-finals, following two close wins to open the series, the Knicks went on the road for Game 3. The Bulls held an 89-70 lead through the first three quarters, but the Knicks charged back in the fourth.

With 1.8 seconds remaining in regulation and Chicago ahead by two points, Patrick Ewing hit a hook shot over Bill Cartwright to tie the game.

Bulls coach Phil Jackson elected to give Toni Kukoc the final shot. The "Croatian Sensation," a twenty-five-year-old rookie at the time, had hit multiple game-winners in his first NBA season.

When Jackson asked Scottie Pippen to inbound the ball, Pippen decided he wasn't going to take the court and sat down on the bench.

As *The New York Times* summed it up, "Andrea Kramer, an ESPN reporter, who was beside the Bulls' bench at this time with a cameraman, quoted Pippen as issuing an expletive and then saying, 'I'm tired of this.' And Pippen then sat down. Some of the other players said, 'Pip, come on, get up, what are you doing?' He refused to come back in the game. Since the Bulls only were sending four men on the court, Jackson had to call a second timeout."

Jackson stacked up four players at the foul line—Kukoc, B.J. Armstrong, Horace Grant, and Steve Kerr—and had Pete Myers inbound the ball. Grant looped around toward the basket while Armstrong and Kerr split off in opposite directions. Kukoc took a few steps back and received the lob from Myers. Kukoc then created enough separation from Anthony Mason to launch a jumper that hit nothing but net and won the game for the Bulls.

The Bulls had used this exact play earlier in the season against the Indiana Pacers with Pippen throwing the pass to Kukoc for a three-pointer for a one-point victory at the buzzer. But this time, Pippen was pouting on the bench as his team won the game. Here's how Pippen explained his decision to *GQ*:

"I don't think it's a mystery, you need to read between the fine lines. It was my first year playing without Michael Jordan, why wouldn't I be taking that last shot? I been through all the ups and downs, the battles with the Pistons and now you gonna insult me and tell me to take it out? I thought it was a pretty low blow. I felt like it was an opportunity to give [Kukoc] a rise. It was a racial move to give him a rise. After all I've been through with this organization, now you're gonna tell me to take the ball out and throw it to Toni Kukoc? You're insulting me. That's how I felt."

So Pippen pulled the race card. In addition, this is from the guy who once accused Kevin Durant of not knowing how to play team basketball.

Durant responded at the time with this tweet: "Didn't the great Scottie Pippen refuse to go in the game for the last second shot because he was in his feelings his coach drew up the play for a better shooter??"

Exactly right, KD.

On the one hand, Pippen charged KD with being selfish for taking all the shots down the stretch in a playoff game. But on the other hand, Pippen couldn't handle it when Phil Jackson wanted someone other than him to take the final shot.

Selfishness can show up in other ways.

In a 2019 game against the Minnesota Twins, the Cleveland Indians' Yasiel Puig hit a grounder directly back to pitcher Jake Odorizzi. Puig immediately turned and headed for the dugout instead of running out the play. A confused Odorizzi opted to jog the ball over to first base after noticing his opponent heading off. Even though Puig was out, the Minnesota home fans, understanding that players are supposed to hustle, gave him a well-deserved booing. Puig was met in the dugout by Carlos Santana, who appeared frustrated with his teammate's behavior.

"Santana was giving me advice that I need to run out every play and I'm 100 percent with him and said sorry to him and said sorry to [manager] Tito [Francona]," Puig explained after the Indians' 5-3 loss, according to MLB.com's Mandy Bell. "I'm supposed to run on that play. I don't know what happened in my mind."

With the Dallas Cowboys well on their way to a 52-17 victory over the Buffalo Bills in Super Bowl XXVII, Dallas's

Leon Lett scooped up a fumble at his own forty-six-yard line and headed toward the end zone. Just before he reached the goal line, he decided to do some showboating, slowing down and holding the ball out to his side. Buffalo's fastest player, Don Beebe, chased him down and knocked the ball loose. The ball bounced out of the end zone for a touchback, Instead of a sixty-four-yard touchdown for Dallas, Buffalo got the ball back on the twenty-yard line. Enduring embarrassment for Lett and a highlight reel that youth sports coaches continue to use for the example of Beebe's never-give-up hustle.

Similarly, at the 2006 Turin Olympics, showboating cost Team USA's Lindsey Jacobellis a gold medal. She was clear of the pack in the women's snowboard cross final, when she grabbed her board on one of the final jumps to add some flair to her victory. The grab caused Jacobellis to fall, giving her opponent just enough time to pass her up for the gold. Jacobellis took home silver.

As the book of Proverbs in the Bible puts it, "Pride goes before destruction, and a haughty spirit before a fall." Sometimes, as with Jacobellis, that axiom is literally fulfilled.

***

"The Non-Denial Denial"

Some athletes would make great politicians. They have mastered the art of the non-denial denial, which the dictionary defines as "a statement that appears to deny that something is accurate but does not constitute a rebuttal of the specific claim or accusation."

Take the case of Yankees pitcher **Gerrit Cole**, who the

Twins' Josh Donaldson accused of doctoring the ball with a sticky substance to get a better grip and more spin. When asked point-blank by a reporter whether he uses an illegal substance on the ball, Cole was silent for five seconds before giving this response:

"Um, I don't . . . I don't know . . . quite know how to answer that, to be honest. I mean, some customs and practices have been passed down from older players to younger players, from the last generation of players to this generation of players. And I think some things are out of bounds in that regard, and I've stood pretty firm in terms of the communication between our peers and whatnot. Again, as I mentioned earlier, this is important to many people who love the game, including the players in this room, fans, and teams. If MLB wants to legislate some more stuff, that's a conversation we can have because, ultimately, we should all be pulling in the same direction on this."

Wow! What a mouthful of nothing. But Cole isn't the first athlete to tiptoe around a direct question.

When **Cam Newton** was the quarterback for Auburn, ESPN reported that a street agent had allegedly solicited money for Newton when he was being recruited out of junior college. Newton said: "I'm not going to entertain something that took place not three months, not six months, not a year but two years ago. I'm not sitting up here and saying anything about it, whether I did or did not, because I don't want to beat a dead horse talking about it. It won't affect me in any way, shape, or fashion."

That reminds one of **Mark McGwire**, who, at a Congressional hearing about his alleged steroid use, repeatedly said, "I'm not here to talk about the past." But the whole point of the hearing was *to discuss his past.*

Tiger Woods called accounts of his sexting "irresponsible" but never attacked their accuracy. Four months later, he apologized for all those actions he once called "rumors."

John McEnroe showed his ability to dance around an issue. When his ex-wife, Tatum O'Neal, said that he had used steroids in 1987, reporters asked McEnroe if steroid use was common in professional tennis. His response: "I, uh, to be honest, I think we're very fortunate in our sport. That's a problem, and we have far other problems. I mean, have I? No. I don't know. Does that mean people haven't done it? No. Of course. I'm sure they have."

He was then asked to confirm or deny his steroid use: "I think it's pretty clear if you read what I said [in the statement], what the bottom line is," he replied. He was then asked to give a yes or no answer to his steroid use. "You need to read the book [his just-published autobiography]," he said. But, a reporter noted, his steroid use isn't in the book, which is why O'Neal brought it up. "Weh, weh, weh, well, I don't understand what that means," he answered. "I made it clear what the answer is, if you read the book, what went on to a large degree. Do I have to spell it out in every ugly, little detail? I don't think so."

Although **Lance Armstrong**, who later admitted to doping, sometimes emphatically denied the claims, at other times, he showed he had mastered the non-denial denial. In a *Nike* commercial, he said, "This is my body, and I can do whatever I want. I can push, study, tweak, and listen to it. Everybody wants to know what I am on. What am I on? I'm on my bike, busting my ass six hours a day. What are you on?" In another, he said, "The critics say I'm arrogant, a doper, and washed up, a fraud. That I couldn't let it go, they can say whatever they want. I'm not back on my bike for them [shots of Armstrong are interspersed with images of cancer patients]."

In 2011, responding to a claim by teammate **Floyd Landis** that he used banned substances, Armstrong replied, "I never lose sleep. It has no effect on my life. That's for other people to deal with. If you're trying to hide something, you wouldn't keep getting away with it for ten years. Nobody is that clever." In none of these instances does he *actually* deny using drugs to enhance his performance.

Then we have "Deflategate," when the **New England Patriots** were accused of using footballs inflated to two pounds less than the minimum required in their victory over the Indianapolis Colts in the AFC Championship game in January 2015. Here are some of the questions and **Tom Brady's** answers at a subsequent press conference:

Q. "When and how did you supposedly alter the balls?"

A. "I didn't, you know, have any, ah, you know I didn't alter the ball in any way."

Note that he says he didn't alter the ball. But that doesn't mean someone else didn't, possibly with his knowledge.

It's a great non-denial denial.

This column first appeared in The Vacaville Reporter *on June 14, 2021.*

* * *

"That's Not Who I Am! (Really?)"

In defense of their bad behavior, sports figures frequently trot out one of the lamest excuses known to humankind, namely, "That's not who I am."

Back in August 2020, Cincinnati Reds announcer **Thom Brennaman** was caught using an anti-gay slur on a hot mic between innings of the first game of a doubleheader against the Kansas City Royals. He apologized during the play-by-play in the fifth inning of the second game just before he was removed from the broadcast. He said, in part, "I can't begin to tell you how deeply sorry I am. That is not who I am, and it never has been. I think maybe I could have some people that can back that up. I am very, very sorry, and I beg for your forgiveness."

But Brennaman's defense caused a stir.

"'That's not who I am' at the end of an apology negates the apology! It implies that you don't think what you're apologizing for requires further self-examination. It is distancing yourself from the error instead of taking responsibility." Hannah Keyster on X

"I love it when people say 'that's not who I am' when they do something dumb. Is there a universal demonic possession going on?" respondent on a *Tech Sideline* message board

"If you're that comfortable using a homophobic slur when the mic's off, it seems like that kinda is who you are. Slurs don't just accidentally come out of your mouth. They're there because you use/think them." Scott McLaughlin on X

Jesus is quoted in the New Testament as saying, "What comes out of the mouth proceeds from the heart, and this defiles a person."

People may be surprised at what just came out of their mouths or what they did, but that reveals who they are. I'm sure all of us have experienced that to some degree. But athletes and sports figures seem particularly good at grabbing headlines with it.

The racist language that Buffalo Bills quarterback **Jake**

Fromm used in 2019 in a text message became public the following year. Fromm responded, "That's not me; that's not who I am. That's not where my heart is."

To get biblical again for a moment, the prophet Jeremiah in the Old Testament said, "The heart is deceitful above all things, and desperately sick; who can understand it?"

In 2018, Broncos running back **Phillip Lindsay** was ejected from a game for throwing some punches after diving late on a pile. "It's my first time getting ejected, so yeah I was surprised," Lindsay told Denver's 7 News. "It's not in my character. That's not who I am." But, as a reader commented, "It was some other Phillip Lindsey dunnit. Bad Phil. He's been expunged and won't be welcomed back into Good Phil's body anymore. Promise."

Back in 2013, All-Pro defensive end **Dexter Manley** of the Washington Redskins (that's what they were called then) used a gay slur to describe Dallas Cowboys Hall of Fame quarterback Troy Aikman. Here is Manley's apology: "While intending to be funny, I used a slur to refer to Troy Aikman. It was wrong and insensitive. Anyone that knows me knows that's not who I am in my heart or mind."

Are we noticing a common theme here?

In 2017, **Baker Mayfield**, then the quarterback for the Oklahoma Sooners, was offended when the Kansas Jayhawks captains refused to shake hands with him at the coin flip at midfield. During the game, Mayfield retaliated by making a lewd gesture toward the KU sideline. He responded (Associated Press): "It's not who I am. I'm not trying to play this ego of being a bad kid. That's not who I am. I'm not someone who's always going to be in trouble. I've had one instance off the field where I've made a mistake. On the field, I'm a competitive guy."

The one instance off the field occurred earlier that year when Mayfield was charged and convicted of public intoxication, disorderly conduct, and fleeing. It is the same Baker Mayfield who planted an Oklahoma University flag at midfield following Oklahoma's big win at Ohio State. Mayfield later apologized: "I did not mean for it to be disrespectful towards any Ohio State people, especially not the team or the players." However, when *GQ* interviewed him in 2019, he admitted that Oklahoma higher-ups had forced him to apologize. Mayfield said, "I was just kinda almost embarrassed for them to tell me to apologize." When GQ asked how heartfelt his apology was, he said it was "zero" on a scale of 1-10.

As John Agnew wrote in the *Fort Myers News-Press*, "What you do spontaneously, including saying hurtful things to amuse your friends—that's who you really are. What you do or say with careful thought and planning, with estimation of possible consequences, that's merely how you want to be perceived by others."

Note: If something I said in this column offended you, please understand it is NOT who I am.

This column first appeared in The Vacaville Reporter *on August 22, 2020.*

***

"Toxic Baseball Teammates Are Nothing New"

It's one thing for ballplayers to show up the opposition. It's quite another when they show up their teammates. But you are wrong if you thought that behavior was reserved for Little Leaguers. It's big-league stuff, too.

Let's start with an incident in a 2021 game between the Toronto Blue Jays and New York Yankees.

Ross Stripling was on the mound for the Jays. He threw a knuckle curve to Giancarlo Stanton, who topped it and sent a slow roller down the third-base line. Toronto third baseman Joe Panik charged and fielded the ball barehanded, but his throw sailed over the first baseman's head, and Stanton was safe. Stripling proceeded to slap the grass and yell in Panik's direction. Panik had made another error earlier in the game, leading to an unearned run, which may have fueled Stripling's outburst.

But that is no excuse. At least, in this case, Stripling was repentant.

Ross Stripling: "It's the most disrespectful thing I've ever done, maybe ever, certainly on a baseball field. I'm completely embarrassed about it, and I let the moment get too big for me. Honestly, I'm mortified by it. I can't stand how it went. I apologized to Joe individually. I even addressed the team because I felt so bad about it. That can't happen. That should never happen. It'll never happen again from me, I promise you that."

Another pitcher who regretted his actions was former Washington Nationals closer Jonathan Papelbon. He didn't think teammate Bryce Harper hustled to first on a flyout to left field. Harper walked back to the dugout as Papelbon stood on the top step and yelled at him. When Harper entered the dugout, Papelbon grabbed him by the throat and drove him into the dugout wall. Both players described the fight as an isolated incident and said it was just a matter of tensions boiling over.

Jonathan Papelbon: "First, I'll say I'm in the wrong there. You know, I grew up with brothers. He grew up with brothers. I view him as a brother of mine. Sometimes, in this game, a lot of testosterone and intensity spills over, and I think that happened today. I can't allow that to happen in the middle of a game. You handle that after the games or enable the manager to handle that. In that light of it, I'm wrong."

Other players have not been so apologetic, etching themselves in the minds of their fellow players and fans as toxic teammates.

Former Chicago Cubs starting pitcher Carlos Zambrano often publicly berated his fielders from the mound for making errors. After a rough outing against the Atlanta Braves in 2007 (he gave up thirteen hits and six earned runs in five innings in the loss), he went after his catcher, Michael Barrett, and Barrett and Zambrano got into a heated exchange in the dugout. Tempers flared, and a Zambrano punch left Barrett with a black eye.

In June 2002, Barry Bonds and Jeff Kent, who had a long-running behind-the-scenes feud, took it public with a brawl in the Giants dugout. It began with Kent yelling at third baseman David Bell over a play at second and then Bonds standing up for Bell. One thing led to another, and a lot of foul language was used, and pretty soon, we had the "Slugout in the Dugout." San Francisco manager Dusty Baker had to separate the two, with Kent shouting that he didn't want to be on the team anymore. Kent signed with the Astros as a free agent after the 2002 season.

Don Sutton and Steve Garvey were Dodger teammates from 1969 to 1980 and even had lockers next to each other. But there was no love lost between them. Their feud came to a head during the 1978 season. In a *Washington Post* article, Sutton said, "All you hear about on our team is Steve Garvey, the All-American boy. But Reggie Smith was the real MVP. We all know it. (Smith) has carried us for the last two years. He is not a facade. He does not have the Madison Avenue image."

Garvey confronted Sutton, asking if the quotes were accurate. Sutton said they were, then leaped at Garvey and flung him against a row of lockers. The two players went down heavily and clawed at one another, trying ineffectually to land punches.

Many Dodgers didn't like Garvey, and apparently, not everyone liked Sutton, either. According to Tommy John, during the brawl someone yelled, "Stop the fight; they'll kill each other!" Catcher Joe Ferguson responded, "Good!"

The Chicago Cubs' double-play combination of Tinkers to Evers to Chance is renowned through a poem. Still, shortstop Joe Tinker and second baseman Johnny Evers, teammates from 1902-1913, didn't talk to each other for thirty-three years, starting in 1905 after the two argued over a cab fare and later fought on the field. The day following the incident, Tinkers told Evers, "Don't talk to me, and I won't talk to you. You play your position, and I'll play mine. Let it go at that."

Words that are heavy with nothing but trouble:
"Tinker to Evers to Chance."
Franklin Pierce Adams, 1910

This column first appeared in The Vacaville Reporter *on June 17, 2021.*

* * *

"Who Says Good Sportspersonship is Passé?"

Great sportspersonship is inspiring, especially when the opposite behavior often makes headlines. Here are several feel-good moments associated with athletes who exhibited graciousness on fields of play.

In August 2020, St. Louis Cardinals pitcher Adam Wainright, who had been beset by injuries and subpar performances, beat the Cleveland Indians 7-2 on his thirty-ninth birthday with a complete game, his first in four years. He was the oldest active player in the major leagues at that time.

"It's just, you know, a lot of hard work from a lot of different people have gone into making me able to pitch this year and pitch well," an emotional Wainwright told ESPN. "You know, when you think you're done three years ago, and you're able to complete a game a couple years later, it's a crazy life, a crazy game." After the final out, the entire Cleveland dugout stood to applaud him. Wainright said, "That was special. I'll never forget it. Appreciate it. Thank you very much, Cleveland."

On June 2, 2012, during the home stretch of the 3,200-meter race at the Ohio High School Athletic Association Division III State Track Meet in Columbus, Ohio, a runner collapsed in front of high school junior Meghan Vogel. Vogel, who had won the 1,600-meter title earlier in the day, could have easily added to her trophy collection by running past her fallen competitor. Instead, she carried the girl across the finish line. "I just figured I'd help her out," said Vogel after the race, "She deserved to finish ahead of me."

In El Paso, Texas, on February 13, 2013, there were just thirteen seconds left in a blowout win for Franklin High over Coronado High. Coronado High's Mitchell Marcus—a special-needs student-athlete—appeared destined to finish his basketball career without a basket. But instead of running out the clock, Franklin High's Jon Montanez turned the ball over to Marcus and said, "Shoot it, it's your time." Marcus took a last-second shot and sank it.

On April 26, 2008, in Monmouth, Oregon, in a softball game between Western Oregon University and Central Washington University, Western Oregon senior Sara Tucholsky hit the first home run of her college career. But she tore her ACL during her home-run trot. If a substitute runner had replaced Tucholsky, her homer would have been reduced to a single. And if any of her teammates touched her, she would have been called out. So, members of the opposing team carried her around the bases.

In Milwaukee, Wisconsin, on February 7, 2009, Milwaukee Madison High senior Johntel Franklin, who had lost his mother to cancer earlier in the day, did not arrive at his high school basketball game against DeKalb High until the second quarter. The referees assessed Franklin with a technical foul because his name was not in the scorebook. Despite DeKalb High's pleas to forfeit the free throws, Coach Dave Rohlman was forced to send one of his players to the line. DeKalb High's Darius McNeal went to the stripe, but he intentionally missed both shots instead of taking advantage of the situation.

At the 1936 Olympics in Berlin, Jesse Owens, the American world record holder in the long jump, had foot-faulted twice in his attempts to qualify for the final. Seeing that his rival was clearly worried, Germany's Luz Long, the European record holder, offered Owens advice on adjusting his run-up to make the qualifying distance. Owens' next jump was successful, winning the gold medal, with Long earning silver. It all occurred in front of Adolf Hitler, who was enraged at Owens' successes. Long was killed in World War II. "You can melt down all the medals and cups I have," said Owens later. "And they wouldn't be a plating on the twenty-four-carat friendship that I felt for Luz Long at that moment."

During the 2005 Rome Masters, in his third-round tennis match against Spaniard Fernando Verdasco, Andy Roddick had match point on Verdasco's second serve. The linesman called out, which gave Roddick the win, but he pointed out the ball mark on the clay. Stunned, the umpire let Roddick overrule him. Verdasco then fought back, held serve, and won the set and then the match. Verdasco later thanked Roddick and called him a great sportsman, saying, "Maybe another player wouldn't have done like Andy."

New Zealand's Nikki Hamblin and Abbey D'Agostino of the US collided with 2,000 meters to go in their second preliminary 5,000-meter heat at the 2016 Rio Olympics. The American got up and tried to help Hamblin to her feet before falling over because she had injured her leg. Hamblin then helped D'Agostino up, and the pair ran most of the rest of the race together before embracing at the finish line. They were reinstated in the final, but D'Agostino could not compete because she had torn her ACL. Hamblin finished seventeenth. The two runners were awarded the Olympic Fair Play Award. "She helped me first," said Hamblin after the race. "I tried to help her. She was pretty bad. That girl is the Olympic spirit right there."

This column first appeared in The Vacaville Reporter *on September 4, 2020.*

* * *

"Kid Gloves for Babe Ruth: The Golden Age of Sportswriting"

Many historians and fans have referred to the decade immediately following World War I as the Golden Age of Sport because of the abundance of sports heroes.

Paul Gallico, a sportswriter with the *New York Daily News* during the twenties, later criticized the sportswriting of the time when he said that its daily function was to "peddle treacle about the baseball heroes and soft-pedal the sour stuff." But that may have been because, as legendary sportswriter Grantland Rice once advised colleague Richards Vidmer, "When athletes are no longer heroes to you it's time to stop writing sports."

An examination of the way the biggest sports hero of the 1920s, Babe Ruth, was treated in newspapers exposes the extent to which the journalists of the Golden Age soft-pedaled the "sour stuff" on his behalf. This naturally leads to the question of how differently the Babe might have been handled by contemporary sports writers.

"Looking back to my youth, I honestly don't think I knew the difference between right and wrong," wrote Ruth. "I spent much of my early boyhood living over my father's saloon in Baltimore—and when I wasn't living over it, I was in it, soaking up the atmosphere. I hardly knew my parents."

As an adult, Ruth indulged himself. He smoked ("He always had something in his mouth," said a contemporary.) He drank heavily and ate gluttonously. He gambled until his heavy losses cured him. He got numerous speeding tickets ("We'd have been in jail more than once on that trip if Ruth didn't know how to be polite to traffic cops," said teammate Lou Gehrig after a barnstorming trip.) He slept around while married, and is reported to have taken on an entire house of prostitution one night in St. Louis.

But much of this never came to light during his career. By diluting the truth or by not telling all of it, the sportswriters avoided impairing Ruth's image as hero in the eyes of the people of the twenties. The writers did not feel this was dishonest reporting. They were following an unwritten code best expressed by Abe Kemp, a San Francisco sportswriter in the twenties. He reflected on his experience with *San Francisco Bulletin* sports editor Hyland L. Baggerly: "When I broke in under Baggerly, the only advice he gave me was 'Abe, I'm not telling you to do this, but if you can't write something nice about a ball player, don't mention his name.' I pursued that policy the rest of my life. I could have written some of the most scandalous stories of all time. But I didn't."

Most of the sports reporters subscribed at least in part to this unwritten code, what Kemp later termed his "Pollyanna" policy. Harold Parrott, another sportswriter of the period, spoke of his admiration for Frankie Graham, who he considered the number one writer of the day: "He was so genteel. He had a code which he held to very rigidly. He never hurt anybody."

The reporters knew the truth about the ballplayers. The sportswriters of the twenties were as close to their subjects as writers have ever been. They traveled with the ballplayers, drank with them, and slept on the same trains and in the same hotels. As a result, the writers were often very close friends with the players. This made impartiality difficult.

John R. Tunis, a sports novelist and freelance writer in the twenties, later commented on this problem: "I always thought it was just as well not to make friends with the players. When you become friendly you inevitably tend to write something favorable about them."

Regarding Ruth, sportswriter Richards Vidmer had this to say: "I could have written a story every day on the Babe. But I never wrote about his personal life, not if it would hurt him. Babe couldn't say no to certain things. Hot dogs was the least of 'em. There were other things that were worse. Hell, sometimes I thought it was one long line, a procession."

How does the modern sportswriter handle the revelation of personal details of an athlete's life that may prove embarrassing?

Fast forward fifty years from the 1920s to a book which kick-started the tell-all style of sports writing in vogue today. Former major league pitcher Jim Bouton opened Pandora 's Box in 1970 when he released his book, *Ball Four*.

Bouton revealed many salacious and personal details about his teammates. What offended his teammates the most was that Bouton never told them he was working on a book all the time he was with them in the clubhouse and on the road.

It is not hard to imagine how Bouton would have written about the personal habits of Babe Ruth. Discretion in sports reporting has become the exception rather than the rule.

As Staci D. Kramer wrote in *The New York Times*:

> *The story goes like this: Two sportswriters are sitting in a dining car when a naked Babe Ruth streaks past followed by a woman wielding a butcher knife. One sports-*

writer turns to the other and says: "I didn't see anything. Did you?"

Instead of being written for the sports pages, the story passes from one sportswriter to another until it becomes folklore.

Today, forget the sports section. The sordid details of Ruth's naked sprint would be splashed all over the nation's front pages with a full color graphic of the railroad car in USA Today.

Like it or not, sportswriting is no longer the art of writing about athletes as though they sprang from Zeus's head and live on Mount Olympus. The unwritten rules of the golden age of sportswriting have been rewritten by the double whammy of electronic media and tabloid journalism. Instead, we have the age of realism or what one observer calls the age of the human side of the athlete combined with the "if I don't write it someone else will" school of journalism.

This column is excerpted from the original, which appeared in Nine: A Journal of Baseball History and Culture, *Volume 33, Number 1, Fall 2024.*

* * *

"Lowell Cohn, Never Boring"

San Francisco Bay Area sports fans either loved Lowell Cohn or hated him. The now-retired sports columnist for the *San Francisco Chronicle* and the *Santa Rosa Press Democrat* had a way with words. Those words could inflame readers but always kept their attention.

Whether or not you agreed with Cohn, you had to

admire his style, wit, courage, and ability to peel back the layers of his subject and get to the heart of the matter.

In his memoir, *Gloves Off: 40 Years of Unfiltered Sports Writing*, Cohn doesn't just publish his previous columns. Instead, he provides insights into his craft via sixty-four short, highly readable chapters on the many Bay Area sports personalities he covered. In it, he pens, "Writing a column, writing anything, means the writer cannot be boring. Not for a single paragraph, sentence, or clause. Not even for a word. How a writer achieves this **not** is the writer's primary business, challenge, and joy—writing lives on the **not**."

No one would ever accuse Cohn of being boring. Although he riled up many athletes and readers, he always clarified his reasoning and was effective because of his objectivity. He was not a fan of any team or athlete. "When people understood that I didn't care if a local team won," he writes, "they would ask why I wrote sports. What was the point? And I said I liked to write about sports, understood that world, simple as that, and I loved bringing up a subject to start a discussion or an argument among readers."

Cohn admits that his chief love, even above sports, is writing.

"When people ask what I like about my job, I say the writing," he states. "They are always disappointed, and they want me to say I'm in love with sports. I am in love with sports, but I love writing more. If it came to that, I could write about a glass of water."

Cohn will probably offend some more readers and athletes in this book. He is not a fan of Colin Kaepernick, for example. He writes: "Disclaimer: My view of Kaepernick may be skewed because I know him and don't like him." Cohn says, "Simple question for Colin Kaepernick, a mere two-word sentence: *Why then?* He had been a mixed-race person all his life facing things a mixed-race person faces and, all of a sudden, six years into his NFL career, it dawned on him that there are monstrous injustices in the American system." Cohn's conclusion: "He dissed the anthem because he wanted attention. Strictly my interpretation. I freely admit that."

Cohn was also no fan of Barry Bonds. He described a scene in the Giants clubhouse where reporters were crowded around Bonds' locker and, without saying a word, Bonds used a bat to herd them away and make a path for himself. "His meaning was clear," writes Cohn. "We were cows or goats or pigs, four-legged subhumans, and we didn't deserve the rudimentary politeness and consideration you would accord a human being."

Cohn writes about Michael Jordan's last game in Oakland during his final farewell tour and how Jordan refused to do the post-game interview in the interview room, instead forcing a horde of reporters to gather around his locker. Then Jordan gave the interview in a whisper, making it impossible for most reporters to capture his words. Cohn writes, "And I looked at Jordan and thought so much of this man is image, packaged, made up. Sure, he may be a good person to those close to him. How would I know? But he isn't acting like a good person now. He's being mean for no reason. To exert power. To disappoint people who came to celebrate him. Why would anyone do that?"

Cohn mentions many local and national sports figures he did like, including Bill Walsh, Steve Young, Vida Blue, Dusty Baker, Floyd Patterson, and Jim Harbaugh. At least in some cases, the feeling was mutual. Young wrote the Foreword to the book, stating, "But in the end, we were better because of

Lowell. There's always a need for a voice like that. It's important. Nothing is worse than internal marketing. It's when we tell each other we're all great and everything is fine. That didn't happen with Lowell. As a truth seeker, he wouldn't allow it." In the Afterword, Harbaugh wrote, "You are a man I truly respect because of your principles and convictions. Your passion and work ethic are at the highest level. And your sense of humor and dry wit were appreciated."

All those characteristics are on full display in this book and, like him or hate him, readers will be fascinated as Cohn shares his insights into people like Reggie Jackson, Tim Lincecum, Baron Davis, Al Davis, Bruce Bochy, Billy Martin, Billy Beane, Randy Moss, Steve Mariucci, and many others.

Cohn lives up to his standard: **NOT** boring!

This column first appeared in The Vacaville Reporter *on February 27, 2021.*

* * *

"Lunches with Lowell Cohn"

People or events sometimes come full circle in our lives. If that circle is negative, some call it bad karma. If the circle is positive, some call it serendipity; religious folks might call it providence.

Whatever you want to call it, the latter type happened to me recently. Let me give you some background.

I am Jewish, and, through a series of what I would call providential events, came to believe in Jesus in August 1978. Gaining a new appreciation for my Jewish heritage after coming to believe in Jesus as the Jewish Messiah, I joined a group called Jews for Jesus and in 1980 relocated 3,000 miles from my New York home to work with them at their San Francisco headquarters.

Almost immediately after relocating, I began reading the sports page in the *San Francisco Chronicle. The Chronicle* had a controversial sports columnist named Lowell Cohn.

In 1978, several born-again Christians on the Giants began to speak out about Jesus in post-game interviews. The Giants, who had been mired in mediocrity for most of the 1970s, came to life that year and led the division until mid-August before a September swoon landed them in third place behind the Dodgers and Reds.

The press didn't trouble the born-again Giants when they talked about Jesus, as they were winning. But the next year, when the Giants reverted to their losing ways, the media dubbed the Christians the "God Squad" and began to take potshots at them.

Cohn, ever the satirist, wrote a column in 1980 called "Can Satan Save the Giants?" in which he recommended that since God wasn't helping the Giants very much, one of them should sell his soul to the devil. A year later, Cohn wrote another column called "Lavelle and the Fiend," in which he said that born-again pitcher Gary Lavelle was intolerant because he had called San Francisco a satanic region (in part because the Church of Satan was founded there by Anton LaVey in 1966).

As I was reading these columns in the *Chronicle,* they irritated me. Of course, Cohn wrote to provoke a reaction. But as a Jesus believer, I felt that he was unfairly picking on the God Squadders.

Some forty years later, after retiring from writing sports for *The* (Vacaville, California) *Reporter* newspaper, I decided to write a book about the God Squad. I wanted to interview

Cohn, but I approached that possibility with fear and trepidation. What were his true feelings about the born-again Christians on the Giants? Did he harbor hostility toward them? Or would he be hostile toward me when I revealed (Cohn is Jewish) that I am a Jewish believer in Jesus?

I expected Cohn's personality to match the acerbic wit of his columns and that he would either refuse the interview, or, if he agreed to it, would slice and dice me. To my surprise and pleasure, Cohn not only agreed to the interview, which we did by phone, but was extremely gracious and wanted to help me, a fellow writer. He had no animosity toward the God Squadders or born-again believers (Jewish or otherwise). We talked for forty minutes and it was one of the best interviews I ever experienced.

My book, *The God Squad: The Born-Again San Francisco Giants of 1978*, was published in November 2023, and I made sure to thank Lowell in the Acknowledgments section. I also sent him a signed copy of my book.

He posted a very nice Tweet about my book on his X account.

Late in 2024, Lowell, who publishes a Substack column three times a week, wrote that he was having difficulty finding a publisher for an autobiographical book he wrote titled *Brooklyn Jew*. I emailed him to let him know that if he continued to strike out with publishers, he might want to try Eric and Peggy Johnson at Alive Book Publishing, who produced my book.

In the spring of 2025, Lowell took my suggestion and met with the Johnsons. He liked them and their publishing house. Eric suggested that Lowell ask me to copy edit his book, which I was more than happy to do, as Lowell had been so helpful to me regarding my book.

I read the book through and Lowell, being an accomplished and wonderful writer, needed little editing. I highly recommend *Brooklyn Jew*. Rather than a straightforward, chronological retelling of Lowell's life, it is a series of fascinating vignettes of some of the indelible moments of his life and career. While I'm at it, I would also recommend his previous book, *Gloves Off*.

To my surprise, to thank me, Lowell treated me to lunch at a great little place halfway between his home and mine. We sat at the backyard outdoor patio and talked for two-and-a-half hours about writing, our lives, and his many encounters with athletes and coaches during his fifteen years at the *Chronicle* and twenty-three years at the *Santa Rosa Press Democrat*.

When the page proofs came back from the publisher, Lowell asked me to read through them. Again to my surprise, he decided to treat me to a second lunch. We talked for another couple of hours, never running out of topics. We found that we have much in common. Both raised in the New York City area (I was born in Manhattan and raised in Hackensack, New Jersey, a New York City suburb), we laughed at the fact that while we should have emerged as tough city guys, we both still have rather sensitive natures. He also found it amusing that I had thought he would be a prickly and intimidating personality before I interviewed him. He explained that although he writes that way, he is not that way as a person. And he is not.

So, forty-plus years after resenting the satirical tone of his columns about the God Squad, I have become good friends with Lowell. Serendipity? Providence? Call it whatever you like. I'm just glad it happened.

***

"In Appreciation of Volleyball"

Before retiring a few years ago, I covered high school sports for *The Reporter*, a newspaper in Vacaville, California. Prior to that job, I had never covered a high school volleyball match. I had much to learn. Here's what I wrote after covering my first volleyball matches:

As I watch the four local girls teams—Vacaville High, Will C. Wood, Vacaville Christian and Vanden—I am learning a lot.

I was way behind the times.

You can score a point when you are not serving? I discovered that in the old system known as side-out scoring, only the team serving could score a point. In the current system, rally scoring, points can be scored by either the serving or the receiving team. The change was made in 1999 to make the matches more predictable in length and more spectator-friendly.

I was watching a local high school match and the serve hit the net but made it over to the receiving team's side. "Do over," I thought, otherwise known as a "let." What, they're still playing the rally? I found out that in 2001 the rule was changed so that a serve that hits the net but still makes it to the other side is playable.

Why is that one girl wearing a shirt that is a completely different color than the rest of the team? She's a *libero*? A what?

I learned that libero is the Italian word for "free," and the position is kind of like the free safety in football, a defensive specialist who is not limited by the regular rules of rotation and stays in the game at all times. But the libero never rotates to the front row.

Why are those three girls standing in a row, stacked up, before the serve? Oh, they are getting ready to switch locations as soon as the ball is served? I don't remember doing that in gym class.

When Vacaville High head volleyball coach Jordyn Adcock started explaining about her team's 5-1 formation versus the 6-2, I stood there nodding my head like I knew what she was talking about. Later I asked her and learned more.

Wood High coach Michaela O'Brien was talking about her team's serve-receive passing game. That just sounded to me like a bunch of verbs strung together. Now I understand that "serve-receive" is one concept, passing is another, all designed to set up the hitter for the best possible shot.

There is a whole lot I still don't understand about this game.

But one doesn't have to understand it all to enjoy it. It is fast-paced, action-packed, edge-of-your-seat, elevated by the enthusiasm of the players and the frenetic cheering of the crowd.

Unlike high school badminton, where there are usually simultaneous matches so the audience has to remain quiet and applause is polite, volleyball fans are LOUD.

I learned something else after watching the first league match this season between Vacaville and Vanden. (The highlight was an incredible second set which Vacaville won, 30-28.)

After the Bulldogs won the match, I was in a quandary. Which player should I interview? It's easy in baseball—grab the winning pitcher or the guy who smacked the game-winning homer. Even in basketball it's not too hard—speak with the girl who scored thirty points and hit seven three-pointers.

But volleyball presented a problem. They were all great. On both teams. Okay, so I'll go with the winning team. But then what? Sure, that tall girl had a lot of kills. But that setter made it possible. And that libero got the balls to the setter. And that other girl was diving headlong for all those digs.

Coach Adcock helped me understand. When I mentioned that the two girls I interviewed seemed to be the key to the match, she politely told me that they are in their roles for a reason. But so are each and every one of her other players.

That's when I finally got it: Volleyball is the ultimate team sport

The experts agree.

Cynthia Barboza, an outside hitter who played for Stanford for four years and led the U.S. national team that won the bronze medal at the 2011 Pan American Games, told Reuters, "You only get one contact before you have to give the ball off to a teammate. It's the synergy of the group that eventually wins the match, not just the all-stars you have lined up there."

Christa Harmotto, U.S. 2012 Olympian and silver medalist, said, "You really have to know your teammates. It is six people and one ball, so you have to know what balls they are going for or how to push them."

The proximity of the six players in that little box makes them totally dependent on each other. You can see it in the camaraderie and teamwork that develop during a match and over the course of a season.

Sure, basketball is also a team sport. But sometimes it's better to just clear everybody out and give the ball to Michael Jordan.

That's not an option in volleyball—the very definition of a team sport.

This column first appeared in The Vacaville Reporter *on September 23, 2019.*

***

"Once a Sportswriter . . ."

Now retired, I am reflecting on how I became a sportswriter.

I loved sports as a kid, especially baseball. Growing up in Hackensack, New Jersey, a suburb of New York City, I played organized baseball from age eight all the way through high school.

I never thought about writing sports, nor did I write for my high school newspaper. But something happened my junior year that would prove significant for my future in journalism.

I played clarinet in our high school orchestra. The director of our orchestra had played clarinet in the New York Philharmonic. So our orchestra was very important to him. I faithfully attended class and did my duty in the marching band for football games.

But in the spring of my junior year I ran into a conflict. I had baseball practice every day after school. On the day when the orchestra would be holding its spring concert that evening, I also had a huge amount of homework. I took my studies seriously, as I graduated number one in my senior class of 550 students. I approached the band director and told him I would not be able to play in the concert. He was very annoyed.

The next week, when I went for my weekly clarinet lesson with his assistant, the director saw me and angrily told the assistant, "Don't give him his lesson!" Whoa! That completely turned me off from continuing to play in the orchestra in the fall. So instead, I took typing.

I was the only guy in the typing class. I took to it well and was soon typing sixty-five words per minute. I did not intentionally take it to help me in college. I just thought it would be good to know how to type.

But when I started college at Cornell, there were so many papers to write. And I was able to do my own typing on my trusty Olivetti-Underwood manual typewriter. This saved me a lot of money I would have had to pay some student to type my papers. And I wouldn't have trusted anyone else to do it anyway, as they might have made typos, and I am a perfectionist about my writing.

While at Cornell, I regularly read the *Cornell Daily Sun* newspaper. As I read the sports page, I said to myself, *I can write better than that*. That may sound boastful, but it was my honest evaluation. So I applied to write for the *Sun*. My test assignment was to watch a baseball game on TV and write the game story. So I watched a Mets game on the TV in our dormitory lounge, wrote the story on my Olivetti-Underwood, and was accepted onto the *Sun* staff.

I covered basketball and baseball for the *Sun* and also had the chance to write my first feature article, a profile of one of the varsity basketball players.

In the two summers I remained in Ithaca, New York (where Cornell is located), I wrote sports feature stories for the weekly *Ithaca New Times*, including an interview with Joe DiMaggio.

During my senior year at Cornell, I had no idea what I

wanted to do after graduation. I was a psychology major, but soured on that because Cornell focused on experimental (lab rats) rather than clinical psychology. But I had enjoyed sportswriting, so I applied to a few schools and received a full fellowship for the master's program in magazine journalism at Syracuse University's Newhouse School of Public Communications.

I learned a lot about feature writing and editing at Syracuse and wrote on a variety of topics for the school newspaper. When I graduated in December 1976 I had no job prospects until, at the last minute, I was contacted by *The Cortland Standard* in Cortland, New York. A sportswriter had just retired and they needed a new one. Apparently someone at *The Syracuse Post Standard* had forwarded my application to the Cortland newspaper.

I jumped at the chance and began covering high school sports of every kind for the *Standard*. Unfortunately, some poor life decisions took me away from Cortland, and my time at the *Standard* came to an end. But out of the dark place to which those decisions led me, I came to believe in Jesus in August 1978. I am Jewish, and with a new appreciation of my Jewishness (Jesus was, after all, a Jew), I came to San Francisco to work with the Jews for Jesus organization.

Although I tried, I could not get back into the sportswriting business. My experience at the Cortland paper was too brief, so San Francisco Bay Area newspapers either turned me down or didn't have openings. I left Jews for Jesus in 1982 and worked in the transportation industry for the next twenty-three years. But all that time, I was writing freelance magazine feature stories about Christian athletes, including Hall of Famer Gary Carter, Brent Jones of the San Francisco

49ers, and Steve Alford of Indiana University basketball fame.

So I still had the writing bug. At age fifty-five, I retired from my transportation job and went back to Jews for Jesus to work as a writer and editor, which I did for the next eleven years. When that job ended, I was almost sixty-six years old but still needed to work for my wife's health insurance (she had retired) until she would turn sixty-five in three years and could get Medicare.

To my amazement, a sports reporter job opened up at *The Reporter*, the Vacaville, California, daily newspaper. I went back to writing high school sports, as I did at Cortland years ago, and I loved it. It made for the perfect sportswriting bookend to my career.

Since retiring from *The Reporter*, I wrote a book, *The God Squad: The Born-Again San Francisco Giants of 1978*. And now I write for *The Sports Column*.

Once a sportswriter, always a sportswriter.

PART 2

Sports and Faith

"How and Why I Wrote a Book about the 1978 San Francisco Giants"

I retired from writing sports for *The Reporter*, a daily newspaper in Vacaville, California, in 2020. Early in 2023, I was driving to my local library in Martinez, California, and I thought to myself, *I'd like to write a book. What could I write about?*

Immediately an idea came to me: I could write about the 1978 San Francisco Giants.

Why that team? Here's the story:

I am Jewish, and, through a series of providential events, came to believe in Jesus in August 1978. Gaining a new appreciation of my Jewishness after coming to believe in Jesus as the Jewish Messiah, I joined a group called Jews for Jesus and moved 3,000 miles across the country to work with them at their San Francisco headquarters in 1980.

I began to read the local sports pages in the *Chronicle* and the *Examiner*, the two main San Francisco papers. The *Chronicle* had two controversial sports columnists, Glenn Dickey and Lowell Cohn. Both were excellent wordsmiths. Cohn was a master of satire. Dickey was blunter, a sledgehammer.

In 1978, a number of born-again Christians on the Giants (there were nine or ten) began to speak out about Jesus in post-game interviews, thanking him for the abilities they had. The Giants, who had been mired in mediocrity for most of the 1970s, came to life that year and led the division until mid-August before a September swoon landed them in third place behind the Dodgers and Reds.

The press didn't trouble the born-again Giants when they talked about Jesus, as they were winning. But the next year, when the Giants reverted to their losing ways, the media dubbed the Christians the "God Squad" and began to take potshots at them.

Dickey called Christianity a crutch and called for the Giants ownership to break up the God Squad, which he called a clique, and trade some of them. Cohn, ever the satirist, wrote a column in 1980 called "Can Satan Save the Giants?" in which he suggested that since God wasn't helping the Giants very much, one of them should sell his soul to the devil.

A year later, Cohn wrote another column called "Lavelle and the Fiend," in which he said that pitcher Gary Lavelle, who had called San Francisco a satanic region (in part because the Church of Satan was founded there by Anton LaVey in 1966), was intolerant.

As I was reading these columns in the *Chronicle,* they irritated me. Of course, Cohn and Dickey intentionally provoke reaction. But as a Jesus believer, I felt that they were unfairly picking on the God Squadders.

In late 1982, the pastor of my church in South San Francisco asked if I could pinch-hit for him and deliver a message to the local chapter of the Fellowship of Christian Athletes (FCA). So I found myself in the home of two brothers, Keith and Drew Petiti (Drew later became my brother-in-law) talking to some college-aged kids about Jesus. After the meeting, Keith told me that their next guest speaker would be Gary Lavelle.

I attended that meeting and afterwards approached Gary to see if I could interview him for an article for the FCA magazine. He agreed, and I met with him in his home, interviewed him and got the article published. In speaking with Gary, I referred to the treatment he was getting from Cohn and Dickey and suggested that the God Squad controversy would make for a good book. He agreed. But we soon realized that neither of us had the time to devote to the project.

Fast forward forty years as I am driving to the Martinez library and have the idea of writing a book about the God Squad. *Are any of those guys still around? What about Cohn and Dickey? If so, would they be willing to talk with me?*

I attempted to reach several God Squad "members"—pitchers Lavelle and Bob Knepper, utility infielder Rob Andrews, shortstop Johnnie LeMaster, outfielder Jack Clark, first baseman Mike Ivie, and others. Some I couldn't reach, others declined, but two said yes—Lavelle and Knepper.

Lavelle was willing because he already knew me. Knepper was reluctant at first because he had been so badly burned by the media during his years with the Giants. But he eventually agreed and we have become very good friends.

I was wary of approaching Cohn. I assumed his personality matched the acerbic tones of his column. Also, Cohn is Jewish. How would he respond to a Jew who believes in Jesus? But I was pleasantly surprised. He was very willing to help a fellow writer and we talked on the phone for a good forty minutes. He was gracious and encouraging and it was one of the best interviews of my career. We too have become good friends.

I learned that Dickey has dementia, so an interview with him was not possible.

In spring 2023, my wife and I traveled to Southern California to be with our daughter as she recovered from back surgery. I spent those days on the couch in her apartment beginning to write my book. It came together so quickly. I started in May and completed my final draft by July. I was able to find an abundance of articles about the God Squad in newspaper archives online—a far cry from my days in journalism school when I had to plow through library microfilm to write my papers.

Finding a publisher was harder than writing my book. But then my pastor at Creekside Church in Martinez told me that we have a book publisher in our congregation—Alive Book Publishing, run by Eric and Peggy Johnson. They were great to work with, and my book, *The God Squad: The Born-Again San Francisco Giants of 1978,* was published in November 2023.

Maybe you have a book in you as well.

***

"Giants of the Faith"

Depending on your spiritual bent, you may have been either thrilled or turned off by University of Connecticut women's basketball star Paige Bueckers talking about her Christian faith in post-game interviews on her way to the semi-finals of the 2024 NCAA tournament.

"I'm a living testimony. I give all glory to God, "she told ESPN. "He works in mysterious ways. Last year [after injury], I was praying to be back at this stage. He sent me trials and tribulations, but it was to build my character. It was to test my faith to see if I was a believer. But I just kept on believing. I did all I could, so God could do all I can't."

Some probably feel, as Beneatha Younger put it in Lorraine Hansberry's play, *A Raisin in the Sun,* "I'm just tired of hearing about God all the time. What has He got to do with anything? I just get so tired of Him getting the credit for things the human race achieves through its own effort.

Now, there simply is no God. There's only man. And it's he who makes miracles."

The media and the public are now accustomed to hearing athletes thank God for the abilities he has given them. But that wasn't always the case. In baseball in the 1950s and 1960s it was extremely rare to hear such pronouncements from athletes. Then in the 1970s in San Francisco, one of the great culture clashes between religious athletes, the media, and the fan base erupted over a group of born-again ballplayers on the Giants who became known as the God Squad.

Giants' relief pitcher Gary Lavelle became a born-again Christian in the winter of 1976. When he returned to the club the next spring, he gradually and quietly began to share his faith with his teammates when they showed an interest. Several, including Bob Knepper, Jack Clark, Rob Andrews, and Randy Moffitt (brother of tennis great Billie Jean King) came to faith, and by the 1978 season there were nine or ten professing Christians on the team.

The Giants, who had suffered through several losing seasons, came to life that year and led the National League West for much of the season, only to fade in a September swoon and finish third. In post-game interviews, the players frequently thanked God for the ability he gave them, and the press raised no objection.

But when the Giants' fortunes faded on the field in 1979, the media was quick to blame the born-again players, claiming their newfound faith had made them passive. The press derisively referred to them as the God Squad.

The cornerstone of that accusation was a quote attributed to pitcher Knepper, who supposedly told manager Dave Bristol it was "God's will" when he yielded a home run that lost a game. Knepper and his Christian teammates have always denied the quote, as did Bristol. But the false story continued to hound them for years.

The media was merciless at times. *San Francisco Chronicle* columnist Glenn Dickey wrote, "It may be that the Giants will have to trade one or two of the most obvious born-agains on the club, to break up the clique. At the very least, their lockers should be separated in the clubhouse."

Another prominent *Chronicle* sports columnist, Lowell Cohn, told me recently that he disagrees with Dickey on that score. However, Cohn, known for his biting satire, penned one of his most provocative pieces, "Can Satan Save the Giants?" in which he recommended that one of the Giants sell his soul to the devil since God didn't seem to be helping the team too much.

Not only did the media blame the God Squad for losing, it also alleged that the Christian athletes caused division in the clubhouse and got two managers fired. These false claims spread to the national media, where prestigious columnists Peter Gammons of *The Boston Globe* and Dick Young of the *New York Daily News* repeated them. One of the more ridiculous accusations was that the Giants had two team buses to take players to the field, one for the God Squad and another for the others,

Mike Ivie, one of the God Squadders, returned to the club from a stint of mental exhaustion and sounded much like Paige Bueckers, who had made a comeback from physical injury.

"He'll put you through trials and tribulations and he'll use every resource to help you find happiness in your heart," said Ivie. "It would have been twice as hard for me to come back if I hadn't believed in the Lord."

Ivie and his teammates commonly made such pronouncements in a liberal San Francisco atmosphere and era that was not conducive to talk about faith. Cohn felt the tension and in his memoirs made this fascinating statement, "Until that day, I believed I was covering a baseball team. I was wrong. I had wandered into the middle of a deep religious debate, one that defined the Giants at that time."

The God Squadders were spiritual pioneers who bore the brunt of attacks by the media. They paved the way for Paige Bueckers and other Christian athletes to speak boldly about their faith.

This column first appeared in The Vacaville Reporter *on May 9, 2024.*

* * *

"Satan and the San Francisco Giants"

Excerpted from my book, The God Squad: The Born-Again San Francisco Giants of 1978 .

San Francisco Chronicle sportswriter Lowell Cohn did not write many columns about the God Squadders, the born-again Christians on the Giants. He was a columnist, not a beat writer, so he wasn't in the Giants' clubhouse every game. Besides, he had to also write about the San Francisco 49ers, the Oakland Raiders, the Golden State Warriors, and the Oakland A's. But when he did approach the topic, he did it with gusto. He wrote a column, "Can Satan Save the Giants?" on May 7, 1980, which made quite a splash.

On the day the *Chronicle* published the column, the Giants were in last place in their division with an 8–18 record. In his satirical piece, Cohn concluded that God must hate the Giants.

Cohn, writing in the *San Francisco Chronicle*: "What does he have against our local heroes? He's downright prejudiced against them. No question about it. He has them so befuddled they can't even count the outs. The irony is that the Giants are a God-fearing bunch, if there ever was one. I'll bet, prayer for prayer, they're the most God-fearing team in major league baseball. It's not for me to say why God has singled out the Giants—His ways are very mysterious to man. But as long as things are already shot to hell, I have a suggestion. Join the other team, fellas. Throw in with the Prince of Darkness—the Big D."

Cohn went on to recommend that at least one Giant sell his soul to the devil to turn the team's season around, just as long-suffering Washington Senators fan Joe Boyd did in the novel, *The Year the Yankees Lost the Pennant*, the inspiration for the 1955 musical comedy, *Damn Yankees*, which in turn generated the movie of the same name (Joe Boyd was transformed into Joe Hardy, Senators' superstar).

"I was joking around," Cohn told this author. "I wrote my satire on the soul because that's what people were talking about. I wasn't accusing them. I was trying to have fun." But, as he would soon discover, some of the Giants didn't get the joke.

In mid-June, the Giants, ten games under .500, were in New York to play the Mets, and Cohn made the rookie journalist mistake of catching a forty-five-minute ride on the team bus from the Giants' hotel in Manhattan to Shea Stadium in Queens. He didn't know that no ballplayer wants a sportswriter on the team bus.

Cohn says he never rode the team bus again. But this time, he did and stood while most of the players sat. Cohn, who had been critical of the Giants, as had other Bay Area writers, told this author: "John Montefusco was in the back. He didn't like me at all. So he started yelling at me. It was more than forty years ago, but I think he said once, "F___ you, Lowell!' The bus stopped at a light in Manhattan. There was a homeless person on the street, and Montefusco yelled, 'See that f___in' bum, that's Lowell's brother!'

"I was still standing up. It happened very quickly. There happened to be an empty seat next to Johnnie LeMaster. He grabbed me and said, 'Sit down here. I'll take care of you.' LeMaster was one of my all-time favorite athletes I ever covered. He is the most decent, lovely person.

"But he was troubled and said to me, 'Why did you write we should sell a soul to the devil?' And I said, 'Johnnie, I didn't mean it. It was satire.' And Johnnie, in the goodness of his heart, said, 'What's satire?' And I'm not putting him down. I love Johnnie. He didn't know. And I tried to explain, you're making a joke, and I don't think I ever adequately explained it to Johnnie. But the point was, even though he disapproved of what I had done, he didn't disapprove of me. And he protected me from what he saw as a verbal onslaught from Montefusco. And by the way, I don't have any hard feelings toward Montefusco. God loves John Montefusco. I'm telling you what happened like forty-three years ago."

Cohn related the story's second half: "So now we get to Shea Stadium, and I already have a migraine headache because of what happened on the bus. So I'm in the dugout, and now Vida Blue—and I didn't even know Vida Blue—comes up, and he doesn't know how to pronounce my name, Cohn [like Cone]. And he says, 'Are you Lowell Cun?' I said yeah. And I thought, *I've already got a migraine, and now this, I've got to deal with Vida Blue.*

"On the contrary, there are all these guys in the dugout. He puts his arm around me and says, 'Lowell Cun, you're okay by me,' letting everybody know, 'Don't screw with this guy.' Then he explained, 'Lowell Cun, I like the God Squadders. But I think they feel losing is God's will, and it troubles me.'

"Vida objected to them. He liked them. How could you not? They were nice guys. But he felt they had a fundamental disagreement. Vida did not accept losing, and I am not saying they did. His perception of them was that they thought losing was God's will, and he wanted everybody to know he approved of the guy, me, who questioned that."

* * *

"Gary Lavelle and the God Squad"

Left-handed reliever Gary Lavelle pitched thirteen seasons in the major leagues, the first eleven with the San Francisco Giants, from 1974-1984. He has pitched in more games (647) than anyone in the history of the Giants, including Christy Mathewson. He is also first for the franchise in games finished (369) and fourth in saves, with 126. He was selected to the National League All-Star team in 1977 and 1983. After retiring from MLB, he became a highly successful high school and college baseball coach in Virginia. This column is based on my interview with him in 1983.

The Fellowship of Christian Athletes gathering had ended and a young woman stopped to chat with guest speaker Gary Lavelle.

"For the first twenty minutes I thought you were a pastor, but when you kept talking about baseball I realized you were a player!" she exclaimed.

At 6-1, 200 pounds it's easy to see why the big lefthander has been mowing them down for nine major league seasons. But the San Francisco Giants ace reliever knows the Bible as well as he does the league's opposing hitters. As the charter member of the Giant's "God Squad" teams of the late 1970s, Gary's helped lead several of his teammates to a personal relationship with Christ.

The youngest of five boys, he was raised on a diet of baseball, football, and basketball in Bethlehem, Pennsylvania, "but baseball was always my first love."

As a high school sophomore Gary tossed his first no-hitter. His senior year he hurled another no-hitter, a bunch of one- and two-hitters, and got a phone call from the Giants. Assigned to their Salt Lake City farm club, Gary began a long climb to the majors. In September 1974, after eight seasons in the minors, he was called up to the parent club.

Gary had married in 1972 and he and wife, Regina, had their first child, daughter Jana, in 1975.

"I'd fulfilled a dream. I had success, money, a beautiful wife, our first child . . . but there was something missing," he said.

At the end of the 1975 season Lavelle went to Venezuela to play winter ball and met former Minnesota Twins pitcher Tom Johnson, who shared about knowing God in a personal way and "answered a lot of questions I had." Gary gave his life to the Lord soon after.

"The hardest thing was coming home," he said about changing his habits. "I didn't want to go into bars anymore." Reporters found the new Lavelle even harder to figure. They were accustomed to the old Lavelle who'd angrily vent his frustration after a poor performance.

"I asked the Lord for strength in both the good times and

bad and before long the press began to report on my newfound composure," he said.

His teammates also saw the change and when opportunities surfaced Gary talked with them about Jesus. "I don't preach. I just share what the Bible has to say about life," he stated.

By 1979 the press had dubbed the Giants the "God Squad" because of the number of professing Christians on the team.

Gary's performance speaks as loudly as his words. Last season his 10-7 mark and 2.67 ERA helped keep the Giants in the pennant race until the next-to-last day of the season.

Coming out of the bullpen in the late innings of a tight game is Gary's specialty, but his biggest challenge came in 1980.

"I'd gotten off to a terrible start and lost my job as the number one reliever. I kept asking the Lord, 'Is this the end of my career?' he recalled. "He gave me the desire to work harder, to go the extra mile."

Gary began a weight training program the next year and by 1982 his arm had returned to form.

"I learned to persevere when the odds are against you, but it also made me realize baseball will end someday and I'll need to go on," he said.

A family man, Gary looks forward to playing ball with his young son Timothy. He relishes family picnics and outings and has recently revived his interest in hunting. When his playing days are over he may go back to school to prepare for a career in business.

"The Lord will guide my path after baseball. I have peace about that."

This column first appeared in Sharing the Victory, *Fellowship of Christian Athletes, July-August 1983.*

* * *

"Jack Clark's Revenge on the Dodgers"

Whitey Herzog called Jack Clark "the greatest fastball hitter of our era." Clark became a born-again Christian in 1977 and was part of the notorious God Squad of the San Francisco Giants. Here is an excerpt about Clark with the Cardinals from my book, The God Squad: The Born-Again San Francisco Giants of 1978.

Before joining the Cardinals in 1985, Clark spent his first ten seasons in the majors with the San Francisco Giants. He may not have been able to propel the Giants to the postseason, but in two of his three seasons with the Cardinals, 1985 and 1987, the team reached the World Series.

"I don't think there's much doubt what he did for us," Cardinals manager Whitey Herzog said in 1990, three years after Clark left the Cards. "We haven't been back to the World Series since, have we?"

But if any felt that becoming a Jesus follower made players passive and gave them the option to excuse every failure as "God's will," Giants fans (bred to be eternal Dodger-haters) will be pleased to hear how Clark felt about hitting his most famous home run, a three-run shot off the Dodgers' Tom Niedenfuer to clinch the National League pennant for the Cardinals in the top of the ninth inning of Game 6 of the 1985 National League Championship Series at Dodger Stadium.

In the seventh inning, with the score tied and Ozzie Smith on third base, Clark struck out against Niedenfuer.

Mike Marshall hit a home run in the eighth inning to give the Dodgers a 5–4 lead.

In the top of the ninth, the Cardinals were down to their last out when Clark came up with Willie McGee on third base and Ozzie Smith on second. Instead of issuing an intentional walk, Dodger manager Tommy Lasorda decided to pitch to Clark. The former Giant smashed Niedenfuer's first pitch into the left-field stands. "It was a good pitch to hit—a fastball, down—and I knew it was gone the minute I hit it," Clark told *UPI* sportswriter Aurelio Rojas.

"I knew first base was open, but I thought they'd come after me because that's what they always did when I was with the Giants because they never respected us," Clark told blogger Jason Peake. "I was having a great series and thought I could hit anything. I was on everything. And I didn't like the Dodgers. I wanted them to go down. They came after me on the first pitch, and I was ready for it. It was a pretty big moment for me, my teammates, Whitey Herzog, and the Cardinal fans, and also for the Giants fans."

As Rojas noted: "The victory washed away unhappy memories both distant and recent for Clark. 'Around the bases, I thought about all the bad times,' said the Cardinals' first baseman, who went through many losing seasons with the San Francisco Giants before being traded to St. Louis in the off-season.

"'As I neared home plate and saw all my teammates there, it dawned on me, "We're going to the World Series, we're going to the World Series." I made the big out before and allowed Marshall to put them ahead,' said Clark, a born-again Christian. 'But I got a chance to redeem myself.'"

Clark told Rick Hummel of the *St. Louis Post-Dispatch*, "There was a lot of payback for many reasons. For all those years in Candlestick Park. Not only was it bad enough just having to play there, but the Dodgers kept whipping up on us every year. I had one mission. To seek and destroy everyone on that team, from Fernando Valenzuela to Orel Hershiser. I wanted it all."

Hummel wrote, "The rage in Clark almost was uncontrollable when he faced the Dodgers."

"I tried to hit it out of the stadium," Clark told him. "I didn't just want a home run. I wanted to have it be shot out of a cannon."

If being born again put out Clark's competitive fire, the Dodgers would sure like an explanation.

* * *

"Mike Ivie, Miracle Man"

Former major league Mike Ivie passed away on July 21, 2023, in North Augusta, South Carolina, at age seventy. A born-again Christian, Ivie was part of the notorious God Squad of the San Francisco Giants during the late 1970s. Here is an excerpt from my book, The God Squad: The Born-Again San Francisco Giants of 1978.

San Francisco's Candlestick Park had a record crowd of 56,103 on May 28, 1978, when the Giants erased a 5-0 Los Angeles Dodgers lead and won 6–5, fueled by a pinch-hit grand slam home run from Mike Ivie. The Giants had been trailing 3–0 going into the bottom of the sixth inning. After the team scored once and loaded the bases, Ivie drilled a shot over the left-field wall to put them ahead 5–3.

From the *San Francisco Chronicle*: "The deafening Candlestick reception for Ivie's home run was what Giants pitcher John Montefusco wanted to discuss. 'I was talking to [trainer] Joe Liscio when Mike got up there and said, "Wouldn't it be unbelievable if he hit one out?" Joe says, "He's gonna do it on this pitch." And sure enough, he did. The ovation Mike got was something I'll never forget. We're going right down to the wire with the Dodgers in every game we play.'"

Ivie, sent up to bat for left-handed Vic Harris in an against-the-percentage move [because the pitcher, Don Sutton, is right-handed], said he was "just looking for a fly ball" against Sutton with one out. "He gave me something I could pull, but I didn't think it was going out. Then the crowd told me it was. The whole feeling is beyond words."

Giants fan Charles A. Fracchia Jr., who was thirteen and at the game that day, said, "He [Ivie] nails that pitch over the fence. The whole stadium rocks like it was an earthquake. The stadium shook. It was unreal. People hugging each other . . . such excitement."

The *San Francisco Examiner*: "I tell ya, this team has so much confidence in each other," said Ivie. "If we get behind, we know we can come back. We believe so much that we can do it. It's a feeling that no other club in the major leagues has got. We have a home-type, unity-type of feeling. It's super. I don't want to be anywhere else but here. I don't want you to misunderstand this, but if we go on the road and win some games, I believe in my heart that we can win the whole thing."

Ivie had a couple of other signature moments later that season.

On July 25 at Candlestick, Vida Blue took a shutout and a 1–0 lead into the ninth inning against the Cardinals, but the Redbirds struck for two runs to take the lead. Bob Stevens of the *Chronicle* described the action in the bottom of the frame: "The Little Miracle of Candlestick Park, and the Miracle Man, struck again last night. With one out in the ninth and a deeply disappointed crowd of 39,289 shuffling quietly toward the exits, Larry Herndon singled, pinch hitter Mike Ivie did his thing—a home run—and the Giants climbed over the St. Louis Cardinals, 3-2. The Giants are 7,020 fans short of hitting the million-mark in attendance."

Rom Fimrite of *Sports Illustrated* covered a four-game series between the Giants and Dodgers at Candlestick in early August, each team winning twice. Fimrite wrote: "And as a team with more than the ordinary complement of born-again Christians—playing in a notoriously sinful city, at that—they appear convinced that the so-called Big Dodger in the Sky who watched so benignly over their opponents a year ago has come over to their side now. In the opinion of the devout Ivie, only divine intervention can account for the Giants' penchant for turning adversity into advantage. 'Too many things are happening our way,' he says, 'too many good things. You have to believe we're being watched.'"

Later that month, Ivie pinch-hit a two-out, two-run ninth-inning home run off ace closer Tug McGraw to beat the Phillies 6–5. The victory kept the Giants one game back of the Dodgers.

In sole possession of first place for much of the season, the Giants had a late-season swoon and finished in third place behind the Dodgers and Reds. Ivie hit .308 that season and belted four pinch-hit home runs, hitting .387 as a pinch hitter. Two of his pinch-hit home runs were grand slams, a single-season record he shares with four other major leaguers. He had an even better year in 1979, smashing 27 home runs and driving in 89 runs to go along with a .286 batting average.

But trials awaited him that would cause emotional turmoil that even his faith was not able to subdue.

* * *

"Boo!"

Johnnie LeMaster was part of the notorious God Squad of the San Francisco Giants in the late 1970s and early 1980s. Here is an excerpt about LeMaster from my book, The God Squad: The Born-Again San Francisco Giants of 1978.

The boos began in 1978 for Johnnie LeMaster, a born-again Christian, who played in the major leagues for thirteen seasons, the first ten with the San Francisco Giants. Baseball writer Sam Miller wrote how booing him began: "The Giants had ace John Montefusco on the mound, and he pitched beautifully, but his teammates managed only a single hit. LeMaster made a throwing error that led to a run, and the Giants lost 1–0. The fans booed LeMaster, and they just . . . never stopped. They developed a habit and never bothered to break it."

Later, Glenn Schwarz of the *San Francisco Examiner* reported: "The first chorus of boos drifted out from the Candlestick stands and reached Johnnie LeMaster's ears a week ago. By the weekend, you didn't need a scorecard to know who was coming to bat for the San Francisco Giants. As the catcalls increased, LeMaster bit his lower lip and told himself to ignore the noise.

"'It's something I have to live with. The fans pay their money and can boo when they want,' the Giants shortstop said. 'You just can't let it get to you.'

"It was no coincidence that it began after LeMaster made a throwing error behind John Montefusco, leading to an unearned run for Atlanta and a 1–0 defeat for the Count [as they called Montefusco back then].

"'I would say the error had a little to do with the boos. Maybe a lot,' LeMaster said, 'But I haven't hit yet either.'"

The Giants had a great year in 1978, challenging the Dodgers and Reds for the division title until a September swoon. Still, when the Giants returned to their losing ways in 1979 (71–91 record), the fans, for some reason, directed their displeasure at LeMaster. As Miller put it, "It would be too emotionally draining, too real, for Giants fans to hate all twenty-five players on their losing club, so they invented a myth that LeMaster alone was the scapegoat."

"The only thing I could figure out is I would make an error at the wrong time of the game or maybe not get a base hit at the right time," LeMaster said. "Our record wasn't the greatest the whole time I played there. Maybe they needed somebody to let their frustration or anger out."

His wife, Debbie, kiddingly suggested he change his name to "Boo." LeMaster ran with the idea and asked equipment manager Eddie Logan to make a jersey with "BOO" on the back in place of his last name. After a couple of weeks, on July 23, 1979, at Candlestick Park, LeMaster got up the courage to wear it in a game. The only teammate who knew LeMaster would pull the stunt was Rob Andrews.

Manager Joe Altobelli didn't have the best eyesight and asked Andrews why LeMaster had "Bob" on the back of his jersey. That broke up everybody in the dugout. The caper was short-lived. LeMaster only got to wear the jersey in the field in the top half of the first inning before General Manager Spec Richardson intervened, fired the equipment manager, and ordered LeMaster to put on his regular jersey.

"But, when the game was over," LeMaster related,

"where do you think every newspaper reporter and TV camera in the San Francisco Bay Area was? And I mean, I had mikes in front of my face like you wouldn't believe. But here's the thing about it. The fans loved it. The reporters loved it. They ate it up. My general manager fined me five hundred dollars for being out of uniform. But it was the best fine that I'd ever had. Eddie Logan got his job back, and everything ended well."

LeMaster had no regrets. Years later, he told the high school baseball players he coached, "Every once in a while, it's not bad to do something a little bit crazy. Sometimes doing something a little crazy makes people realize you're as human as they are."

* * *

"Dave Dravecky's Unforgettable Game"

This is an excerpt from my book, The God Squad: The Born-Again San Francisco Giants of 1978.

The second version of the God Squad included five pitchers—Atlee Hammaker, a Giant from 1982 to 1990, Scott Garrelts (1982–1991), Dave Dravecky (1987–1989), Jeff Brantley (1988–1993), and Craig Lefferts (1987–1989). Outfielders Brett Butler (1988–1990), Kevin Bass (1990–92), and Candy Maldonado (1986–1989), catcher Gary Carter (1990), and utility men Dave Anderson (1990–91) and Greg Litton (1989–92) were also born-again Giants. And Houston traded Bob Knepper back to the Giants in 1989.

In September 1989, the *Santa Rosa Press Democrat* reported that as many as fifteen Giants out of the twenty-four-man roster attended chapel services.

A year earlier, misunderstanding had grown between the God Squadders and some teammates, fed, in part, by the press. Dravecky described it:

After a while, the "God Squad" term became a pejorative. It certainly made life difficult for us in the clubhouse as reporters constantly probed other ballplayers about their feelings regarding the "religious" pitchers on their team. Scott, Jeff, Atlee, and I read anonymous quotes from our teammates questioning whether we had what it took to be winners. Some felt that we were too "passive" or "weak" because we shrugged off defeat, thinking it must have been "God's will."

That was a bunch of baloney because I know I fought with everything I had when I was on the mound . . . If the media has a weakness, it's called writing from the "template." The template for Christian ballplayers is that we are too nice to be winners, that we lack intensity and determination at crunch time, and that when we lose, we shrug our shoulders and mumble, "Praise the Lord."

Dravecky received support from his manager, Roger Craig. After the southpaw spun a two-hit complete game shutout against the Cardinals in Game 2 of the 1987 National League Championship Series, he was led to a media room next to the locker room, where Craig was answering questions. When the manager looked up and saw Dravecky, he said, "They say Christians don't have any guts. Well, this guy's a Christian and he's not afraid of anything."

Dravecky demonstrated that courage in a remarkable chain of events that began in 1988. He had surgery to remove a cancerous tumor in his pitching arm in October. The surgeon removed half of the deltoid muscle and froze the humerus bone in an attempt to eliminate all the cancerous cells. In what many called a miraculous return to baseball, Dravecky pitched eight-innings in a 4–3 victory over the

Cincinnati Reds on August 10, 1989, at Candlestick Park in front of 34,810 roaring fans.

Writing in 1999 for the *San Francisco Chronicle*, Henry Schulman recalled that game played ten years earlier:

Dravecky did not exactly fit the San Francisco mold. His politics were right of Ronald Reagan's, and he was a born-again Christian. But . . . when Dravecky returned to the mound at Candlestick Park for the first time after battling cancer in his arm for more than a year, everyone—politics and religion not withstanding—felt a kinship with the man. On a beautiful afternoon, with not a wisp of wind in the air, the applause began as soon as Dravecky stepped out of the tunnel to begin his pregame warmups. The applause turned into an ovation, one of many he got that day as he not only pitched, but won, beating the Cincinnati Reds. There were lumps in tens of thousands of throats.

Five days later, while pitching in Montreal, Dravecky felt a tingling sensation in his arm in the fifth inning. The next inning, on his first pitch to Tim Raines, Dravecky's humerus bone shattered, the sound heard throughout the stadium as Dravecky collapsed on the mound.

San Francisco Chronicle sportswriter Bruce Jenkins wrote about Dravecky's equanimity when the pitcher met with the Bay Area press the morning after his injury:

He had the same calm, relaxed look on his face, the same glow in his eye, the same attitude that said, "My life is going just great." That's the Dravecky we've always known, and it's the one we've got today. If you are put off by the open preachings of Christian athletes, then maybe his story is not for you. But Dravecky's beliefs are at the heart of his strength. That became abundantly clear in the wake of an injury that sent shock waves through the baseball world.

Jenkins noted how Dravecky's born-again teammates

rallied around him when the pitcher returned to his hotel room the night of his injury: "Within minutes, his best friends on the team were there: Garrelts, Bob Knepper, Jeff Brantley, and Greg Litton. The five of them, all of whom share a vigorous belief in Christianity, stayed in Dravecky's room from midnight until 5 a.m., talking things over."

Although Dravecky had felt there was division between the Christians and non-Christians in 1988, he said that was not a problem on the 1989 team.

"I think there's camaraderie on this club," he said near the close of the 1989 regular season. "I also think there's a genuine respect from the players on the team that might not choose to attend [chapel], and that's obviously important."

Dravecky's cancer returned and his left arm and shoulder had to be amputated in June 1991. On July 16, the Associated Press reported on the first time Dravecky spoke publicly after the operation:

Looking fit and rested, Dravecky said, "There's adjustments that I have to make, but there's nothing out there that I don't want to do." Although his future won't include baseball, Dravecky said he will swim, play golf and tennis, and engage in other sports he was unable to enjoy in the past because of his baseball contract. He also has a full schedule of speaking engagements.

* * *

"Gary Carter Thanked Jesus and Turned Heads"

Hall of Fame catcher Gary Carter passed away in 2012 at age fifty-seven from brain cancer. My interview with him for this column took place in 1990 at Candlestick Park when he was a San Francisco Giant.

It was the 1986 World Series, the New York Mets versus

the Boston Red Sox—and Gary Carter, catcher for the Mets, played a key role. In Game 4, he hit two home runs to tie the Series at two games each. But his biggest contribution came in the tenth inning of Game 6 in one of the most exciting comebacks in World Series history.

The Mets trailed in the Series, three games to two. They were losing 5-3 as they batted in the last of the tenth. With two outs and nobody on base, Carter came to the plate. The Red Sox were one out away from winning the World Series.

"I felt that God was going to bat with me," Carter said of that moment "I felt so confident."

He lined a base hit into left field. The next two Mets also got hits. Then, after a passed ball allowed the tying run to score, Mookie Wilson hit a ground ball that went through the legs of Red Sox first baseman Bill Buckner, giving the Mets a 6-5 victory. New York went on to win Game 7 and become the World Series champions.

During the post-game celebration in the Mets clubhouse, Bob Costas of NBC called Carter to the microphone for an interview.

"They had me up on the platform," Carter remembers, "and he [Costas] said, 'Well, Gary, what do you think about all this?' And I said, 'Well, first of all, I want to give all the glory and praise to Jesus.'"

Carter's remark caught Costas off guard and probably surprised many in the national television audience as well.

But this eleven-time All-Star catcher has never held back; he is quick to give the credit for his success on the ball field and in life to his personal relationship with Jesus Christ.

From 1990-2021, Carter held the National League record for most games caught. Twice named the Most Valuable

Player of the All-Star game, he also won the Gold Glove award three times.

Nicknamed "The Kid" for his enthusiasm for the game of baseball, Carter is seldom at a loss for words. He is also rarely too busy to sign an autograph or to talk with a young fan.

Carter lost his mother to leukemia when he was twelve years old and said he will always have a place in his heart for any child who has lost a parent. His faith in God actually arose out of the doubts that he experienced after his mother's death.

"We were a church-going family," Carter said, "and we had known the Lord as a loving God. I didn't understand why the Lord would take someone away as dear as Mom at age thirty-seven, who was loved by her family. Why would this tragedy happen?"

With these questions in the back of his mind, Carter immersed himself in sports during his teenage years. He was captain of the baseball, basketball, and football teams as a junior and senior at Sunny Hills High in Fullerton, California. He also excelled as a student, graduating in the top fifty of a class of 550.

A high school All-American quarterback as a sophomore and junior, Carter signed a letter of intent to play football at UCLA. But when he tore the ligaments in his right knee while playing football his senior year, he decided instead to sign a professional baseball contract with the Montreal Expos.

In 1973 Carter went to his first major league spring training camp, where he was assigned to room with another catcher, John Boccabella.

"He was twice my age," Carter said. "And I figured I

could learn a lot from him. He taught me a ton about baseball. But what really stood out to me was how he lived his life."

They became good friends, and Carter talked with him about losing his mother. Boccabella gave him Bible verses to read and shared with him that the secret of the peace he experienced was a personal relationship with God through Jesus Christ.

Soon after getting to know Boccabella, Carter asked Christ into his life and finally came to terms with his mother's death.

"Since that day," Carter said, "everything in my life has taken on new meaning. I have learned I don't have to run away from my problems, because God gives me the power to face up to them. The best decision I ever made was asking Christ into my life."

After ten highly productive seasons with the Montreal Expos, Carter was traded to the New York Mets in 1985. He drove in one hundred or more runs his first two seasons with the Mets, and his inspired play helped lead the Mets into the World Series against the Red Sox in 1986.

Carter said that it's not unusual for him to feel that God is with him as he goes to bat In fact, he enjoys the pressure situations.

"I just pray in my heart about it," he says, "then I go up there, and I feel like he gives me something extra."

The San Francisco Giants signed him prior to the 1990 season, and he shared the catching duties most of the season with Terry Kennedy. He hit a respectable .254 and also belted nine home runs in less than 250 at-bats.

Carter believes that a ballplayer's faith should make a difference in his on-the-field performance.

"As athletes, we're blessed with the ability to play the game," he said. "If you're able to look in the mirror and say, 'Hey, I gave it my very best,' it's between you and God. And if you're shortchanging yourself, you're the one to blame. So I've always taken that out on the field every day, and it's made me a better ballplayer. Because I don't ever try to underachieve. I always try to overachieve."

This column, which has been contemporized, first appeared in Teen Quest, *November 1991.*

* * *

"In His Own Words: Brett Butler's Story"

Brett Butler, who had a career .290 batting average, 2,375 hits, and 558 stolen bases, is considered one of the best leadoff hitters of the 1980s and early 1990s. This is his story, as told to me at Candlestick Park in 1989 when he was a San Francisco Giant.

I had just completed one of the best seasons of my baseball career. I scored over 100 runs, batted .311, stole 47 bases, and led all American League outfielders in fielding percentage.

So that winter at my home in Atlanta, I was relishing the off-season and looking forward to the year ahead. But on January 16, 1986, my baseball future almost came to a sudden end.

While I was playing racquetball, the ball smashed into my right eye, breaking my protective goggles. My eye hemorrhaged and my vision was impaired. For five days, I lay on my back in the hospital with patches over both eyes.

I knew my career might be over. But, being a Christian, I put everything in God's hands. I told him, "If it's your will for me to do something else, I'll accept that.

When the doctors removed the bandages, they were amazed. My injured eye had cleared up. God had healed me. It was a miracle.

I hadn't always been so submissive to the will of God. Although I grew up attending a Christian church, it wasn't until I was a sophomore in high school that I understood I needed to accept Jesus into my heart in order to go to heaven. That year, at a Fellowship of Christian Athletes conference, I received Christ as my personal Savior. But total dedication didn't come until later.

After graduating high school, I played junior varsity baseball at Arizona State University. Then I transferred to Southeastern Oklahoma State University, where I was an All-American my junior and senior years. In 1979, I was drafted by the Atlanta Braves and began my climb through their minor league organization.

I saw how God was directing my steps and turned to him for help in various matters. I even cut out drinking and tried to stop swearing. But there was one area of my life that hadn't changed—my relationship with women.

I enjoyed wining and dining, and if it led to anything, I figured that was all right. But then I'd feel bad. I'd feel guilty because the Lord was convicting me of the fact that I was wrong.

As I struggled with this weakness, I asked God

to put a Christian woman in my life. So in 1982, in Richmond, Virginia, I met Eveline Balac, who had become a Christian just a few months earlier. Three days after we met, we knew we were getting married.

We were married that same year and the Lord solidified that aspect of my life. He dealt with the one weakness I couldn't give up by putting a Christian woman in my life. It's made my entire walk with God stronger.

The Lord has blessed us with four healthy children, and they're all gifts. For me it is essential to be with your family. The constant travel in baseball makes this tougher, but we try to keep the family as close together as possible.

In life we are faced with many tests and trials, and believe me, baseball players are not exempt. If you look at athletics as a whole, there's a lot of pressure. Some people turn to drugs, to drinking, to women, or whatever it may be.

Some people have a misconception about ballplayers who are Christians. They talk about us being passive. But if Jesus Christ was a ballplayer, he'd have been the best there is. Look at Orel Hershiser or other Christian athletes who play very, very hard. You can't tell me that these are passive individuals.

I've always tried to give it my very best in baseball. But, as I've discovered, even your best is no guarantee of job security. In 1983, my first full season with the Braves, I was the starting center fielder and the lead-off man. I set an Atlanta single-season record with 39 stolen bases, led the major leagues with 13 triples, and got 5 hits in one game against Montreal.

But late that season I was traded to the Cleveland Indians. It was a tremendous shock to me, as I'd been with the Atlanta organization since 1979.

With God's help, I was able to let the past go and gave it my all for the Indians. In 1984, I became the first player in Cleveland history to steal more than fifty bases and score more than one-hundred runs in the same season. I had four solid years with the Indians, averaging forty-one stolen bases a season and leading the majors in triples again in 1986. But after the 1987 season, we couldn't agree on a contract. So I decided to become a free agent.

I try to let God direct my steps, so I just said, "Okay, Lord, wherever you want me to be." I never expected San Francisco.

But I really enjoy it with the Giants. I grew up across the Bay in Fremont, so it's almost like coming home. In my first season with the new club, I led the league in runs scored and the team in stolen bases.

So, even through the unexpected changes in my career, the Lord has blessed me unbelievably.

My career didn't end the day I was playing racquetball, but it might have. Being blind for five days is a very humbling experience, but it helped me to put life in perspective.

As it Is, I'm not going to be in baseball very much longer—five or six years, maybe. And I don't know what the future holds. All I can do is take it one day at a time and live the way God wants me to live. When the game is over, I'll cross that bridge when I come to it.

This column first appeared in Full Gospel Business Men's Voice, *July 1989.*

* * *

"Struggles and Successes of Scott Garrelts"

Scott Garrelts pitched for the San Francisco Giants from 1982-1991, compiling a 69-52 won-loss record with a 3.29 ERA. This column is based on my 1990 interview with him.

As a boy growing up in Illinois as a Chicago Cubs fan, Scott Garrelts never dreamed he would be on the mound at Wrigley Field ready to pitch against the Cubs in the first game of the 1989 National League Championship Series.

The twenty-eight-year-old San Francisco Giants pitcher beat the Cubs in that game, helping to propel his team into the World Series. Though the Giants fell to the Oakland Athletics four games to none in the earthquake-interrupted Series, 1989 was the best year of Garrelts' career.

The 6-4 righthander compiled a 14-5 won-lost record and led all National League starting pitchers with a 2.28 ERA.

Things haven't always gone so smoothly for Garrelts. Between an All-Star season as a reliever in 1985 and 1989's heroics, life in the big leagues has been a roller coaster ride.

In 1988 he had a season that most pitchers would like to forget.

"I had a 6.21 ERA the first half," Garrelts says of his efforts as a relief pitcher. "I was blowing saves and struggling."

When the media and fans started to criticize his performance, the situation went from bad to worse.

"I kept trying to prove to the Giants, to prove to everybody, what I could do," Garrelts recalls. "And I kept spinning my wheels, kept getting deeper and deeper."

As the frustration grew, Garrelts talked with two of his closest friends on the Giants, pitchers Dave Dravecky and Atlee Hammaker. Like Garrelts, Dravecky and Hammaker are born-again Christians. They had also struggled with trying to please everybody when they pitched.

"We talked about what am I really playing for," says Garrelts. "I stopped trying to pitch for everybody, and when I did that, I could accept myself and just do my best."

In his last twenty games of 1988, Garrelts allowed just four earned runs in 32 2/3 innings (a 1.10 ERA), recording four saves and two wins, salvaging a season that had almost become a nightmare.

Even as a boy growing up in Buckley, Illinois, a town of six hundred people, Garrelts didn't attain instant success in baseball.

"I was nothing spectacular," he says. "My first two years in high school were not that big of a deal. My sophomore year I actually pitched terrible. I got beat up all over the place."

But in his junior year, he began to improve. In a game for Buckley-Loda High, he struck out twenty-two batters in the seven-inning contest. If you know a little baseball and a little math, you realize those numbers don't compute—unless the catcher dropped a third strike, allowing the batter to advance to first base.

"Actually, he dropped two," Garrelts explains. "There was one guy who put the ball into play. He bunted it back to me in the air."

After that eye-opening no-hitter, the scouts started showing up. When Garrelts graduated from high school in 1979, the Giants made him their number one selection in the free-agent draft.

After six seasons of minor league ball, he burst onto the Giants' scene in 1985 with an outstanding season. As a reliever, he posted a 9-6 mark with a 2.30 ERA and 106 strikeouts in 105 innings. He was the only Giant selected to the National League All-Star Team.

Garrelts was promoted to a starting role in 1986. But he didn't win consistently and was moved back to the bullpen by July. He did better as a reliever, and the following year he led all National League relievers with 127 strikeouts.

Then came the nearly disastrous 1988 season.

"Without Jesus in my life," says Garrelts of that year, "I don't know if I could have made it. I was struggling, the people around me knew I was struggling, yet there was still that comfort that I had. I was still at ease."

Although Garrelts attended church with his family throughout his youth, it wasn't until his years in the minor leagues that God became real for him. The pivotal time was during a trip to the Dominican Republic to play winter baseball.

"In 1984, we were down in the Dominican, and we had no TV, no telephone, no radio, no anything, and I had taken my Bible down there. I was reading one night in the book of John, and I knelt down beside the bed and prayed to receive Christ."

Garrelts says that although he grew in his faith, progress was slow until 1987, when Dravecky arrived in a trade with the San Diego Padres. The following year, center fielder Brett Butler came to the Giants from the Atlanta Braves, and the three of them plus Hammaker formed an accountability group. In 1989, another Christian, Bob Knepper, was traded to the Giants from the Houston Astros and joined the group.

In 1989 the Giants decided to try Garrelts as a starting pitcher again. After a minor injury caused him to miss a few pitching turns, he came back in mid-July and won eight games in succession, the last of them a crucial victory over the second-place San Diego Padres in mid-September. He had become the Giants' most consistent starting pitcher.

"Throughout my minor league career, I always felt like I was a .500 pitcher. I'd win a game, lose a game, win two, lose two—because I always had that feeling that I'm going to lose. It wasn't until I got into the major leagues that I realized that God doesn't want you to lose. He wants you to be successful. And it wasn't until I realized that, that I was able to overcome the fear of being a .500 pitcher and to excel and to be more than that. It helped me not to think on the negative things. It helped me concentrate on what I had to do."

This column first appeared in Teen Quest *in March 1991.*

* * *

"Jesus at the Bat"

The following is an excerpt from my book, The God Squad: The Born-Again San Francisco Giants of 1978.

When a baseball player brings Jesus into his life, can it improve his performance? One could look at batting averages and ERAs before and after a player became a Christian to try to answer the question. But too many other factors can affect those statistics. Increased experience in the big leagues can lead to improvement. Conversely, age can lead to decline. Even something as simple as a change in one's slot in the batting order can impact a player's statistics for a season.

So the only source to test the theory is the player himself. Let's hear what they had to say.

Catcher **Mike Matheny**, who went on to manage the St. Louis Cardinals and the Kansas City Royals, told this author that he had such a dreadful spring training before his first season with the Cardinals in 2000 that he worried he wouldn't make the cut.

"My walk with God was as strong as it had ever been," he said, "but my baseball was terrible."

He spent a lot of time in prayer, talked with his wife, Kristen, and came to realize the problem.

"I had been playing not to fail," he explained, noting that he was too concerned about making his new team. He dove back into baseball with new boldness. He not only made the team but was the starting catcher on opening day and went on to win his first Gold Glove.

Another catcher, Hall of Famer **Gary Carter**, shared with this author his thoughts about the relationship between faith and performance. In Game 6 of the 1986 World Series, Carter's Mets were one out away from losing the series, four games to two, to the Boston Red Sox. Boston led 5–3 as New York batted in the last of the tenth inning. With two outs and nobody on, Carter came to the plate.

"I felt that God was going to bat with me," he said. "I felt so confident."

He lined a base hit into left field. The next two Mets also got hits. Then, after a wild pitch allowed the tying run to score, Mookie Wilson hit a ground ball that went through the legs of Red Sox first baseman Bill Buckner, giving the

Mets a 6–5 victory. New York went on to win Game 7 and become the World Series champions.

Carter said it was not unusual for him to feel that God was with him as he went to bat. In fact, he enjoyed the pressure situations.

"I just pray in my heart about it," he said. "Then I go up there, and I feel like he gives me something extra."

After retiring from baseball, Carter elaborated in 1997 on his at-bat that inning:

"While in the on-deck circle, I really felt the presence of God right there. I normally prayed while in the on-deck circle, but this time I prayed maybe just a little more. With divine intervention, I was able to line a base hit into left field, which led to a rally and our winning the game 6–5. We then won Game 7 and the World Series. Without God in my life, that moment may have never happened."

Nick Peters of the *Sporting News* wrote this about San Francisco Giant **Jack Clark**:

"Ask Jack for the main reason behind his change of attitude and impressive statistics in 1978 and he doesn't hesitate to answer.

"'I've accepted God,' he said. 'I wasn't getting fulfillment out of baseball last year, so I turned to the Lord and let him guide me. I enjoy telling people about my involvement with the Lord and how he blesses my life. I find some people turn around and walk away when I start talking about it. But that's their problem.'"

There are times when it would be better for a born-again player to remain silent. In June 1985, the *Omaha World-Herald* reported:

"St. Louis Manager Whitey Herzog has stuck with catcher Darrell Porter, who has yet to throw out a would-be base stealer. But when Porter took ten fastballs while striking out four times the other night, Herzog told Porter, 'Darrell, you've got to do better than that.'

"A born-again Christian, Porter reassured Herzog that the Lord was with him.

"'You better listen to me,' Herzog replied. 'The Lord's a terrific guy, but he doesn't know anything about hitting.'"

Lowell Cohn of the *San Francisco Chronicle* had a humorous take on the issue. In May 1980 he wrote:

"I was browsing through the *Sporting News* last week when I came upon the following headline: 'Foster Finds Faith a Positive Factor.' The article tells how George Foster of the Cincinnati Reds first noticed a change in himself when he went to a hypnotist. The article goes on, 'the biggest change in Foster came when he 'took God into my life.'

"Some guys get every edge. Not only is Foster one of the most awesome power hitters in baseball, not only does he regularly pump up his already mighty muscles with weights, not only does he consult a hypnotist—but, now we find out he also has God on his side. It hardly seems fair. Ordinary guys like Darrell Evans and Marc Hill could use a little help from the deity just to nudge their averages above .250—how else are they going to do it? Superstars like Foster ought to have the good taste to go it alone."

Hall of Fame manager Sparky Anderson expressed his skepticism:

"So many baseball teams have their 'God Squads' these days," said Anderson, "players who after they hit a home run credit God with their good swing . . . like, 'God made me hit that home run.' You hear that a lot these days. I look at it this way: If God let you hit a home run last time up, then who struck you out next time at bat?"

Four-time National League batting title champion Bill Madlock put it in perspective: "It's sort of misleading to say, 'Well, because we have this Christian element on the club, we are winning.' I think our faith helps us handle situations more effectively and helps us to play to our capabilities, that's all."

* * *

"Punching Back at Depression"

Sidhu Kshetri from India holds the Guinness world record for consecutive hours hitting the heavy punching bag—fifty-five and fifteen minutes.

Now there's someone out to break that record—sixty-year-old Lou Sandoval. But he's not just out to break a record. He began this quest to combat depression in his own life and to inspire others to punch back at depression.

Sandoval has already gone twenty-four hours straight punching the bag. Now he is gearing up for thirty-three consecutive hours, beginning on April 15, 2025.

Sandoval, who was raised in the Catholic faith, is doing this in part for Lent, in preparation for the celebration of Jesus' resurrection on Easter Sunday.

He notes that the path to healing from depression begins with human connection. His began when, through the help of Craig Syracusa, the Diocese of Brooklyn commissioned Sandoval, who is an artist in many media, to do a sculpture. Syracusa, a writer and director, is making a documentary film about Sandoval's punching bag quest.

Sandoval points out that if you watch the video of Kshetri's fifty-five-hour marathon, he is barely tapping the bag, "kissing it," as Sandoval describes it. In contrast,

Sandoval is hitting the bag with force. For this reason, Syracusa is asking Guinness to create a new category for punching the bag with force so that Sandoval's thirty-three hours will establish a new standard.

Born and raised in Gallup, New Mexico, Sandoval and his family attended the Catholic church.

"We were just going through the motions as a Catholic family," Sandoval recalls. "But when I was ten years old, the charismatic Catholic movement hit. My parents became very active in it. When I was twelve, I got baptized into the Holy Spirit."

Sandoval says it is the Holy Spirit who has led him on his punching bag quest.

As a young man, Sandoval moved to Los Angeles to pursue an acting career. He gained membership in the Actor's Studio there, which gave him access to the New York studio branch. Once in New York, he turned to sculpting and other art projects, eventually leading to the sculpture for the Brooklyn Diocese and his friendship with Syracusa. When he gets commissioned for a sculpture, he usually travels back to Gallup, where his dad had set up a workshop, which Sandoval describes as a "sacred place."

His punching bag mission developed from a personal, Job-like crisis.

"This was nowhere on the horizon six months ago," he says. "But a little over a year ago, I was experiencing severe depression. I was living in the Palm Springs area because my fiancée was there helping her mother. Within a month my truck died, three commissions dried up within ten days, and I was forced to be separated from my fiancée and go back to my hometown with nothing but a broken heart.

"I had been fasting and praying through my running,

and I had to give myself a goal physically that would take me out of the anger of the depression. I said I'd try for ten percent body fat. The plan was to build a good foundation through resistance training the first six to eight weeks. Then I would go into boxing training for cardio. When it came time to do the boxing training, I fell into the early morning roadwork, the speed bag, jumping rope. But I discovered an unusual capacity to hit the bag for longer than I ever had before.

"I was asked by someone at the gym if I knew if there was a world record for hitting the heavy bag. And I didn't know, I mean, never even considered it. A couple of days later, I'm hitting the bag and I'm in my third hour and I heard a voice that says, 'Why don't you see if you can go four hours? Maybe you can go six.'"

Sandoval says that inner voice was the prompting of the Holy Spirit. Sandoval became familiar with the Guinness rules for the record: The participant goes for an hour and then has the option of resting for five minutes or foregoing that rest, banking it and continuing, and, for example, in three hours having fifteen minutes rest.

When he reached twelve hours straight, he felt a breakthrough. Suddenly the record seemed achievable.

Sandoval says the physical key is the development in the brain's anterior cingulated cortex (ACC), which is involved in higher-level functions such as attention allocation, reward anticipation, decision-making, impulse control, and emotion.

"Neurologists have discovered it as the seat of the will," Sandoval explains. "How it grows is us choosing to physically do something we don't want to do. That can be as simple as making amends or doing some notes on the piano.

It's also by not doing something that you're absolutely pulled to do, which is about addiction. It's spiritual combat.

"This discovery of hitting a bag or even to think about doing it for more than two hours, I could never do more than forty-five minutes before. But it's because of my spiritual connections. But on a medical level, the hour-to-hour connection trying to develop that cortex."

His motivation, rather than personal achievement, is to highlight the issues of depression and addiction. He notes that men in particular are told, "'You just take it on the chin, you've got to be macho. Vulnerability is a weakness.' That is essentially pride. And pride will get you killed."

"It [Lou's quest] gives you the inspiration to speak openly about your struggle with depression," says Syracusa. "And that is what Lou is doing. It's not about the bag or the fists or the time. It's something about the man himself."

Note*: The event was live streamed on April 15, 2025 on Syracuse's Walk in Faith YouTube channel. Sandoval achieved his goal of thirty-three consecutive hours punching the bag. Sandoval eclipsed the fifty-five-hour record and punched the bag for sixty consecutive hours on September 11, 2025. Syracusa's documentary of Sandoval's experience, which is in progress, will also feature interviews with experts, doctors, and mental health professionals, as well as with others who have suffered from depression and have fought back.*

* * *

"Faith Sustained Brent Jones During Times of Adversity"

Brent Jones played for the San Francisco 49ers from 1987-1997 and was on three Super Bowl championship teams. One of the top players in franchise history, Jones helped revolutionize the concept of the pass-catching tight end. This column is based on my interview with him in 1992.

San Francisco 49er tight end, Brent Jones, caught a pass and headed up field. The 49ers were playing the Minnesota Vikings in the first round of the NFL play-offs on a fateful January afternoon in 1988. San Francisco was heavily favored to win the game, and many, including Jones, expected the 49ers to go on to capture their third Super Bowl Championship.

As Jones looked for room to run, a Minnesota defender crashed into his left knee, snapping it back, and Jones went down. He would not play again that game. The Vikings went on to beat the 49ers 36-24, eliminating San Francisco from post-season play.

Jones's knee was so badly injured that it required reconstructive surgery.

"I thought I was going to the Super Bowl. I couldn't believe it," said Jones of the injury. "I think for the most part, people thought I'd never play again."

Remarkably, his knee healed in five months. But at training camp he injured his *other* knee. This one required arthroscopic surgery.

As Jones waited for his knee to heal, Bill Walsh, the 49ers' coach at the time, brought an unwelcome message.

"He said they were just going to keep two tight ends on the roster," Jones recalled, "and it was going to be these other two guys. I wasn't going to be around."

But, for some strange reason, the 49ers put Jones on the injured reserve list instead of cutting him from the squad. Then some even stranger things began to happen. One of the other tight ends suffered an injury, and Jones got some playing time. He did so well that he moved from third string to second string. After the end of the season, John Frank, the 49ers' starting tight end, announced his retirement.

Suddenly, the first-string tight end job was up for grabs. Jones grabbed it. The twenty-nine-year-old San Jose native has now been the 49ers' starting tight end for three seasons and has collected two Super Bowl rings in the process. In 1990, Jones set single-season team records for reception and yardage by a tight end.

Ironically, Walsh, who turned to broadcasting after retiring as 49ers head coach in 1990, emphasized Jones's importance to the team during; a telecast of a 49ers game last season.

Jones was out with still another knee injury, and Walsh explained that, although most fans know about 49er receivers Jerry Rice and John Taylor, it is Jones, the third weapon in the team's pass-catching arsenal, who keeps defenders honest. Because of Jones's great pass-catching ability, defensive backs can't just key on Rice and Taylor.

As if to make a prophet of Walsh, the 49ers, who had been struggling with a four-and-five record, went on to finish the season a respectable ten-and-six after Jones returned to the line-up.

His biggest thrill was catching a pass for the second touchdown of the game in San Francisco's 55-10 victory over the Denver Broncos in Super Bowl XXIV in 1990. But his best game as a 49er was in a 19-13 victory over the Atlanta Falcons the following season. He caught five passes for a career-best 125 yards, including a 67-yard touchdown pass.

Besides success, the one thing that has characterized Jones's career is adversity—and his uncanny ability to come back from it.

In the second game of the 1991 season against the San Diego Chargers, Jones tore a ligament in his left knee. The doctors said it would be eight to ten weeks before he could play again, yet after five weeks the knee had healed, and he was cleared to play. Although Coach George Seifert decided to rest his star tight end for two additional weeks to play it safe, Jones had come back from his fourth major injury in professional football.

What stands out is his attitude during those times of recovery.

"A lot of people say, 'How can you handle that? How can you be so up about having a knee injury? How come you're not down and frustrated?'" Jones related.

The answer, he said, is his faith in God.

"I can't even begin to take credit for what I've done or what I've been through," he said. "There's just no way. I would have never been able to handle it."

He said his faith has sustained him in adversity, especially in recovering from injuries.

"Going through it, there's times of frustrations," he said. "But Christ has really brought me through the tough times."

Jones feels that his success as a football player is directly related to his faith.

"I think that God had a plan for my life," Jones explained. "There's no way I could have become a professional football player had it not been for that commitment [to Christ]. There were so many events in my life—having them move me to tight end in college, and finally getting my chance. I was a good athlete, but you could talk to any one of my friends from high school. I was the farthest thing from a pro football player."

Jones feels that many athletes turn to God because of the emptiness they experience in the midst of success.

"A lot of times athletes have everything," he explained. "They have the fast cars, the big money, all the women, if they wanted that. And I think so many guys climb that mountain and see that there's really nothing there. They realize that money and the world's view of success can't buy true happiness."

For Jones, true success is to honor God in everything he does. So his faith pervades every aspect of his life, including his actions on the football field.

"I play as hard as anybody out there," he said. "That's how Christ wants me to play. But I'll help guys up on other teams."

This column first appeared in Teen Quest, *September 1992.*

* * *

"Brian Sipe: Get Off the Bench!"

The Kardiac Kids were at it again. The 1980 Cleveland Browns, led by quarterback Brian Sipe, earned that nickname for their uncanny ability to come from behind for a heart-stopping victory. Sipe, facing a third and twenty from the Green Bay Packers' forty-six yard line with sixteen seconds left to play and the Browns trailing, found wide receiver Dave Logan downfield for the winning touchdown,

In the final game of the regular season, the Browns beat the Cincinnati Bengals on a field goal with 1:25 left. The victory secured a division title for Cleveland and put them in the playoffs for the first time since 1972. Sipe passed for 4,132 yards and thirty touchdowns and was named the National Football League Most Valuable Player.

Today, Sipe is still leading his team to the playoffs—not as a player, but as a coach. He has been the head coach for seven years at Santa Fe Christian High School in Solana Beach, California, just north of San Diego. The Eagles' record with Sipe as coach is 66-10, including four section championships. There are only 385 students at Santa Fe Christian, making it a Division 5 school, the smallest. But in 2005 Sipe decided to compete against Division 4 schools, which can have a student body of up to 1,700,

Then he went a step further. He scheduled the first game that season against Torrey Pines, the two-time defending Division 1 champion, with a student population of 3,300 at the time. The two schools are neighbors, just four miles apart.

"I think that the kids got tired of hearing people say, 'Oh,

Santa Fe Christian, you've got a great program, for a small school.'" Sipe says. "We decided to take a shot at Torrey Pines."

This David and Goliath story didn't quite turn out as the biblical account. The Eagles lost to Torrey Pines. But Sipe could not have been more proud of his team.

"If we played mistake-free football, we could beat those guys," Sipe says. "But we turned the ball over five times, and to lose to them 28-14 with five turnovers—we gave them all they could handle."

In 1985, when Sipe retired from football, he and his wife, Jeri, started to attend church because they thought it would be good for the family.

"I was confronted with the truth," Sipe remembers. "It was a message with authority. I decided that I needed to be honest about what the Bible was saying, or I needed to throw it in the trash."

The Bible did not end up in the garbage. Instead, Sipe took seriously what it said, that Jesus had died for him and his sins, that he rose from the dead and that by believing in him he could have eternal life.

Today, as Sipe grows in his relationship with God, he has an impact on his players.

"I recognize that God allowed me to have all those experiences in the NFL," Sipe says, "to have some credibility with these boys that a lot of other men would have to struggle to achieve. People want me to say that coaching football is a ministry. It's not a ministry any more than anything else we do.

"Who I am and my relationship with Christ is my ministry. And these boys have an opportunity to see me during the pressure of games and making decisions, my relationship with the coaches, all those different things. They want me to take them to a championship. And that's my job. But along the way I want them to see a man who is leading them through those stressful times and does it in a way that glorifies God."

The Eagles have a motto: "To be my best, alongside our best, against their best, as a warrior in the service of our King." Sipe says that the motto stresses each player's responsibility to his teammates and to God. Sipe's football program requires that each member of the team see his role in relation to his teammates, not as an individual. The motto is intended to awaken the players to their future roles as a husband, father, and friend. His coaching philosophy is that every player has to contribute.

"Every week I challenge the players to get off the bench," Sipe explains. "That means you've got to figure out some way to contribute. The longer you are on the bench, there's somebody out on that field longer than he should be. And he's getting tired. The more people who play, the fresher we are, the better football team we are."

Sipe has given some thought to what it is to honor God as a football player.

"There's a team that's our archrival, another Christian school," Sipe relates. "And sometimes it's the down-and-dirtiest, nastiest football we play all year. The kids push the envelope in their demeanor and their sportsmanship.

"I was challenged by this idea of what does God-honoring football look like. The conclusion I came to is that when you're playing football, you really can't be thinking about God. It's like life. And I think we can beat ourselves up and say, 'Oh, I'm a lousy Christian because I should be thinking about Jesus from the moment I wake up until the moment I go to sleep.' But the truth is, life is a distraction. And nothing's more distracting than having a guy across the line from you who wants to tear your head off.

"To me, God-honoring football is football where the kids made a commitment to prepare and to be the best that they can be so that when they are alongside their teammate, the two of them together can work and be the best that they can be. To honor your commitments, to do it in an upright way—I think that brings him glory."

This column first appeared in Breakaway *magazine in January 2008.*

* * *

"Mickey Marvin: On the Line for the Lord"

Longtime fans of the now Las Vegas Raiders know that the team won the Super Bowl in 1977, 1981, and 1984. For fans longing for those glory days, below is my 1981 column about one of the key members of the solid offensive line that helped the team win Super Bowl XV that year—Mickey Marvin.

Before sharing my thoughts, here is what renowned *San Francisco Chronicle* sports columnist Lowell Cohn wrote about Marvin in 1983:

"Mickey Marvin came over. 'Don't leave without visiting,' he said. I went back to his locker. We made small talk for a while, and then the conversation shifted to religion. It always does with Mickey. He is a fundamentalist Christian and he sees every particle of life through the filter of his beliefs. With some guys, I find that oppressive. With him I don't.

"'Do you believe in the devil?' I asked.

"His face grew red and he leaned back in awe. 'I take the devil very seriously,' he whispered. 'I believe in the devil as surely as I

believe there's a heaven and a hell. The devil is very powerful. Make no mistake about that. But the Lord is more powerful.' A glow passed over Mickey's face as he contemplated the Lord's omnipotence."

Cohn, who doesn't believe in the devil and also happens to be Jewish, likes to write tongue-and-cheek. But he genuinely respects Mickey. Here's my story:

When Mickey Marvin weighed in at a whopping eight pounds, eleven ounces in Margaret R. Pardee Hospital in Hendersonville, North Carolina, his proud parents should have known there were "big" things in store for him. But they probably would never have guessed that twenty-five years later their son would help bring a Super Bowl championship to the Oakland Raiders.

Marvin, a 6-5, 275- pound offensive guard for the Raiders, is entering his fifth season in professional football. When Oakland dispatched the Philadelphia Eagles, 27-10, in the Superdome last January, Marvin and his fellow linemen went virtually unnoticed. The headline stories were Jim Plunkett's brilliant passing, Cliff Branch's sensational catches, and Rod Martin's Super Bowl record three interceptions.

But did you notice how lonely Plunkett was when he dropped back to pass? An Eagle jersey in the Raiders' backfield was as rare as a polar bear in the Sahara. Oakland's fearsome fivesome dominated the line of scrimmage, and on some plays they gave their quarterback an unheard-of eight seconds to pass.

Marvin and his linemates received little recognition for their role in Super Bowl XV, but that's of no great importance to Marvin. He says the glory should go to God.

An only child, Marvin grew up in the small town of

Hendersonville with a respect for the church. At the age of eight, he asked Jesus into his heart.

"I knew what I was doing when I accepted Christ," Marvin says, "but as I grew older and I grew in the Lord, I came to appreciate and understand that decision a lot better."

Mickey was also growing in size and stature. Because he was so much bigger than the other kids his age, he was prohibited from playing organized football until he was in eighth grade. By then he weighed 195 pounds and had to practice with the high school team.

In high school, Mickey threw the shot and discus for the track team and was the heavyweight wrestling champion of North Carolina in 1972. But he was at his best on the football field. As an offensive and defensive lineman, he earned All-County and All-Conference honors his junior and senior years and was selected to the All-State team as a senior.

Marvin went on to play football at the University of Tennessee, where he started at guard for three years and played in the Gator Bowl and the Liberty Bowl. He was named to All-American teams his last two seasons.

In 1976 Marvin was drafted by the Raiders in the fourth round, and he proved himself quickly. In 1978 he became the only second-year player in a decade to start regularly on the Raiders' offensive line. Although he was injured the next season and played in just two games, he was back at full strength in 1980 as the Raiders roared to a 15-5 overall record and the Super Bowl championship.

Marvin says his faith in God was important "from beginning to end" this past season. It must have been especially important in the beginning, when some prognosticators were picking the Raiders to finish last in their division. When Oakland struggled to a 2-3 start, it looked like the experts might be right.

But from that point on, the underdog Raiders rattled off six straight victories and scrapped their way into a wild-card playoff berth. Then they shocked the football world as they knocked off Houston, Cleveland, and San Diego *en route* to the Super Bowl win over the Eagles.

"The guys started to believe in something other than themselves," Marvin says of the Raiders' championship season. "It's an infectious attitude. I really and truly believe that the Lord helped each and every one of us—all in a different way. We had to work and sacrifice, but Jesus is the one who is most responsible.

"I take Jesus with me every time I go out on the field. People always ask me how I can be a Christian and play football. I get up on the line and I say, 'Thank you, Jesus'—just for the opportunity to play. When the ball is snapped, I knock my man on the seat of his pants. Then I go back to the huddle and I say again, 'Thank you, Jesus!'

"I don't hate anybody and I'm not mean. I have a job to do, and I do it the best I can. I like to physically dominate the opposing lineman and try to wear him out. But it's not that football is just a job for me. I've always loved football."

This column first appeared in the July/August 1981 edition of Venture *magazine.*

* * *

"Steve Alford, Then and Now"

Steve Alford, a college basketball coach for over thirty years, was a two-time consensus All-American playing for the Indiana Hoosiers and an NBA player for four seasons. I interviewed him for this column in 1989 when he was a Golden State Warrior.

Steve Alford, the son of a high school basketball coach, claims he learned to count on a basketball scoreboard. At age nine, he began attending the summer basketball camp run by Indiana University coach Bob Knight. He dreamed of playing for the Hoosiers, and he worked for countless hours on his shooting and other basic skills.

At New Castle High, Alford played for his dad's team. As a senior, he averaged thirty-eight points a game and won Indiana's Mr. Basketball Award as the best high school player in the state. When Bob Knight called to say he wanted Alford to play at IU, it was the first of many dreams come true. He became a starter at Indiana as a freshman and led the team in scoring. In the NCAA tournament that year, Alford scored twenty-seven points in one of the biggest upsets in tournament history, a 72-68 win over top-ranked North Carolina, a team featuring Michael Jordan and Sam Perkins.

After that season, Alford was selected for the United States Olympic Team. Playing alongside Jordan, Perkins, Patrick Ewing, Chris Mullin, and other college stars, he averaged more than ten points a game, shot 64 percent from the field, and helped lead the U.S. to a gold medal.

In the following years at Indiana, Alford became the target of special defensive tactics. Opposing coaches assigned bigger, stronger players to guard Alford, who was on the small side at 6-1. But with the help of Coach Knight's system, he still found ways to get open and score.

The sharpshooting guard won Indiana University's Most Valuable Player award four years in a row, and the team had a 92-35 record during his college career. In his senior year, Alford was named a first-team All-American. Indiana finished with a 30-4 record that season, capped by a dramatic 74-73 win over Syracuse for the NCAA title.

"We worked hard for four years as a team," says Alford, "and Coach Knight tried very hard to get us to that level of championship play. To end my career at Indiana like that was a great thrill."

Playing for Bob Knight was no picnic. The great college coach had a volatile temper and often used criticism to motivate his players. But Alford remained cool under Knight's fire. He used his coach's comments as a springboard for improvement. "He brought out more abilities than I thought I had," Alford says of his coach. "He made me a better player and person and ensured that I graduated on time."

Alford earned a degree in business at Indiana. He was married shortly after graduation and was drafted in the second round by Dallas in 1987. Alford made the team but found himself in a position he was not accustomed to—on the bench as the Maverick's twelfth man, and he was getting very little playing time. "Even though it was a blessing just to be in the NBA," says Alford, "not being able to play or do things that I'd done in the past was very frustrating."

The 1988-89 season didn't start much better. Although Alford was one of just six 1987 second-round college picks remaining in the NBA, he still wasn't getting much playing time. He credits his wife, Tanya, and his parents for helping him through that time.

Then the next shock wave hit. On December 13, 1988, Dallas released him. The Golden State Warriors signed him as a free agent three days later. "It was a blessing in disguise," he says. "That's the funny thing. God works in mysterious ways."

The primary difference was playing time. Warriors coach

Don Nelson utilized Alford's shooting ability and hustle in Golden State's free-wheeling offense, and the young guard responded, averaging 6.4 points in about fifteen minutes of action per game.

Alford's belief in a loving God goes back to his childhood.

"My brother and I were raised in a home where my parents always took us to church on Sundays and taught us the proper morals and values. So when I came of age and could make that independent decision, that's when I accepted the Lord." That time was his junior year in high school.

Alford describes the experience of asking Jesus Christ to come into his life: "There wasn't any thunder and lightning," he recalls. "What changed was my outlook on life. The things that I took for granted, now I appreciated more—the abilities I had to play basketball. But more than that, I appreciated my parents and friends more, being more appreciative of things around me that God had been so gracious in giving me."

He says being a Christian influenced his approach as a basketball player. "I didn't pray before each game for points or big plays or wins because I don't think God really cares about that," he explained. "I think he's more concerned about the way you conduct yourself. I try to play in a sportsmanlike manner, and I work hard at the game."

Note: *I interviewed Alford years ago when he played for the Warriors. Since 1991, he has devoted his career to college coaching, serving as head coach at six schools, including high-profile UCLA and Iowa. Today, Alford is the head men's coach of the University of Nevada, Reno. Alford has won over 65 percent of 1,000+ games during his head coaching career.*

This column first appeared in Venture, *September/October 1989.*

* * *

"Kelenna Azubuike's Rough Road to the NBA"

Kelenna Azubuike, bypassed in the draft, played five seasons in the NBA, the first four with the Golden State Warriors under head coach Don Nelson. Here's Azubuike's story.

Golden State trailed the Denver Nuggets by six with three minutes left in the second quarter at the Warriors' Oracle Area. The Warriors' Kelenna Azubuike leaped over Carmelo Anthony to grab a defensive rebound, threw an outlet pass, ran downcourt, and set up just behind the three-point line. Monta Ellis whipped a pass to Azubuike, who nailed the three.

That play highlighted Azubuike's great leaping ability, aggressiveness, and three-point shooting touch. It also typified the frenetic style that carried the Warriors to their first playoff appearance in thirteen years in 2007 and a stunning 4-2 victory over the Dallas Mavericks in the first round of the Western Conference playoffs. It was the first time in NBA history that a No. 8 seed had defeated a No. 1 seed in a best-of-seven series.

Don Nelson, who has the second most wins of any coach in NBA history, brought a free-wheeling style to Golden State when he returned to coach the Warriors in 2006 (he had previously coached the team from 1988-1995). Azubuike, who at 6-5 can play both guard and small forward, was a model player in Nelson's scheme.

"He's a pretty good all-around player. His No. 1 thing is

that he has some shooting range," said Nelson. "He works on defense, he's a pretty good rebounder and fits right into our system."

In 2006-07, Azubuike's .430 three-point field-goal percentage was second among NBA rookies. He averaged 7.1 points in sixteen minutes per game. The next season he played more, providing quality play off the bench to ease the load on star players Baron Davis and Stephen Jackson.

"I've got to bring a lot of energy when I come in," Azubuike said, "and do whatever we need at the time, whether it's getting rebounds or shooting threes if the right shot is there."

Azubuike's path to the NBA is as incredible as the Warriors' resurgence from doormat of the league to one of its most exciting teams. Raised in Tulsa, Oklahoma, Azubuike led Victory Christian High School to the state basketball title as a sophomore. He topped the state in scoring in each of his final three high school seasons, averaging 39.1 points and 13.3 rebounds as a senior.

After three years at the University of Kentucky, including two trips to the NCAA Elite Eight, Azubuike decided to enter the 2005 NBA draft. No team selected him.

He was devastated, but the Cleveland Cavaliers asked him to play in their summer league.

"I decided I wasn't going to give up. I'm not going to let my dream die here," he recalled. "I decided I belong in the NBA. So I just kept working hard to stay focused. I realized that I had a tough road ahead of me, but I was ready."

There were more bumps in the road. Azubuike played the preseason for Cleveland, but the Cavaliers waived him before the season began. He signed with Fort Worth in the NBA Development League, where he shot over fifty percent for the season and helped the Flyers win the regular season D-League title. Then the Houston Rockets invited him to training camp.

"I played well there, but they had too many guys," says Azubuike."They signed Bonzi Wells late, so that wasn't good for me. I realized that I probably wasn't going to make the team. I just kept working hard, and I was ready if they cut me to go to the D-League and then try to get back up."

Houston did cut him. Azubuike went back to Fort Worth and played with passion. After twelve games with the Flyers, he was leading the league in scoring at twenty-six points per game. Fort Worth coach Sydney Moncrief, a former NBA All-Star who became the Warriors' shooting coach, recommended Azubuike to Nelson. The Warriors signed him on January 2, 2007.

"He [Moncrief] told me about him, and I just basically took his word," Nelson recalled. "I had never seen him play. He came in, and he was everything Sydney told me he was."

Many players have been called up from the D-League, but not many have thrived in the NBA.

"There are other players who have failed their first time around in the NBA," Nelson noted. "He is one of the guys that the D-League looks to as a success story."

Azubuike easily could have quit, especially after coming up empty in the NBA draft.

"It was definitely depressing, and you get tempted to get down on yourself and give up," Azubuike acknowledged, "but my family was huge. They gave me a lot of support and encouraged me to keep going. And my relationship with Jesus Christ, that was definitely huge too. I could go pray and read the Bible and just get back strong again."

Azubuike's parents nurtured his faith as a child, and he

remembers when he was five or six asking Jesus to forgive his sins and come into his life.

"My parents kept me in church, they raised me right, they read the Word a lot," he said. He admits it is not easy to maintain that spiritual discipline in the NBA.

"It can be a challenge, trying to get into the Word every day," he explained. "A lot of times we're on the road, you got early practices or early shoot-arounds. It's tough to keep your routine going. And not just make it a routine, but get something out of it."

Azubuike regularly attended the Warriors chapel services, where he was joined by teammates Al Harrington, Troy Hudson, Patrick O'Bryant, and assistant coach Keith Smart, all fellow believers.

Azubuike said that making it to the league the hard way gave him plenty of motivation to stay there. "You've got to bring it every game," he said.

And he does.

This column first appeared in the May/June 2008 edition of Sports Spectrum *magazine.*

* * *

"Alvin Davis: The Big Decision"

Alvin Davis, known as Mr. Mariner, played nine major league seasons, including his first eight with Seattle. Davis ended his career with a .280 lifetime batting average and 160 home runs. Here's his story, as told to me in 1987.

When I was named the American League's 1984 Rookie of the Year, it was a dream come true.

At the beginning of the year, I had just hoped to be a

starting player with the Seattle Mariners' minor league team in Salt Lake City. So to become the Mariners' starting first baseman, to be named to the All-Star team and to be selected as the Rookie of the Year all in one season was a tremendous experience.

Looking back, however, I realize that my baseball dream could have become a nightmare.

My sophomore season at Arizona State I batted .370 and hit ten home runs. That summer I played ball in Fairbanks, Alaska, and hit about .400 with eight home runs. This early success motivated me to work especially hard during the fall and winter to prepare for the 1981 season.

But when the season began, I didn't hit for any power. I couldn't figure out what the problem was. I ended up batting .395, but I hit only four home runs and didn't drive in many runs.

After that season, the pro scouts didn't have many good things to say about me. I might have started believing those reports were it not for a physical exam that revealed I had been suffering from a couple of viruses that had sapped my strength.

But now it was time for the baseball draft. And when the money's on the line, the scouts are looking for players who are going to *produce.* I was supposed to have been a first-round draft pick. But after my below par season, I wasn't drafted until the sixth round.

The club that drafted me offered me a contract for about $40,000, and I wanted to sign so badly. But I didn't like the things that the man I was dealing with was saying about my ability. He told me there was no way I'd have a better season my senior year. He probably did what he does with all ballplayers to get them to sign, but it turned me off.

Yet it was a tough decision. And I knew this: Whatever decision I made, it would affect me for the rest of my life.

That's when a verse from the Bible came to mind that my mother had quoted as I was growing up: "Trust in the LORD with all your heart; and lean not on your own understanding. In all your ways acknowledge him, and he shall direct your paths" (Proverbs 3:5-6).

I had to ask myself at that point, "Am I trusting God to guide me? Am I even acknowledging him in my life?"

My father died when I was nine years old, so my mother raised my two brothers and me by herself to have faith in God. I knew that Jesus had died for my sins. When I was ten years old, I asked him into my heart.

But when I went off to college, I wasn't spending time reading the Bible. I wasn't depending on God to help me and direct me. Now I was about to make a very important decision. And I took that verse to heart. As I thought things over, I felt that the spirit of the negotiations just wasn't right. I took it as a challenge. I turned down their offer and decided to come back for my senior year at Arizona State.

A lot of people thought I was crazy not to sign. I can't say there were no doubts—even as to whether or not I was supposed to play professional baseball. For one thing, I didn't know if my body could take it. I was sick.

But I committed myself to studying the Bible and to start relying on Jesus totally to guide my life. And it was kind of miraculous all the things that I accomplished my senior year. I was one year and six units short of graduating, but I went to summer school, worked hard at my studies during the regular year and completed my degree in finance by the spring. My health returned to normal, and my bat came to life again. I hit thirteen home runs and drove in ninety-one runs.

The scouts showed interest, and I signed a contract with the Seattle Mariners. In my first year, I batted .284 and drove in fifty-six runs in seventy-four games for the Mariners' Double-A team in Lynn, Massachusetts. The next year I played for their farm team in Chattanooga, Tennessee, where I hit eighteen home runs with eighty-three RBI's.

I played winter baseball in Venezuela following that season. There I met two strong Christians, Jesse Barfield of the Toronto Blue Jays and Kevin Bass of the Houston Astros. We had Bible studies together and really grew in our faith. I think the results were evident on the field. I became a more consistent player, had a great mental attitude, and it carried over into the I984 season.

When the year began, I was assigned to the Mariners' Triple-A team in Salt Lake City. But three games into Seattle's season, the starting first baseman broke his hand and the Mariners called me up. I hit eight home runs in my first fifteen games, and they made me the regular first baseman.

I was selected to the American League All-Star team. I finished the season with 27 home runs and 116 runs batted in. I also drew 97 walks.

But baseball is too inconsistent to tie your life into. There are weeks in between those home runs sometimes, and there are strikeouts in between those RBI's and base hits. Your faith has got to be in God. That's where my faith must remain to be successful and have joy in this life.

This column first appeared in the May/June 1987 edition of Venture *magazine.*

* * *

"Ray Burris's Nightmare Season"

Ray Burris pitched in the major leagues from 1973 through 1987 for seven different teams. This column is based on my interview with him in 1983.

Ray Burris finished off the 1981 season in high style.

His team, the Montreal Expos, won the division championship that year, then faced the Los Angeles Dodgers in the National League Championship Series. In Game 2 at Dodger Stadium, he pitched against Fernando Valenzuela and beat him, 3-0. Burris pitched the final game and went eight innings. The game was tied, 1-1 when they took him out.

"We eventually lost it, 2-1, but those two performances were very special to me—my most exciting moments in baseball," Burris recalls.

The next spring, when he won five games without a loss in exhibition season, it looked like 1982 would be even better. ·

"I had no idea what was in store for me," the 6-5 righthander says. "In my first three games of the season, I gave up just one run but lost all three games—1-0, 1-0, and 2-1. I had the best earned-run average in the league, but my record was 0-3."

After that Burris began to think a lot. "I began to worry. I would go out to the mound thinking, *Well, what's going to happen today? How many runs are they going to score for me? Are they going to make the plays for me today?*

"I began losing my concentration. I would defeat myself before I even took the mound. What I was thinking, I was believing, and my mind was in a rut. Although I was a Christian, I wasn't allowing Christ to work in my life, and it showed up even on the mound."

By mid-May Bμrris had yet to pitch a winning game. His record was 0-7, and he was dropped from the starting rotation.

"I did a little better as a relief pitcher, but I lost four more games as a starter and ended the season with a disastrous record—4-14," he recalls.

"I knew my attitude had not been what it should have been as a Christian. So that winter I sat down and analyzed what happened. As I looked at the films of the games I had pitched, one stood out from all the rest. It was the game in the 1981 playoffs against Valenzuela in Los Angeles."

As he watched that tape, Burris was able to re-experience that game. "I remember exactly how I was mentally, what I went through, what I was thinking on every pitch."

Burris saw himself doing all the things a big-league pitcher is supposed to do—being aggressive, throwing strikes, staying ahead of the hitters, keeping the ball down, staying within his game plan. That game told him what he *didn't* do in 1982 in terms of mental preparation.

"So that winter I began to tell myself, *I've got to block all those negative things out of my mind. If I'm going to throw a pitch low and away, I pick that target out and I* ***throw*** *it! I don't try to guide it. If I throw it there, even if I miss the target, I'll have that extra hop on the ball, and the batter might pop it up. I have to allow myself a* ***chance*** *to be successful.*

"I also did some preparation on the physical level. I had gotten into some bad eating habits and weighed 230 pounds when I lost my job as a starter. It was almost impossible to get the snap I wanted on the ball.

"So I stopped eating between meals and stopped eating just for the sake of eating. When the 1983 season began, I was at 195 pounds and was ready physically and mentally. In spring training, I could feel the difference. Pitching was fun again."

Although he wasn't given a spot in the starting rotation, Burris didn't find himself worrying about it. "I simply told myself, *I'm in the ballclub, and I'm contributing even by coming out of the bullpen. I'm just going to go out, give my best effort, do the things I know I can do, and let everything else take care of itself.*"

As the season progressed, Burris encouraged the starting pitchers. "I wanted them to do well. If they do well, everybody benefits. I enjoyed seeing them be successful."

Then in June the Expos began to use Burris as a starter again. In a game against the New York Mets, he pitched eight innings and only gave up one run, though the Mets won in seventeen innings. But the big moment came on June 20 against the Philadelphia Phillies in Montreal. Burris pitched the entire nationally-televised contest—the first time since that day in Dodger Stadium against Valenzuela. He only gave up three hits and ended the game by striking out future Hall of Famer Mike Schmidt.

"I leaped off the mound in joy, and the fans at Olympic Stadium gave me a standing ovation," he recalls. "We won 5-0, and I was especially pleased because I had maintained my concentration throughout. It was a confirmation to me that I had recaptured the right mental attitude.

"In 1982 I had not allowed Christ to be in control of me. So he couldn't work anything good for me. Now I've given him back control of my life. And now he's making good things happen for me and it shows up even out on the mound.

"There are people constantly watching you to see how you handle adversity, to see how you handle trials and tribulations. God has brought trials and tribulations my way, and he's given me the strength to handle them and to know that he'll always be there with me. The season I went through last year, on a mental level, was very hard. But I learned that if you do what you know you have to do well enough, it will pay off."

This column first appeared in Venture, *March 1984.*

* * *

"Mike Matheny, Gold Glove Catcher"

Mike Matheny caught in the major leagues for thirteen seasons, earning four Gold Gloves. He owns the catching record of 1,565 consecutive fielding chances without an error (does not include passed balls). With the San Francisco Giants in 2005, he won his fourth Gold Glove and set a Giants single-season team record for catcher's fielding percentage at .999. He went on to manage the St. Louis Cardinals and the Kansas City Royals. I interviewed him in 2005 when he was a Giant.

The dangerous Ryan Klesko was at the plate for the San Diego Padres in the top of the eighth inning with men on first and second, two outs, and the Padres leading the San Francisco Giants 5-3. A hit by Klesko could break the game wide open. The count went to 3-1, and then Klesko fouled off a pitch. Giants' catcher Mike Matheny took the opportunity to visit relief pitcher Scott Eyre on the mound. When Matheny went back behind the plate, he never gave a signal for the next pitch. Eyre busted a 3-2 curveball, Klesko swung and missed, and the Padres threat was over.

Matheny had gone to the mound to tell Eyre to throw a curveball on the next pitch. He did not want to give the runner on second base the chance to steal the signal and relay it to Klesko.

"My true joy comes from working behind the plate, working with the pitcher," Matheny says. He calls the pitcher and catcher's duel with the batter "the game within the game."

Matheny is not as well known for his offense. But he is a clutch hitter and a tough out. In a game against the Milwaukee Brewers earlier this year, with the Giants trailing in the ninth and in desperate need of a base runner, Matheny fouled off half a dozen consecutive pitches before being hit by a pitch to get on base. In a game at Pittsburgh a week later, he hit a solo home run to beat the Pirates 3-2.

"I want to get the big hits," Matheny says. "I want to contribute in the small ways—get the guy over, get the bunt down, get that big RBI."

Matheny spent the last five years with the St. Louis Cardinals, where he took a trip to the 2004 World Series. The Cards fell to the Red Sox in four straight games.

"It was disappointing that we didn't play the kind of baseball that we knew we could play," Matheny says of the World Series. But he was glad to make it to the Fall Classic. "I know a lot of people that have had much better careers than I've had and have never had that opportunity, so it's something I feel very grateful for."

Matheny left a legacy as a leader in St. Louis. He quickly gained the same reputation in 2005 with his new team, the

Giants, In spring training pitchers were regularly stopping by his locker to talk baseball.

"He called a couple of 3-2 curveballs that I hadn't thrown in a while," Eyre told the *San Francisco Chronicle.* "I was thinking, 'Are you serious? Okay, here goes.' You throw with confidence because he puts his finger down and pulls it away before you have a chance to say no."

The only person who does not see Matheny as a leader is Matheny.

"I don't necessarily claim to be a leader," he says. "I think a lot of times the people that do are the people who aren't. I just see myself as a servant, as a helper to these guys, seeing how I can give them the best chance to be successful."

His humble attitude stems from his Christian faith, which he says he puts "in the center of everything." He grew up in a Christian home, but learned that he had to enter into his own relationship with God.

"A lot of times you grow up in a Christian home, the whole process becomes a religion instead of a personal faith. It did for me, even at an early age. I realized that I was missing something, something wasn't quite right. I explain to kids that just because you're born in a garage, it doesn't make you a car. The same thing goes for your faith.

"I got challenged one night in a revival in a church in Columbus, Ohio. The pastor was telling each of us, regardless of our position in the church, where do we stand with Jesus. Who is he to us individually? And I realized that it was just a name and a ritual, going to church, standing up, singing the songs.

"I was eight years old, but old enough to know that

God was talking right to me. I went home, asked a bunch of questions, and I remember my parents leading me to Christ, kneeling in front of our couch."

He was the team captain for both the baseball and football teams at Reynoldsburg High in Ohio. But his faith lay dormant. Matheny says he was a "closet Christian" during that time.

"There was a period in high school and college when I went on under the radar," he says. "It wasn't until minor league baseball that I was challenged to really step out and be bold in my faith."

He came to see baseball as a mission field, where he could be a witness "not necessarily to the masses, but more importantly to the guys in the clubhouse." Matheny does not preach at his teammates, but says he tries to "keep it real" by building friendships so that they can "find out who Christ is and that he can change lives, and there is a better way out there than what this world offers."

Matheny's former manager at St. Louis, Tony La Russa, is certain that Matheny would make a great manager. Matheny is not sure what he wants to do after his playing career ends, but you can be sure that whatever he does, he will follow the Scripture that is inscribed on the stand that holds a baseball in his locker: "Whatever your hand finds to do, do it with all your might" (Ecclesiastes 9:10).

* * *

"Jim Essian's Biggest Decision"

The San Francisco Giants of the late 1970s and early 1980s gained notoriety as the "God Squad." But across the Bay, the Oakland A's had just as many born-again Christians on the team. One was catcher Jim Essian, a major leaguer from 1973-1984. He managed the Chicago Cubs in the 1991 season. This article is based on my interview with him in 1984.

Ten years as a major league catcher would make just about anybody angry at the world. How would you like to wake up each morning knowing that a base runner is going to try to separate your head from your shoulders on a close play at the plate? Or that you might break a few fingers trying to catch your ace pitcher's forkball?

It's not all glory being a catcher. And it's a lot of hard work. But if you thought all those guys behind home plate had to get meaner and nastier to survive in the majors, then you haven't met Jim Essian of the Oakland A's.

Essian, now in his tenth season in the big leagues, is about as nice a guy as you'll ever meet. But if you're trying to cross home plate and he's got the ball, don't expect tea and crumpets. The 6-1, 187-pound catcher will make you pay the price.

A starter for the Chicago White Sox in his early years, Essian now works mainly in a reserve role for the A's. When called upon, the thirty-three-year-old veteran can still do the job. Earlier this season, when A's starting catcher Mike Heath was injured, Essian caught seven games in a row and Oakland won five of them. A little later in the year, another opportunity came along and Essian blasted a game-winning home run.

One of thirteen children, Essian was always active in

sports. The Detroit native played football, basketball, baseball, and hockey in high school. He attended Arizona State, but only for a semester, as the Philadelphia Phillies signed him to a professional contract in 1970.

After five years in the Phils' farm system, Essian was traded to the White Sox. In 1977, his first year as a starter in the big leagues, he batted .273 with ten home runs in 114 games.

The next spring, however, the Sox traded Essian to Oakland. It was a time when he began to do some serious thinking, not just about baseball, but about life.

"I was pretty much wrapped up in myself," he recalls. "And yet there was something in me that was searching for answers."

The answers came through a friend, teammate Wayne Gross, now with the Baltimore Orioles.

"He invited my wife and me to Bible studies at his house," Jim remembers, "and I began to hear the truth of God's Word. I had some questions answered about God, about sin, about salvation.

"I got my first Bible that summer and began to read for myself. At the end of that season I knew I had a decision to make—that I was either going to come to the Lord, or not. I knew what I had to do. I had heard the truth, and I knew that God was tugging on me. So I gave my heart to the Lord in a simple prayer."

Essian's wife, Janey, also asked Christ into her life shortly afterward. Since then, the Essians, who have two children, have built their lives with God as the center.

After receiving Jesus as his Lord and Savior, Essian immediately got involved in reading the Bible, praying, and attending church on a regular basis.

During the baseball season, the players' schedules make regular attendance at any one church impossible. But Essian and a number of his teammates are faithful attendees of the Sunday services offered at the ballpark by Baseball Chapel.

Essian stresses the fact that the Christian life is a relationship with God.

"I'm learning more and more about God's will for my life," he says, "and more and more about how to rely on his strength. This is an everyday thing. Every day, if you're relating to God, he's going to show you something."

One thing Essian is learning about is how to share his faith in Jesus Christ with others, including his teammates and other ballplayers.

Essian admits that his natural inclination is not to mingle.

"Oftentimes I'll be wanting to go off in the comer and be by myself," he said. "But God's showing me to put the newspaper down . . . that he wants me to be a people person. He's showing me not to be a 'respecter of persons.' It's easy for us to minister to certain types of people and to forget about the others—those less attractive or less fortunate."

Essian confesses that not being a starting player is a tough adjustment.

"It's difficult," he says. "But it's a role they want me to play—that of being someone able to come off the bench. Being a Christian enables you to handle all these different circumstances."

Essian has some definite ideas about what he wants to do when his playing days are over.

"I want to manage a ballclub," he says. "I believe in my heart that there'll be a position open for me, so I'm preparing for that."

In the off season, Essian likes to relax by reading and playing golf. He's also quite a music fan.

"I love Christian music," he shares. "I think it's the greatest music in the world."

Essian is quick to point out that the Christian life is one of commitment.

"You've got to be on one side or the other," he stresses. "You're either going to run out on your own, or you're going to do it God's way, with his help. If we build our foundation on the Rock, we're going to stand, and we're going to stand firm."

This column first appeared in Venture, *September/October 1984.*

* * *

"David Newhan: Nothing to Hide"

Maybe it wasn't quite Lou Gehrig replacing Wally Pipp, but when David Newhan got to play for the Baltimore Orioles in the summer of 2004, he made the most of it. The left-handed swinging sparkplug belted a 435-foot pinch-hit home run in his first at-bat for Baltimore on June 18. Previously a utility player, Newhan became a fixture in the lineup, hit an inside-the-park home run against Pedro Martinez, and was hitting .400 by late July.

Orioles fans bombarded the *Baltimore Jewish Times* with calls and emails demanding an article about "the new Jewish hero." The *Times* is the "go-to" paper for Jews in the greater Baltimore area. When the newspaper obliged with a feature story on Newhan, revealing that he is a Jewish believer in Jesus, enthusiasm turned to hostility.

"Instead of explaining that Newhan is an apostate Jew who has left the faith," one reader wrote, "[the article] gives his ideas legitimacy, sure to add fodder to Hebrew-Christian propaganda."

The editors replied, "So why did we write about it, and why did we let Mr. Newhan speak of Jesus and Jewish symbols on our pages? The answer is simple: penetrating the heart of our craft. It's because you were talking about it and kept asking us."

When Newhan joined the New York Mets in 2007, people still talked about it. After noting that Newhan was one of the team's three Jewish players, *The New York Times* wrote, "Newhan's religious odyssey, however, has taken him so far outside the Jewish mainstream that many Jews probably no longer consider him Jewish."

Newhan found that reasoning absurd. Many of the Jewish baseball players he knows are agnostic, non-practicing, or dabbling in Eastern religion. Ironically, Shawn Green, the baseball idol of Jewish kids until he retired in 2007, did not attend Hebrew school or have a *bar mitzvah*. Newhan did both.

The controversy even spilled over into the world of baseball cards. *Jewish Major Leaguers*, a company that issues an annual set of Jewish player cards, discontinued Newhan's card in 2008. Newhan's dad, Ross (who does not believe in Jesus), called Martin Abramowitz, the company's president, and expressed his unhappiness with the exclusion. He told Abramowitz that his son is a Jew and that both Ross and his wife, Connie, are Jews. Abramowitz said he would "reinstate" David and would be pleased if Ross would write the bio for David's card.

You would think that would have settled the matter,

especially because Ross Newhan is a Hall of Fame baseball writer who wrote for *The Los Angeles Times*. However, when no David Newhan card appeared in 2009, and this author asked Abramowitz why, he replied via email: "At some point, we learned that he had become identified with Messianic Judaism (Christ as the Savior), so we stopped including him."

Ross Newhan: "The position of Mr. Abramowitz and his card company is utterly ridiculous. David was born to Jewish parents. He was a bar mitzvah. He has read thoroughly about Judaism and celebrates the Jewish holidays. I became so frustrated trying to explain all this to Mr. Abramowitz that I finally told him to do what he saw fit. However, to exclude him is wrong. His card collection is incomplete."

Not all Jewish baseball aficionados dismiss Newhan. Howard Megdal, who ranked all Jewish players in the history of baseball by position in his book, *The Baseball Talmud,* rated Newhan No. 4 among second basemen. As to why he included Newhan, who he knew to be a Messianic Jew, Megdal displayed a sense of humor: "We as the Jewish people cannot afford to cast aside middle infielders."

Newhan grew up in Yorba Linda, California (near Anaheim) in one of the few Jewish families in the neighborhood. The Newhans went to a nearby Conservative synagogue, but David stopped attending after his bar mitzvah. Though he was one of the top high school hitters in the area, his 5-8 frame may have given the scouts pause. He played one year of community college baseball, transferred to Georgia Tech, then to Pepperdine. He hit .313 with 15 home runs and 71 RBIs in 103 games in his two years at Pepperdine and was drafted by the Oakland A's in 1995.

While at Pepperdine, a Christian university, students

talked with him about Jesus, which piqued his spiritual interest. "Here I am, this Jewish kid going to Pepperdine, of all places," he recalls. "And then, when I signed and played pro ball, I started looking into things more. I just never felt complete or whole, and it seemed like there must be more to life. I even read books on Buddhism."

While in the minor leagues, he met Karen Letizia, who talked about having a personal relationship with Jesus. As Newhan's relationship with Karen developed, he spoke about spiritual things with the pastor of her church, Roger Friend. A friend encouraged Newhan to talk with Rabbi Barney Kasdan, the leader of a Messianic synagogue in San Diego.

"The more I read the Bible and passages in Isaiah and Daniel that spoke of Messiah, the more it made sense to me," Newhan says. "I couldn't deny that Jesus fit the bill, and I just believed. That was the train that came into the station, and I liked where it was leading. When I received *Yeshua* [Jesus] into my life, I felt it was completed."

He and Karen married in 2001 and began to attend Shuvah Yisrael, a Messianic congregation in Irvine, California. His parents were accepting, though not thrilled, with his new beliefs.

Newhan broke into the big leagues with the San Diego Padres in 1999 and was traded to the Phillies after two seasons. In 2001, he tore the labrum in his right shoulder and missed most of that year and the entire 2002 season. He came back and hit .348 for the Colorado Rockies' minor league AAA team in 2003 and .328 for the Texas Rangers' AAA team in 2004 but was not called up. Then the Orioles grabbed him, and he took full advantage. His hot hitting may have surprised others, but Newhan says he always expected to succeed in the major leagues.

"In my mind, I did well because that's the only chance I was given to play daily," says Newhan. "When I got the at-bats, I hit."

It looked like Newhan was going to settle into a career in Baltimore. He had a great start as the regular left fielder in 2006 but broke his leg while stealing second base and missed most of the season. He was traded in 2007 to the Mets, where he experienced more frustration.

"I understood that I would not be playing regularly," says Newhan, "but [manager] Willie Randolph used me only as a pinch hitter for about six weeks—and I play five or six positions. You're facing the other team's best pitcher when you're pinch hitting, and you go six weeks without getting more than one at bat in a game, it's tough."

Picked up by the Houston Astros the following year, Newhan showed again that he could do the job. He significantly contributed to one of the hottest second-half teams that season. He latched on with the Phillies in 2009 but played all year in AAA.

His hopes to make it back to the majors almost ended permanently. In late September 2009, near his home in Oceanside, California, Newhan, a lifelong surfer, dove off his board into shallower water than he realized. He broke three bones in his C2 vertebrae, an injury almost identical to the one that left Christopher Reeve paralyzed and which has killed others instantly.

"I should have died or, at the very least, been in a wheelchair," says Newhan. "It's very much a miracle." He never needed surgery, removed his neck brace in early February, and has made a full recovery.

His trust in God has helped him through his career's many ups and downs. "There's so much frustration and failure in baseball," he says, "it just helps to have faith that everything's going to work for the good."

David, Karen, and their two young children, Gianna and Nico, attend Vista Christian Fellowship, the same church where Pastor Friend married them. They also celebrate the Jewish holidays and visit Shuvah Yisrael when they can.

While people question why he, as a Jew, follows Jesus, David finds it strange that more Christians don't understand the Jewish roots of their faith. "The Jewish holidays are biblical, and there are ties to Yeshua in every one of them," he says. "At Passover, the lamb shank represents the Lamb of God, and Jesus is that lamb."

As for Newhan's future, he says, "One thing I learned from the surfing accident is that I'm not in control—Yeshua is. I'm just praying that he shows me what he wants of me and opens the doors where he wants me."

This column first appeared in ISSUES: A Messianic Jewish Perspective, *Volume 18:5, 2010. In addition to personal correspondence with the author, other sources drawn on for this article include 'Editorial,"* Baltimore Jewish Times, *August 6, 2004, 42; "No Place,"* Baltimore Jewish Times, *August 13, 2004, 47; Ben Shpigel, "His Father May Write About It, but Newhan Plays the Game,"* The New York Times, *February 22, 2007; and Howard Megdal,* The Baseball Talmud: The Definitive Position-by-Position Ranking of Baseball's Chosen Players *(New York: Harper, 2009), xii.*

* * *

"Honoring Jewish Ballplayers"

In a scene from the 1980 movie *Airplane!* the stewardess approaches an elderly lady passenger and asks, "Would you like something to read?" "Do you have anything light?" the lady asks in return. "How about this leaflet? 'Famous Jewish Sports Legends,'" the stewardess replies.

Of course, *Airplane* is fiction.

Meanwhile, in the real world, Alex Bregman, Joc Pederson, and Harrison Bader are current Jewish major league baseball players.

Moreover, historically, many Jewish baseball players have stood tall in our National Pastime. Here are a few.

Hank Greenberg, the first Jewish player to be elected to baseball's Hall of Fame, led the league in home runs four times, drove in an incredible 184 runs in a season, and won two MVP awards in a thirteen-year career. He is the all-time Jewish home run king with 331 dingers. He did not play on Yom Kippur in 1934, predating the more famous decision by **Sandy Koufax** by thirty-one years.

In 1965, the first game of the World Series between the Los Angeles Dodgers and the Minnesota Twins fell on Yom Kippur, the holiest Jewish holiday. Ordinarily, Koufax would have pitched that game, but he decided not to play on the holiday. Don Drysdale pitched for the Dodgers and lost. When manager Walter Alston came out to the mound to take the ball from Drysdale, the pitcher quipped, "I bet you wish I were Jewish too."

Koufax's 1963-66 statistics are hard to believe: three Cy Young Awards, an MVP, three strikeout titles, four ERA titles, and ninety-seven wins. The southpaw won four World

Series, was elected to the Baseball Hall of Fame, and is considered one of the greatest pitchers ever.

Then there's third baseman **Al Rosen**, who made his mark in only seven full seasons in the majors in the 1950s. Hall of Famer Early Wynn once told Roger Kahn, author of *The Boys of Summer*, "Believe me, the two best clutch hitters in the game are [Yogi] Berra and Rosen." Rosen led the league in home runs twice, made four straight All-Star teams, and won the 1953 MVP award. As general manager for the Giants, Rosen became the first former player to win Executive of the Year honors.

At his peak, outfielder **Shawn Green** regularly hit 35-45 homers and stole 20 or more bases a year playing for teams such as the Los Angeles Dodgers, Toronto Blue Jays, and New York Mets. He batted .283 in his fifteen-year major league career and is one of only sixteen players to hit four home runs in a game. In 2002, against the Milwaukee Brewers, he registered nineteen total bases, which is still an MLB record (tied with Nick Kurtz).

Sid Gordon played thirteen years in the big leagues in the 1940s and 1950s. He made two All-Star teams and was an exceptionally disciplined hitter, walking over twice as much as he struck out. The outfielder had a career batting average of .283.

There has been a spate of excellent Jewish ballplayers in the major leagues in recent years. June 8, 2018, was the most productive day for Jewish batters in Major League Baseball history—five Jewish ballplayers combined to hit six home runs to help their respective teams to victory. **Ryan Braun** hit two round-trippers for the Brewers. **Kevin Pillar** (Blue Jays), **Alex Bregman** (Astros), **Ian Kinsler** (Angels), and **Joc Pederson** (Dodgers) hit one apiece.

One of the more interesting Jewish baseball stories is about former big leaguer **David Newhan**, mainly because some did not accept Newhan—a Jew who believes in Jesus—as Jewish. When Newhan was traded from the Orioles to the Mets in 2007, *The New York Times* wrote, "Newhan's religious odyssey has taken him so far outside the Jewish mainstream that many Jews probably no longer consider him Jewish."

Newhan found that reasoning absurd because many of the Jewish ballplayers he knew were agnostic, non-practicing, or dabbling in Eastern religion. Ironically, Green, the baseball idol of Jewish kids until he retired in 2007, did not attend Hebrew school or have a *bar mitzvah;* Newhan did both.

The controversy even spilled over into the world of baseball cards. Jewish Major Leaguers, a company that issues an annual set of Jewish player cards, discontinued Newhan's card in 2008.

David's father, Ross Newhan, a Hall of Fame baseball writer for *The Los Angeles Times,* told this reporter, "The position of (owner) Mr. Abramowitz and his card company is utterly ridiculous. David was born to Jewish parents. He was a bar mitzvah. He has read thoroughly about Judaism and celebrates the Jewish holidays. I became so frustrated trying to explain all this to Mr. Abramowitz that I finally told him to do what he saw fit. However, to exclude him is wrong. His card collection is incomplete."

Not all Jewish baseball aficionados dismissed Newhan. Howard Megdal, who ranked all Jewish players in the history of baseball by position in his book, *The Baseball Talmud,* rated Newhan No. 4 among second basemen. As to why he included Newhan, who he knew to be a Messianic Jew,

Megdal displayed a sense of humor: "We as the Jewish people cannot afford to cast aside middle infielders."

This column, which has been contemporized, first appeared in The Vacaville Reporter *on April 9, 2020.*

***

"Jewish Baseball Players and the High Holy Days"

We Jewish people are proud when a Jewish athlete succeeds, but a few have gained even more respect for refusing to play ball on the holiest day of the Jewish calendar.

Hank Greenberg, the first Jewish player to be elected to baseball's Hall of Fame, led the league in home runs four times, drove in an incredible 184 runs in a season, and won two MVP awards in a thirteen-year career. He hit 58 home runs in 1938 and 331 in his career.

He did not play on Yom Kippur in 1934, predating the more famous decision by **Sandy Koufax** by 31 years. Greenberg recalled his 1934 decision:

"Both Rosh Hashanah and Yom Kippur came in September and since we were in the thick of the pennant race, the first for Detroit in many years, it became a national issue whether or not I should play. The question was put before Detroit's leading rabbi, Rabbi Leo Franklin. He consulted the Talmud and announced that I could play on Rosh Hashanah because that was a happy occasion on which Jews used to play ball in the streets long ago. However, I could not play on Yom Kippur. So I played on Rosh Hashanah and, believe it or not, I hit two home runs."

Koufax is considered by some to be the greatest left-handed pitcher in baseball history. His 1963-66 statistics are hard to believe: three Cy Young Awards, an MVP, three strikeout titles, four ERA titles, and ninety-seven wins. The southpaw won four World Series and was elected to the Baseball Hall of Fame,

In 1965 Koufax was scheduled to pitch the first game of the World Series for the Los Angeles Dodgers. But the game fell on Yom Kippur. Koufax refused to play, but, as he pointed out, "There was never any decision to make because there was never any possibility that I would pitch. The club knows that I don't work that day."

Shawn Green regularly hit 35-45 homers and stole 20 or more bases a year playing for the Los Angeles Dodgers, Arizona Diamondbacks, Toronto Blue Jays, and New York Mets. He batted .283 in his fifteen-year major league career and is one of only sixteen players to hit four home runs in a game. In 2002, against the Milwaukee Brewers, he registered nineteen total bases, which is still an MLB record (tied with Nick Kurtz). He also played and coached for the Israeli national baseball team.

As a Dodger in 2001 Green elected not to play on Yom Kippur. By sitting out the game, Green ended his streak of having played in 415 consecutive games. He said, "I felt like it was the right thing to do. I didn't do this to gain approval. I thought it was the right example to set for Jewish kids, a lot of whom don't like to go to synagogue."

In 2004 the Dodgers faced a key weekend series against the San Francisco Giants in the September pennant race. Yom Kippur began at sundown on Friday, September 24. On Thursday, Green announced that he would play the Friday night game but sit out on Saturday. Although some rabbis accused Green of trying to have it both ways, Koufax was more understanding.

"That kind of call is totally up to Shawn," he said. "There's no way anyone can advise you on something like this."

Matthew Ceryes, who worked clubhouse security for the Giants and was assigned to the Dodgers clubhouse when they came to town in 2004, has a great story about Green sitting out that Yom Kippur Saturday game. The whiteboard in the visitors' clubhouse generally contained innocuous messages, like "Batting practice moved up one hour today." But on Saturday, Ceres saw this message scrawled on the board, perhaps by Manager Jim Tracy or a teammate: "Win this one for the Kippur."

To play or not to play—what would you do if you were in their place?

A version of this column first appeared in ISSUES: A Messianic Jewish Perspective, *Volume 18:5.*

PART 3

Legends, All-Stars, the Great and Not-so-Great

"My Interview with Joe DiMaggio"

This column was first published in the Martinez News-Gazette. *Martinez, California, is the home town of Joe DiMaggio.*

In the summer of 1974, between my junior and senior years at Cornell University, I was freelancing for the *Ithaca New Times*, a weekly newspaper in Ithaca, New York. My editor suggested I write a feature story about the Oneonta Yankees, a New York Yankees farm team in the New York-Penn League.

The NY-P, founded in 1939 as a Class D League and called the PONY (Pennsylvania-Ontario-New York) League, became a Class A league in 1963. The NY-P was the oldest continuously operated Class A league in professional baseball until its demise after the 2019 season.

Oneonta is about a two-hour drive from Ithaca. My only problem was that I didn't have a car. But back then, many young people hitchhiked. It was not yet considered very dangerous (although in 1973 the FBI put out a poster warning drivers that a hitcher might be a "sex maniac" or a "vicious murderer"). I guess I didn't look like either, so I managed to hitch a ride to Oneonta.

Oneonta is a small town (around 16,000 people then and now) nestled in the foothills of the Catskill Mountains. In the 1940s and 1950s, the town supported the Oneonta Red Sox, a Boston farm team in the now-defunct Canadian-American League. Frank Malzone, the Golden Glove third baseman for Boston in the 1950s and 1960s, played at Oneonta in 1949.

The Yankees took over the franchise in 1967. Notable Oneonta Yankees alumni include Don Mattingly (1979),

Bernie Williams (1987) and Jorge Posada (1991). During my visit in 1974, the roster included Dennis Werth, a catcher who played in the big leagues for parts of four seasons and whose stepson is Jayson Werth, the retired All-Star outfielder. Also on the squad was Mike Heath, then a shortstop, who spent fourteen seasons in the major leagues, mostly as a catcher. The president of the team was Sam Nader, cousin of the famous consumer advocate Ralph Nader.

The team played at the well-groomed Damaschke Field, where attendance averaged around 1,000 a game. Admission was $1.25 for adults and sixty cents for children.

I had intended to just spend the day, do my interviews and hitch a ride back home. But General Manager Nick Lambros informed me that I happened to arrive the day before Famous Yankee Night, an annual promotional event when the team brings in a former Yankee star.

The star that year was Joe DiMaggio. The next evening 3,000 people jammed into Damaschke Field to see Joltin' Joe before the game. He signed autographs, talked with the fans, and took a few swings for old times' sake.

I wouldn't be able to stay that late, but Mr. Lambros invited me to a small press conference the next afternoon on his backyard patio. So, after sleeping the night on the floor of an apartment shared by some of the players (one of them was Lou Turco, a pitcher I had played semi-pro baseball with in New Jersey), I headed over to the press conference.

As we sat on the patio sipping lemonade, Mr. Lambros emerged through the screen door of his home and announced, "Ladies and gentlemen, Mr. Joe DiMaggio." And behind him came the dapper, dignified Yankee Clipper himself.

As a twenty-one-year-old cub reporter, I was in awe as

DiMaggio sat down in a lawn chair right next to me. He would turn sixty in November, but apart from the silver hair, he looked like he could still be playing center field for the Bronx Bombers.

As I wrote in my August 24, 1974, article for the *Ithaca New Times*, "Even if he can no longer hit that high inside fastball, the grace and dignity that characterized him on and off the field still shine through." What impressed me most was how unassuming and approachable and congenial he was. Here was the great Joe DiMaggio in a tiny town with just a few folks out on the patio, and he treated me and the others with the utmost respect, taking time to fully answer all our questions.

Here's the portion of the article from my interview with him that day:

The Yankee Clipper reminisced: "I think I played in one of the most beautiful eras in baseball. At that time you had a different type of fan and a different type of ballplayer. We used to sit in the hotel lobbies and talk baseball for hours. Nowadays all the players have business interests and other things on the side to think about. But I don't blame them for that.

"As far as ability, that's hard to say. There were only eight teams in each league when I was playing. Today you have twelve, and I believe that's diluted the talent a bit. Also, they're bringing along young ballplayers a little too quickly, so that they come out of the minor leagues unrefined. I remember when I was coaching for Oakland and Reggie Jackson first arrived. He couldn't catch a fly ball. We'd hit it to him, he'd pound the glove a few times, and the ball would drop twenty feet behind him. I'm not kidding."

Jackson has come a long way since then, and DiMaggio claims it's because he's a hard worker. He feels that natural ability goes only so far. "There's no perfect ballplayer," said the man who may have been the closest to it. "We all strive for it but there's no one who ever gets there. I worked for hours and hours in practice just charging ground balls."

After talking a little about his famous fifty-six-game hitting streak, his daffy roommate Lefty Gomez, and the great Yankee manager Joe McCarthy, DiMaggio was goaded into answering one of the most frequently asked questions: "What was your greatest thrill in baseball?"

"I'll tell you one of them," he replied. "Putting on the New York Yankees pinstripes in spring training for the very first time."

It was such a thrill to interview the Yankee Clipper that day. Who knew that forty-four years later I would move to Martinez, Joltin' Joe's home town, and get to share this story with readers of the *Gazette*? Hope you enjoyed it.

* * *

"Gary Carter: A Fielder Turned Catcher Became a Hall of Famer"

I conducted an interview with Gary Carter for this column in 2007. Carter, inducted into the Hall of Fame in 2003, held the record for most games caught by a National Leaguer from 1990-2021, when his record was broken by Yadier Molina. Carter died from brain cancer in February 2012 at the age of fifty-seven. Sports Illustrated *baseball writer Tom Verducci reminisced about Carter following his death, "I cannot conjure a single image of Gary Carter with anything but a smile on his face. I have no recollection of a gloomy Carter, not even as his knees began to announce a slow surrender . . . Carter played every day with the joy as if it were the opening day of Little League."*

Not many people remember that Hall of Fame catcher Gary Carter played more games in the outfield than behind the plate his first two seasons in the major leagues. Montreal Expos manager Gene Mauch stayed with established catcher Barry Foote and put Carter in the outfield.

That's where Carter had his first major baseball injury.

He was in right field with Pepe Mangual in center in a game against Atlanta in June 1976. Braves' batter Darrel Chaney hit a liner into right-center field.

"I came running over," Carter recalls. "I was yelling, 'I got it' and Mangual was yelling 'Yo tengo,' and I didn't hear anything, the crowd's yelling and everything. And we collided, and my thumb was almost back to my wrist. And I knocked him out. He missed three games, but I missed six weeks."

That same season, Carter cracked his eleventh and twelfth ribs when he robbed the Phillies' Dave Cash of a home run. Carter says he felt safer behind the plate than in the outfield.

"It was getting frustrating," he says of the wide open spaces in right field. "Once I went back behind the plate and was more accustomed to the position, I don't feel like I had anywhere near the injuries."

Carter has had eleven knee surgeries, eight on the right and three on the left. But all of those surgeries stemmed from an injury he sustained to his right knee as a football player his senior year in high school. Even the surgeries to his left knee were the result of overcompensating for his bad right knee. The knee surgeries were due to deterioration from his many years of catching. The eleven-time All-Star believes some of that wear and tear could have been prevented.

Carter caught 2,056 games, more than any catcher in the history of the National League until Molina broke his record. He averaged 146 games behind the plate his first eight years as a catcher for the Expos and the New York Mets (not counting the strike-shortened 1981 season). Nobody does that anymore.

"There's no question I was overused," states Carter. "Nowadays catchers are a lot more protected. The average that a starting catcher will catch might be around 130 games."

One way to preserve a catcher's longevity is to use him at first base from time to time. But that only happened once during Carter's prime, his final year with Montreal in 1984. He played 159 games that season, but twenty-five of them were at first base under manager Bill Virdon.

"Virdon said, 'You deserve to play, to keep your bat in the lineup, but play another position,'" Carter remembers. He usually played first base on a day game following a night game. He feels his career would have been lengthened had the Expos and the Mets made that a regular practice.

Fortunately, Carter landed on his feet, so to speak, after retirement. He was a broadcaster for the Expos and Florida Marlins for seven years, then worked for the Mets as a catching instructor and minor league manager. He also began the Gary Carter Foundation, which has raised over $250,000 to support eight underprivileged schools in south Florida.

Carter's theory that the safest place for him was behind home plate gained some support when he suffered a freak accident on the golf course. Carter, an avid golfer and member of the Celebrity Players Tour, was playing in a tournament in the Bahamas several years ago when a tropical storm blew in.

"We had just gone through a devastating rainstorm, a major deluge," he recalls. "I was keeping everybody under cover, and I was walking back to my cart and to my golf bags to put the umbrella back in, and this kid just inadvertently backed up [Carter's golf cart] and hit my knee and blew my medial collateral ligament out again."

The good news is that in October 2004 Carter had knee replacement surgery on that right knee, which has enabled him to freely participate in many activities that had previously caused him great discomfort. That includes throwing batting practice, hitting fungos, and coaching at third base during the two years he managed in the Mets' minor league system in Florida.

"I'm able to get back in and work out and do those things on a pretty regular basis," says Carter, "and I'm very grateful for that."

Would Carter do it all over again if he knew his baseball career would result in so much physical pain?

"I have no regrets whatsoever," he says. "Injuries are part of a career. It happens to everybody. It's just a matter of how you overcome them, and how you handle them."

This column is excerpted from one that first appeared in Sports Spectrum, *September-October 2007.*

* * *

"Willie Mays May Have Been the Greatest Ever"

Was Willie Mays the greatest baseball player ever? Many who played with or against him think so. It was common for radio announcers calling Giant games to say, "The only man who could have caught that ball just hit it [after Mays hit a ball]."

I grew up in New York City in the 1950s, but Willie and the Giants left town for San Francisco when I was five, so I never saw him play for the New York Giants. I did see him play against the New York Mets on June 1, 1962, on Willie Mays night at the Polo Grounds, the great center fielder's first trip back to play in New York.

But I didn't have the privilege of seeing Mays regularly in person or on television until he was traded to the Mets in 1972, where he played two seasons until he retired at age forty-two.

I learned much about his greatness from my father, a native New Yorker who saw Mays play for the New York Giants when the *Say Hey* kid arrived in 1951. My dad was at the Polo Grounds when Mays hit his first home run, a 450-foot blast off Warren Spahn.

Perhaps the best way to appreciate Mays is to hear from those who played or managed with or against him. So here are some Willie Mays stories.

Joe Torre (catcher): "Willie didn't like to wait in the box. He wants you to throw the ball right now. Sometimes, I'd put a sign down, but I wouldn't put anything down. And Willie would talk to you. He'd say, 'I know what you're doing. I know what you're doing.' It was impossible not to love him even though he scared you to death because he was so good. One time, I tried to distract him by talking to him. I asked him a question at the plate. I don't remember what it was about, maybe about a restaurant, and he hit the ball out of the ballpark while answering the question. Then he made a half turn to me as he started to first base and told me, 'I'll finish the story later.'"

Leo Durocher, Mays' first big-league manager: "If somebody came up and hit .450, stole one-hundred bases, and performed a miracle in the field every day, I'd still look you right in the eye and tell you that Willie was better. He could do the five things you must do to be a superstar: hit, hit with power, run, throw, and field. He also had the other magic ingredient, which turns a superstar into a super Superstar. Charisma. He lit up a room when he came in. He was a joy to be around."

Don Zimmer: "In the National League in the 1950s, there were two opposing players who stood out over all the others—Stan Musial and Willie Mays. I've always said that Willie Mays was the best player I ever saw. He could have been an All-Star at any position."

Gil Hodges: "I can't very well tell my batters don't hit it to him. Wherever they hit it, he's there anyway."

Harvey Haddix: (to his catcher with Willie Mays at bat): "Look at him. He knows he's going to hit me, and I know he's going to hit, so I'm going to walk him."

Reggie Jackson: "You used to think if the score were 5-0, he'd hit a five-run homer."

Bill Rigney: "As a batter, his only weakness is a wild pitch."

Willie McCovey: "I played with him. People have a false impression of what a great player is nowadays. If somebody puts up great numbers, they think he's great. But if you saw Willie play, you would see games where he would win it for us, and he wouldn't even get a hit. He did things that nobody else did. That's what makes a great ballplayer."

Steve Stone, former Giants pitcher: "He was the best center fielder in the game when he was thirty-nine. It's truly amazing how long he maintained his skills."

Johnny Bench: "And he never missed one. He was so effortless. Back then, you wanted to put mustard on him. But that was just his natural ability and his grace in performing. In almost every game, it seems like he made an amazing play. You could have had two outfielders, put the other in the infield because Willie covered it all."

Felipe Alou (who played left or right field next to Mays): "I sometimes found myself watching the game like a fan would watch a game. A ball would be hit, and I would say, like a fan or a broadcaster, 'Is he going to catch this one?' He had an amazing first step. He was covering half of the field by himself."

Peter Macgowan, former Giants president: "He would routinely do things you never saw anyone else do. He'd score from first base on a single. He'd take two bases on a pop-up. He'd throw somebody out at the plate on one bounce. And the bigger the game, the better he played."

Dusty Baker: "I thought I had a pretty good arm. I thought I would throw Willie out at third base one day. I had him out. He ran right in the way of the ball, and it hit him in the shoulder. I got an error, and he scored. I swear he looked back, saw where the throw was, and ran right into the ball's path. I told the umpire, 'He can't do that!'"

Sandy Koufax: "I can't believe that Babe Ruth was a better player than Willie Mays. Ruth is to baseball, what Arnold Palmer is to golf. He got the game moving. But I can't believe he could run as well as Mays, and I can't believe he was any better an outfielder."
Say Hey!

This column first appeared in The Vacaville Reporter *on May 6, 2021.*

* * *

"Roberto Clemente, Best Ever?"

I couldn't believe my eyes. As a ten-year-old with my dad at the Polo Grounds in New York in 1963, I watched the Pittsburgh Pirates warm up before taking on the Mets in a weekend afternoon contest. Roberto Clemente was shagging flies in right field. He caught a ball on the warning track and unleashed a throw that carried on a fly into the catcher's mitt at home plate. Then he did it again.

Today, Major League Baseball holds a Roberto Clemente Day every September. All players and coaches on the Pirates and their opponent for the day wear 21 on their jerseys. Additionally, Puerto Rican players and any past Clemente Award winners and nominees can wear the number 21 on the backs of their jerseys. All other players, coaches, and umpires wear a No. 21 patch on their sleeves. Since Clemente's death, no Pirates player has worn 21 on the field of play other than on this special day.

Clemente died in a plane crash at age thirty-eight on New Year's Eve 1972 as he accompanied a cargo plane departing San Juan, Puerto Rico, in an attempt to bring humanitarian aid to people affected by a devastating earthquake in Nicaragua. Months later, Clemente became only the second player in MLB history to have the mandatory five-year waiting period waived for Hall of Fame induction. He was the first Latin American player elected to the Hall.

Before our sabermetric era, baseball players were evaluated using five tools: *speed, arm strength, fielding ability, hitting for average,* and *hitting for power.* Clemente had them all. Paul Ladewski of *Stadium Talk* applied a combination of Gold Glove Awards (Clemente won twelve), Defensive Wins Above Replacement (dWAR), Total Zone Runs (an estimate of runs saved in the field), Range Factor per nine innings and *YouTube* clips, and rated Clemente the best defensive right fielder of all time.

He led the National League in outfield assists five times and, since 1904, ranks second in career assists as a right fielder, with 255. He didn't try to steal many bases, but his speed in taking the extra base was phenomenal. Nobody ran from first to third with more wild abandon. He was a fifteen-time All-Star, an MVP in 1966, and a World Series MVP in 1971. He helped the Pirates win the World Series in 1960 and 1971, hitting a combined .362. A notorious bad-ball hitter, he also won four batting titles. He had exactly 3,000 hits, a career .317 batting average, a .359 on-base percentage, a .475 slugging percentage, and .834 OPS. He hit 240 homers and knocked in 1,305 runs.

Clemente spent all eighteen major league seasons in Pittsburgh, where he didn't get the media attention afforded to big-city stars like Willie Mays, Mickey Mantle, and Joe DiMaggio.

That said, consider the attention Clemente garnered from his fellow Latinos. Former St. Louis catcher Yadier Molina told *ESPN,* "For all us Latinos who have played major league baseball and have had to deal with so many obstacles, difficulties, and challenges, Clemente is the source of inspiration we need to move forward and pursue our dreams and be an example to others on and off the field."

Tony Bartirome, Clemente's former trainer with the Pirates, told the *Baseball Hall of Fame,* "When Clemente came to spring training in 1969, the Pirates had just built Pirate City. It was basically for the minor league players. All the major league players stayed at Longboat Key (a popular island resort off Florida's west coast). Clemente wouldn't do that. He would stay at Pirate City. Believe me, the food was horrible. I asked, 'Why are you staying here?' He shrugged his shoulders. I made it my business to find out why."

He discovered that Clemente didn't want his teammates to go through the same struggles he had encountered as a rookie in 1955. Clemente was staying there for the young Latin ballplayers.

Bartirome added, "Every night after dinner, he would sit in the front of the building and teach the players how to order off a menu and to communicate with the other players. He did that every spring, and no one knew about that."

Former teammate Al Oliver told the Hall, "To hear Roberto was like listening to my dad. He preached like a Baptist minister. He would say, 'How can the rich have so much [money] and people are starving?' This was his mindset, his spirituality."

Back to the ball field, Jerry Green of *The Detroit News* once wrote, "Roberto Clemente might not have been the perfect baseball player, but no other player in the game's 140 seasons has been closer to perfection." His one fault concluded Green—he played in Pittsburgh.

This column first appeared in The Vacaville Reporter *on September 9, 2020.*

***

"Yin and Yang of Barry Bonds"

Vallejo, California, resident Matthew Ceryes was a security guard at Pac Bell Park (which became SBC Park in 2004) from 2003 to 2005. He had a bird's-eye view of the Giants' inside goings-on, including those of Barry Bonds. In his own words, Ceryes relates a couple of incidents that show the good and the bad of the controversial star.

"During the 2004 season, two well-dressed eleven-year-old boys approached me pre-game at the 'velvet rope' line at the Giants' clubhouse, where folks with expensive tickets can actually wait while Giants cross the concrete tunnel," Ceryes said. "Players go down steps to then go up steps to the dugout and field. It was rare, but now and then, one of the stragglers would sign an autograph or pose for a picture. But these kids wanted neither. One politely asked me to go in and tell 'Uncle Barry' his nephews were here.

"This used to happen occasionally, with the fakers always smiling or giving away the game with a laugh. I was just about to, 'O yeah?' in the little Caucasian kid's face when his very focused eyes and my 'little voice' simultaneously told me this wasn't a joke."

Ceryes took his name, left a guard at the doors and went in to tell Barry. He respectfully approached his "compound" in the corner. Bonds was shirtless on the edge of his recliner close to his TV (pre-flat screen), on top of which a teammate or coach had added a small, yellow and black warning sign, "CAUTION: 40-year-old having a senior moment." Ceryes then said, "Barry, your nephews are here to see you . . . " ending with a confidence-fading, question-mark inflection ("?").

Bonds jumped to his feet, slipped on a black athletic fleece, and said, as Ceryes left, that he would be there. When Bonds came out to the line, the kids instantly lit up and Barry brought them to his side with cordial greetings and genuine warmth. Then he bent down, grabbed each kid's face with his two large hands, and kissed them squarely on the lips.

"I silently congratulated my little voice for not blowing this the ten different ways I could have," said Ceryes, "reminding myself of Barry's first marriage and, finally, admiring the loving and affectionate side of his personality. No hard feelings with the ex's family apparently, wow."

However, Ceryes said during a 2004 game versus the Pirates, Mr. Bonds made a very different display while Ceryes was holding down the fort at the visitors' clubhouse. Riding shotgun in a golf cart down the long concrete tunnels, Bonds was going with the Giants doctors for what Ceryes thought was a knee appointment and/or MRI at the under-stadium medical office.

"Slowing down to make the right-handed turn past my post," recalled Ceryes, "Barry proceeded to rage out incoherently and physically at somebody who wasn't there. Kicking over stanchions with a metallic crash and dragging the velvet rope with him for a short ride of ten more feet or so, he screamed from the cart, 'Tell that so-and-so McClendon [Pirates manager] he's such a so-and-so and he can so-and-so-this/that and so-and-so OFF!!'"

"Then just like that, they made the turn, he flipped the rope back toward me, and the cart sort of faded away. I looked around to find myself completely alone, which in-game was fairly normal. But just who the heck was that for? Lloyd McClendon was busy above us, managing his heart out from the Pittsburgh dugout. No one from the Pirates heard a word of what Barry said, and between the shock of the crashes, I didn't understand half of what he said either, and I was standing right there."

Ceryes then picked up three stanchions one at a time and clicked the green velvet line's golden hooks back into their spots. He reset the fan viewing area for the visiting team and waited for the post-game crush, after which he would catch the N-Judah line back home to the Outer Sunset.

In 2001, when Bonds hit 73 home runs, he earned this review from *ESPN's* David Halberstam: "He has also been one of the most difficult to like. The stories have always been quite shocking. They are not, it should be noted, about a distant, somewhat aloof, relatively private young man who keeps himself apart from the amiable pre-game byplay that can make baseball fun. Rather, they are about unprovoked, deliberate, gratuitous acts of rudeness towards people, other players, and distinguished sportswriters. They are of a handsomely rewarded young man of surpassing talent, going out of his way to make the ambience in which he operates as unpleasant as possible and to diminish the dignity and pleasure of other men (and now women) who also work for a living, even if their talents are somewhat smaller than his."

In 2016, when Bonds was serving as hitting coach for the Miami Marlins, he admitted to some of his bad behavior, particularly with the media. Here's what he told Terence Moore of *Sports on Earth.*

Barry Bonds: "It's on me. I'm to blame for the way I was

[portrayed] because I was a dumbass. I was straight stupid, and I'll be the first to admit it. I mean, I was just flat-out dumb." Bonds added, "The one thing that I would never, ever reflect on and talk about changing from the past is my ability with what I did on the field. I did that right when it came to [preparing for and playing the game]. But I didn't do it the right way regarding my attitude and handling things. There were times during my career when I did try, but I wasn't given the benefit of the doubt because I had already created the monster."

This column first appeared in The Vacaville Reporter *on September 22, 2020.*

***

"Is Shohei Ohtani the New Babe Ruth"

In 2021, I wrote "It is way too early in Shohei Ohtani's major league career to compare him to Babe Ruth, who many consider the greatest baseball player of all time. But the comparisons are fun to make."

Now it may be time to make those comparisons.

Here's one that blows my mind:

Babe Ruth: 159 home runs in his first 674 career games; W-L 35-18 in his first 455.0 career innings pitched.

Shohei Ohtani: 160 home runs in his first 674 career games; W-L 35-19 in his first 455.0 career innings pitched.

Ruth was a starting pitcher for the Boston Red Sox and pitched a bit for the New York Yankees after that infamous trade. But he was too good a hitter to only play every four days, so the Yankees made him their starting right fielder.

Back in May 2021, Ohtani pitched seven innings of one-run ball and struck out ten Houston Astros hitters while serving as the Los Angeles Angels' No. 2 hitter. In the bottom of the eighth, with the score tied and his spot due up the next half-inning, rather than pull him from the game, Angels manager Joe Maddon moved him to right field to keep him in the lineup.

On the mound, he became the first pitcher in the modern era, which dates back to 1900, to strike out forty or more batters and allow fewer than a dozen hits over his first five starts of a season.

"I don't think I've ever seen anybody who's that skilled at both things," White Sox manager Tony La Russa told ESPN.

La Russa, like most people still alive today, never saw Ruth play. But some forget what a unique talent the Bambino was on the mound. He had a lifetime record of 94-46 and an ERA of 2.28.

In 1916, Ruth won twenty-three games and posted a league-leading 1.75 ERA. He also threw nine shutouts—an American League record for left-handed pitchers that still stands (the Yankees' Ron Guidry tied it in 1978). In Game 2 of the World Series, Ruth pitched all fourteen innings, beating the Brooklyn Dodgers, 2-1. Boston beat Brooklyn in the series four games to one.

On May 6, 1918, in the Polo Grounds against the Yankees, Ruth played first base and batted sixth. It was the first time he had appeared in a game other than as a pitcher or pinch-hitter and the first time he batted in any spot other than ninth. Ruth went 2-for-4, including a two-run home run. The next day against the Senators Ruth was moved up to fourth in the lineup—he hit another home run—where he stayed for most of the season.

Manager Ed Barrow wanted Ruth to continue pitching

but Ruth would feign exhaustion or a sore arm to keep that from happening. But he did throw over one hundred innings in his final season with the Red Sox in 1919.

When Ruth came to the Yankees in 1920, he made the switch from pitcher to everyday player full time. He threw four innings during a spot start that year and pitched nine more across two games in 1921. But after that, he appeared done with it.

Late in the 1930 season, the Yankees seemed destined to finish third in the American League. The Red Sox were even further back in the standings. So there was not much on the line when the Yankees went up to Boston to end the season on September 28.

Ruth approached manager Bob Shawkey with an idea to draw fans to the meaningless game: he would pitch the season finale. Shawkey agreed, and after nearly nine years, Ruth was given the ball. To add to his mystique, he pitched a complete game and got the win. He scattered eleven hits and allowed three runs.

As a side note, after hearing that Ruth was going to pitch, Lou Gehrig offered and was allowed to take Ruth's position in left field.

Three years later, Ruth similarly got the start in a meaningless final game of the season against the Red Sox. He again threw a complete game as the Yankees won 6-5.

So it seems the Curse of the Bambino was alive and well.

Now Ohtani is building his own mystique.

"That's so unusual what he was able to do tonight," Maddon said of the outing when Ohtani switched to right field and stayed in the lineup. "He does it so easy that we have to understand it's not so easy to do what he's doing."

Ohtani, a right-handed thrower, sustained a right UCL

(elbow) tear during a start for the Angels on August 23, 2023. He had surgery on the elbow that September, but his timeline to return to pitching hit a road black when he suffered a labrum tear in his left shoulder while trying to steal a base in the 2024 World Series.

He is back on the mound, in limited pitches per game, in 2025.

Babe Ruth said, "I don't think a man can pitch in his regular turn and play every other game at some other position and keep that pace year after year. I can do it this season all right, and not feel it, for I am young and strong and don't mind the work. But I wouldn't guarantee to do it for many seasons."

Ohtani and his Los Angeles Dodgers manager Dave Roberts may want to take Ruth's words to heart.

In the meantime, it's a lot of fun to watch this highly gifted Japanese import do his thing.

This column, which has been contemporized, first appeared in The Vacaville Reporter *on May 19, 2021.*

***

"Omar Vizquel Belongs in Baseball's Hall of Fame"

Vizquel didn't make it during the most recent Hall of Fame voting (January 2025). I'll keep writing, "He deserves to be in the Hall," until he is. Here's what I wrote in 2021.

On January 26, 2021, the Baseball Writers of America Association will announce the results of its 2021 Hall of Fame voting live from Cooperstown on MLB Network. Electees will be inducted during Hall of Fame Weekend on Sunday, July 25, in Cooperstown.

This writer believes former shortstop Omar Vizquel should be making his acceptance speech in July. But he probably won't, even though he played more games at shortstop than any other man in the history of baseball.

His career spanned four decades and twenty-four seasons, over which he won eleven Gold Gloves. His career fielding percentage of .9847 is the best for all major league shortstops. He had 2,877 career hits and a career batting average of .272, ten points better than the .262 of Ozzie Smith, who is in the Hall.

Also, Vizquel was a master at handling the bat. With 256 sacrifice hits (bunts) and 94 sacrifice flies, he has the most combined sacrifices (350) since 1954, the first year *Baseball-Reference* measured sacrifice flies.

Statistics guru Bill James came up with what he calls a "similarity score." The players most similar to Vizquel in offensive production are Luis Aparicio, Rabbit Maranville, Smith, Bill Dahlen, Dave Concepción, Luke Appling, Pee Wee Reese, and Nellie Fox. Only Concepción and Dahlen are not in the Hall of Fame.

As writer Chris Bodig notes, "Vizquel is on the Hall of Fame ballot for the fourth year and is at the center of the debate between the community of sabermetricians and people who follow their instincts when evaluating a player's Hall of Fame candidacy. He may run into a sabermetric wall of detractors that keep him under the magic number (75 percent of the votes) and thus force his case to be considered years later by the 'Today's Game' Eras Committee, the modern version of the Veterans Committee."

Sabermetricians who make the case against Vizquel claim that some defensive metrics don't back up Vizquel's reputation as an all-time premier defender. But, as Bodig points out, defense is more difficult to quantify than offense. Vizquel's detractors point to a statistic called **Range Factor**, which is computed this way: nine times (putouts plus assists) divided by innings played. In his career, Vizquel's range factor per nine innings was 4.62. The league average over those twenty-four seasons was 4.61.

The idea behind the **Range Factor** is that a player involved in many plays must be able to cover a wider portion of the field. But, as an article on *pennantchase.com* states, "Anyone who has watched a lot of baseball knows that a fielder involved in many plays doesn't necessarily have good range. Maybe he's an infielder playing behind a lot of ground-ball pitchers. Maybe he's an outfielder playing in a large ballpark. One player might accumulate more opportunities for many reasons than his peers."

Detractors make the case that Vizquel did not help his teams offensively, primarily based on his career **Wins Above Replacement** (WAR) score. **WAR** is a difficult statistic to describe. It seeks to answer the question: "If this player got injured and their team had to replace him with a freely available minor leaguer, how much value would the team lose?"

However, **WAR** is another controversial statistic, so much so that in 2016, the MLB Players Association scheduled a meeting after the MVP and Cy Young winners were announced because they believed **WAR** was weighted too heavily in the decision-making process. A more meaningful statistic is **OPS-plus**, which combines on-base and slugging percentages, adjusted for ballparks and seasons. Vizquel's score of 82 equals that of Hall of Famers Aparicio and Maranville and is just below that of Smith.

So, should Vizquel be in the Hall of Fame? Bodig writes,

"Essentially, it was a **WAR** test vs. an eye test." Let's hear from four baseball writers who saw Vizquel play.

Andrew Baggarly, *The Athletic Bay Area*: *"My small Hall includes Vizquel. Go ahead and torch me for that, but I believe that longevity matters—especially at the most grueling position on the infield—and there aren't metrics that can adequately assess the transcendent joy he brought to anyone who watched him play."*

Henry Schulman, *San Francisco Chronicle*: *"Face it, Vizquel was his generation's Ozzie Smith or the closest facsimile. Stats are important, and newer metrics that better compare players through different eras are valuable. But they are the sum of a player's career. If you use numbers alone to shunt Vizquel into that mythical Hall of the Very Good, it's a fair bet you did not see him play. Sometimes a man is a Hall of Famer because he just is."*

Bill Madden, *New York Daily News*: *"I have two straightforward Hall of Fame criteria: The first is the 'see' test. In watching a player for ten or more years, did I say to myself: 'I'm looking at a Hall of Famer?' The four greatest fielding shortstops I ever saw were Vizquel, Ozzie, Luis Aparicio, and Mark Belanger. Ozzie had the flair and the backflips, but Vizquel, for me, was the best. Made every play look easy."*

Bob Ryan, *Boston Globe*: *"A consummate fielder—I said consummate—fielder, and teamed with Hall of Famer Roberto Alomar to form the best DP combo I ever saw. Yes, I am partial to defensive whizzes, and I refuse to apologize for it."*

I agree. Those of us who had the pleasure of watching Vizquel play shortstop knew we were seeing greatness.

Here's hoping that more baseball writers trust their eyes as much as their calculators when they vote next time.

Note: *Claims of domestic abuse and sexual harassment (involving different people, separate cases) by Vizquel could play a role in Hall of Fame voting.*

This column first appeared in The Vacaville Reporter *on July 9, 2021.*

* * *

"The Baseball Actors All-Star Team"

Vacaville Reporter reader Keith Abernethy suggested I assemble an all-star team of actors from baseball movies. Here are my picks.

Pitcher: Dennis Quaid (as Jimmy Morris) in *The Rookie,* **Sammi Kane Kraft** (as Amanda Whurlitzer) in the remake of *Bad News Bears,* **Tatum O'Neal** (as Whurlitzer) in the original *The Bad News Bears,* **Ronald Reagan** (as Grover Cleveland Alexander) in *The Winning Team,* **Brendan Fraser** (as Steve Nebraska) in *The Scout,* **Tim Robbins** (as "Nuke" LaLoosh) in *Bull Durham,* **Kevin Costner** (as Billy Chapel) in *For Love of the Game,* **Lori Petty** (as Kit Keller) in *A League of Their Own,* **Charlie Sheen** (as Ricky Vaughn) in *Major League,* **Billie Dee Williams** (as Bingo Long) in *The Bingo Long Traveling All-Stars & Motor Kings,* **Thomas Ian Nicholson** (as Henry Rowengartner) in *Rookie of the Year*

Catcher: Geena Davis (as Dottie Hinson) in *A League of Their Own,* **Kevin Costner** (as Crash Davis) in *Bull Durham,* **Tom Berenger** (as Jake Taylor) in *Major League,* **Robert De Niro** (as Bruce Pearson) in *Bang the Drum Slowly.*

First base: Tom Selleck (as Jack Elliot) in *Mr. Baseball,* **Gary Cooper** (as Lou Gehrig) in *The Pride of the Yankees,* **Bernie Mac** (as Stan Ross) in *Mr. 3000.*

Second base: Jackie Robinson (as himself) in *The Jackie Robinson Story,* **Megan Cavanaugh** (as Marla Hooch) in *A League of Their Own,* **Chadwick Boseman** (as Jackie Robinson) in *42.*

Third base: Corbin Bernsen (as Roger Dorn) in *Major League,* and **Rosie O'Donnell** (as Doris Murphy) in *A League of Their Own.*

Shortstop: Mike Vitar (as Benny "The Jet" Rodriguez) in *The Sandlot*

Left field: Robert Redford (as Roy Hobbs) in *The Natural*

Center field: Anthony Perkins (as Jimmy Piersall) in *Fear Strikes Out,* **Wesley Snipes** (as Willie Mays Hayes) in *Major League,* **Thomas Jane** (as Mickey Mantle) in *61.*

Right field: William Bendix (as Babe Ruth) in *The Babe Ruth Story,* **John Goodman** (as Babe Ruth) in *The Babe,* **Tommie Lee Jones** (as Ty Cobb) in *Cobb,* **Barry Pepper** (as Roger Maris) in *61.*

Manager: Tom Hanks (as Jimmy Dugan) in *A League of Their Own*

Scout: Clint Eastwood (as Gus Lobel) in *Trouble with the Curve,* **Albert Brooks** (as Al Percolo) in *The Scout.*

Announcer: Bob Uecker (as Harry Doyle) in *Major League*

NOTE: If you're wondering why none of the actors from *Eight Men Out* made the squad, that's because the players they portrayed were all thrown out of baseball for life. That's also why **Ray Liotta** (as Shoeless Joe Jackson) in *Field of Dreams* didn't make the cut.

This column first appeared in The Vacaville Reporter *on May 12, 2020.*

* * *

"My Two-Sport All-Star Team"

Reader Keith Abernethy suggested I form an All-Star team of major league baseball players who also played in the NFL. I have expanded that to include those ballplayers who played in the NBA.

Here are the two squads. Selections are based not just on the players' baseball careers (some were very short) but also on their performance in their other sport.

NATIONAL LEAGUE

Infield

Catcher, Vic Janowicz—The first Heisman Trophy winner to play in both the NFL and MLB, he logged two seasons with the Pittsburgh Pirates and played halfback for the Washington Redskins.

First base, Chuck Connors—Known better for his starring

role in TV's *The Rifleman*, the 6-6 Connors played 53 games for the Boston Celtics and baseball for the Brooklyn Dodgers and the Chicago Cubs.

Second base, Chuck Corgan—He played baseball for the Brooklyn Robins (later named the Dodgers) during the 1925 and 1927 seasons and played football for the Kansas City Blues/Cowboys, Hartford Blues, and New York Giants from 1924 to 1927. He died from cancer in 1928.

Third base, Chuck Dressen—He played primarily for the Cincinnati Reds in his eight-year major league career and later managed the Brooklyn Dodgers. At 5-5, Dressen played quarterback for the Decatur Staleys in 1919, the precursor to the NFL's Chicago Bears, and then joined the NFL's Racine Legion for two seasons.

Shortstop, Dick Groat—He played for four NL teams and was named the league's MVP in 1960 after winning the batting title with a .325 average for the World Champion Pirates. A two-time All-American basketball player at Duke University, he played one season as a guard for the Fort Wayne Pistons in the NBA.

Outfield

Jim Thorpe—The Olympic gold medalist played pro baseball, football, and basketball, though football was his most decorated sport. He began his career with the Canton Bulldogs in the inaugural 1920 NFL season and played for six NFL teams. Thorpe played for the New York Giants, Cincinnati Reds, and Boston Braves for six MLB seasons.

Deion Sanders—Although he began his MLB career with the Yankees, Sanders spent more time in the National League, chiefly with the Reds and Braves, in his nine-year career. He played in the NFL for fourteen seasons, won two Super Bowls, and is in the NFL Hall of Fame.

Brian Jordan—Jordan played three seasons as a defensive back with the Atlanta Falcons. Following his time in the NFL, Jordan played fifteen seasons of major league baseball, primarily for St. Louis and Atlanta. He had a lifetime .282 batting average and had more hits (1,454) than any other MLB-NFL athlete.

Pitchers

Gene Conley—The 6-8 Conley played eleven seasons from 1952 to 1963 for four major league teams and played forward in the NBA in the 1952–53 season and from 1958 to 1964. He is the only athlete to win championships in two of the four major American sports (MLB, NBA, NFL, NHL), one with the Milwaukee Braves in 1957 and three Boston Celtics championships from 1959 to 61.

Ron Reed—Reed spent two seasons as a power forward for the Detroit Pistons before deciding to dedicate himself to baseball. The 6-6 righthander spent nineteen seasons in the majors, compiling a 146-140 won-loss record and a 3.46 ERA.

AMERICAN LEAGUE

Infield

Catcher, Charlie Berry—Berry started his major league career with the Philadelphia Athletics in 1925 but didn't return to the majors until after his football career ended, playing for the Red Sox, White Sox, and Athletics. In 1925–26, he starred for the Pottsville Maroons of the NFL, leading the league in scoring in 1925 with 74 points.

First base, Cotton Nash—Nash had a three-year MLB career with the White Sox and Twins. He played collegiate basketball for the University of Kentucky, where he was named a first-team All-American in 1964. He went on to play in the NBA for the Los Angeles Lakers and the San Francisco Warriors during the 1964–65 NBA season.

Second base, Danny Ainge—Ainge is the only person named a high school first-team All-American in football, basketball, and baseball. While still in college, Ainge played parts of three seasons with the Toronto Blue Jays. He was then drafted into the NBA by the Celtics. Ainge was later the general manager and president of basketball operations for the Boston Celtics.

Third base, Drew Henson—Henson played eight games for the Yankees from 2002-2003. The Houston Texans drafted the quarterback in the sixth round of the 2003 NFL Draft. He played briefly for the Dallas Cowboys and Detroit Lions.

Shortstop, Jim Levey—Levey was a Jewish shortstop who played from 1930 to 1933 for the St. Louis Browns. He also was a halfback for the Pittsburgh Pirates of the National Football League from 1934 to 1936.

Outfield

Bo Jackson—The only professional athlete in history to be named an All-Star (or All-Pro) in baseball and football, Jackson won the Heisman Trophy in 1985. He played in the NFL for the Los Angeles Raiders and in the MLB for the Kansas City Royals, Chicago White Sox, and California Angels. A 1991 hip injury on the gridiron ended his football career, and his baseball career ended in 1994.

George Halas—Although he only played twelve games for the New York Yankees in 1919, Halas makes up a huge portion of the Chicago Bears' history. He founded, coached, played, and picked the team's colors. He also played defense and offense and handled ticket sales.

Tom Brown—Brown briefly played for the Washington Senators early in the 1963 season and then was a defensive back in the NFL for six seasons with the Green Bay Packers and Washington Redskins.

Pitchers

Dave DeBusschere—Elected to the NBA Hall of Fame and named one of the fifty greatest players in the history of the NBA, DeBusschere also pitched in 1962 and 1963 for the Chicago White Sox. He played twelve years in the NBA for the Pistons and Knicks and was named to eight NBA All-Star teams.

Steve Hamilton—Hamilton was primarily used as a relief pitcher during his twelve MLB seasons. In 421 career games from 1961 to 1972, he had a 40–31 record with 42 saves and a 3.05 earned run average. From 1958 to 1960, he was a power forward/center for the Minneapolis Lakers.

This column first appeared in The Vacaville Reporter *on July 15, 2020.*

* * *

"Baseball Stars Who Have Played Around"

Many major league ballplayers ended up in different positions than they started out.

Stan Musial was a minor league pitcher for the Cardinals for three seasons. He had control problems and then a shoulder injury forced him from the mound. That worked out quite well for St. Louis. The Hall of Famer hit 475 home runs.

Rick Ankiel pitched for the Cardinals from 1999 until 2001 when he got the yips and couldn't find home plate. After trying to regain his pitching form in the minors and briefly returning to the majors in 2004, he switched to the outfield in early 2005 and developed his skills as a hitter and fielder in the Cards' minor-league system. He returned to the big club on August 9, 2007. As a Cardinal through 2009, Ankiel hit forty-seven home runs as an outfielder.

Tim Wakefield, the famed knuckleballer who won 200 games in the majors, was an eighth-round pick as a first baseman. But he hit just .189 in his first season in the minors. He also annoyed his manager by constantly throwing a knuckleball during infield practice. Luckily for baseball, his coaches eventually let him try it from the mound.

Jack Clark was drafted as a pitcher by the San Francisco Giants. But in the Rookie league he walked nineteen batters in fifteen innings while hitting .321. The Giants quickly converted him to an outfielder.

In 2005, the Angels selected a right-handed pitcher out of Lee County High School named **Gerald Dempsey Posey III** in the fiftieth and final round of the Draft. But Posey elected to keep playing for Florida State University instead of signing. Three years later, the Giants drafted Posey—better known as Buster—with the fifth overall pick in the 2008 Draft. By then, the future Hall of Famer had converted to catcher and become one of the top collegiate baseball players in the country.

Eddie Murray is one of only seven players in MLB history to be in both the 3,000 hit club and the 500 home run club. He was elected to the Baseball Hall of Fame in 2003 in his first year of eligibility. Bill James ranks him as the fifth-best first baseman in major league history. But Murray was drafted as a catcher out of high school by the Orioles in 1973.

Former Oakland A's slugger **Matt Stairs** began his career as a second baseman and third baseman who even played shortstop at times. It was not until he reached the majors at age twenty-four that he converted to the outfield.

Former San Francisco Giant **Michael Morse** started out

in the majors as a shortstop, playing fifty-seven games at that position. But he literally outgrew it. He became so big that the only logical places to put him were at first base, outfield, or designated hitter.

Jason Giambi came up with the Athletics as a third baseman. Oakland already had a guy named Mark McGwire at first. So Giambi played the hot corner, left field, and DH. It wasn't until 1997 that he was moved to first base.

Dave Stieb, who won 176 games on the mound in his major league career, all but one of them with the Toronto Blue Jays, played the outfield for Southern Illinois University. But he was only drafted because he happened to pitch in relief on a day that major league scouts were at a game. Stieb was sure he could make it as an outfielder. But he only hit .192 in one hundred plate appearances in the minors and finally agreed to switch to the mound. Two years later he was in the Blue Jays starting rotation.

Todd Helton was a pitcher and outfielder at the University of Tennessee (also a quarterback). In the Rockies minor league system, he played both first base and outfield. But once he made the majors, he played the outfield just fifteen times as a rookie and never played there again. He became Colorado's first baseman, playing solely for the Rockies for seventeen seasons, the greatest player in franchise history.

And then, of course, there is **Babe Ruth**.

George Herman Ruth began his major league career in 1914 with the Boston Red Sox as a starting pitcher. He had a lifetime 94-46 won-lost record and a 2.28 ERA. In 1916 he went 23-12 with a 1.75 E.R.A. In the World Series against Brooklyn that year, he pitched the longest complete game in World Series history, a fourteen-inning 2-1 victory over the Dodgers.

The Red Sox couldn't help but notice how well Ruth hit the ball when he was in the lineup on the days he pitched. So Boston started to play him in the outfield on some days he was not pitching.

By 1918 they had him in the outfield pretty much every day he was not on the hill. He hit .300 that year. The next year he hit .322 and led the league with 29 home runs.

In 1920 he was traded to the Yankees and the rest, as they say, is history.

Ruth first played baseball at St. Mary's Industrial School for Boys in Baltimore. He was a left-handed catcher. Since the school only had a right-handed catcher's mitt, Ruth would catch the ball with his left hand. If a runner attempted to steal, he'd toss the glove aside, catch the ball in the air and throw it to second base with his left hand.

One can't mention Ruth without bringing up **Shohei Ohtani**, who from his youth has been a remarkable pitcher and batter. Ohtani's prime major league seasons have been considered among the greatest in baseball history, with some comparing them favorably to the early career of Ruth.

Sometimes we forget that first and foremost, baseball players are athletes. The ones who make it to the majors are exceptional athletes with more than one set of skills. It shouldn't surprise us when they succeed at another position, even one they have never tried before.

This column, which has been contemporized, first appeared in The Vacaville Reporter *on August 8, 2019.*

***

"Remembering Arthur Ashe"

More than fifty years ago, Arthur Ashe defeated Jimmy Connors in the Wimbledon finals.

I watched the July 5, 1975, match on TV and couldn't believe my eyes. Ashe, the prohibitive underdog, was dinking and lobbing and outsmarting Connors, the reigning Wimbledon champ and No. 1 ranked men's player in the world who had gone 99-4 in 1974.

Connors had just destroyed hard-serving Roscoe Tanner in the semis, 6-4, 6-1, 6-4 and seemed unstoppable. Ashe also had a huge serve and was a hard hitter who took no prisoners. But Connors was a master counterpuncher who was predicted to decimate Ashe.

The two had some unpleasant history. Two years earlier, Ashe was one of the leaders of the Association of Tennis Professionals (ATP) Wimbledon boycott to put the players mostly in control for the first time. Connors, then twenty, who would benefit from the strike, ignored the boycott and made it to the quarterfinals.

Connors had refused to play in the 1974 Davis Cup, which irked Ashe. Connors and his manager, Bill Riordan, filed a lawsuit against Ashe, who, according to them, had damaged Connors' image by claiming that his Davis Cup absence was unpatriotic.

To get into Connors' head, Ashe walked onto Centre Court wearing red, white, and blue sweatbands and his Davis Cup team jacket, with USA across the back.

Connors was not the most popular player, especially among his peers. As Tony Kornheiser described him in a

New York Times article, "His outcries during the early stages of a match are usually self-directed and funny. But if he starts losing, he turns malicious. First with a leer, then with obscene gestures and, finally, with a descent into runaway vulgarity."

As Richard Evans wrote in *Open Tennis,* "The political background had obviously added spice to the occasion, but even without that the match would have attracted an unusual amount of interest, because Ashe had already established himself as one of the most articulate and popular athletes in the world, while Connors was the perfect anti-hero—brash, vulgar, and threatening."

Many were rooting for the humble Ashe, age thirty-two, to upend the brash, cocky Connors. But how?

Tennis commentator Bud Collins said he was "scared to death that Arthur was going to be terribly embarrassed."

But Ashe walked onto the court brimming with confidence.

"I had the strangest feeling that I couldn't lose," he said later on.

Between the semis and final, Ashe had a meeting of the minds with his agent (and U.S. Davis Cup captain) Donald Dell and his friend and fellow player Dennis Ralston. They devised a plan based on the strategy that Muhammad Ali had used to take back the heavyweight championship from George Foreman in October 1974. Ali labeled the tactic "rope-a-dope" (a none-too-subtle dig at Foreman's intelligence), a defensive shell used to tire an opponent out. Frequently on the ropes from round two onward, Ali allowed Foreman to pound away with enormous blows intended for head and body, most of which Ali blocked. He also picked his moments to counterpunch, and then, in the eighth round came away from the ropes full force and knocked out Foreman to reclaim the title.

Now Ashe, like Ali, facing a younger and stronger opponent, gave up his signature style of hard-hitting, hard-charging tennis. Like a pitcher who knew a good fastball hitter would send his pitch out faster than it came in, Ashe knew that Connors' returns would come back harder than Ashe's serves.

Instead of smacking the flat serve he favored, and which Connors loved to smack back with his two-handed backhand, Ashe would bend his serve out wide. Rather than try to slug it out, Ashe would slice and dice, dink and dunk and lob.

His strategy worked to perfection. He kept the ball low, softly rolled it, chipped it. He moved Connors from side to side, and his forehand volley, unreliable in the past, was precise. He gave Connors nothing to work with. Ashe won the first two sets by an astonishing 6-1.

Connors eked out the third set 7-5 and went up a break in the fourth. But Ashe, closing his eyes to meditate during each changeover, did not change his plan. At the end, much like Ali against Foreman, Ashe uncorked two vicious backhands to break serve. Minutes later, he completed the incredible upset with a perfectly-placed serve that Connors could only weakly backhand to the net, where Ashe plunked it for the 6-4 winner, set and match.

Ashe would never again play the style he did that day. As Evans wrote, "It was all biff and bang and glorious technicolor winners for the rest of his career."

Ashe became the first and so far only African-American man to win a Wimbledon title. Ashe said, "Among Blacks, I've had quite a few say [the win] was up there with Joe

Louis in his prime and Jackie Robinson breaking in with the Dodgers in 1947."

Steve Tignor, writing for tennis.com, noted, " . . . to win a Wimbledon title on Centre Court was to show, like his fellow pioneer Althea Gibson had shown, nearly twenty years earlier, that there was no place in tennis where African-American players couldn't succeed. He was the rare athlete who transcended all boundaries, and he inspired whites and blacks alike. Ashe showed that thought and courage do matter in tennis, and with enough of both, anyone can be beaten."

Ashe helped create inner-city tennis programs for youth and spoke out against apartheid in South Africa—successfully lobbying for a visa so he could visit and play tennis there.

Ashe died at age forty-nine in 1993 from AIDS-related pneumonia. Ashe and his doctors believed he contracted the virus from blood transfusions he received during his second heart surgery.

Let's take a moment during Wimbledon each year to remember the great Arthur Ashe.

* * *

"The Fight of the Century Lived Up to the Hype"

March 2026 marked the fifty-fifth anniversary of the first heavyweight championship fight between Muhammad Ali and Joe Frazier.

The March 8, 1971, contest, billed as the Fight of the Century, was the first heavyweight title fight between two undefeated fighters and lived up to all of its publicity. At that time, the fight, which took place at New York's Madison

Square Garden, was probably the most hyped and highly anticipated event in the history of sport.

For those readers who weren't alive at the time or who don't recall the outcome, I will just say that Ali's prediction that he would knock out Frazier in the sixth round did not come true and that the fifteen-round battle went the distance.

I don't want to spoil the enjoyment for those who might want to watch the fight in its entirety for free on YouTube. For that matter, I won't tell you how the second Ali-Frazier contest (Super Fight II), also at Madison Square Garden, and the third Ali-Frazier bout (the Thrilla in Manila) turned out. You can watch both those fights in their entirety on YouTube as well.

There was considerable drama around the first fight due to the political climate of the times.

Born Cassius Marcellus Clay in Louisville, Kentucky in 1942, Ali won the gold medal at the Rome Olympics in 1960 and in February 1964 became world heavyweight champion by defeating Sonny Liston. The day after he defeated Liston, Ali rejected the name Clay given to his family by a slave owner and said he had joined the Nation of Islam.

In the mid-1960s America was being torn apart by the issues of the Vietnam War and civil rights. When Ali was ordered to report to the draft board, he was confronted by reporters. He asked them why he should travel thousands of miles to kill people on behalf of a nation that treated him and his fellow African Americans as second-class citizens.

On April 28, 1967, Ali made his refusal to join the armed forces official, claiming conscientious objector status. That same day, the New York State Athletic Commission took away his boxing license and stripped him of his title. Boxing commissions across the nation would not let Ali fight, effectively banishing him from boxing.

In late 1970, when the tide of public opinion had turned against the Vietnam War, the city of Atlanta allowed Ali to return to the ring, where he stopped Jerry Quarry in three rounds. Ali then knocked out Oscar Bonavena in the fifteenth round at Madison Square Garden in December of that year. After the win, Ali shouted "I want Joe Frazier!"

Two courts had upheld the government's refusal to accept Ali as a conscientious objector and the case was headed to the Supreme Court in June 1971. Ali, expecting the Supreme Court to decide against him, was eager to fight Frazier for the title before that date. He got his wish with the bout in March of that year with Frazier, who had ascended to the throne in Ali's absence.

The two fighters were polar opposites. Ali was talkative, brash, and boastful and an anti-establishment hero. Frazier just went about his business in the ring. Broadcaster Tim Ryan described Frazier as "a workaday guy, who lived the way he fought: just get in there, throw a hundred punches, be strong, and mind your own business."

Frazier never made any political statements. He actually helped Ali financially during his exile and appealed to President Richard Nixon to grant Ali clemency. But Frazier became the hero of the establishment, just because he was not Ali. As author Jerry Izenberg wrote, "many whites who disliked Ali on racial grounds adopted Frazier as their designated Black representative."

Ali, as he always did, poured fuel on the fire. He unfairly called Frazier an "Uncle Tom" and said he was too ugly and stupid to be heavyweight champion. Izenberg described the fight as the hippies against the hardhats, but noted that "as dramatic as the story was, this was still just a prizefight between two very good heavyweight boxers."

The fight lived up to all the hype. The pace of the fight, especially for heavyweight fighters, was incredible. Both fighters showed they could take extreme punishment and engaged in verbal sparring as well.

In the fifteenth and final round, Ali taunted Frazier, saying, "Fool! Don't you know that God's ordained I be champion?"

"Well, God's going to get his ass whupped tonight," retorted Frazier.

For those who don't want to watch the entire fight, just watch the fifteenth round.

Three months later, Ali won his battle with the U.S. government when the Supreme Court ruled 8-0 that the government had not provided good reason to deny Ali conscientious objector status.

As noted in an article on the fight on history.com, "In the end, for all the import and symbolism that had been assigned to it, the Fight of the Century was . . . just a fight. The Vietnam War continued for another four years; 54 years later America remains riven by racial injustice and sports figures continue to use their platforms to call for social and political change."

This article, which has been contemporized, first appeared in The Vacaville Reporter *on March 23, 2021.*

* * *

"Baseball Heroics"

In June 2019, one day after breaking his nose while fouling back a bunt attempt into his face in batting practice, **Max Scherzer** of the Washington Nationals pitched seven shutout innings in a 2-0 win over the Philadelphia Phillies. His face looked awful, black-and-blue around the eye sockets, nose all banged up, but it did not affect his pitching. Or maybe it motivated the big right-hander, already known for his toughness.

Scherzer is not alone. There have been other notable one-game heroics by injured baseball players.

Curt Schilling's bloody sock is now in the Baseball Hall of Fame. In Game 6 of the American League Divisional Series against the Yankees in 2004, he took the mound even though he had torn his tendon sheath earlier. He pitched seven innings of one-run ball to help Boston win and even the series at three games apiece. By the end of his outing, TV viewers could see blood soaking through his sock. Boston won the seventh game and went on to win the World Series.

A's fans would rather forget, but in Game 1 of the 1988 World Series, the Dodgers' **Kirk Gibson**, who had a torn hamstring in his right leg, ligament problems in his left knee and could hardly walk, came out to pinch hit in the ninth inning against Dennis Eckersley. With the Athletics hanging on to a 4-3 lead. Gibson guessed right on a 3-2 slider, leaned over, and hit a two-run walk-off homer, which fired up the Dodgers for the rest of the Series, which they won four games to one.

Scherzer, Schilling, and Gibson played amazingly

through their injuries in those heroic games. But how about **Jim Abbott**, who played every game with a congenital defect? Born without a right hand, he pressed on toward his dream of playing major league baseball. Abbott would lay his glove on his right forearm, throw the pitch, and then put the glove on his left hand in time to field any ball hit or bunted his way. Selected in the first round of the 1988 MLB draft by the California Angels, Abbott was in the big leagues the following year. He played ten seasons and won eighty-seven games, including a no-hitter with the New York Yankees in 1993.

Abbott's accomplishments represent baseball heroics that were the product of long-term, not one-day, feats. Here are other examples.

Known as the "Iron Horse," Yankee legend **Lou Gehrig** played in 2,130 consecutive games over 15 years before he was diagnosed with ALS, now commonly known as Lou Gehrig's disease. His farewell speech was one of baseball's most heart-wrenching yet most amazing moments.

Cal Ripken Jr. eclipsed Gehrig's record on September 6, 1995, when he played in his 2,131st consecutive game. For good measure, he hit a deep home run to left field during that game. He went on to play a total of 2,632 straight games.

Other baseball heroes played through intense mental pressure.

In the case of **Roger Maris**, it came through the media and the baseball establishment in 1961 when he broke Babe Ruth's single-season home run record, belting his sixty-first on the season's final day. Maris was a relative newcomer to the Yankees and shy, and the media wanted the popular Mickey Mantle to break the record. And he might have.

Mantle had fifty-four home runs heading into September but injured his hip.

In July, when it became evident that either Mantle or Maris or both might hit more than sixty home runs, baseball commissioner Ford Frick, a pal of Babe Ruth, announced that he wouldn't consider the record broken unless the player did it in 154 games, the length of the season in Ruth's era. Major League Baseball, due to expansion, began the 162-game season in 1961.

The pressure on Maris caused him to lose great clumps of hair and chain-smoke as he chased the Babe's record. But he let nothing deter him. It was a magical season for those like me who lived in the New York area at the time.

So, as far as MLB was concerned, there were two records—Ruth for the 154-game season and Maris for the 162-game one. Finally, in 1991, six years after Maris died of cancer, an MLB committee voted to remove the distinction and award the record fully to Maris.

Just as difficult, if not more so, was what **Hank Aaron** endured en route to breaking Ruth's career home record 714 in 1974. Aaron had ended the previous season with 713 home runs. All winter, he received hate mail and death threats just because he was a Black man trying to break Ruth's record.

Hammerin' Hank let nothing stand in his way, hitting home run number 715 off the Dodgers' Al Downing on April 8 in front of a sellout crowd of 53,775 at Atlanta-Fulton County Stadium. Here's what Mantle said about Aaron: "As far as I'm concerned, Aaron is the best ball player of my era. He is to baseball of the last fifteen years what Joe DiMaggio was before him. He's never received the credit he's due."

In breaking baseball's color barrier, **Jackie Robinson**, a fiery competitor, had to control his emotions, especially in his first year, 1947, and avoid fighting back on the field when opponents threw at him or tried to spike him. He had to brave constant threats and mass taunts from fans, even opposition from his Brooklyn Dodger teammates, until shortstop Pee Wee Reese led by example in accepting Jackie. Robinson won Rookie of the Year that year. To perform at the level under that intense pressure and scrutiny was incredibly courageous. His number 42 is retired throughout baseball.

There are different kinds of baseball heroes, and they are heroes all.

***

"Great Individual Comebacks in Sports"

Sports fans love a good comeback story.

In baseball one thinks of **Tommy John**, who had a surgery named after him. John, perhaps one of the best pitchers not in the Hall of Fame, threw primarily for the Chicago White Sox at the beginning of his career. In 1974, he was dominating with the Los Angeles Dodgers and had a 13-3 record. He then damaged the ulnar collateral ligament in his elbow, which at the time was essentially career-ending. He was given the surgery that now bears his name and pitched fifteen more seasons. He was even better after the surgery, compiling three seasons with twenty or more wins.

There are other great stories of athletes rising from the dead. Here are a few who made great comebacks—not from injuries, necessarily, or we would be discussing **Tiger**

Woods winning the Masters or **Willis Reed** coming out to play Game 7 of the 1970 NBA finals for the Knicks against the Lakers or **Curt Schilling** and his bloody sock.

Here we're going to remember a few athletes who everybody said were washed up but who refused to believe it.

Hunter Pence, who had enjoyed a stellar career and three All-Star selections, seemed to have run out of gas when, at age thirty-five, he hit .226 in 2018 for the San Francisco Giants. He received zero contract offers from major league teams that winter. Everyone thought he was through.

Everyone except Pence.

He overhauled his swing and played winter ball in the Dominican Republic to test out his reinvented batting approach. The Rangers took a shot and signed him to a minor league contract. Pence went to spring training and won a spot on the opening-day major league roster. He made the All-Star team as a designated hitter and batted .297 with eighteen homers in 2019.

If you've seen the movie *Cinderella Man*, you know the story of boxer **Jim Braddock**.

A successful light heavyweight turned heavyweight, Braddock couldn't find regular work and his boxing career went downhill when the stock market crashed in 1929 and sent the nation into the Great Depression. He lost sixteen of twenty-two fights, quit boxing, and had to file for government relief to feed his family.

But in 1934 he was given a chance to fight an established fighter, John "Corn" Griffin, because of a cancellation To everyone's amazement, Braddock knocked Griffin out in the third round. That led to an opportunity to fight John Henry Lewis. Again, the experts said Braddock had no chance. But he won a ten-round decision.

The ascent continued as Braddock beat Art Lasky to earn a heavyweight championship bout against Max Baer, one of the hardest hitters of all time.

If you haven't seen the movie, spoiler alert: On June 13, 1935, at Madison Square Garden, Braddock, a ten-to-one underdog, beat Baer in a fifteen-round decision to become heavyweight champion of the world.

How about a football comeback story?

When **David Akers** missed two field goal attempts for the Philadelphia Eagles in their 21-16 loss to the Green Bay Packers in a January 2011 Wild Card playoff game, most people didn't know how much he had on his mind.

He had been swindled out of $3.7 million in a Ponzi scheme by Triton Financial. He got none of it back. He had many sleepless nights as he pondered his family's future.

After twelve years of outstanding play for Philadelphia and five Pro Bowls, Akers was waived by the Eagles after that loss to Green Bay.

The 49ers grabbed him. In 2011, Akers set NFL league records by a kicker with 44 field goals and 166 points for San Francisco and was selected to his sixth Pro Bowl.

Back to boxing.

George Foreman won a boxing gold medal for the U.S. in the 1968 Olympics and knocked out Joe Frazier in the second round to become heavyweight champion in 1973. Foreman fought for a few more years after losing the title in a stunning loss to Muhammad Ali in Zaire in 1974, then retired in 1977.

But ten years later, at age thirty-eight, he returned to the ring, eventually earning a title shot. On November 24, 1994, Foreman, age forty-five, became boxing's oldest heavyweight champion by defeating twenty-six-year-old Michael Moorer.

Moorer went into the fight with a 35-0 record.

Foreman was wearing the same red trunks that he had had on the night he lost to Ali.

Let's bookend this column with a comeback story about another pitcher, former San Francisco Giant right-hander **Ryan Vogelsong**.

Vogelsong rebounded from ten years of pitching more in the minors and Japan than in the majors to make the 2011 All-Star team as a Giant.

Then at age thirty-five in his first ever World Series appearance, he beat the Detroit Tigers in Game 3 of the 2012 Fall Classic. He escaped the first and third innings by getting double-play ground balls from Prince Fielder and Quintin Berry. In the fifth inning with the bases loaded and one out, Vogelsong struck out Berry and induced the dangerous Miguel Cabrera to pop out to short. Tim Lincecum and Sergio Romo closed out the 2-0 shutout in relief.

That postseason, Vogelsong gave up only three runs in four starts in 24 2/3 innings. He was only the second pitcher in baseball history to yield one run or less in his first four postseason starts lasting five innings or more.

The other was a fellow named Christy Mathewson.

That's pretty good company for a guy everybody had given up on. Everybody except the guy himself.

This column first appeared in The Vacaville Reporter *on July 8, 2019.*

* * *

"Baseball Records That Will Never Be Broken"

Usually, when someone says a record will never be broken, it is a subjective opinion. **George Sisler** had 257 hits in 1920, which seemed unapproachable—until **Ichiro Suzuki** spanked out 262 in 2004. **Lou Brock's** 118 stolen bases in 1974 seemed untouchable—until **Rickey Henderson** stole 130 in 1982.

Douglas Jordan took an analytical approach in a story he wrote for the *Baseball Research Journal* (Fall, 2015). He defined "never be broken" as *the record will not be broken over the next 110 baseball seasons played under rules similar to today's rules.* Then, he went about computing the probability of certain records being eclipsed.

Jordan used **Cal Ripken's** record of 2,632 consecutive games played as the standard against which other records are compared when examining the likelihood of broken records. Ripken played more than sixteen straight seasons without missing a game. Reynolds looked at records from 1903 on. In addition to Ripken's, here are some single-season and career records that should stand the test of time:

Let's start with **Rickey Henderson's** 130 steals. He stole three bases in six games and had three incredible games in which he stole four. He had a games-played-per-stolen-base average of 1.15. The next highest stolen-base total in the twenty-first century is 78 by **Jose Reyes** in 2007, with a games-played-per-stolen-base average of 2.05. So Henderson was almost twice as productive as Reyes on a per-game basis.

In addition, baseball has come to revolve around the long ball rather than the stolen base, and teams are reluctant to let a star like **Mike Trout** take the pounding of stealing many bases during the season. It is safe to say that Henderson's mark will never be broken.

Regarding career records, **Henderson's** total of 1,406 stolen bases is absurd. It is 468 more stolen bases (fifty percent better) than Lou Brock's second-place total of 938.

Suzuki's 262 hits are also in that category. An analysis of **George Sisler's** 257 hits shows that he played in every game, made 692 plate appearances, struck out only 19 times, walked 46 times, and batted .407. Suzuki played in all but one of the Mariners games (161), led the league in plate appearances (762) and batting average (.372), struck out just 63 times, and walked only 49 times.

These numbers show that to challenge the hits record, a player has to play in almost every game of the season, have a very high number of plate appearances, hit for a high average, and not walk very much. A high average alone will not do the job. For example, even with the fifty-six-game hitting streak in 1941 and a .357 batting average, **Joe DiMaggio** had 193 hits. **Ted Williams** had 185 hits that same year when he batted .406. It is unlikely anyone will ever match Suzuki's incredible season.

There are several reasons **Hack Wilson's** record of 191 RBIs in 1930 should stand forever. One is that **Woody English** and **Kiki Cuyler** batted in front of Wilson that season and had OBAs of .430 and .428, respectively. But take nothing away from Wilson—he batted .356 and led the league in home runs (56) and slugging (.723). He had two games with six RBIs, three with five RBIs, seven with four RBIs, and fifteen with three RBIs. He drove in twelve runs in the last five games of the season.

Barry Bonds' remarkable 232 walks in 2004 is unlikely

ever to be broken. **Babe Ruth** is the next best player on the walk list records, with 170 in 1923. The only player to pass 170 is Bonds, who did it thrice between 2001 and 2004.

John "Chief" Wilson's record of thirty-six triples in 1912 is just as safe. That mark is 38 percent better than the next highest post-1902 total (26). **Curtis Granderson's** twenty-three in 2007 is the most recent high for triples, with most modern-day years having a high well under twenty triples. The Pirates' home ballpark in 1912, Forbes Field, helped Wilson. The center field wall was an astounding 462 feet from home plate.

Here are two pitching records that will never be touched—**Ed Walsh** pitched 464 innings in 1908, and **Jack Chesbro** had forty-one wins in 1904. These totals are out of reach today since starting pitchers have a maximum of about thirty-five starts during a season.

Hank Aaron's 2,297 career RBIs will probably never be bettered, though **Albert Pujols** came close with 2,218. Aaron reached 118 or more RBIs in nine seasons, with a career-high 132 in 1957. He had two other seasons with over 100 and seven seasons between 86 and 97.

It staggers the imagination to think that anybody will ever equal **Peter Rose's** 4,256 career hits. To get 4,000 hits, a player has to play twenty seasons with 200 hits each season. As great as **Derek Jeter's** twenty-year career was, his 3,465 career hits are almost 800 short of Rose's record.

So, should Rose be in the Hall of Fame? That's a topic for another day.

This column first appeared in The Vacaville Reporter *on July 22, 2020.*

* * *

"Why Should One Bad Play Define a Career?"

When **Bill Buckner** passed away at age sixty-nine, journalists nationwide urged readers to remember the player—not the one who lived in Red Sox infamy. But where were those journalists in 1986 when Buckner needed them?

Boston, looking for its first World Series title since 1918, was up three games to two as it faced the Mets at Shea Stadium in Game 6 of the 1986 Fall Classic. The Red Sox led 5-3 going into the bottom of the tenth inning. The Mets had two outs and nobody on but had tied it with two runs and had Ray Knight on second base as Mookie Wilson faced Boston pitcher Bob Stanley.

After working a 3-2 count, the speedy left-handed batting Wilson bounced a slow roller up the first-base line. Buckner moved to his left, went down to field the ball behind the bag, and watched it roll through his legs into right field. Knight scored, the Mets won, then took Game 7 to win the Series.

Some feel Wilson would have beaten Buckner to the bag anyway. In any case, it's too bad most journalists in Boston weren't telling the fans to remember the player—not the play—back then. Buckner played twenty-two seasons in the majors, was an All-Star once, and won the batting title in 1980.

But Boston wouldn't forgive him. When he retired in 1990, he and his family stayed in Massachusetts. However, fans and the local media continued to taunt him, so Buckner moved his family to Idaho, where he bought a ranch.

Bill Buckner to the *Boston Globe*: "I had to forgive, not the fans of Boston, per se, but I would have to say in my heart I had to forgive the media for what they put me and my family through. So, you know, I've done that, and I'm over that."

Wilson, who became close friends with Buckner, told *NBC Sports*, "I felt bad for some of the things he went through. Bill was a great baseball player whose legacy should not be defined by one play."

It's sad that a player's entire career can be defined by one bad play. It is seldom determined by one good play, but a few exceptions exist.

Bill Mazeroski will be remembered for hitting the only seventh-game walk-off home run in baseball history, defeating the Yankees in 1960. **Kirk Gibson** will be memorialized for hobbling to the plate in the first game of the 1988 World Series and belting a two-run, walk-off home run to defeat the A's and propel the Dodgers to win the Fall Classic. Say "**Joe Carter**," and most baseball fans will think of his walk-off home run in Game 6 of the 1993 World Series that iced the championship for the Toronto Blue Jays over the Philadelphia Phillies.

Interestingly, none of those three players was a flash-in-the-pan. All were outstanding veteran players before their big moment. But few players are remembered just for one great moment on the diamond. They are evaluated on their body of work—career home runs and/or RBIs, reaching three hundred wins as a pitcher, batting titles, and All-Star selections. But in the case of a blown play, somehow that body of work gets thrown out the window.

Ralph Branca was a three-time All-Star. The right-handed pitcher won eighty-eight games during his twelve-year major league career, including twenty-one for the Dodgers in 1947. But his achievements were overshadowed by one game he lost—the third and deciding game of a playoff for the National League pennant in 1951. Branca yielded the "Shot Heard 'Round the World" to Bobby Thomson, a three-run walk-off home run for a 5-4 New York Giants victory over the Brooklyn Dodgers.

In Game 4 of the 1941 World Series, with the Yankees holding a 2-1 series lead over the Dodgers, Brooklyn catcher **Mickey Owen** dropped the third strike of what would have been the final out, allowing Tommy Heinrich to reach base. The Dodgers had been leading 4-3, but the Yankees went on to score four runs after the passed ball and won 7-4 for a 3-1 series lead. They won the next game to clinch the world championship.

Owen, a four-time All-Star, had a .995 fielding percentage that season—a team record at the time—and set a National League record for catchers with 476 consecutive chances without an error. He had only two passed balls during the entire 1941 regular season.

Let's go back to 1908 when the New York Giants' **Fred Merkle** committed an infamous baserunning blunder. With less than two weeks left, the Giants and Cubs were tied for first place and playing a crucial game at the Polo Grounds. With the score tied 1-1 in the bottom of the ninth, the Giants had a man on first with two outs. Merkle, a nineteen-year-old rookie making his first major league start, singled to right to put runners on the corners. The next batter, Al Bridwell, lined a ball that fell onto the right-field grass, apparently winning the game for the Giants.

The hometown fans rushed onto the field to celebrate, and Merkle, like most players, wanted to get into the clubhouse as quickly as possible to avoid them. But he raced off the field before he touched second base. Unfortunately for the rookie, Cubs second baseman Johnny Evers noticed. He somehow retrieved the ball (or, some say, any ball he could find), stepped on second, and alerted umpire Hank O'Day, who called Merkle out, nullifying the run. The game ended in a tie because of darkness.

The two teams ended the season with identical records, so the game had to be made up. The Cubs won the game and the pennant.

Merkle went on to a long and distinguished major league career, but he was forever known as "Bonehead."

"I wish I'd never gotten that hit that set off the whole Merkle incident," Bridwell later told Lawrence S. Ritter in the book *The Glory of Their Times*. "I wish I'd struck out instead. If I'd have done that, I would have spared Fred a lot of unfair humiliation."

"Unfair humiliation." Buckner, Branca, Owen, Merkle, and many others have lived with that.

This column first appeared in The Vacaville Reporter *on July 18, 2019.*

PART 4

Sports Books, Movies, Philosophy, Stats, and Rule Changes

"*Ball Four* Opened Pandora's Box"

When Jim Bouton passed away at age eighty from a brain disease linked to dementia, I was prompted to reread *Ball Four,* the iconic diary of the pitcher's 1969 season with the Seattle Pilots and the Houston Astros.

If you are of the same generation as modern-day major leaguers, you may have never heard of Bouton or *Ball Four.* That's what sportswriter Thom Loverro of the *Washington Times* discovered when he queried some of the Washington Nationals.

The book was first published in 1970 and has sold more than five million copies. In 1995, the New York Public Library selected *Ball Four* as one of about 150 Books of the Century, alongside such works as Anne Frank's *Diary of a Young Girl* and F. Scott Fitzgerald's *The Great Gatsby*. It is the only sports book on the list.

Is it a great book? In terms of impact, yes. As John Feinstein, author of *A Season on the Brink,* his journal of the 1987 season he spent with Bobby Knight and the Indiana University basketball team, said in a tribute to Bouton in *The Washington Post,* "Bouton proved the importance of firsthand reporting, of truly getting inside a subject. Besides *All the President's Men,* no book influenced me more as a reporter."

The library editors noted that Bouton's book "was the first ripple of a tidal wave of 'tell-all' books that have become commonplace not only in sports, but also in politics, entertainment, and other realms of contemporary life."

Is it excellent writing? Bouton was no Steinbeck or Kafka, but he wrote well, and many of his stories are hilarious. Sportswriter Leonard Shecter edited the original version, and Bouton added *Ball Five, Ball Six,* and *Ball Seven.*

But there is one way in which the book is not so great—nobody on the team knew that Bouton was writing it.

As Joe Morgan, Bouton's teammate on the Astros, told Mark Armour of the Society for American Baseball Research, "I always thought he was a teammate, not an author. I told him some things I would never tell a sportswriter." Similarly, according to Bouton's *Ball Six*, Rich Rollins, who was Bouton's teammate on the 1969 Pilots, told a Seattle newspaper, "What offended me more than anything was that no one was aware what he was writing."

When Feinstein wrote his book about Knight, the coach had given him unprecedented access to the locker room and team for that season. Nothing Feinstein wrote should have surprised Knight, although, characteristically, Knight still found things to be upset about when the book was published.

Bouton revealed many salacious and personal details. For example, he wrote about his teammates' "beaver-shooting" (trying to look up the skirts or into the hotel windows of attractive women) and popping greenies (amphetamines). And he didn't stick to that 1969 season. He went back to his years with the New York Yankees and revealed that Mickey Mantle was the ringleader of the Peeping Tom unit and had a significant problem with alcohol.

Bouton's book was not the first baseball book of that genre. Years before, Cincinnati Reds pitcher Jim Brosnan chronicled two seasons, 1959 and 1961, in his books *The Long Season* and *Pennant Race*. As Mike Durell wrote in his review of those books, "There are still numerous moments of candor regarding drinking and, somewhat more discreetly, skirt-chasing. For readers accustomed to every sordid detail of an athlete's sordid acts being disseminated worldwide seconds after they occur, *The Long Season* and *Pennant Race* may seem somewhat tame. Still, to older readers they will seem refreshingly discreet. There is something to be said for discretion and implication. More is not always better."

Bouton read *The Long Season* as a twenty-one-year-old pitcher for the Yankees' Greensboro, North Carolina, farm club. He loved the book, which inspired him to write *Ball Four*. In my opinion, he went too far.

As Connie Ray Godwin wrote in his review of *Instant Replay*, the diary of the 1967 Green Bay Packers season by Jerry Kramer, "Kramer violates the 'what happens in the locker room stays in the locker room' ethos, but not to a flagrant or irresponsible degree. Kramer exercises discretion and deftly straddles the boundary between being candid and destroying the reputations of his teammates, coaches, and opponents."

In *Ball Six*, Bouton wrote: "I must admit that it pains me to hear that some former teammates are still angry about *Ball Four*. But I'm not surprised. They see the book as an invasion of their privacy. And maybe they're embarrassed by something they said or did. Those players don't realize that nobody thinks badly of them, no matter what they say or do, especially after twenty years. But they don't have that perspective."

I think the person who needed perspective was Bouton. The players saw it as an invasion of privacy because it was. And how could Bouton know what other people thought of the players? His revelations did lower my opinion of Mantle, my first childhood baseball hero.

Bouton did regret that his book spawned a host of sports tell-all books, each vying to be more revealing than the last.

For example, Jose Canseco became baseball's public enemy number one after he wrote *Juiced* and named ballplayers allegedly using steroids.

As Paul Sullivan of *The Chicago Tribune* wrote of Canseco's book and others like it, "It proves that the adage 'What's said here stays here' no longer applies when someone feels the urge to cash in on old stories for a memoir."

And that's a shame.

This column first appeared in The Vacaville Reporter on July 22, 2019.

* * *

"What Was the Big Deal about *The Jordan Rules*?"

The Last Dance, the docuseries about Michael Jordan's last season with the Chicago Bulls, mentions a controversial book, *The Jordan Rules*, which was published in 1992 about the 1991-92 Bulls season. Controversial because it painted an unflattering portrait of Jordan as a teammate.

But it was actually the media's reaction to the book which set off the firestorm, as well as condemnations from people who hadn't even read the book.

After watching *The Last Dance* (which I heartily recommend), I decided to read *The Jordan Rules: The Inside Story of a Turbulent Season with Michael Jordan and the Chicago Bulls*, written by Sam Smith, who covered the Bulls for *The Chicago Tribune*.

And I was shocked—shocked at why this book was considered so evil by so many at the time.

Unlike Jim Bouton's *Ball Four*, the book does not delve into the personal affairs of the players. It just chronicles their interactions with Jordan and each other over the course of the season. It wasn't a hit-and-run piece, as Smith traveled with the team all season and continued to do so for years to come.

In an introduction to a later edition of the book, Smith wrote, "I told every player about the book before I wrote it, although Jordan later said he didn't recall that. I sat down with every one of them at lunch or dinner and explained this was a book about basketball, not private lives. I remain proud of the book because it didn't hurt anyone in that way. And to this day I remain friendly with most of those players."

Apparently it is almost impossible to write a book like this without creating misunderstanding. When John Feinstein wrote *A Season on the Brink* about Bobby Knight's 1985-86 season with Indiana University's basketball team, Knight gave Feinstein permission to immerse himself in the program, giving him the chance to attend meetings and practices, to travel with the team, and even to sit on the bench during games.

Nevertheless, Knight complained to the *Chicago Sun-Times* that Feinstein "wrote the book completely outside the parameters that were set. The book was supposed to be about the players, but it was about me, starting with the cover and going right on through."

Feinstein claimed that Knight knew from the outset that he would be the focus.

Similarly, Jordan was upset with the book.

"There was no question he was angry then," wrote Smith, "though I felt it was more because of the negative publicity from portions of the book that were taken out of context by others. My guess is Jordan never read the book.

But people who read it now ask me why it was such a big deal then."

Count me among that number. The book is tame to the point of being PG by today's tell-all standards. It is well-written and fair. It paints all the players, including Jordan, as merely human and simply portrays the inevitable conflicts and jealousies that arise when twelve people are so close to one another day in and day out for an entire basketball season.

All Smith did was write about the players' thoughts and feelings, which they freely shared with him.

"There's always been this mystery and guessing game about *The Jordan Rules*," wrote Smith. "Who was the source, the Deep Throat. I've always hated that since the implication is someone handed me all this information and I sat around and just waited. There was no secret source. Everyone was the source."

The title of the book conveys the fact that Jordan was treated differently from the other players. Looking back, that was no great revelation.

As Smith explained, "The Jordan Rules wasn't a difficult story to get if you looked. For several years, players would tell me something about how Jordan had held someone up to ridicule, or skipped a mandatory workout of some sort. Phil [coach Phil Jackson] had explained publicly, which was part of his brilliance, that the pretty girl gets kissed. In other words, some people just get better treatment because society sees them as more special than others."

At the time, the public didn't want to burst the bubble of the Michael Jordan mystique. Everyone wanted to "be like Mike." But Smith felt he might have done MJ a favor.

"Michael Jordan had been marketed as perfect," Smith

wrote. "And he looked the part with that magnificent smile and spectacular game. I always figured *The Jordan Rules* took some pressure off him by showing he wasn't perfect and he didn't have to be, and that the fans will still love him. Not that the book did him any favors. But he always worried about being unloved and unpopular, and here I was writing about him being a real guy, hardly a criminal but difficult at times. How dare me! And you know what, they still loved him. Maybe even more."

The Jordan Rules is well worth the read and a great companion to *The Last Dance*. I felt the docuseries glossed over some of Jordan's faults and that the book was more honest and less biased. In any case, if you haven't already, check them out.

This column first appeared in The Vacaville Reporter *on July 25, 2020.*

***

"Lost Ballparks, Part One"

Dennis Evanosky and Eric J. Kos created a marvelous coffee table book titled Lost Ballparks: A Celebration of Baseball's Legendary Fields. *The book features stunning photographs of fifty-eight no-longer-standing ballparks. The stories recounted here are from their book.*

Ketchikan Harbor Ballpark, Alaska, dredged away, 1935

In the early 1900s, there wasn't much else to spend leisurely time in small Alaskan towns other than the game of baseball. In Ketchikan, the ballpark doubled as a harbor depending on whether the tide was in or out. The return of the tide could end a ballgame early.

There were special rules. Balls hit into the adjoining sawmill yard were doubles. Any ball hit too far out to sea as the tide rolled in was a home run. Ketchikan resident Harriet Hunt's dog Toby was one of the best outfielders, paddling out to retrieve any ball a human could not reach.

Ketchikan built a new dry-land ballpark in 1921. During the Depression, the city received federal funding to improve its harbor facilities. By 1935, the old ballpark had been dredged out of existence and is known today as Thomas Basin.

Ebbets Field, Brooklyn, razed in 1960

The Brooklyn Dodgers were active in the major leagues from 1884 until 1957, after which they moved to Los Angeles. The team's name derived from the reputed skill of Brooklyn residents at evading the city's trolley streetcar network. The Dodgers played in two stadiums in South Brooklyn, each named Washington Park, and at Eastern Park in the neighborhood of Brownsville before moving to Ebbets Field in the Flatbush neighborhood in 1913.

The name "Brooklyn Dodgers" did not appear on the team's uniforms until 1932. In the 1890s and early 1900s, newspaper reporters bestowed many nicknames on the club, including Trolley Dodgers, the Bridegrooms (seven players got married in the same year), the Superbas, and the Robins.

Charles Ebbetts became the team's first president in 1898, and when Ebbetts Field was completed, he achieved his goal of building a fireproof stadium of steel, glass, brick, and concrete. The stadium's capacity was eighteen thousand, rising to 31,902 in 1952.

Although the team finally won a World Series in 1955, Dodger President Walter O'Malley was concerned about its future in the old ballpark. Ebbetts Field was too hemmed in by urban development to meet the demand for more seats and bigger parking lots. O'Malley wanted to move to a larger site in downtown Brooklyn, but New York City only offered a spot in Queens.

Los Angeles provided over three hundred acres in Chavez Ravine. The Brooklyn Dodgers played their last game at Ebbets Field in September 1957 and became the Los Angeles Dodgers the following year.

Polo Grounds, New York, razed 1964

The New York Giants originally played on polo grounds, and the name of their adopted ballpark stuck. They moved into a second version of the park in 1889 and a third in 1891, situated below Coogan's Bluff in Harlem. This site served as the team's home until 1957.

When the stadium was packed, those fans without tickets gathered atop Coogan's Bluff to watch the game for free. Harry M. Stevens single-handedly revolutionized ballpark concessions at the Polo Grounds by popularizing scorecards and inventing the hot dog.

The third Polo Grounds, made entirely of wood, burned on April 14, 1911. Construction began immediately on a new, ornate one with a horseshoe-shaped, steel, concrete grandstand and thirty-four thousand seats. The Polo Grounds had the deepest center field in baseball, but the right-field foul pole was just 257 feet from home plate.

From 1913 through 1922, the Giants shared the Polo Grounds with the Yankees. And it was here, not Yankee

Stadium, where Babe Ruth had his greatest seasons. He slugged .796 from 1920 to 1922, while the Yankees were the Giants' tenants.

In 1956, with the Giants' attendance figures suffering badly, Dodgers owner Walter O'Malley talked to Giants owner Horace Stoneham about moving to San Francisco. The New York Mets, an expansion team intended to replace the Giants and Dodgers, played poorly in the Polo Grounds under manager Casey Stengel in 1962 and 1963.

The stadium fell to the wrecking ball in 1964. An enormous housing project now sits below Coogan's Bluff, where the ballpark once stood.

Astrodome, Houston, partially demolished in 2013

Billed as the Eighth Wonder of the World, the Astrodome, which opened in April 1965, was the home of the Houston Astros (formerly the expansion Colt .45s). The city broke ground on the stadium by shooting Colt .45 pistols into the ground.

The Astrodome was the world's largest enclosed space and the first fully enclosed and climate-controlled domed stadium. It held sixty-six thousand people and had a $2 million programmable scoreboard. It became one of the nation's most popular domestic tourist destinations, behind only the Golden Gate Bridge and Mount Rushmore.

Mickey Mantle, who played for the Yankees against Houston on opening night in an exhibition game, said of the stadium, "It reminds me of what I imagine my first ride would be like in a flying saucer."

The field was originally grass, but the dome restricted proper lighting, so the Astros developed their trademark playing surface called AstroTurf, which is used worldwide today. The turf was initially kept clean by men in spacesuits known as "Earthmen."

Muhammad Ali, Elvis, The Rolling Stones, Evel Knievel, The Who, Pink Floyd, and The Jacksons all appeared at the Dome.

Although the facility received a $100 million overhaul in 1987, the thrill was gone by the mid-1990s, and the Astros migrated to Enron Field (today Daikin Park) in 1999.

Parts of the Dome were demolished in 2013, and much of the interior was gutted—bench seats and other memorabilia were auctioned off to the public. Harris County commissioners are considering proposals to raise the floor level of the Dome and create parking space underneath.

...to be continued in Part 2

This column is condensed from columns that first appeared in The Vacaville Reporter *on April 21 and 23, 2020.*

***

"Lost Ballparks, Part Two"

Dennis Evanosky and Eric J. Kos created a marvelous coffee table book titled Lost Ballparks: A Celebration of Baseball's Legendary Fields. *The book features stunning photographs of fifty-eight no-longer-standing ballparks. The stories recounted here are from their book.*

Kingdome, Seattle, imploded 2000

After one year, the Seattle Pilots expanded to Milwaukee in 1970 and became the Brewers. The Pilots had played in Sick's Stadium, but the city wanted a stadium for baseball and football, as it had the prospect of attracting a football expansion team. From its completion in 1976 until its implosion in 2000, the Kingdome was home to the NFL Seahawks and Mariners. The 1979 MLB All-Star game was held there.

It was built as a football stadium that could be converted to baseball. Seattle teams have a reputation for having loud fans, and the cavernous Kingdome served them perfectly. With eleven men on the football field, the fans became known as the 12th Man and the Kingdome as the loudest stadium in football. The jersey number 12 was retired in the fans' honor during the 1984 season.

As time wore on, the stadium's deficiencies began to emerge. Both the Seahawks and Mariners wanted their own stadium. Ceiling tiles collapsed onto the seating area during a Mariners game, and lobbying began for a new venue. Safeco Field (now T-Mobile Park) was built a block away for the Mariners, complete with a retractable roof, and was ready for play in July 1999.

When it imploded in 2000, the 250-foot-high concrete shell of the Kingdome collapsed in 16.8 seconds.

Yankee Stadium, New York, demolished 2008

In 1913, the Yankees shared the Polo Grounds with the New York Giants. The Yankees' acquisition of Babe Ruth early in 1920 resulted in bigger crowds than the Giants, who asked them to leave.

The owners decided on a ten-acre former lumberyard in the Bronx. It was built in just 284 days. Ironically, the Polo Grounds across the Harlem River was within sight. The gentle curving latticework that ran around the grandstand's roof was known as the Frieze and was commissioned by the owners to give the stadium an air of dignity.

Opening day was April 18, 1923, before a capacity crowd. Twenty-five thousand fans were turned away. The Yankees beat the Red Sox 4-1, with Babe Ruth christening the "House that Ruth Built" with a three-run homer into the right-field bleachers.

By the mid-1960s, the imposing triple-decked structure had been allowed to deteriorate. The stadium closed for renovation on September 30, 1973, and the Yankees played the next two seasons at the Mets' Shea Stadium.

The Yankees beat the Minnesota Twins 11-4 in front of 52,613 fans in reopening the refurbished park on April 15, 1976. By the 1980s, owner George Steinbrenner was already discussing the need for a new ballpark. The site chosen was just across the street from the existing stadium. The groundbreaking ceremony occurred on August 19, 2006, and the new stadium opened on April 2, 2009. The new ballpark was closely modeled on the original, including the dimensions of the field of play.

The site of the old Yankee Stadium is now a public park complete with a baseball diamond overlooked by a giant Louisville Slugger baseball bat.

Candlestick Park, San Francisco, erased 2015

Although the Giants played two seasons in Seals Stadium, it was never intended to be their permanent home field. Part of the deal with the Giants moving west from New York was that the city would build the team a new stadium.

The city bought sixty-five acres at Candlestick Point and

settled on the name Candlestick Park on March 3, 1959, after a name-the-park contest. Architect John Bolles designed the park like a horseshoe, open in the outfield, which turned the stadium into a virtual wind tunnel. The place was so cold and windy that some fans returned their season tickets for refunds.

Candlestick was the first modern baseball stadium built entirely of reinforced concrete. It served well until the Loma Prieta Earthquake struck during Game 3 of the "Bay Bridge" World Series on October 17, 1989.

The outfield area was fully enclosed when the 49ers moved from Kezar Stadium to Candlestick Park in 1971. However, the enclosure did not tame the wind as it swirled around the stadium's interior. The Giants played their last game at Candlestick on September 30, 1999, before moving to AT&T Park (now Oracle Park). The 49ers played at Candlestick until December 23, 2013. With no more tenants, the stadium would face the wrecking ball, but not before Paul McCartney played a concert there on August 14, 2014, some forty-eight years after he had sung at Candlestick as a Beatles member.

This column first appeared in The Vacaville Reporter *on April 25, 2020.*

* * *

"A Baseball Movie that Gets it Right"

I don't like most baseball movies because they get so much wrong. The players look like they never swung a bat, the baseball strategy is wrong, or, in the case of historical movies, the history is wrong.

But the 1988 movie, *Eight Men Out,* about the 1919 Chicago Black Sox scandal, nearly bats 1.000 on all counts.

That's why I was surprised to read the late Roger Ebert's review. The great movie critic only gave the film two out of four stars and had many negative things to say about it.

He wrote, "It tells the story of how the stars of the 1919 Chicago White Sox team took payoffs from gamblers to throw the World Series, but if you are not already familiar with that story you're unlikely to understand it after seeing this film. It's an insider's movie, a baseball expert's film that is hard for the untutored to follow."

First of all, it is unlikely that many non-baseball fans would go to see this movie. One would have to have at least some interest in the game. But one does not need to be a "baseball expert" to appreciate it. I watched the movie the other night with my adult daughter, a baseball fan, who had only heard of the scandal when I mentioned it to her several days ago. She followed the movie just fine and understood what was happening.

Yet Ebert wrote, "If you're going to make a movie about a baseball scandal that happened before most of the audience was born, you'd better start by making it understandable."

Ebert also complained, "By the half-hour mark in *Eight Men Out*, I had little idea who the individual players were, and I wasn't helped by the fact that many of the actors seemed to resemble each other."

Granted, there are eight ballplayers to keep track of, but does Charlie Sheen really look like John Cusack? My daughter was able to identify the key participants and who the bad guys (the gamblers) were.

Ebert wrote, "The Sox players are so obviously throwing the game, with deliberate and not even subtle errors, that it's hard to imagine that anyone could have been fooled, even for a second."

Certainly the way the Sox played created suspicion, especially as they were a huge favorite to beat the Cincinnati Reds. But not all the mistakes were obvious, such as when pitcher Ed Cicotte, on a comebacker, threw off the mark to second base on what should have been a double play ball.

For those who are not "experts" on this episode of baseball history, the Sox played for a cheap owner, Charlie Comiskey, and were tempted to make big money by throwing the Series. Supposedly eight of them conspired, but, as the movie shows, it is not clear whether third baseman Buck Weaver and outfielder Shoeless Joe Jackson tried to play poorly.

The manager, Kid Gleason, is puzzled by his players' poor performance, as they drop the first two games to the Reds in the best of nine game series. But in Game 3, Dickey Kerr, who is not party to the plot, throws a three-hit shutout and Gleason is happy again. The Sox, with Cicotte pitching, lose Game 4, his second loss of the Series. The Sox drop Game 5, the second loss by pitcher Lefty Williams, one of the eight.

The Black Sox had purportedly arranged to receive their bribes in five $20,000 installments—one after each loss—but the gamblers had failed to deliver the full amount. This apparently spurred the cheating ballplayers to pull a double-cross, as they beat the Reds in Games 6 and 7 to pull within four games to three in the Series, Cicotte winning Game 7.

But the gamblers are said to have threatened some of the eight and their families prior to Game 8. The movie shows a hood threatening pitcher Williams, and Williams got just one out in the first inning and gave up four runs before Gleason pulled him. We don't know if Williams was one of those threatened, but I can live with that poetic license.

The only historical inaccuracy I found was a brief conversation in which one of the players says he saw Gleason throw a no-hitter against Christy Mathewson. Gleason never threw a no-hitter.

The eight did face a courtroom trial, and Ebert complained that it "is less about baseball than about the standard cliches of all courtroom scenes." But the trial was dramatic. A contemporary *New York Times* account described the scene this way, "The spectators added to the bleacher appearance of the courtroom, for most of them sweltered in shirtsleeves, and collars were few. Scores of small boys jammed their way into the seats, and as Mr. Gorman [the prosecutor] told of the alleged sell-out, they repeatedly looked at each other in awe, remarking under their breaths: 'What do you think of that?' or 'Well, I'll be darned.'" And all the paper records relating to the players' grand jury confessions vanished under mysterious circumstances.

The movie includes the classic line of the boy looking up at Shoeless Joe Jackson, imploring, "Say it ain't so, Joe!" *The New York Times* reported that when Jackson left the grand jury room, "a crowd of small boys gathered round their idol and asked: 'It isn't true, is it, Joe?' Shoeless Joe replied: 'Yes, boys, I'm afraid it is.'"

I like the movie's grammar better.

Just for fun, I re-created the first game of the 1919 World Series using the identical lineups on my favorite computer simulation game, Old Time Baseball. The Reds won 4-1. Two of Cincinnati's runs were unearned thanks to a throwing error by Swede Risberg, one of the notorious eight. Did he do it on purpose? I don't think the computer programmed the game for cheating. But you never know . . .

* * *

"The Saint of Second Chances"

I just watched a wonderful baseball documentary called *The Saint of Second Chances*. Recommended by my adult daughter, we watched it together. There are many facets to this 94-minute movie, one of which is the close bond that a father and daughter formed around baseball, close to my heart because of the similar bond my daughter and I have formed around the game.

It chronicles the life of Mike Veeck, son of baseball owner Bill Veeck, who is in the Hall of Fame. Bill Veeck was the ultimate showman and promoter. As he put it, he was a hustler, not a con man, because a hustler believes. Perhaps his most famous stunt was when, as owner of the St. Louis Browns, he signed a little person, Eddie Gaedel, who stood three feet, seven inches tall to pinch hit in a game. Veeck instructed Gaedel to crouch which, according to Veeck, gave him a strike zone of one and one-half inches. Gaedel ignored that instruction, but the pitcher still walked him on four straight pitches, all high.

Striving to follow in his father's footsteps, Mike Veeck assisted his dad when Bill owned the Chicago White Sox. The son because the manager of promotions and thought he had hit on a great one with Disco Demolition Night on July 12, 1979.

In the late 1970s disco had become the most popular form of music in the United States. But disco sparked a major backlash from rock music fans—an opposition strong enough that the White Sox, seeking to fill seats at Comiskey Park during a lackluster season, engaged Chicago shock jock and anti-disco campaigner Steve Dahl for the promotion at the doubleheader. In fairness to Mike, he had previously held a promotion for disco fans. He just thought it would be fun to have one for those who hated disco.

But it did not turn out fun. Admission was just 98 cents for anyone who turned in a disco record. Between games, Dahl would destroy all of the vinyl in an explosion. At least 50,000 packed the stadium, and several thousand were turned away. After Dahl blew up the collected records, thousands of fans stormed the field and remained there until dispersed by riot police. The second game was initially postponed, but, by order of the president of the American League, was forfeited to the Tigers the next day. Some accused the Veecks of racism and homophobia, since disco was popular with Blacks and gays.

This event broke both of the Veecks emotionally, Mike in particular. His dad took responsibility, but Mike's life fell apart after the event, spiraling down into a failed marriage and drug use. He yearned to get back into professional baseball promotion, but no one was calling. It seemed as if the Disco Demolition Disaster had defined his career for prospective employers.

His big break came when he became the president of an independent league team (a step below the minors), the St. Paul Saints. He went all out with promotions, training a pig to bring the balls to the umpire, bringing in the San Diego Chicken mascot, signing pitcher Ila Borders, the first woman to pitch in professional baseball since Mamie Johnson in the Negro Leagues. He held a "Nobody Night," where no fans were allowed in the park until the official attendance of zero was announced in the fifth inning. Veeck brought Minnie Miñoso out of retirement to play for the Saints on July 16, 2003, at age seventy-seven, making him the first player to appear in professional games in seven different decades. The Saints played a game with no professional umpires; instead, a "jury" of Little League baseball players made the calls.

At forty-one years old, Hall of Famer Jack Morris, a Saint Paul native, pitched ten games for the Saints and went 5-1 with a 2.69 ERA.

Another remarkable facet of this movie is the resurrection of Darryl Strawberry's baseball career by a summer stint with the Saints in 1996 at thirty-four years old. Drugs had destroyed Strawberry in both his baseball and personal life. He said that at this time he was just existing, not having any joy in life and no desire to play baseball. When an agent approached Mike Veeck about signing Strawberry to play for the Saints, Veeck turned him down, afraid that Strawberry's drug problems would taint the Saints' image. Veeck's second wife, Libby, lit into him, calling him a hypocrite. After all, hadn't Veeck been given a second chance after his life blew up? Veeck saw the light and signed Strawberry.

Strawberry loved the atmosphere at the Saints' ballpark and also bonded with teammate Dave Stevens, a congenital amputee. Veeck didn't sign Stevens as a stunt. Stevens had an incredible will to compete. In a touching moment, Strawberry, who had already hit three home runs in the game, was due up. Everyone was hoping he would hit a fourth. Instead, he insisted that Stevens pinch hit for him. The Saints restored Strawberry's love for baseball, and later that summer the New York Yankees signed him. The Yanks won the World Series that year.

In 1998, Mike Veeck's dream of returning to the major leagues was fulfilled when the Tampa Bay Rays hired him as senior vice president in charge of marketing and sales. He was working sixteen-hour days. When he told Libby he needed to work seventeen-hour days, she filled a glass of wine and sardonically suggested that they toast to the fact that he won't have a relationship with his second child. That hit Veeck hard, as he had missed out on many years with his son from his first marriage. So he quit his job and devoted much of his time to his daughter Rebecca, who had been diagnosed with Batten disease, which eventually left her blind. She died at age twenty-seven in 2019 from complications from the disease.

This movie is heartwarming and well worth your time.

* * *

"2012 Film *Knuckleball* is Well Worth the Watch"

I just watched a fascinating baseball documentary, *Knuckleball*, from 2012.

The film focuses on the last two great major league knuckleball pitchers, Tim Wakefield and R.A. Dickey. The movie documents Wakefield's last season in MLB, with the Boston Red Sox, and his quest to win two hundred games, which he reached at Fenway Park on September 13, 2011.

Dickey's knuckleball was so good in 2012 that he won the Cy Young Award with a record of 20-6 and a 2.73 ERA.

The movie also features interviews with Hall of Fame knuckleballer Phil Niekro, who won 318 games, and others who relied on the specialty pitch, including Charlie Hough, Tom Candiotti, and Jim Bouton.

Knuckleball is a misnomer, as the ball is not thrown with the knuckles resting upon it. Rather, the fingernails dig into the ball, often resting on the seams. When thrown correctly, the ball has zero spin, causing it to dart and move erratically. The pitcher doesn't even know where it's going, and catchers have a miserable time corralling it.

Knuckleballers are told to forget everything they have ever been taught about pitching. Trained to try to dominate with hard stuff, they are now throwing a ball which ranges in speed from the high fifties to eighty miles per hour. In clutch situations, when their instinct is to throw harder, they have to learn to throw softer to better control the pitch. That requires great trust and patience.

Managers also need a huge level of trust and patience. Some days the knuckleball is dazzling hitters; on other days it is eminently hittable. The good managers stick with their knuckleballers through thick and thin, believing that in the long run they will produce more wins than losses. Managers learn to live with passed balls and stolen bases, hoping the effectiveness of the pitch will counteract those inevitable drawbacks.

Knuckleballers are a tight-knit fraternity, and Wakefield and Dickey attribute their success to advice from their mentors—Wakefield from Hough and Candiotti, and Dickey from Niekro. Dickey also got valuable tips from Wakefield. As Dickey put it, "Knuckleballers don't keep secrets."

All knuckleballers have to overcome the stigma of relying on what others look at as a novelty pitch, or, as Dickey describes it, a "circus" pitch. They are often not respected as real pitchers, even though all of them came up as regular hurlers. They realized they did not have as good stuff as the younger hurlers advancing in the ranks, and the knuckleball saved their careers. In fact, most knuckleballers improve with age, coming into their own in their thirties. And they can pitch a long time—Wakefield retired at age forty-five,

Hough at forty-six, Niekro at forty-eight.

It was painful to watch Wakefield giving up a home run to the Yankees' Aaron Boone in the eleventh inning of Game 7 of the 2003 American League Championship Series at Yankee Stadium. Wakefield had started and won Games 1 and 4, and was called upon to pitch the tenth and eleventh innings in Game 7, so he went from hero to goat with one pitch. With a knuckleball, all it takes is one pitch that hangs instead of dances.

Wakefield first got interested in the knuckleball from playing catch in his backyard with his dad, Steve.

"If he asked me to go out in the yard and play catch, I always said yes," Steve recalled. "But then he'd want to play and play and play, so I started throwing knuckleballs at him. He didn't like it. Eventually, he's say, 'OK, I've had enough.'"

Drafted as a position player by the Pittsburgh Pirates in 1988, Wakefield was flailing at the plate, hitting below .200. His minor league manager in extended spring training, Woody Huyke, had seen him fooling around with the knuckleball while playing catch with a teammate and saw how difficult it was to catch. So the Pirates made him a pitcher. When the Pirates called him up to the big league club at the end of July 1992, Wakefield's debut was a complete game, 3-2 win with ten strikeouts. He finished the season 8-1 with a 2.15 ERA.

But he struggled mightily in 1993, going 6-11 with a 5.61 ERA and ended up back in Triple-A for all of 1994. The Pirates released Wakefield at the start of the 1995 season, and the Red Sox were smart enough to sign him. Wakefield, who worked tirelessly at his craft, had a great year with the Sox, and the rest, as they say, is history.

Dickey, who had been a power pitcher with the Texas

Rangers, began to lose velocity on his fastball in 2004 and 2005 to a maximum of eighty-six mph. That's when pitching coach Orel Hershiser advised him to abandon every other pitch and throw the knuckleball exclusively. That advice turned his career around.

As an aside, Jim Bouton should have followed that advice when he faced me in a semi-pro league game after his retirement from major league baseball. Eating me up with his knuckler, he made the mistake of throwing a fastball. I lined a base hit over his head.

Wakefield and Dickey agreed that the toughest batters to face were contact guys like Bill Buckner. The free-swingers like Albert Pujols were easy pickings for the knuckleballers.

The film also pays tribute to knuckleball pioneers Hoyt Wilhelm and Wilbur Wood. After Wakefield retired, Dickey carried the knuckleball torch until his retirement after the 2017 season. The only current major leaguer to rely on the knuckleball is Matt Waldron of the San Diego Padres, but his career record is 8-15 with a 4.86 ERA.

Knuckleballers may get a bad rap (pun intended), but to withstand the ups and downs of the fortunes of their unique pitch takes courage. As Dickey put it, "You may hit me. You may knock me around and knock balls out of the park. But I am always going to get back up and keep coming at you."

* * *

"You're Killing Me, Smalls!"

It just dawned on me that although my kids loved the movie, *The Sandlot*, I only caught bits and pieces of it from when they watched. I had never watched the entire movie. So today I did.

I am a big baseball fan and grew up playing the game. But I must confess that I don't like a lot of baseball movies because they always get something wrong. Sometimes the actors don't look like they ever played the game. Or the situations on the diamond are unrealistic. Or the screenwriters get baseball history wrong.

The Sandlot sinned in that last regard, right off the bat, so to speak. The narrator, the adult Scotty Smalls, describes Babe Ruth's famous "called shot" in the 1932 World Series as happening in the ninth inning with two outs, a full count, and the tying run on base. In truth, the home run he hit to center field, where some believe he pointed to, came in the fifth inning of a tie game.

But I forgive *The Sandlot* for this transgression, because they got so much else right about baseball, especially as seen through the eyes of kids.

I identified with the movie right away. Scotty Smalls had just finished fifth grade and was probably eleven years old when he moved to the San Fernando Valley in Southern California in 1962, identified as the year that Maury Wills of the Dodgers broke the single-season record for steals. I was nine years old that year, growing up playing baseball in sandlots and in Little League in Hackensack, New Jersey, a suburb of New York City. In the summer of 1963, we flew to Southern California to visit our relatives in the San Fernando Valley, where I played baseball with my cousins Rich and Rob in their backyard, which adjoined a schoolyard and had a high chain link fence. We would toss pop flies to each other against the fence and pretend we were robbing home runs from major leaguers.

That was the kind of impromptu baseball depicted in *The Sandlot*, where eight boys who played baseball all day long on their neglected, unwatered field, brought newcomer Smalls onto their squad to complete the team.

I loved some of the touches in the movie, such as pitcher Kenny DeNunez, the only Black kid on the team, wearing the baseball cap of the Kansas City Monarchs, the team for which the legendary Satchel Paige pitched. The star of the sandlot squad, Benny "The Jet" Rodriguez, wore a Los Angeles Dodger cap, and at the end of the movie is shown playing for the Dodgers and stealing home. Another sandlot kid wore the hat of the Los Angeles Angels, an expansion team that was established in 1961.

Another great shout-out was the scene where Benny meets Babe Ruth in a dream in Benny's bedroom, and, as the Babe is leaving, he spots a baseball card of Hank Aaron, who of course was destined to break the Babe's career home run record. The Babe says, "Henry Aaron. I don't know why, but can I have this, kid?"

And all the kids know how to play ball. Kenny throws like a real pitcher and all the kids can swing the bat, slide, and play the field.

The drama centers on the boys attempting to retrieve a ball that Smalls borrowed from his stepdad's trophy room—a ball autographed by Babe Ruth. Smalls hits the ball for a homer over the fence into the yard of Mr. Mertle, played by James Earl Jones, who owns an old junkyard dog named Hercules. The boys call Hercules "The Beast," as he is purported to have eaten a kid who tried to retrieve a ball.

The movie brilliantly magnifies the fears all kids had who played ball in the streets or sandlots or backyards of retrieving a ball from a neighbor's backyard. Was the neighbor mean? Would the neighbor scream at them? Arrest them? Shoot them?

They discover that not only is Mr. Mertle, who they greatly feared but had never met, a nice old man, but in a shout-out to the Negro Leagues, he shows the boys a photo of him standing between Babe Ruth and Lou Gehrig, probably during a barnstorming tour that the Yankees did in the off season. And, to replace the Babe Ruth autograph ball that Hercules had chewed up, Mr. Mertle gives Smalls a ball autographed by the entire 1927 New York Yankees team, which included Ruth and Gehrig. Benny correctly refers to "Murderers' Row," the first six hitters in the lineup. Props to the screenwriters for recognizing that team as perhaps the greatest of all time.

The nostalgia for me and others of the Smalls' generation is the concept of sandlot baseball. I know it is hard for young people today to imagine, but we would go down to our local worn-out field and assemble two full squads for a pickup game that went for hours, and nobody seemed to care much about the score. Some of us also played Little League, but some didn't. We just had fun.

I worry that perhaps the fun of baseball has been drained by parents exerting pressure on their kids to get college scholarships or major league contracts. I distinctly remember after completing Little League at age twelve that I just wanted a breather from organized ball. The feeling waned, and I went on playing Babe Ruth League and high school baseball.

But if I had that feeling, how about the kids who are playing not only Little League and higher division ball, but are also on travel ball teams and spending all their waking hours in batting cages and baseball camps? They can nail all the technical skills, but are they losing the joy of the game in the process? Ninety-six percent of high school athletes never go on to play college ball.

The best baseball memories are those when you were having fun. Like in *The Sandlot*.

***

"*The Catcher Was a Spy* is Stranger than Fiction"

Moe Berg is not exactly a household name among baseball fans. The catcher played fifteen seasons for five different teams in the 1920s and 1930s, with a cumulative batting average of .243. His best weapon was his brain, as he was a heady backstop recruited by his manager to serve as a coach for the Boston Red Sox in his final few seasons.

What makes Berg different from the typical baseball player is that brain. He knew ten languages, graduated from Princeton University, and got a law degree from Columbia University. That language prowess helped him get a position with the Office of Strategic Services (OSS), a predecessor to the CIA, when World War II broke out.

Berg, who was Jewish, drew a singular assignment: arrange a meeting with German scientist Werner Heisenberg to determine if Heisenberg's work with nuclear energy was assisting the Germans in developing a nuclear bomb. If Berg determined that it was and that the Germans were close, he was to kill Heisenberg.

If this sounds like movie material, it is.

Based on the book of the same name, *The Catcher Was a Spy* was released in 2018 and details Berg's captivating story. The opening credits come with the proviso, "based on a true story," and Hollywood takes its usual liberties.

For example, because Berg was a lifetime bachelor, the movie hints strongly that Berg was homosexual. But Aviva

Kempner, who produced a documentary on Berg entitled *The Spy Behind Home Plate*, dispels that notion. Kempner told the *Los Angeles Times*, "You know, Hollywood makes their movies with a kind of script development. I call this [documentary] the real story. The players who played with him talked about all these girlfriends, and then the testimony of Babe Ruth's daughter saying [in "The Spy Behind Home Plate"], 'I danced with him; he came onto me.' He had a long-time relationship."

The movie does show Berg with a girlfriend, so they get that part right. Berg's cousin, Denise Shames, posited an interesting theory as to why Berg and his two siblings never married. "I think there's a reason for that," Shames told the *Los Angeles Times*. "I think it was an agreement they all made. It didn't mean they didn't have relationships; some were long-lasting. My mother told me that when Sam (Mo's brother) was in medical school, he was studying genetics and understood something in the family should not be passed through to children."

"I think Moe Berg is best explained as a mystery," Major League Baseball historian John Thorn told the *Los Angeles Times*. "Berg is such an odd duck. He's learned. He has a sense of humor and women like him. Yet he was a loner." Casey Stengel once described Berg as "the strangest man ever to play baseball," and actor Paul Rudd captures Berg's enigmatic personality in the film. Thorn also pointed out that Berg's closet was filled with identical black suits, so he dressed the same daily.

I have to confess that I'm not a big fan of baseball movies because, with some exceptions, they never seem to get the baseball right. I'm more interested in baseball movies with an interesting plot—like *Eight Men Out* about the Chicago

Black Sox scandal of 1919. Interestingly, *The Catcher Was a Spy* only has one baseball scene. It's passable, although the players' skill level is suspect. But that's not the focus of the movie, a spy thriller made more interesting because it is true. The film builds to the climax of Berg's dramatic meeting with Heisenberg in 1944—again, most likely ratcheted up by Hollywood.

The irony of Berg, a Jew, spying on the Nazis increases the tension. "If he had been caught, can you imagine what would have happened to him?" asked Kempner. "He would have been assassinated on the spot."

Despite his law degree and offers to coach in the major leagues after the war, Berg elected to live with his brother, Dr. Samuel Berg, in New Jersey. He spent the rest of his life unemployed, living off the goodwill of family and friends. When people asked Berg what he did for a living, he would slowly draw his finger to his lips as if to silence both the question and answer, giving the impression that he was still a spy, which he was not.

"You know how many people peak very early in life?" asked Shames of Berg's behavior. "They live on those laurels for a long, long time."

The book on which the movie was based was written by Nicholas Dawidoff and spent seven weeks on *The New York Times* bestseller list, which described the biography as "The life of Moe Berg, big-league catcher, O.S.S. agent, lady's man, and freeloader." If you like baseball and spy stories, this book and/or movie is for you.

Berg died on May 29, 1972, at age seventy, of an aortic aneurysm. His last words were a question to his nurse: "How are the Mets doing today?" He died before she could answer.

This column first appeared in The Vacaville Reporter *on June 15, 2021.*

***

"A Movie that Swings for the Fences"

Disclaimer: This is not a sports movie.

Having said that, Troy Maxson, the main character in *Fences,* is a Black man who claims he would have made it to the major leagues but never got the chance because of the color barrier. That injustice has turned Maxson into a bitter man who turns that sour spirit on his son, Cory, a high school football player who is being recruited to play in college. Since Maxson's dream of professional sports was squelched, he wants Cory to work after school rather than attend football practice.

If that sounds like a sports movie, it is only because I haven't told you the other elements of this powerful drama, which was first a play.

I had never heard of the movie or the play until I took a trip to the post office the other day. I wanted to buy a book of stamps and the postal worker apologized because she had a limited selection—three different types of Christmas stamps and a stamp commemorating someone named August Wilson under the heading, "Black Heritage."

I told the clerk that I would take the August Wilson stamps and that I had never heard of him. The clerk, who is Black, told me that Wilson wrote the screenplay for the 2016 movie *Fences,* which she said was very good. I told her I would check it out.

I was not disappointed.

Wilson wrote the screenplay and Denzel Washington, who plays Troy Maxson, directed the movie.

I did a little research and discovered that the late August Wilson, alongside Eugene O'Neill, Edward Albee, and Tennessee Williams, was one of the greatest American playwrights. He won two Pulitzer Prizes and *Fences* is one of ten plays in Wilson's magnum opus, "The Pittsburgh Cycle." The cycle focuses on African-American life in the twentieth century, each play taking place in a particular decade. *Fences* is set in the late 1950s.

Wilson has done his baseball homework. If you follow some of the players and statistics the characters or the radio rattle off, you can place the early part of the movie in 1957. The movie is set in Pittsburgh and Troy and Cory are Pirates fans. In one scene, the radio is tuned to a Pirates game and the announcer says that Roberto Clemente is at the plate. He says Clemente is batting .249 with 4 homers and 24 RBIs. A quick check at baseballreference.com reveals that Clemente finished the season with a .253 average, 4 homers and 30 RBIS. So we know we are hearing a game late in the 1957 season.

Cory mentions that Hank Aaron has forty-three homers. Aaron finished the 1957 season with forty-four round-trippers, so again we know that we are nearing the end of the season in September.

Troy claims he hit seven home runs off Satchel Paige when they were both in the Negro Leagues. The film doesn't identify Troy's teams, but he probably played for the Pittsburgh Crawfords (named after the Crawford Grill, a prominent nightclub) or the Homestead Grays, another Pittsburgh team.

Troy is no fan of Jackie Robinson. He claims there were one-hundred Black players better than Robinson who never got a chance to make the big leagues because they played earlier than Robinson. Troy is also not impressed by Aaron. He says that Clemente doesn't get as much playing time as his white teammates because he is Puerto Rican.

Troy tells his friend and co-worker Jim Bono, "Take that fellow playing right field for the Yankees back then. Selkirk. Man batting .269. What kind of sense that make? I was hitting .432 with 37 home runs."

Wilson got that detail right—George Selkirk played outfield for the Yankees in 1940 and hit .269 that season.

Troy's critical spirit is fed by the fact that he is a garbage collector rather than a big-league ballplayer. We find out that he was in jail for fifteen years and played baseball there, but by the time he got out he was forty-three. His wife, Rose, played by Viola Davis, reminds him that he was too old at that point to play professional baseball. But Troy refuses to accept that obvious fact.

Troy keeps a baseball bat in the backyard along with a baseball suspended by a rope from a tree. He and Cory smack the ball around from time to time. At one point Troy says, "Death ain't nothing but a fastball on the outside corner." He then takes his bat and swings at that suspended baseball.

He uses baseball as a metaphor for life throughout the movie. He tells Rose, "You born with two strikes on you before you come to the plate. You got to guard it closely, always looking for the curveball on the inside corner. You can't afford to let none get past you. You can't afford a called strike. I fooled them, Rose. I bunted. When I found you and Cory and a halfway decent job, I was safe. Couldn't nothing touch me, I wasn't gonna strike out no more."

This is a very potent movie and the performances are astounding. Washington and Davis won Tonys when they played these parts for the Broadway play. Davis won an Oscar for Best Supporting Actress in the film version.

It's not a sports movie, but sports are used as a framework and a metaphor for the fences that Troy is trying to break out of. The film is a great reminder of the fences that have hedged in African Americans, not only on the baseball field, but in life.

This column first appeared in The Vacaville Reporter *on February 5, 2021.*

***

"Situational Hitting. What's That?"

When Major League Baseball introduced the concept of placing a man at second base with no outs in extra innings, I hoped that the experiment would not last. I hate it. I am a baseball traditionalist. Unfortunately, the experiment stuck.

But I wondered, would ballplayers be able to resurrect the art of situational hitting? Would players be able to bunt a man over, advance him on a ground ball, execute the suicide squeeze, loft a sacrifice fly?

They may still remember the latter, since everybody is trying to launch the ball for a home run anyway. However, bunting or making an out to advance a runner? That is a foreign concept to most professional ballplayers.

Contact rates across the majors have been at a historic low, with MLB hitters making contact less than 80 percent of the time.

Prior to the DH becoming universal when adopted by

the National League, Chipper Jones, a former NL MVP, World Series champion, and eight-time All-Star, told CBS Sports Radio that the state of the game leaves much to be desired.

"You don't see the fundamentals practiced all that much," he said. "Pitchers can barely get down bunts anymore. You're certainly not asking one of your position players to do that. The hit-and-run, the straight steal, the days of guys stealing 75, 80, 100 bases a year and manufacturing runs so that you can win games 3-2—everybody is sitting back and waiting for the two- or three-run home run that's going to break the game wide open.

"Look, it's just the way the game is evolving. You've got a lot of smart guys that are heading up and general managing baseball teams now that never really played the game. But they're relying on a lot of this information and a lot of this data to build their ball clubs. Some of them have done some great jobs over the last few years. Just like I tell hitters there are a thousand different ways to hit a baseball, there are a bunch of different ways to put a ball club together—and this just seems to be the hot fad right now."

There used to be players whose trademark was bunting.

Hall of Famer Eddie Collins, who played twenty-five years in the majors (1906-1930) had 512 sacrifice bunts—the most in major league history—to go along with 3,000 plus hits and over 700 stolen bases.

Brett Butler, who played for the Giants and Dodgers among other teams, has the most bunt base hits in MLB history—188. The outfielder reached base successfully on 48.8 percent of his bunt base hit attempts. He holds the single-season record with twenty-nine bunt base hits with the Dodgers in 1992.

There are some current ballplayers who still honor the craft of bunting. Boston Red Sox outfielder Jarren Duran, who had a 50 percent ground-ball rate in his minor league career, told FanGraphs, "I can't beat out a fly ball. That would be a waste of my speed, so why not use the tool that I have?"

A skilled bunter, he had something to say on that subject.

"Everybody wants to talk about hitting, but nobody wants to talk about bunting anymore," he said. "The bunt is a lost art in this sport. Except for guys like Dee Gordon and Billy Hamilton, who can get away with it. I mean, bunting is harder than you think."

He considers bunting a multi-faceted art form.

"You've got the push bunt to third, and the one where you drag it past the pitcher toward the second baseman," he explained. "And then you've got one that's called 'walk the dog,' where you literally walk it down the first-base line and just have to beat the ball."

There are also exceptions to the managerial approach of waiting for the long ball.

Joe Maddon, who last managed in the big leagues in 2022, told ESPN, "In today's game, everyone is working off the same sheet of music. I think there's a reason why fans have been turned off a bit by our game. That's because the game looks the same no matter where you go. I want to reestablish our own identity here."

Angels' owner Arte Moreno said, "You really get caught a little bit in the whole analytical part of the game. To me, you need to be in the fun part of the game."

Maddon was not opposed to analytics but also liked a balance between that approach and what he called the "heartbeat" approach, which includes gut instinct and small ball. He proudly declared that the Angels were "gonna bunt this year."

So I wondered, would anybody be able to bunt the man on second over to third when the tenth inning gets underway? As Bruce Jenkins pointed out in the *San Francisco Chronicle,* bunting is "hardly an easy task against pitchers who throw ninety-eight mph fastballs, sweeping sliders, nasty cutters and drop-off-the-table changeups."

Retired Hall of Fame pitcher John Smoltz was optimistic. He told ESPN, "You get to extra innings and everybody's trying to end the game with a home run. We won't see that with the new rule, and I like that part of it."

Sorry, John. Contrary to his expectations and mine, bunting has not increased in extra innings. In fact, leadoff batters are swinging around 89 percent of the time in extra innings. The clubs that embrace sabermetrics—all of them to some degree—don't want to give away an out.

Taylor Bechtold stated in a 2023 article, "While teams that choose to bunt have scored one run in the inning 46.4 percent of the time since 2020 compared to 33.1 percent of the clubs that don't, teams that swing away have been more likely to have a big inning than those that have opted to square around."

The battle between traditionalists and sabermetric gurus continues.

This column, which has been contemporized, first appeared in The Vacaville Reporter *on July 7, 2020.*

* * *

"Baseball's Unwritten Rules Stir Controversy"

I thought when Ken Griffey Jr. made his "Let the kids play" ad for MLB before the 2018 postseason we were done with denouncing bat-flips and other gray areas of baseball etiquette. No such luck.

In the eighth inning of the Padres/Rangers game in August 2020, the Padres' Fernando Tatis Jr. swung at a 3-0 fastball with a 10-3 lead. He belted a grand slam off Rangers reliever Juan Nicasio. Tatis had missed a take sign, but the Rangers didn't approve with the Padres holding such a big lead. Ian Gibaut replaced Nicasio and threw his first pitch behind Manny Machado's head.

"I didn't like it, personally," Rangers manager Chris Woodward said of Tatis' 3-0 swing. "But the norms are being challenged on a daily basis. So just because I don't like it doesn't mean it's not right. I don't think we liked it as a group."

This raises the whole issue of baseball's unwritten rules, one of which is don't swing at a 3-0 pitch when you have a big lead. But a bunch of big leaguers and ex-big leaguers jumped to the defense of Tatis Jr.

Hall of Famer Johnny Bench tweeted, "So you take a pitch . . . now you're 3-1. Then the pitcher comes back with a great setup pitch . . . 3-2. Now you're ready to ground out into a double play. Everyone should hit 3-0. Grand slams are a huge stat."

Retired MLB infielder Trevor Plouffe tweeted, "Ya we were taught that coming up but it's ok to change when you learn that the things you were taught are stupid."

Former big league pitcher Ron Darling spoke about the

trouble with the unwritten rules: "I'm old enough that I grew up in a game that a lot of older guys had all the power and they would tell you how to act, what to do, and you did what they told you to do because that's how it was. Unwritten rules only work if everyone knows the unwritten rules. By their very definition, nobody knows an unwritten rule, so what you have now is you're trying to make a decision that a 3-0 count in a seven-run game is off-limits. I'm just not with that at all."

Let's take a look at some of baseball's unwritten rules. As Joe Garagiola put it, "Baseball is a game played by human beings and governed by unwritten laws of survival and self-preservation."

Don't take too long rounding the bases after a home run

In 2015, Machado hit a home run off of Jonathan Papelbon, and Papelbon thought that Machado took too much time admiring his handiwork. The next time they faced each other, Papelbon threw at Machado's head. Bryce Harper, Papelbon's teammate, objected to Papelbon's reaction. When Harper didn't hustle on a flyout, Papelbon confronted Harper in the dugout, leading to a fight. Harper later called for an end to the unwritten rules.

Do not spend time admiring your homer

Jose Bautista brought this unwritten rule to a head with his emphatic bat flip in the 2015 American League Division Series between the Toronto Blue Jays and the Texas Rangers. Rangers pitcher Sam Dyson took offense and told Toronto's Edwin Encarnación to tell Bautista to "respect the game."

The next year, Bautista slid into the Rangers' Rougned Odor, leading to a fight.

The same day as the Tatis Jr. debacle, Juan Soto of the Nationals blasted a 445-foot home run off Braves reliever Will Smith. Soto admired his home run for a second or two—not as long as he has gazed at some of his other shots—and Smith then screamed an expletive at Soto. That just led to an even slower trot around the bases.

ESPN's David Schoenfield noted, "It's important to understand the cultural aspects here, however. Tatis and Soto are both Dominican, and Latin players often do play the game with more flair—no different than, say, the Korea Baseball Organization, where bat flips are almost an artistic aspect of the game."

Do not disrespect the pitcher in any way

Bob Gibson once beaned an opposing batter for a perceived slight that occurred fifteen years earlier. Stan Williams, who pitched during the 1960s, wrote the names of players he felt he had to retaliate against on the inside of his baseball cap. Nolan Ryan threw beanballs at hitters who bunted to him, making him field his position.

Do not steal bases when your team has a big lead

In 1994, while playing in the minor leagues, Michael Jordan stole third base even though his team had an 11–0 lead. His manager, Terry Francona, explained the unwritten rule to him after the game.

Do not bunt to break up a no-hitter

In a 2001 game, with the Arizona Diamondbacks Curt Schilling just five outs away from a perfect game, San Diego's Ben Davis bunted for a single. Some of the Diamondbacks spent the rest of the game peppering Davis with obscenities. After Schilling completed a three-hitter for a 3-1 win, manager Bob Brenly called Davis' move "chicken."

Never mind that San Diego was only down 2-0 at the time and desperately needed a baserunner to bring the tying run to the plate. Forget trying to win the game, apparently. Davis broke the unwritten rule.

Brenly later admitted that the bunt fell into the gray area of unwritten rules.

"That's the way I was raised in the game," Brenly said. "That doesn't mean that I'm right and they're wrong, that's just the way I was taught how to play the game. It's all very subjective. It depends which side of the fence you're on."

This column first appeared in The Vacaville Reporter *on August 20, 2020.*

* * *

"The War about WAR and Baseball's Hall of Fame"

Ichiro Suzuki, CC Sabathia, and Billy Wagner were inducted into baseball's Hall of Fame in 2025. There was no controversy over their selection. The only disappointment is that Ichiro wasn't a unanimous selection. One baseball writer didn't vote for him.

But past selections have caused quite the uproar, highlighting the chasm between those voters who rely on traditional metrics and sabermetric aficionados.

Case in point: the 2019 Hall of Fame selections.

I had no argument with that year's choices—Harold Baines, Edgar Martinez, Mike Mussina, Mariano Rivera, Lee Smith, and the late Roy Halladay. But I knew someone would.

Jon Tayler, *Sports Illustrated*: "[Baines] represents one of the most baffling and poor Hall of Fame choices in decades."

Ben Lindbergh, *The Ringer*: "Statistically speaking, Baines is probably the worst player to qualify for the hall in forty-two years, and his election is shocking in an era of relatively enlightened evaluation."

Ah, the era of "enlightened evaluation." Translated: Those who believe sabermetrics and WAR trump any other means of assessing a candidate.

WAR (Wins Above Replacement) is an attempt by the sabermetric baseball community to summarize a player's total contributions to their team in one statistic. As explained on FanGraphs website, "WAR offers an estimate to answer the question, 'If this player got injured and their team had to replace them with a freely available minor leaguer or a AAAA player from their bench, how much value would the team be losing?'"

AAAA player is an outstanding player at the AAA level who has trouble succeeding at the major league level.

In any discussion about Hall of Fame merit, one will invariably run into two camps: the sabermetric folks and the so-called "old school" baseball people.

Rob Neyer of *SB Nation* wrote this about Bruce Jenkins of the *San Francisco Chronicle* and other members of the Hall of Fame Expansion Era Committee of 2013: "Nearly everybody on that committee honestly believes that everything they need to know about baseball, they learned in kindergarten."

One of Jenkins' sins, in Neyer's eyes, was writing this about the 1970s in his column about the committee: "Within that realm, players, managers and writers treated wins, RBIs, batting average and ERA as invaluable measuring sticks—and never really felt compelled to adjust."

With Baines, as Gary Peterson noted in *The Mercury News*, "The criticism was instant and combustible, focusing on the three-man caucus that punched Baines' ticket. One is Jerry Reinsdorf, who has owned the Chicago White Sox for thirty-five years, including the fourteen years Baines played on the South Side. Another is Pat Gillick who was GM of the Orioles during two of the seven seasons Baines spent in Baltimore. La Russa managed Baines for seven seasons in Chicago, and three more in Oakland."

NBC Sports' Craig Calcutta said, "It's hard to view it as anything other than a product of cronyism and a conflict of interest on the part of the Hall of Fame and the Today's Game Committee."

Tayler of *Sports Illustrated* wrote, "The result is the Hall inducting a sub-standard player through a committee that clearly doesn't care about or understand advanced statistics or anything more than basic numbers."

Who is better qualified to evaluate a player than someone who has seen him play day-in and day-out over the course of several seasons—like LaRussa, Reinsdorf, and Gillick?

Tayler went on to say, "That's of a piece with last year's election by the Modern Game Era committee of Jack Morris, who was passed over by the writers but immediately ushered into the Hall in his first year of consideration despite being a mediocre starter whose claim to fame—like Baines—was extreme durability."

That kind of denigration always makes me wonder—did

they ever see them play? And I don't mean a bunch of YouTube clips.

Before we talk about alleged "mediocre starter" Morris, let's hear what LaRussa said in defense of his choice of Baines to the Hall of Fame.

In an interview with Christopher Russo on MLB Network's "High Heat," Russo asked if LaRussa thought that a Hall of Famer should have a couple of MVP awards under his belt. LaRussa gave a straightforward "no."

Tony Gwynn never won an MVP Award and went in with 97.6 percent of the vote, the eighth-best all-time. Eddie Mathews, who hit 512 home runs and was elected to the Hall in 1978, never won the MVP. Also, the MVP is often awarded to players on teams that make it to the postseason, so it's not an even playing field.

LaRussa noted that Baines had knocked in over one-hundred runs early in his twenty-two-year career (1982 and 1985) and late (1999). He also said that "in game-winning RBIs, he's up there with the best of them." The GWRBI, an official MLB statistic from 1981 to 1989, was discontinued after that decade.

FanGraphs admits that WAR does not consider that factor: "WAR is entirely context neutral. It doesn't take into account that some hits are more important in games than others. And it doesn't take into account that some relievers pitch in key, high-leverage situations, making their results more important than, say, the appearances by the team's long reliever."

Which brings me back to Morris, the guy that Tayler called a "mediocre starter."

As Kevin Eck wrote for the Pressbox, "If you deem Morris not Hall of Fame-worthy because of his 3.90 ERA, you clearly don't know Jack. The right-hander was the winningest pitcher of the 1980s, a three-time twenty-game winner, a five-time All-Star, the MVP of the 1991 World Series with the Minnesota Twins."

If you saw his ten shutout innings for the Twins over the Braves in Game 7 of the 1991 Fall Classic, you learned everything you needed to know about Morris. He was the definition of a clutch performer.

And if you were a pitcher, Baines is not the guy you wanted to face with runners in scoring position and the game on the line.

Something WAR can't tell you.

This column, which has been contemporized, first appeared in The Vacaville Reporter *on August 1, 2019.*

* * *

"Searching for Rickey Henderson"

On August 27, 1982, the Oakland A's Rickey Henderson set a new single-season record by stealing his 119th base against the Brewers in Milwaukee. After four pickoff throws, Henderson stole second—on a pitchout. He stole three more bags that day, including one of third base.

Henderson finished the season with 130 thefts, an MLB record that still stands today and may stand forever.

Of course, there have been other great base stealers, such as Vince Coleman, Maury Wills, and Ty Cobb. Coleman, who stole more than Robin Hood, swiped 110 bases for the St. Louis Cardinals in 1985, 107 in 1986, and 109 in 1987. Wills stole 104 for the Dodgers in 1962 and 94 in 1965. Cobb had 95 thefts for the Detroit Tigers in 1915. Lou Brock's 118 in 1974 held the record until Henderson came along.

But that was then. In 2024, the Reds' Elly De La Cruz led the majors with 67 stolen bases; the Braves' Ronald Acuna had 73 in 2023.

Base stealing, like writing thank-you notes, is becoming a lost art. It's because teams gauge the risk-reward of the steal. They don't want to take unnecessary chances in a game where the number of outs is finite. Instead, they are sitting back and waiting for the three-run homer. Even the little guys who could hit .300 swing from their heels, more than willing to strike out frequently in exchange for eventually knocking one over the wall. The data tells teams they are more likely to win that way.

But not everyone agrees. Whit Merrifield stole 45 bases for the Kansas City Royals in 2018 and 40 in 2021 and led the American League both seasons. Here's what he told *Athlon Sports*:

"Base stealing is a lost art, in my opinion, because of how people view analytics these days. I guess they don't like stolen bases or don't value the risk-reward in their algorithm. A lot more goes into stolen bases than being successful or not. Numbers can't quantify that—a guy being on first base, taking the pitcher's attention away from the hitter, getting the hitter more fastballs because they're scared of throwing a slider and bouncing it. There are a lot of things that go into being a threat on the bases that benefit a team. People forget about it. But I haven't forgotten about it."

Hall of Fame manager Tony La Russa said that because of the concentration on the home run, teams are neglecting to practice defending the steal. And a steal can be the difference-maker in a close game. "Stolen bases are more possible with average runners now until teams pay attention to it," he told *Athlon*. "It's a skill. You can teach these things. You should still be interested in adding a run, but if they think the only way to do that is swinging from their [butts], they won't."

There is also the risk of injury. The Angels' Mike Trout stole 24 bases in 26 attempts in 2018 for a 92.3 percent success rate, the best in baseball. But in 2017, he lost six weeks when he tore a ligament in his thumb while sliding on a stolen base attempt. However, he dove headfirst into second base, which isn't the wisest move if you don't want to get hurt. Also, it has been demonstrated that you don't get to the base any faster that way.

Jack Perconte, a middle infielder for a few major league teams in the 1980s, has the fourth-best all-time base-stealing percentage at 85.714. He said on his website: "The final key to successful base stealing is the ability to slide as late as possible, so little speed is lost from the friction of the ground. The pop-up slide seems to be rarely used now for base stealing, but I believe it should be."

But perhaps we will again see what fans once took for granted. For example, back in the early 1980s, people used to go to the Oakland Coliseum to see Henderson chase stolen base records. There was great excitement in 1980 when "The Man of Steal" became just the third player in baseball history to steal 100 bags in a single season. Jackie Robinson, Coleman, Brock, and Wills used to drive pitchers to distraction when they reached base.

Everyone knew they would steal and succeed far more often than not. Even if they didn't go, sabermetrics can never calculate the effect of the threat on infielder positioning, pitch selection, and the pitchers' nerves.

The good news is the pendulum seems to be swinging back with the numbers Acuna Jr. and De La Cruz have put up recently. Most fans know Shohei Ohtani for his big bat (54 homers in 2024). How many know he stole 59 bases that season, No. 2 across the Majors?

As Cobb told the *Detroit Free Press in the* July 31, 1921, edition (the season when Babe Ruth would smash 59 homers), "With the sluggers of today, base stealing is a back number. But the hitting will pass. Then, we will return to the pitching and base running cycles. Five years from now, my baserunning marks may be eclipsed by some youngster now in grammar school."

Indeed, maybe somebody playing Little League ball today will be the next Rickey Henderson. At least we can hope.

This column, which has been contemporized, first appeared in The Vacaville Reporter *on August 15, 2019.*

* * *

"Strong up the Middle"

One of baseball's axioms is that teams that are strong up the middle win championships.

What is strong up the middle? It means that your catcher, shortstop, second baseman, and center fielder are all outstanding defensive players.

Bill James used Win Shares (a complicated formula he developed to determine a player's value to a team) to demonstrate that championship teams do tend to be stronger at catcher, second base, shortstop, and center field than at first base, third base, left field and right field.

For each season of major league baseball from 1900 through 2003, James selected three teams from each league to represent a championship team, an average team, and a bad one. He then compared the amount of value each team received at each position. The result was that championship teams were 98 percent better than bad teams up the middle, and only 73 percent better than bad teams at the remainder of the positions.

Dan Turkenkopf used another complicated formula, Win Shares above Bench, and came up with the same conclusion: concentrating your resources on players who play the skill positions seems to lead to more wins.

James and Turkenkopf took into account the up-the-middle players' offensive as well as defensive performances. But a case can be made on defensive prowess alone. More balls are hit up the middle than to the corner spots in the infield and outfield. And a catcher's ability to call a good game for the pitchers and to throw out would-be base stealers is key to a good defense.

For example, the 1959 Dodgers, who beat the Chicago White Sox in the World Series, batted the league average of .257, seventh best among the sixteen major league teams. But at .981 they were the best team in the majors in fielding percentage. Second baseman Jim Gilliam won a Gold Glove. Don Zimmer and Maury Wills shared shortstop duties, and both were solid. Don Demeter patrolled center field. An outstanding defensive player who could field multiple positions, Demeter once played 266 consecutive errorless games in the outfield, a major league record that stood for almost thirty years. John Roseboro is considered one of the best defensive catchers of the 1960s and won two Gold Gloves.

The 1969 New York Mets, who defeated the Baltimore Orioles in the World Series, were also offensively challenged. They ranked fourteenth out of the twenty-four teams in batting average, below the league average. They ranked seventeenth in home runs. They finished next-to-last in the National League in slugging and OPS (.351 and .662, respectively). But defensively up the middle, they were stout. Catcher Jerry Grote would have won a Gold Glove if Johnny Bench never existed. Bench won the Gold Glove every year from 1968 to 1977. Shortstop Bud Harrelson won a Gold Glove in 1971, finished with a career .969 fielding percentage and is the Mets' all-time leader in defensive WAR at 13.7. He played fifty-four consecutive errorless games in 1970, at the time a record for a shortstop. Second baseman Ken Boswell, shaky at second base when he entered the league in 1967, had steadily improved. In center field, Tommie Agee was a two-time Gold Glove winner and made two incredible catches against the Orioles in Game 3 of the 1969 Fall Classic that potentially saved five runs. The Mets won 5-0.

The 1976 Cincinnati Reds are the best offensive team of all time. But let's not overlook their defense, especially up the middle. Bench, as was mentioned, won ten consecutive Gold Gloves. Second baseman Joe Morgan won five Gold Gloves. So did shortstop Dave Concepción. As Bench noted, if not for the arrival of Ozzie Smith, Concepción probably would have won ten Gold Gloves. Center fielder Cesar Gerónimo won one of four consecutive Gold Gloves in 1976.

Not to compare my 1971 Hackensack, New Jersey, high school baseball team with any of the above-mentioned teams, but we too were strong up the middle. Anchored by first team All-County catcher Art Sarro and first-team All-County shortstop Tom D'Arminio, we had a solid defense all around, including the middle positions. I was a first team All-League second baseman and Joe Pistono, the best center fielder I ever played with or against and among the top hitters in the league, probably would have received league honors had he been a senior instead of a junior.

When Joe and I played together on the junior varsity team the year before, he made a play that I will always remember. Passaic Valley had a runner on third with less than two outs. Their batter hit a fly to medium-to-deep center field and the runner tagged up on third. It seemed like a sure successful sacrifice fly. But Joe uncorked a perfect, one-hop throw to home plate that, to the amazement of all, nailed the runner at home.

In the last game of the 1971 regular season, our record was 15-2 and we were playing the second-place team, Wayne Valley, with a record of 14-3. So we had to win to claim the championship outright.

In the first inning, Wayne Valley's fastest runner was aboard. He lit out to try to steal second, and Art threw a perfect strike to me covering second. Out!

The next inning, Art hit a tremendous home run to left field that rolled forever (we had no fences on our home field). I followed with my first and only home run in my high school career, a shot that also rolled a long way. Back-to-back homers.

In the fifth inning, Wayne Valley scored once to cut our lead to 3-1 and had runners on first and second with one out. But the next batter grounded to short, and Tom and I pulled off a 6-4-3 double play to end the threat.

We went on to win 4-1. Joe caught the final out, a fly ball to center field.

Fittingly, the four of us had all played a part in the victory.

Strong up the middle.

* * *

"Baseball's 'Brave New World'"

British author Aldous Huxley described his 1931 novel, *Brave New World*, as a "negative utopia," a parody of novels which portrayed a hopeful vision of the future. Set in a futuristic World State whose citizens are environmentally engineered into an intelligence-based social hierarchy, the book lays out a dystopian society that is challenged by two protagonists, Bernard and John.

Allow me to play protagonist in opposition to the Brave New World experiments that MLB is conducting in the minor leagues in the hopes of importing them to the majors.

For some changes, I am too late. We already have the pitch clock, which speeds up the game but takes away the tension of dramatic moments when the pitcher might need extra time to compose himself. Some pitchers work faster than others. Does anyone remember Luis Tiant's endless windup or Mark "The Bird" Fidrych talking to the ball or Al "The Mad Hungarian" Hrabosky walking off the back of the mound, then turning back and charging to the rubber? Now we have uniformity—baseball's Brave New World.

MLB has already increased the size of the bases (which Red Sox manager Alex Cora says look like pizza boxes); eliminated defensive shifts; extended the designated hitter rule to the National League; limited mound visits; imposed a three-batter minimum for relief pitchers (greatly reducing the lefty-righty mental chess that managers employ and I enjoy); allowed managers to signal for an intentional walk instead of making the pitcher throw four balls (doing away with the possible drama of a wild pitch); required batters to keep one foot in the batter's box during their at-bat (eliminating the natural tendency for a batter to step out to refocus in a tense moment); limited the pitcher to three pick-off attempts; and the crown jewel—started extra innings with a man on second base, which I put right up there with Huxley's depiction of citizens being engineered through artificial wombs.

MLB is not done yet. They have experimented in the minors with moving the rubber one foot back, increasing the pitching distance to sixty-one feet, six inches. MLB can sure spin a ridiculous gimmick, calling the change "meaningful without being disruptive." Fortunately, MLB hasn't adopted that one yet.

The goal is fewer strikeouts.

I would like someone to chart a graph. The Y-axis would be the number of strikeouts. The X-axis (although too subjective to chart) would be the number of hitters who are more concerned with launch angle and hitting the ball out of the park than getting on base.

I predict the graph would show a direct correlation.

Baseball has become "hit a home run, strike out, or walk" and neither the players nor the managers—and especially not the sabermetric-guided general managers—seem to care much about the strikeouts.

The reason everyone is striking out is that they are jumping out of their spikes trying to hit the ball out of the park. It is simple geometry to recognize that when you are uppercutting rather than swinging on an even plane, your odds of hitting the ball decline drastically. Also, if you are holding the bat down at the knob, you have less control and are less likely to make contact.

I see this tendency at the high school level in softball and baseball where even the smallest hitters hold the bat down at the very end, resulting in a longer time to move the bat through the strike zone.

Yes, pitchers have increased velocity and spin rate. But I'm sure bat speed has increased for all these MLB hitters who lift weights and work out year-round. They just need to apply that speed to making contact instead of trying to go yard with every swing.

I used to care a lot if I struck out. It is something that is actually under the control of the batter to a great degree by simply prioritizing making contact. But players don't seem too bothered by getting rung up anymore.

MLB has also experimented in the minors with a designated pinch runner who can be substituted at any point into the game as a baserunner—does anyone remember sprinter Herb Washington who played in 105 MLB games for the Oakland A's without batting, pitching, or fielding, playing exclusively as a pinch runner?—and a "double-hook" designated hitter, which would eliminate a team's right to use a DH if the starting pitcher doesn't go five innings, meaning pitchers would then have to hit for themselves.

The goal, according to ESPN, is "to see starters pitch longer into games, creating more value for them and increasing late-game strategy."

Isn't that what National League fans have been saying all along, that the DH killed not only late-game but all in-game strategy? So all of a sudden MLB wants that strategy back?

Next up: the Automated Ball-Strike (ABS) System. In other words, robot umpires. Rather than completely remove the umpire from the process, MLB experimented in this year's spring training games with a hybrid challenge system. Umpires called the game as usual, but each team had two chances to challenge a pitch per game. When challenged, the ABS system determined whether the call should be overturned. I can live with that, just as I already live with the timeouts for challenges in the NBA. But this could be the slippery slope to ABS for every pitch, thus eliminating the human element. I enjoy watching batters, pitchers, and managers react to the occasional awful umpire call.

Coming soon: the automated check-swing call. The only problem is that the MLB rulebook doesn't define a checked swing. It just says a swing is "an attempt to swing at the ball."

But I'm afraid all my protests, like those of Bernard and John in *Brave New World*, will be in vain. Baseball rules are not set in stone like the Ten Commandments. But neither should they be at the mercy of today's sabermetric gurus.

***

"Why Does Baseball Have a Pitcher's Mound?"

The other day I went with two friends to see the A's play in their minor league park in Sacramento. Don't tell anyone, but for the last two innings we snuck from our seats way down the left-field line to great seats close to the field and just to the right of home plate.

As I gazed out onto the field, my eyes fell upon the pitcher's mound. And I wondered, why does baseball have a pitcher's mound? Was there always a pitcher's mound? How would pitchers fare if there were no mound?

Here is what I found out.

In the earliest days of the game, there was no mound. Pitchers merely lobbed the ball underhand. There were no balls and strikes. The focus was on the batter hitting the ball.

A pitcher would throw as many pitches as needed until the batter struck the ball.

In the mid nineteenth century, the front of the pitching area was forty-five feet from home plate. The pitcher could not cross over the line. But pitchers began looking for ways to gain an advantage over the hitter. They started to take a running start, much like the bowler in a cricket match.

To reduce the pitching advantage, by 1864 a pitching box was employed to limit the pitchers' freedom. The three- by twelve-foot box prevented pitchers from taking a running start. In addition, they were also required to pitch with both feet on the ground.

Pitchers found new ways to gain an edge, putting movement on the ball and changing speeds to throw off the batters' timing. As a result, in 1881 the front of the pitching box was moved back to fifty feet instead of forty-five. In 1884, pitchers were allowed to throw overhand. In 1887 the distance was further extended to fifty-five feet, six inches.

In 1893, the box was replaced with a raised mound and a rubber slab twelve inches long and relocated further back to sixty feet, six inches from home plate. Pitchers had to touch the rubber with their back foot.

Baseball officials were trying to achieve a balance between hitter and pitcher. Increasing the pitching distance helped the batter, while instituting a raised mound helped pitchers, as it allowed them to gain momentum as they pitched downhill, adding velocity to their throws and making it more difficult for batters to square up.

The extra five feet was significant, as it cut down on the angle of the pitches. The league batting average increased thirty-five points in 1893 and another twenty-nine points in 1894.

Between 1893 and 1950, the only rule regarding the height of the pitching mound was that the top could be no more than fifteen inches above the playing field. Teams used this loose rule to their advantage, changing the height of the mound to play to the home team's pitching strengths or to throw off pitchers from visiting teams.

For example, as Arthur Dailey wrote, "As a means of utilizing to the full the blinding side-arm speed of Walter Johnson, Washington leveled off the 'mound' so completely that it was almost a depression instead of an elevation."

Bill Veeck, while general manager of the Cleveland Indians, had Emil Bossard, "the Michelangelo of grounds keepers," custom craft the Indians' mound to the preferences of the pitcher of the day. Veeck wrote, "Bob Feller always liked to pitch from a mountaintop, so that he could come down with that great leverage of his and stuff the ball down the batter's throat."

These adjustments were legal prior to 1950, when MLB made a rule that all mounds be exactly fifteen inches above playing field level.

Groundskeepers could still tinker with the contours of the mound. But with the growing use of relief pitchers, a mound customized for the starter did not always suit the home team's subsequent hurlers.

Ryne Duren, a relief pitcher for the Yankees, said, "Bob Turley wanted the mound at Yankee Stadium to be flat and since he was the top gun of the staff in 1958, the grounds keepers kept it that way. I preferred it to be sloped. One day I threw my first pitch and my foot hit the ground and I thought my knee was going to hit me in the chin."

Combined with a 1963 rule change that expanded the strike zone, pitchers began to dominate hitters in the extreme. 1968 is referred to as "The Year of the Pitcher," because average run scoring per game per team that year was merely 3.42, with 21 percent of the games ending in one of the teams getting shut out. Bob Gibson recorded a miniscule ERA of 1.12 and Denny McLean won thirty-one games.

In response, in 1969 MLB attempted to shift the balance in favor of the hitters by lowering the mound five inches to a height of ten inches. MLB also restored the smaller strike zone that was the standard before 1963. It worked; in 1969 the average run scoring per game jumped to 4.07 and then to 4.34 in 1970.

MLB has made no further adjustments to the mound height since 1969. However, there were discussions about adjusting the pitching distance to address the increasing strikeout rates. In 2021 an experiment was conducted in the independent Atlantic League in which the distance was increased to sixty-one feet, six inches to see if it could restore the balance between pitchers and batters.

The experiment was discontinued after that year. According to ESPN, "The sixty-one-foot, six-inch distance to the mound appears dead. Neither the data nor feedback from players or coaches in the Atlantic League last season suggests the extra foot had much effect."

I, for one, am glad to hear it. Adjusting the height of the mound is one thing. Changing the pitching distance, which has been the same since 1893, would offend me almost as much as the automatic runner at second base in extra innings.

* * *

"Bring Back the (Real) Intentional Walk"

In 2017 in its continual effort to speed up the game, MLB took away the need for a pitcher to throw four intentional balls outside the strike zone for a walk. Instead, the manager can just signal to the umpire for an intentional base on balls.

As with other modern-day MLB changes, that took a lot of fun out of the game.

Believe it or not, some pitchers who can paint a ninety-five-mile-per-hour fastball on the outside black of home plate get the yips when they have to soft toss an intentional ball. This can lead to some embarrassing moments, as in a September 2016 game between the Tigers and Twins.

With Tigers' pinch hitter Erick Aybar at the plate in the top of the ninth and runners on second and third—after they had advanced on a wild pitch earlier in the inning—Twins pitcher Pat Light uncorked intentional ball four over the head of catcher Juan Centeno. Justin Upton scored from third, opening up the floodgates for the Tigers, who scored six runs in the inning.

At other times, the pitcher seems unable to throw the ball far enough outside the strike zone. On June 22, 2006, the Marlins' Miguel Cabrera was being walked intentionally by the Orioles' Todd Williams when he took a surprise swing at the first pitch, just off the plate outside, and came through with an RBI single, knocking in the go-ahead run and sparking the Marlins to an 8–5, ten-inning victory.

Said Cabrera, "I looked at it and saw it was too close to the plate. And decided I would swing at it. It wasn't planned. They gave me time to wait and get ready to hit it. I've never done that before."

In September 2016, with runners on second and third, the Rays decided to intentionally walk formidable Yankee rookie Gary Sanchez and pitch to struggling shortstop Didi Gregorius. But when Enny Romero left a pitch close enough to the plate, Sanchez decided to swing and drove the pitch to the centerfield wall for a sacrifice fly, scoring Brett Gardner.

Spoiler alert, if you've never seen the 1976 movie, *The Bad News Bears*. In the last inning of the championship game, the Bears' Kelly Leak is up with the bases loaded and his team down four runs to the Yankees. The Yankees' coach doesn't want to take any chances and tells the pitcher to walk Leak. But Bears' coach Buttermaker tells Kelly to swing away on a 3-0 count. Kelly bombs one into right-center field. The three runners score and Kelly heads home. The Yankees' relay the ball to the catcher as Kelly slides. Unfortunately, the ump calls him out and the Bears lose by one run.

Then there was the intentional walk ruse, in which the pitcher and catcher appear to be throwing an intentional ball, then try to slip a strike by the batter. The most famous successful deployment of this technique was in the 1972 World Series, when the Oakland A's Rollie Fingers nailed a called third strike past the Reds' Johnny Bench after appearing ready to put him on base. Oakland manager Dick Williams played his part perfectly, coming out to the mound to talk with Fingers and pointing to the on-deck circle and first base, making it seem certain that they intended to walk Bench.

Similarly, back in July 1996, Cleveland's Dennis Martinez was on the mound and Tony Pena behind the plate. With a 3-2 count on Toronto's John Olerud, Pena walked out in front of home plate to signal for an intentional ball four.

Pena returned behind the dish, signaled again, and Olerud relaxed just enough to allow Martinez to slip a called third strike by him.

The traditional intentional walk resulted in some comical moments. In 1976, the Twins' Rod Carew was being walked with a runner on second in the eleventh inning. Carew had hit .350 or better in each of the last three seasons, so the strategy made sense. But Carew swung at the first two pitches just to get two strikes on him and encourage the other team to go after him. But they went ahead with the intentional walk.

I will also miss the home crowd booing the manager of the other team when the opposition decides to intentionally walk their player. The crowd is accusing the opposing team of being chicken. What San Francisco Giants fan wants to see Barry Bonds intentionally walked? The booing was a lot of fun.

Speaking of the intentional walk, we must mention the two times since the end of World War II when the manager elected to issue a free pass with the bases loaded. The first was to Bonds in 1998 and then to Josh Hamilton a decade later. Both cases were late in games with the pitching team ahead by two and four runs respectively. The strategy succeeded in both cases, with the next batter making the final out of the game.

There's at least one other aspect of the game that the new intentional walk has eliminated. Did you ever notice the box behind home plate? It's wider than the plate itself, but the catcher is supposed to remain within it. Here's the MLB rule:

5.02 (4.03) Fielding Positions

The catcher shall station himself directly back of the plate.

He may leave his position at any time to catch a pitch or make a play except that **when the batter is being given an intentional base on balls, the catcher must stand with both feet within the lines of the catcher's box until the ball leaves the pitcher's hand.**
PENALTY: Balk.

If you go back and watch intentional walks on YouTube, you will see that the catcher regularly steps out of the catcher's box before the pitcher releases the ball. But the umpires almost never called it. That curious rule is no longer needed. But nobody will miss it.

* * *

"MLB Pitchers Who Would Have Loved the DH"

There have been some great-hitting major league pitchers, like Babe Ruth. It's a good bet that the Babe would have hated the DH rule when he was still just a pitcher. On the other hand, there have always been the automatic-out kind of pitchers who spurred people like Connie Mack as far back as 1906 to advocate for a designated hitter.

The idea finally caught on in the American League in 1973 and the National League in 2022. Here are some of the best arguments for the DH (meaning, these guys were *really* lousy hitters).

Ron Herbel: 1963-1971, .029 Lifetime Batting Average: Herbel must have been embarrassed to step to the plate on a Giants team that boasted Willie Mays, Willie McCovey, and Bobby Bonds. In 206 lifetime at-bats, Herbel collected a total of six hits. He struck out 125 times and only walked eight times, giving him an on-base percentage of .065 and making him the worst-hitting pitcher in Major League Baseball history.

Don Carman: 1983-1992, .057 Lifetime Batting Average: Carman was used as a starter until 1990, when he became a fixture in the bullpen. National League fans were probably grateful, as they no longer had to watch him attempt to hit a baseball. In 209 total at-bats, Carman had a whopping total of twelve hits, all singles. In 1986, Carman went the whole season, thirty-one at-bats, without a hit.

Luke Walker: 1965-1974, .059 Lifetime Batting Average: Luke Walker pitched for the Pittsburgh Pirates during eight of his nine seasons and mercifully pitched for the Detroit Tigers in 1974, his final season, when he didn't have to pick up a bat. In 188 total at-bats, Walker struck out 107 times. All of his eleven career hits were singles. To put his batting average in perspective, imagine going to the plate twenty times and getting one hit.

Dean Chance: 1961-1971, .066 Lifetime Batting Average: A great pitcher, Chance won the American League Cy Young award in 1964 with the Los Angeles Angels, compiling a 20-9 record with a 1.65 ERA, fifteen complete games and eleven shutouts. He had a 2.92 career ERA. But he was as bad at batting as he was good at pitching. In 662 career at-bats, Chance struck out an astounding 422 times, giving him a 63.4-percent strikeout rate.

Clem Labine: 1950-1962, .075 Lifetime Batting Average: Clem Labine gained fame during the 1955 season for the Brooklyn

Dodgers, winning thirteen games, mostly out of the bullpen, and helping the Dodgers to win their first-and-only World Series title while in Brooklyn. But he couldn't hit his way out of a wet paper bag, as his minuscule average testifies. He did, however, hit three home runs in his career.

Dick Drago: 1969-1981, .077 Lifetime Batting Average: Drago was superb in the Boston Red Sox bullpen in 1975 when he helped them reach the World Series against the Cincinnati Reds. He spent his entire career in the American League and must have been grateful when the DH came along in 1973. He only had one plate appearance after that. But he compiled a dreadful batting record before then. In 274 total at-bats, Drago had twenty-one total hits, just four of them for extra bases.

Ben Sheets: 2001-2010, .077 Lifetime Batting Average: It's too bad Sheets didn't join the Milwaukee Brewers before they moved from the AL to the NL in 1998. That would have spared him much humiliation attempting to hit a baseball. In 436 total at-bats, Sheets collected three extra-base hits and struck out an impressive 206 times against just eighteen walks.

Mike Bielecki: 1984-1997, .078 Lifetime Batting Average: Except for one year in his fourteen-season career, Bielecki played in the National League, where opposing pitchers must have salivated every time he came to the plate. In 282 total at-bats, Bielecki recorded twenty-two singles and no extra-base hits.

Bill Hands: 1965-1975, .078 Lifetime Batting Average: You would expect a pitcher to have a good knowledge of the strike zone, and Hands at least demonstrated that, walking forty-eight times during his career. He wasn't very good at hitting strikes, however. In 472 lifetime at-bats, he had a 52.7 percent strikeout rate.

Doug Davis: 1991-2011, .083 Lifetime Batting Average: Davis was not a great pitcher. Generally the fourth or fifth starter, he compiled a career record of 92-108 with a 4.44 ERA. But he was far worse in the batter's box. In 412 total at-bats, Davis had six total extra-base hits and drew only four walks. He struck out 175 times.

Jeff Fassero: 1991-2006, .083 Lifetime Batting Average: From a batting standpoint, it was lucky for Fassero he went from being a starting pitcher to a reliever, where he didn't get many more opportunities at the plate. He struck out 151 times in 276 career at-bats for a whiff rate of 54.7 percent.

Wilbur Wood: 1961-1978, .084 Lifetime Batting Average: The great knuckleballer probably felt like he was trying to hit his own pitching when he stepped to the plate. In 322 official at-bats, Wood had just two extra-base hits and struck out a remarkable 189 times for an outrageous 58.9-percent strike-out rate.

This column first appeared in The Vacaville Reporter on June 30, 2020.

* * *

"MLB Pitchers Who Would Have Hated the DH"

In my previous column on this topic, I wrote about MLB pitchers who would have welcomed the designated hitter. Here, I identify pitchers (both living and passed on) who likely would have wanted to sustain their presence in the batting order.

Babe Ruth: With the Boston Red Sox from 1915-1918, Babe won seventy-eight games as the best left-handed pitcher in the American League. He was twice among the top ten in pitching and hitting categories for a single season: 1915 (wins; homers) and 1918 (ERA; everything). One hardly needs to prove his batting prowess, but here are the figures: 714 home runs, 2,217 RBIs, a .342 batting average, a .474 on-base percentage, and a .690 slugging percentage.

Micah Owings: In his six-year National League career (2007-2012), the 6-5 righthander was a credible pitcher, compiling a 32-33 record with a 4.86 ERA. But he stood out at the plate. In his rookie season, he hit .333 with four homers in sixty at-bats. The following year, he hit .304 in fifty-six at-bats. He was a .283 career hitter with nine home runs in 205 at-bats.

Ken Brett: Like Owings, the lefty was a solid pitcher, compiling a record of 83-85 over fourteen seasons with a 3.93 ERA. But he is remembered more for his prowess at the plate (after all, he is George Brett's big brother). Ken had a .262 career batting average with ten home runs in 347 at-bats with a .406 slugging percentage. His .310 batting average in

1974 was higher than six of the eight starting position players on his Pirates, a team that won the National League Eastern Division title.

Wes Ferrell: In 1931, the righty remarkably hit as many home runs (nine) as he surrendered on the mound. That year, he also threw a no-hitter against the St. Louis Browns while driving in four runs with a double and a homer. His thirty-eight career homers still stand as the record among players who pitched their entire career (home runs as a pitcher in the game, not as a DH like Shohei Ohtani). He had a lifetime batting average of .280 and drove in 208 runs.

Red Lucas: Here's a guy who defies all the stereotypes of pitchers that led to the dark day when the American League adopted the DH rule. Lucas pitched from 1923-1938 in the National League with a 157-135 record and a 3.72 ERA. But what made him stand out was that he was used regularly as a pinch-hitter. He had 437 at-bats and 114 hits as a stand-in, both top-ten among pinch-hitters. He also had a .281 career batting average.

Jim Tobin: The Boston Braves starter became the only pitcher to ever hit three successive home runs in a game on May 13, 1942. In his fourth at-bat, he forced outfielder Ducky Medwick to the left-field fence for what was almost home run number four. Tobin was a career .230 hitter.

Bob Gibson: The Hall of Fame pitcher was also a threat with the bat. He compiled a career .206 batting average with twenty-four home runs and 144 RBIs. In his 1968 MVP season, when he compiled a minuscule 1.12 ERA, he also had the same on-base percentage (.233) as the batters he faced. He batted just .170 that year, but that was only .014 lower than his opponents' average—.184.

Rick Wise: The highlight of the righthander's eighteen-year career was June 23, 1971. He shook off the after-effects of the flu to no-hit the Reds in Cincinnati, driving in three of the four Philadelphia runs with two home runs. As a pitcher, Wise was 188-181 lifetime with a 3.69 ERA. He hit .195 for his career with fifteen home runs.

Don Drysdale: Since 1901, the career Dodger is one of only four players in baseball history to at least twice record a higher OPS (on-base percentage plus slugging average) than any of the position players on their squad: .852 in 1958 and .839 in 1965. Drysdale had a 209-166 career mark as a pitcher with a 2.95 ERA and 2,486 strikeouts. He also hit twenty-nine home runs.

Walter Johnson: The Big Train threw 38 1-0 shutouts and was the only man to win twenty games and hit .400 in the same season (1925, when he hit .433). The Hall of Famer's career pitching line is incredible: 417 wins against 279 losses, a 2.17 ERA with 3,509 strikeouts. But he was no slouch at the plate, turning in a career .235 batting average with twenty-four home runs, 255 RBIs, and a .342 slugging percentage.

Don Newcombe: Newcombe threw right and hit left and did both well. His 149 career wins against 90 losses gave him a .623 winning percentage along with a 3.56 ERA. He had a .271 lifetime average at the plate, belted fifteen home runs, and knocked in 108 in his ten-year career. Like Lucas, Newcombe was often used as a pinch hitter.

Shohei Ohtani: Ohtani is an anomaly for this column, as he loves the DH. He is a starting pitcher and DH for the Los Angeles Dodgers. The left-handed-hitting, right-handed-throwing Ohtani hit .310 for the Dodgers in 2024 with 54 homers and 130 RBIs. He didn't pitch in 2024 but was again a two-way player in 2025.
This column, which has been contemporized, first appeared in The Vacaville Reporter *on June 26, 2020.*

* * *

"So You Think You Know the Strike Zone?"

There is always something new to learn about baseball.

I thought I understood the strike zone. The other day, I watched a left-handed pitcher throw a sharp breaking ball to a left-handed batter. It appeared the pitch would be way inside, but it broke at the last minute over the back of the plate before it plunked into the catcher's mitt.

"Strike three!" called the umpire.

I thought that the ball had to cross the front of the plate to be a strike. Not so. Here is the MLB definition of a called strike:

"The official strike zone is the area over home plate from the midpoint between a batter's shoulders and the top of the uniform pants—when the batter is in his stance and prepared to swing at a pitched ball—and a point just below the kneecap. In order to get a strike call, **part of the ball must**

cross over part of home plate while in the aforementioned area."

So, the ball just needs to cross over any part of home plate. Maybe you already knew that; I didn't. A pitch passing outside the front of the strike zone but curving so as to enter the zone farther back is sometimes called a "back-door strike." I knew the term but had never realized just how back-door a back-door strike can be.

The advantage for that left-handed pitcher is that he threw a pitch that was virtually impossible to hit. The same is true when a right-handed pitcher throws a sweeper than starts way outside to a left-handed hitter, then breaks over the outside and back part of the plate at the last minute. That pitch is also almost impossible to hit. Ted Williams, one of the greatest hitters of all time, said the pitch on the low outside corner is the most difficult to hit. He calculated if he swung at that pitch regularly he would hit .130. Imagine then trying to hit the sweeper I just described.

Of course, no pitcher can always execute these kinds of pitches. But those who can with some consistency will handcuff batters.

This got me interested in the history of the strike zone.

In the mid 1800s, there was no negative consequence if the batter did not swing. Since the called strike did not exist, batters could wait all day for "their" pitch. In 1858, the National Association of Baseball Players, the first organization governing baseball, declared, "Should a striker stand at the bat without striking at good balls repeatedly pitched to him, for the purpose of delaying the game or of giving advantage to a player, the umpire, after warning him, shall call one strike, and if he persists in such action, two and three strikes.

When three strikes are called, he shall be subject to the same rules as if he had struck at three balls."

In 1886, the American Association adopted the first rule leading to the creation of a defined strike zone. The rule stated that the ball must be delivered at the height called for by the batsman—high (between waist and shoulders), low (between waist and at least one foot above the ground), or fair (between the shoulders and at least one foot above the ground). If at such height it passes over any part of the plate it is a strike. The following year, the National League eliminated the batter's right to call the height of the pitch and created the full strike zone, requiring the umpire to call a strike on any pitch that "passes over home plate not lower than the batsman's knee, nor higher than his shoulders."

In 1907, after the American League formed in 1901, Major League Baseball defined a "fairly delivered ball," or strike, as one that passes over **any portion** of the home base, before touching the ground, not lower than the batsman's knee, nor higher than his shoulder."

In 1950, MLB redefined the strike zone as "that space over home plate which is between the batter's armpits and the top of his knees when he assumes his natural stance."

St. Louis Browns' owner Bill Veeck, a showman known for publicity stunts, signed a little person, Eddie Gaedel, three feet, seven inches tall, to a contract, and had him bat in a game against the Detroit Tigers on August 19, 1951. Veeck trained Gaedel to assume a tight crouch at the plate. He measured Gaedel's strike zone in that stance and claimed it was just one and a half inches high. But when Gaedel came to bat, he abandoned the crouch. It didn't matter. The pitcher threw four straight balls, all high. That was

Gaedel's first and last appearance in a major league baseball game.

After Roger Maris's record home run year in 1961, MLB increased the top of the strike zone in 1963 from the armpit to the top of the shoulder. Pitchers began to dominate, as in 1968 when Denny McLain won 31 games, Bob Gibson posted a 1.12 ERA, and Carl Yastrzemski was the only American League hitter to bat over .300.

To help the dwindling offense, in 1969 MLB lowered the height of the mound from fifteen inches to ten inches and reduced the size of the strike zone to extend from the batter's armpits to the top of the knees.

In 1988, the strike zone was redefined as an area over home plate, the upper limit the midpoint between the top of the shoulders and the top of the uniform pants, and the lower level the top of the knees.

MLB expanded the lower end of the strike zone in 1996, moving it from the top of the knees to the bottom of the knees.

As automated balls and strikes (ABS) marches toward MLB acceptance, the system will have no problem adjusting to any future changes in the strike zone. But I will have trouble adjusting to a robot making the calls.

* * *

"Ode to a Foul Pole"

A few days ago at Fenway Park, Boston's Trevor Story sliced a fly ball down the right field line. Cleveland Guardians right fielder Jhonkensy Noel pursued the ball and reached out for it just in front of the foul pole. The ball bounced off his glove, hit the foul pole, bounced back into his glove, and then was jarred loose when his glove hit a fan.

The umpires called it a foul ball, but Red Sox manager Alex Cora asked for a review. The umps changed the call to a home run. Since Noel caught the ball in fair territory and the foul pole knocked it out of his glove before he established possession of the ball, causing the ball to touch the pole, it was ruled a home run.

That foul pole has a history. It is known as the Pesky Pole, in honor of Johnny Pesky, an infielder for the Red Sox in the 1940s and 1950s. Former Red Sox lefthander Mel Parnell is believed to be the first person to refer to Fenway's right-field foul pole as "Pesky's Pole." Parnell, a Sox broadcaster in the 1960s, enjoyed talking about how Pesky, a power-challenged lefthanded hitter, benefited from an occasional fly ball that would hit the pole and go for a home run.

The pole is just 302 feet from home plate. Story's shot would not have been a home run in any other major league park.

The foul pole, in general, has an interesting history.

Beginning in 1860 a foul ball post was to be placed 100 feet from both third and first base in line with home base. The post was used to help the umpire judge whether a batted ball landed in fair or foul ground. A more fitting name would be the fair ball post, since a ball striking the post is fair. In 1861 a new rule stated that "a line connecting home and first and home and third" must be marked by the use of chalk or other suitable material. That line is called the foul line, but again, would be more aptly named the fair line, since any ball that hits it is ruled fair.

In 1874, the foul ball posts were moved to the limits of

the ground, but the foul lines were not extended. In 1878 the foul lines were extended to the length of the field.

The foul pole serves as a visual aid. Its height and materials have evolved over time. The first foul poles were made of wood and not standardized in height. Today, foul poles in major league parks are metal and must be at least 30 feet tall, with 45 feet the recommended height.

When I attended an A's game at their temporary minor league park, Sutter Health Park, in Sacramento, California, last week, I noticed that the foul poles were not very high, perhaps closer to 30 feet than 45. This would make it difficult for an umpire to judge if a long fly ball is a home run or just a long foul.

But even in major league ballparks, there have been many cases of balls hit so high that the foul pole is of no help to the umpire. A famous instance happened at Montreal's Olympic Stadium in 1977, when slugger Dave Kingman hit a ball against the technical ring (the large concrete structure that surrounds the opening in the roof) in left field, over a hundred feet above the fence. The ball was ruled foul, but the umpires instructed ground crews to paint a line on the ring to demarcate fair from foul territory before the next day's game.

There have been other notable foul-pole related incidents in baseball history. In July 2012, at PNC Park, Garrett Jones and Neil Walker pulled back-to-back home runs off the right field foul pole.

Howie Kendrick hit a two-run home run off the right field foul pole at Houston's Minute Maid Park to give the Nationals a 3-2 lead over the Astros in Game 7 of the 2019 World Series. It is one of the most dramatic Game 7 homers in World Series history. The Nats went on to win 6-2 to take the crown.

Speaking of Pesky's Pole, in the eighth inning of Game 1 of the 2004 World Series at Fenway Park, with the Sox and Cardinals tied at nine apiece, Mark Bellhorn hit a two-run homer off the pole to propel Boston to an 11-9 win. The Sox swept the next three games to win the Fall Classic.

In Game 2 of the 2017 American League Division Series between Cleveland and New York, Francisco Lindor clobbered a grand slam off Chad Green off the right-field foul pole at Cleveland's Progressive Field in the sixth inning to draw the Indians to within 8-7 of the Yanks. The Indians went on to win 9-8 in 13 innings. Unfortunately for the Tribe, New York came back to win three straight and take the series,

Not as famous, but very dramatic was a two-out, three-run walk-off homer by the A's Marco Scutaro off the Yankees Mariano Rivera that hit the left field foul pole in Oakland in April 2007 to give the A's a 5-4 victory.

No discussion of foul pole dramatics is complete without revisiting Carlton Fisk's 12th inning, game-winning home run at Fenway Park in Game 6 of the 1975 World Series. Fisk pulled the ball down the left-field line and jumped up and down and waved his hands to the right, willing the ball fair. It clanked off the pole, which was later christened the "Fisk Pole."

Why did the camera stay on Fisk, despite the fact that cameramen were instructed to follow the flight of the ball? Because Lou Gerard, distracted by a nearby rat and unable to follow the ball, kept the camera on Fisk instead.

Guess who congratulated Fisk from the first-base coaching box? Johnny Pesky.

***

"Is it Time we Reviewed Replay Review?"

Video review in sports has become as controversial as the calls it is meant to settle.

First introduced in the NFL in 1986, it became universal in college football in 2004. While the system, now used in most major professional sports, has undoubtedly overturned wrong calls by officials, it has also slowed down the game and taken away the joy of many fans.

As Bob Ford wrote in the *Philadelphia Inquirer*, "The problem with replay came when it went from being a part of the telecasts to actually being a part of the games. Using replays to review decisions made by umpires, referees, and officials is totally understandable on one level—let's have a fair outcome by getting the calls right—but it also removes the human element of those outcomes and introduces a tyranny of technology."

Trevor Denton put it this way in the *Daily Trojan*: "Instant replay can be a good thing. It can help clear up controversial scoring plays and make sure teams don't get away with egregious fouls or penalties. But when overused, video replays make games choppy and often add new layers of dispute—exactly what they are supposed to prevent."

In any case, the use of this technology is here to stay and will probably expand. Major League Baseball may take it one step further and introduce robot umpires. Let's take a look at some infamous blown calls that almost certainly would have been overturned by video review had it existed at the time.

Diego Maradona's "Hand of God"

In the 1986 World Cup quarterfinal between England and Argentina, the late legendary Maradona initiated an attack that ended when England defender Steve Hodge sliced at the ball, causing it to fly into the air. Maradona, who had continued his run into the box, leaped into the air to contest the ball with England keeper Peter Shilton. Maradona reached the ball first and appeared to head it into the net.

Replays show that he actually punched the ball into the goal with his left hand, a move which he labeled the "Hand of God." Maradona struck again three minutes later, leading Argentina to a 2-1 victory. Argentina later captured its second World Cup.

Video technology would have caught the violation and Maradona may well have been given a red card.

Don Denkinger's blown call in the 1985 World Series

The St. Louis Cardinals were up 1-0 in Game 6, three outs away from a title. Kansas City's Jorge Orta led off the ninth with a slow roller that Jack Clark fielded and tossed to pitcher Todd Worrell, who stepped on first base a clear half-step ahead of Orta. Denkinger called Orta safe.

The Royals rallied for two runs and won the game 2-1. They took Game 7 the next night with Denkinger working behind the plate. He received a slew of hate mail, including some death threats, which eventually got the FBI involved.

Briana Scurry stops China's penalty kick in 1999 World Cup

Neither team could score a goal after 120 minutes, which meant penalty kicks decided the match at Pasadena's Rose Bowl.

After each team made its first two penalty shots in the shootout, Scurry stopped China's Liu Ying. The U.S. responded to Scurry's save with three more successful penalty shots, including Brandi Chastain's clincher to give the team its second World Cup title.

The U.S. might not have won if Scurry hadn't charged a few feet off the line before the ball was kicked. Goalkeepers are supposed to keep at least one foot on the goal line while a penalty kick is being taken until the ball is struck.

Scurry later admitted she broke the rule.

"Everybody does it," she told the *Los Angeles Times*. "It's only cheating if you get caught."

Missed pass interference: Saints vs. Rams on Jan. 20, 2019

In the NFC championship, the Saints had the ball on the Rams thirteen-yard line with 1:48 to play and the score tied 20-20. Drew Brees dropped back and threw a pass to Tommylee Lewis, who was met by Rams cornerback Nickell Robey-Coleman.

Robey-Coleman made contact long before Lewis had an opportunity to catch the ball. The pass fell incomplete. None of the refs threw a penalty flag and the Saints had to settle for a field goal. The Rams then tied the game before winning in overtime.

A pass interference call would have given the Saints a first-

and-goal with a chance to run the clock all the way down before a potential game-winning touchdown or field goal.

This play led to a rule change that made offensive and defensive pass interference calls and non-calls reviewable.

The perfect game that wasn't

In June 2010 in a game between the Tigers and Indians, veteran umpire Jim Joyce was assigned to first base. Detroit's Armando Galarraga was one out away from pitching a perfect game when Cleveland's Jason Donald hit a routine ground ball to the first baseman and Galarraga covered first base. He clearly received the ball before Donald's foot hit the bag. But Joyce called Donald safe.

After the game when Joyce saw the replay, he broke down in tears and admitted to reporters that he cost Galarraga a perfect game. In fact, last year Joyce and Galarraga told *The Athletic* that they would like Major League Baseball to overturn the call.

Of course, if MLB decided to do that, it would open Pandora's Box to everyone who ever had a call go against them.

Although the above examples can be used as a strong case for replay review, perhaps, as Ford concludes, we have created a monster: "Sports played by humans should be officiated by humans. It's that simple. If we can live with a fielder dropping an occasional fly ball, we should be able to live with a bang-bang missed call at first base. Trying to achieve perfection in an imperfect world never works, and there are centuries of history that can be replayed and reviewed to prove that."

This column first appeared in The Vacaville Reporter *on January 6, 2021.*

PART 5

Appreciating Baseball, the Thinking Person's Game

"Baseball's Dumbest Plays"

Even major leaguers make dumb mistakes. Here are some of the more memorable ones—mental lapses, not physical errors.

The Ultimate Bad Hop

On May 29, 2010, the Angels' **Kendry Morales** hit a walk-off grand slam in the tenth inning to beat the Mariners, 5-1. Unfortunately, when he took a celebratory jump onto home plate, he fractured his left ankle. He would miss the rest of the 2010 season and all of 2011 after several setbacks in his attempted return.

"It'll change the way we celebrate," said Angels manager Mike Scioscia. "It sure is exciting, but you always wonder if it's an accident waiting to happen."

The Tag that Never Was

On May 27, 2021, in the top of the third inning—with two outs and Wilson Contreras on second base—Cubs Javier Báez hit a routine ground ball to third base. Pirates third baseman Erik Gonzalez threw wide to first, pulling first baseman **Will Craig** off the bag. Baez stopped in his tracks so that Craig could not tag him. Craig, instead of merely retreating to the bag to end the inning, decided to try tag Báez.

As Craig pursued, Báez kept retreating until he was a few steps away from home plate. Meanwhile, Contreras was charging toward home plate attempting to score. Craig flipped the ball to the catcher, but Contreras slid in safely. Báez then took off for first base. The second baseman was late covering the bag and, as the throw sailed into right field, Báez took second base.

Said Craig after the game, "I messed up. I just kind of lost my mind for a second."

Maury Wills his Team to Defeat

Or, as another journalist put it, "Where there's a Wills, there's no way." Wills lasted less than a year as manager of the Seattle Mariners, making a series of horrendous decisions.

On August 6, 1980, in Wills' second game as manager, the Mariners were ahead of the Angels 4-3 as the Angels batted in the bottom of the eighth. With runners on second and third and two outs, pitcher Dave Heaverlo was facing anemic-hitting Rick Miller with even worse-hitting Dan Whitmer on deck. Wills decided to walk Miller intentionally. Angels manager pinch hit for Whitmer with Jason Thompson, who was batting .317. Thompson doubled to defeat the Mariners, 5-4. Asked why he gambled on the possibility of Thompson batting rather than pitching to Miller, Wills replied, "I was hoping Thompson wouldn't hit for Whitmer."

Managing by hope.

Fiddle While Rome Burns

On May 22, 2010, Washington Nationals center fielder **Nyjer Morgan** ran back on a ball hit to the wall by the Orioles Adam Jones. As Morgan leaped up to make the catch, the ball hit off his glove. Thinking the ball went over the wall for a home run, Morgan spiked his glove into the ground in disgust and began to stomp around. Little did Morgan realize the ball actually stayed inside the park and was sitting on the warning track while he was having his tantrum. Left fielder Josh Willingham raced over to grab the ball and throw it in, but Jones beat the relay home for an inside-the-park home run to put the Orioles ahead, 4-2.

Oops, kid! Give me that ball back!

On August 12, 2000, **Benny Agbayani** etched his name into New York Mets infamy. In the fourth inning, with the Mets leading 1–0, the San Francisco Giants loaded the bases. With one out, Bobby Estalella lifted a fly ball to Agbayani in left field. Agbayani, thinking his catch was the third out, sauntered over to the stands and gave the ball to a child, Jake Burns, and began to trot toward the dugout. Upon realizing his mistake, Agbayani sprinted back to the stands, pulled the ball from the hands of Burns, and, after more confused delay, threw toward home plate. Unfortunately for Agbayani, once the ball left the field, the play was dead, and all three runners were awarded two bases—causing the Giants to take the lead, 2–1. The Mets came back to win the game, 3–2, and Agbayani gave another ball to Burns.

The Third Time's the Charm

I know I said I would not include physical errors, but of the three errors **Tommy John** made on one play, the last was mental. So he makes the cut.

On July 27, 1988, John was pitching for the New York Yankees in a game against the Milwaukee Brewers. With Jim Gantner on first base, Jeffrey Leonard squibbed a ball back toward the mound. John muffed the grounder for the first error, then threw the ball wildly past first base for the second. Yankees right fielder Dave Winfield retrieved the errant throw and unleashed what looked like a perfect strike to home that would have nailed Gantner. But John, who should have let the throw go through, inexplicably intercepted it and then threw wildly past the catcher for his third error on the play, allowing Leonard to also score.

The three errors on one play tied the record for pitchers. Tommy John surgery is not the only thing the lefty is known for.

I've got to throw this one in

This is not from the major leagues, but I wouldn't put it past a big leaguer to do this.

My cousin Brian Sieger sent me a video of his son Luca, who recently graduated high school and is playing in the summer Atlantic Collegiate Baseball League. The video shows two Luca at-bats. In the first, he smacks a line drive to left. You can hear the center fielder yelling to the left fielder "In! In! In!" as the ball drops for a single. No harm there. But in the next at-bat, you can hear the center fielder yelling to the right fielder, "In! In! In!" The ball flies over the right fielder's head and Luca cruises into second base with a double. Apparently the center fielder likes to call "In!" at every opportunity.

* * *

"Baseball Gaffes Keep Us Entertained"

As the poet Alexander Pope said, "To err is human, to forgive divine." So, let us be charitable to the miscreants of our national pastime, even as we laugh at their foibles.

The Pittsburgh Pirates' **Ke'Bryan Hayes** gave us two for the price of one on a June night in 2021. Hayes lined an opposite-field drive in the first inning against the Dodgers' Walker Buehler that cleared the right-field wall inside the foul pole. Running hard and with his eyes on the ball, Hayes missed first base with his left foot by a couple of inches and kept going. After completing what he thought was his home-run trot, the Dodgers challenged, and after a brief video review, Hayes' home run was changed to an out.

But Hayes wasn't finished. In the third inning, he singled to center with one out. Pirates center fielder Bryan Reynolds then hit a fly ball to left field that AJ Pollock caught for the second out of the inning. Hayes tagged up and ran to second base. He made it in time but fell off the bag, where Chris Taylor tagged him for the final out of the inning.

The Pirates had earlier entertained us in May of that year with a play that has to be seen to be believed (you can find it on YouTube). With the Chicago Cubs' Willson Contreras on second base and two outs in the third inning, Javier Baez hit a routine ground ball to third baseman Erik Gonzalez. His throw to first baseman **Will Craig** was a bit up the line, pulling Craig off the bag. Baez stopped running to avoid Craig and backtracked toward home plate. Craig made the mistake of chasing him. All Craig had to do was touch first base for the final out of the inning,

Meanwhile, Contreras rounded third and sprinted home. Craig attempted a flip to catcher Michael Perez, but Contreras slid under the tag. Knowing he still had to reach first base safely for the run to count, Baez took off for first. No one was covering first base, and as second baseman Adam Frazier tried to get there, Pérez's throw sailed past him, allowing Baez to reach first safely and advance to second.

Craig, who had the reputation of being an outstanding fielder in the minor leagues, told reporters after the game, "I guess I'm going to be on the blooper reels for the rest of my life."

If video were available throughout the history of baseball, he would be in good company.

In 1931, in an April 26 game against the Washington Senators, the Yankees' **Lou Gehrig** hit what should have been a home run with Lyn Lary on first base. Lary thought the ball had been caught and did not run to second. Not paying attention and assuming Lary would be rounding the bases ahead, Gehrig passed Lary at first. If the rear runner passes the lead runner on the bases, the rear runner is called out. So, when Gehrig passed Lary at first, he was called out and given a single rather than a home run. That gaffe cost Gehrig the outright home run title because he finished tied with teammate Babe Ruth with forty-six round-trippers at the end of the year.

The **1926 Brooklyn Dodgers** pulled off one of the most famous baserunning blunders, now known as the "three men on third" incident. With Dazzy Vance on second and Chick Fewster on first, Babe Herman hit a long drive that fell in the outfield. As Herman rounded second base, the third-base coach yelled for him to return because Fewster had not yet reached third. Vance, who had just rounded third, misunderstood and returned to third. Fewster continued towards third, and Herman ignored the instructions and kept going to third. So now, Vance, Fewster, and Herman were all standing at third base, and the third baseman got the ball. Fewster and Herman decided to let Vance have possession of third and headed back toward second, but both were tagged out. The Dodgers, who could have had runners at second and third with nobody out and a run in, instead had a runner on third with two outs.

In 2003 at Pac Bell Park, the San Francisco Giants' Ruben Rivera represented the potential winning run as a pinch-runner for Andrés Galarraga at first base with a 2–2 score and one out in the ninth inning. Marquis Grissom hit a ball to deep right-center field. Rivera advanced to second base but reversed course two steps beyond it and ran back to the first-base side of second base, thinking that right fielder David Dellucci had caught the ball. Realizing that Dellucci had missed the ball, Rivera ran past second base but missed it, returned to retouch it, and headed to third. The relay throw by second baseman Junior Spivey would have been in plenty of time to nail Rivera at third, but the throw was low and bounced off third baseman Alex Cintrón's glove towards shortstop Tony Womack. Rivera then tried to score, but Womacks's throw nailed the sliding Rivera at home plate by five feet.

Giants broadcaster Jon Miller, who called the play, deemed it "the worst baserunning in the history of the game." You can find that one also on YouTube.

This column first appeared in The Vacaville Reporter *on June 10, 2021.*

* * *

"Baseball Bloopers Not Found on YouTube"

While it's fun to watch baseball bloopers on YouTube, some of the best bloopers were never captured on film or aren't available for public viewing. Here are a few of my favorites.

The 1962 New York Mets were so bad it wasn't even worth playing their two makeup games (they finished the season 40-120). They remained terrible through most of the decade. The right side of the infield was so clumsy that first baseman Dick Stuart was known as *Dr. Strangeglove,* and second baseman Chuck Hiller was called *Dr. No.* But the man who captured the hearts of New Yorkers with his ineptitude was first baseman **Marvin Eugene Throneberry** (his initials spell MET), better known as *Marvelous Marv.* Marv merits his own blooper show, but one example suffices to give you an idea.

At home at the Polo Grounds on June 17, 1962, the Mets gave up four runs to the Cubs in the top of the first, partly because Throneberry was called for obstruction during a rundown play. He appeared to have made up for it in the bottom of the frame when, with the Mets trailing 4-1, he knocked in two runs with a triple. But he was called out on appeal because he missed first base. When Mets manager Casey Stengel jumped out of the dugout to argue the call, the ump told him, "Don't bother, Casey. He missed second base, too."

Fred Merkle was a pretty good baseball player. Unfortunately, he is mainly remembered for a baserunning mistake on September 23, 1908, at the Polo Grounds when his team, the New York Giants, hosted the Chicago Cubs during a tight pennant race between the two squads. The score was 1-1 in the bottom of the ninth when Merkle, then nineteen, singled with two outs to put runners at the corners for New York.

Giants shortstop Al Bridwell then hit what appeared to be a game-winning single. But Merkle, seeing fans swarm onto the field in celebration, headed toward the clubhouse without touching second base. Cubs second baseman Johnny Evers retrieved the ball (or whatever ball he could find in the madhouse on the field) and stepped on second base. Merkle was ruled out, negating the run. When the umpires couldn't clear the field, they called the game because of darkness. The game was replayed on October 8 and became a pennant tie-breaker. The Cubs won 4-2 and went on to win the World Series.

Some thought the title was tainted, as the Cubs didn't win another World Series for 108 years.

Speaking of base-running gaffes, the great **Babe Ruth** has a pretty bad one to his credit. Ruth could run but would have done better not to in this situation.

The 1926 World Series between the New York Yankees and the St. Louis Cardinals came down to a deciding Game 7 at Yankee Stadium. The Yanks trailed 3-2 in the bottom of the ninth, with Ruth at first with two outs and Bob Meusel at the plate. Meusel had hit .315 that year and batted in 81 runs in just over 100 games. With Grover Cleveland Alexander pitching in relief, Ruth decided to try to steal second base. Catcher Bob O'Ferrell threw him out on a close play, and Meusel was left looking at the end of the season without ever swinging the bat.

Another notable blunder on the basepaths belongs to Philadelphia Phillies catcher **Tim McCarver**. In the first game of a doubleheader against the Pittsburgh Pirates on July 4, 1976, McCarver came up to face Larry Demery in the top of the second with the bases loaded. McCarver smacked a deep fly that cleared the fence for what should have been a grand-slam homer. But McCarver, running fast out of the box, passed teammate Garry Maddox, who was waiting between first and second base to see if the ball had cleared the fence. The umpire called McCarver out. Fortunately, there were less than two outs, so McCarver still got credit for a hit and three RBIs—a grand-slam single.

In 1895, New York Giants third baseman **Mike Grady** made four errors on one play, a record that still stands today. Grady bobbled a ground ball, ensuring the runner would reach first. He threw the ball anyway, which sailed wide of the bag and enabled the runner to advance to second for error No. 2. The right fielder retrieved the ball, saw the runner rounding second, and threw to Grady at third. Grady dropped the throw (error No. 3), the ball rolling away toward left field. Grady scrambled after the ball and attempted to throw the runner out at home. He threw it over the catcher's head—error No. 4.

Before Game 4 of the 1985 National League Championship Series between the Dodgers and the Cardinals, St. Louis outfielder **Vince Coleman** was warming up on the field when he did not notice the automatic tarp had been deployed and was subsequently rolled up in the tarp. The injury ended his season, and he was unable to play in the World Series when the Cards advanced. St. Louis eventually lost to the Kansas City Royals in that year's Fall Classic.

Joel Zumaya, a middle reliever and setup man for the Tigers, had a fastball that could reach 104 mph. Unfortunately, that fastball wasn't available to Detroit in the 2006

American League Championship Series against the Oakland A's. Zumaya couldn't pitch because of a sore wrist that Tiger General Manager Dave Dombrowski later disclosed was due to Zumaya playing too much *Guitar Hero*, the PlayStation 2 video game.

Okay, you can go back to *YouTube* and your video games now. But watch out for *Guitar Hero*.

This column first appeared in The Vacaville Reporter *on March 26, 2020.*

* * *

"When Major Leaguers Don't Know the Rules"

It never ceases to amaze me how so many major league baseball players don't know some of the basic rules of the game. The infield fly rule is a great example.

With fewer than two outs and runners on first and second, or bases loaded, an infield fly is ruled an automatic out at the discretion of the umpires, regardless of whether the fielder catches the ball. The batter is out, and the runners advance at their own risk. The rule was implemented in the 1890s to prevent infielders from intentionally dropping a pop fly to try to get a double play.

On June 9, in a game between Tampa Bay and Boston at Fenway Park, the Rays had Yandy Diaz on second and Jonathan Aranda on first with no outs when Junior Caminero popped the ball up near home plate along the third base line. Red Sox third baseman Marcelo Mayer misjudged the ball and dropped it. Then the fun began.

Diaz did not know that he did not have to run, so he took off for third base when Mayer dropped the ball. Catcher Connor Wong picked it up and threw to shortstop Trevor

Story, who was covering third base. The throw arrived well ahead of Diaz. But evidently Story didn't know the rule either. He just stepped on the bag and threw to second base, where second baseman Kristian Campbell took the throw and tagged out Aranda, who also did not have to run and was advancing on his own risk, but did not reach second in time.

Story's mistake is that since the batter is automatically out on an infield fly, there is no force play in effect, and Story needed to tag out Diaz. So Diaz was safe. The play made it evident that Diaz and Story did not know the rule, and Aranda is also suspect, as he didn't try to slide into second, probably because he also thought it was a force play. He would have been safe if he had slid.

On May 13, 2003, the San Francisco Giants were hosting the Montreal Expos. With one out and the bases loaded in the fifth inning, Barry Bonds lifted a pop-up in front of home plate. Home plate umpire Jim Joyce called it an infield fly. Four Expos converged on the ball, but no one touched it as it hit the turf. Neifi Perez, who was the runner on third base, apparently did not know the rule, as he ran toward home plate when the ball dropped. He would have been an easy out, as Expos third baseman Fernando Tatis picked up the ball a few feet in front of home plate. However, instead of tagging Perez (since the force play was off), Tatis stepped on home plate. Perez, who had stopped ten feet from home, tiptoed over to the plate and touched it and was ruled safe, since no one had tagged him. The Expos players, not knowing the rule, started arguing with Joyce. While they did so, the Giants runners on first and second also advanced a base.

Expos manager Frank Robinson came out of the dugout yelling—not at the umpire, but at his players for not knowing the rule.

On April 8, 2016, the Phillies and Mets were playing in New York. The Phils had Cesar Hernandez on first and Freddy Galvis on second with one out. Odubel Herrera hit an infield fly. Mets third baseman David Wright tried to catch the ball but lost it to the wind. Hernandez lit out for second base, even though he did not have to. Realizing his mistake too late, Hernandez stopped between first and second base. Wright picked up the ball and wisely ran right at Hernandez to make him commit. Hernandez, caught in the rundown, ran back toward first. Wright threw to the first baseman, who then threw to the second baseman, who tagged Hernandez out to complete the double play.

How about when an umpire doesn't know the rule? On September 26, 2021, the Cubs were hosting the Cardinals. With one out in the ninth inning and Austin Romine on second and Rafael Ortega on first for the Cubs, Frank Schwindel popped a ball up along the third base line. Third-base umpire Gabe Morales immediately raised his right hand to signal an infield fly. Cardinals third baseman Nolan Arenado slipped and fell, and the ball landed in fair territory on the infield grass.

Arenado picked the ball up and threw to shortstop Paul DeJong covering third because Romine, evidently not knowing the rule, was trying to advance. But DeJong didn't know the rule either, because he just stepped on the bag instead of tagging Romine.

DeJong then threw to second base to Tommy Edman, covering, as Ortega was trying to advance. But Edman didn't know the rule either, as he just stepped on second base instead of tagging Ortega. But second base umpire Doug Eddings called Ortega out, even though it wasn't a force play. Ortega, thinking he was out, jogged a few steps past second base. That's when Cardinals first baseman Paul Goldschmidt told Edman to tag Ortega.

However, before Edman could tag Ortega, Eddings called time, realizing that he had blown it by calling Ortega out on a force play. That meant that Edman's tag on Ortega did not count. So Ortega was safe at second and Romaine safe at third.

Home plate umpire and crew chief Bill Miller told the Associated Press that Eddings did not realize an infield fly had been called. But how could a major league umpire see a popup in the infield with runners on first and second and one out and not know the infield fly rule was called?

As reporter Dave Adam summarized, "The only people demonstrating understanding of the play and the rule were [umpire] Morales and Goldschmidt. Several professional athletes and umpires didn't know what to do about a rule they all learned in Little League."

* * *

"Worst Managerial Decisions in Baseball History"

Having recently purchased Baseball Mogul, a great computer simulation game, I am gaining new appreciation for how difficult it is to be a good manager. As I play the games in managerial mode, I am seeing how crucial good bullpen management and other strategic decisions are to the outcome. I have already managed to blow some late leads for my teams with poor pitching substitutions.

So let us give some grace to these major league managers who made some of the worst decisions in baseball history.

John McNamara keeps Bill Buckner at first base in Game 6 of the 1986 World Series

Every baseball fan remembers when Buckner let a ground ball by Mookie Wilson go through his legs in the tenth inning to hand Game 6 of the 1986 World Series to the New York Mets, who went on to defeat the Red Sox in Game 7. Many feel Buckner should never have been out there.

In Games 1, 2, and 5, Red Sox manager John McNamara had replaced Buckner with Dave Stapleton late in the games for defensive purposes. Buckner had been battling severe ankle injuries and Achilles tendonitis for years, and 1986 was a particularly bad season for his injured legs. Also, by the end of Game 6, Buckner was hitting just .179, so there was no point keeping him in the game for his offense.

McNamara has always defended his decision. He said, "Buckner was the best first baseman I had. And Dave Stapleton had taken enough shots at me since he didn't get in that ballgame, but Dave Stapleton's nickname was Shakey. And you know what that implies. I didn't want him playing first base to end that game, and it was not any sentimental thing that I had for Billy Buck."

Then why did he replace Buckner with Stapleton in the late innings of those three previous games?

Grady Little sticks with Pedro Martinez in Game 7 of the 2003 ALCS

It's the Red Sox again. I'm not trying to pick on them, but manager Grady Little's decision ranks up there with the worst. Martinez got the start, and Boston was leading New York 5-2 heading into the bottom of the eighth inning at

Yankee Stadium. Pedro had already thrown over 100 pitches, but Little let him start the inning. No big deal there. He got the first batter out. Then Derek Jeter doubled and Bernie Williams singled him home to make it 5-3. Pedro had now thrown 115 pitches.

Next up was left-handed hitting Hideki Matsui, who had already hit a double off Pedro in this game. The Red Sox had left-handed reliever Alan Embree ready to go. Little came out to the mound, but left Pedro in. Matsui hit another double, moving Williams to third. Little still stuck with Pedro. Jorge Posada blooped a flare into shallow center field. Three Red Sox fielders converged on the ball, but it dropped in and tied the score at 5-5. It was Pedro's 125th pitch. Finally, Little removed Pedro. Then Aaron Boone won the game for the Yankees with an eleventh inning home run.

Dusty Baker removes Russ Ortiz in Game 6 of the 2002 World Series

The San Francisco Giants led the Anaheim Angels 5-0 heading into the bottom of the seventh in Anaheim. Ortiz had been masterful, allowing just two hits on ninety pitches. After getting the first out, he gave up back-to-back singles. Dusty came out and, to the surprise of many, including some Giants players, replaced him with Felix Rodriguez, who promptly gave up a three-run homer to Scott Spiezio. The remaining Giants relievers fared no better, as the Angels scored three more in the eighth inning to win the game, 6-5. They went on to win the next game and the Series.

After Ortiz handed Baker the ball and began to leave the mound, Dusty stopped him and, in an unusual move, handed him the ball as a memento. Though some have claimed this gesture irked the Angels and fueled their comeback, Angel Tim Salmon dispelled that claim. He said he didn't see it, and if anyone else in the Angels' dugout saw it, they didn't talk about it.

Gene Mauch overuses starters, Phillies collapse

On September 21, 1964, the Philadelphia Phillies were in first place by six-and-one-half games with just twelve remaining. They then lost ten straight and the pennant, overtaken by the Cardinals. Mauch started right-handed ace Jim Bunning and left-handed ace Chris Short in seven of those ten games, four of them (two each) on just two days rest. Even if the Phils had somehow won enough games to make it to the World Series, what short of shape would their pitching have been in?

Yogi Berra pitches Tom Seaver on short rest in the 1973 World Series

The New York Mets led the Oakland A's three games to two, with Game 6 to be played in Oakland. Manager Berra decided to go with Seaver on three days' rest, something Seaver had done rarely in his career. But this meant if the Mets lost, Jon Matlack would also have to pitch on three days' rest in Game 7. That's exactly what happened, and the A's battered Matlack and won the Series.

But Berra had another option: George Stone. Stone was a starter for the Mets who had gone 12-3 with a 2.80 ERA in 1973. As Game 6 was not do-or-die for the Mets, Berra could have started Stone, leaving a better-rested Seaver for Game 7, with Matlack available out of the bullpen. Although

Seaver pitched well in Game 6, giving up just two runs in seven innings, the A's Catfish Hunter pitched better, and the A's won 3-1.

Reggie Jackson, who beat Seaver with a pair of RBI doubles, said, "That wasn't the same Seaver we saw in Game 3, except in heart and fortitude."

Tough decisions. That's why I'd rather manage in my computer simulation world than try the real thing.

* * *

"Baseball's Dumbest Trades"

Let's look at some of the worst trades in baseball history.

I've picked my top ten. They are not in any particular order, although the Babe Ruth trade has to be first on any list. It's hard to grade stupidity. On the other hand, hindsight is always 20/20.

Babe Ruth for mortgage on Fenway and $125,000 cash

The Babe had led the Boston Red Sox to three world championships in five-plus years when in 1919 owner Harry Frazee sold him to the New York Yankees for $125,000 and a $300,000 loan (Fenway Park as collateral) to produce a Broadway show. The next year Ruth hit fifty-four home runs; the Sox hit twenty-two as a team. The Babe would lead the Yanks to four championships and seven pennants. Boston would not win another World Series until 2004.

Nolan Ryan for Jim Fregosi

On December 10, 1971, the New York Mets dealt Nolan Ryan and three others to the then-California Angels for former All-Star infielder Jim Fregosi. The Mets were in desperate need of a third baseman and the young Ryan was erratic. He posted a 29-38 record over five seasons with the Mets, walking 344 and striking out 493.

Fregosi lasted less than two seasons, batting just .233 before being shipped off to Texas. Ryan turned into one of the best pitchers in the game. The Hall of Famer threw seven no-hitters.

Lou Brock for Ernie Broglio

When the Chicago Cubs traded Lou Brock to the St. Louis Cardinals for pitcher Ernie Broglio in 1964, it seemed like a smart move by the Cubbies. Broglio went 21-9 in 1960. Brock had batted .251 in 1963, slightly worse than the .262 he batted in 1962.

But after the trade, Brock batted .348 the rest of the year and helped the Cards win three pennants and two World Series over the next fifteen seasons. He stole 938 bases on his way to the Hall of Fame. Broglio played a little more than two seasons with the Cubs, compiling a 7-19 record before retiring.

Frank Robinson for Milt Pappas

On December 9, 1965, the Cincinnati Reds traded Frank Robinson to the Baltimore Orioles for pitchers Milt Pappas, Jack Baldschun, and outfielder Dick Simpson. Reds General Manager Bill DeWitt thought Robinson was "an old 30."

In his first year with the Orioles, the Hall of Famer won the American League Triple Crown, led his team to a World Series championship and was named AL and World Series MVP. Pappas went 30-29 over the next two-plus seasons before being shipped off to Atlanta. Baldschun and Simpson accomplished little with the Reds.

Joe Nathan and Francisco Liriano for A.J. Pierzynski

The Giants thought catcher A.J. Pierzynski was the missing piece to a playoff run in 2004. They sent Joe Nathan, Francisco Liriano, and Boof Bonser to the Twins. Nathan became one of the best closers in the game, and Liriano had some great seasons in Minnesota. Bonser was a serviceable arm for the Twins for a short time.

Pierzynksi was best known for being a cancer in the Giants' clubhouse and for grounding into double plays. He was dealt to the White Sox the next season and strangely enough, Chicago won the World Series with Pierzynksi as the backstop.

Pedro Martinez for Delino DeShields

The Los Angeles Dodgers traded Pedro Martinez to the Montreal Expos in 1993 for second baseman Delino Shields. Shields spent three unproductive years with the Dodgers, while Martinez became one of baseball's best starting pitchers.

Martinez won fifty-five games and lost thirty-three in four seasons with the Expos, winning the first of his three Cy Young Awards in 1997. In 1998, the cash-strapped Expos sent Martinez to Boston for Carl Pavano and Tony Armas

Jr. The Expos could not afford Martinez and would have lost him to free agency anyway.

Expos trade Randy Johnson to Mariners

In 1989, the Expos dealt Johnson, Brian Holman, and Gene Harris for Mark Langston and Mike Campbell. Langston was a solid pitcher, but the Big Unit went on to win five Cy Young Awards, make ten All-Star appearances, win more than 300 games, win a World Series, pitch a perfect game, and rank second all-time in strikeouts.

George Foster for Frank Duffy and Vern Geishert

On May 29, 1971, the Cincinnati Reds traded shortstop Duffy along with pitcher Geishert to the Giants for Foster. Geishert, who had played briefly in the majors in 1969, never played in the majors again. Duffy played just twenty-one games for the Giants before being dealt to the Cleveland Indians.

Foster became an essential cog in the Big Red Machine. He tore up the league with the Reds through 1981 and added four more respectable seasons with the Mets until retiring after the 1986 season.

Dennis Eckersley for three minor-leaguers

On April 3, 1987, the Cubs, who considered starter "Eck" washed up, dealt him to the Athletics for three prospects who never reached the majors. Converted to a closer by the A's, Eckersley became one of the greatest relievers in baseball history. He saved 387 games over the next twelve seasons, winning the Cy Young Award and MVP in 1992. In 2004, Eckersley was inducted into the Hall of Fame.

Mets trade Tom Seaver to the Reds

The Mets would not pay Seaver what he thought he was worth and just before the trade deadline decided to deal him to the Reds for minor league outfielders Steve Henderson and Dan Norman, pitcher Pat Zachry, and utility infielder Doug Flynn. None of the players did a whole lot for the Mets and the Reds got one of the best pitchers in major league baseball history. The deal became known as "the midnight massacre."

This column first appeared in The Vacaville Reporter *on April 18, 2020.*

* * *

"Great Goofs in Pro Sports"

To err is human, to forgive is divine.

But when our professional sports teams blow it, it is tough for us fans to forgive.

As Scott Janovitz noted in Bleacher Report, "Combining pressure with the spotlight can do crazy things to the mind. In fact, it's the primary reason the history of competitive sports is so littered with mental meltdowns and mishaps."

In a Week Two NFL game in 2020 between the Dallas Cowboys and the **Atlanta Falcons** in Dallas, the Falcons showed the world how not to handle an onside kick.

After scoring a touchdown to get within two points of

the Falcons with 1:49 left in the game, Dallas tried the onside kick. Greg Zuerlein kicked without a tee and the ball started slowly rolling forward. While the rules state that the Cowboys could not recover their own onside kick until it went at least ten yards, the Falcons' players could have recovered the ball at any point. But three Falcons stared at the ball as it trundled ten yards and Dallas's CJ Goodwin pounced on it. The Cowboys then advanced downfield and kicked a field goal to win the game as time expired.

"They definitely know the rule," said Falcons head coach Dan Quinn of his players after the game. But it sure didn't look that way.

Here are a few more notable goofs:

Fred Merkle was a pretty good baseball player. Unfortunately, he is mostly remembered for a baserunning mistake he made on September 23, 1908, at the Polo Grounds when his team, the New York Giants, hosted the Chicago Cubs during a tight pennant race between the two squads.

The score was 1-1 in the bottom of the ninth when Merkle, then nineteen, singled with two outs to put runners at the corners for New York.

Giants' shortstop Al Bridwell then hit what appeared to be a game-winning single. But Merkle, seeing fans swarm onto the field in celebration, headed toward the clubhouse without touching second base. Cubs' second baseman Johnny Evers retrieved the ball (or whatever ball he could find in the madhouse on the field) and stepped on second base. Merkle was ruled out, negating the run. When the umpires couldn't clear the field, they called the game on account of darkness. The game was replayed on October 8 and turned out to be a pennant tie-breaker. The Cubs won 4-2 and went on the win the World Series.

In the first game of the 2018 NBA Finals, with 4.7 seconds left and the Cavs down to the Warriors 107-106, George Hill tied the game with his first free throw but missed the second. **J.R. Smith** grabbed the rebound, but instead of lofting a quick put-back, dribbled the ball back toward halfcourt.

A wide-open LeBron James pointed back towards the hoop while yelling at Smith. With the clock nearly out, Smith finally passed to Hill, who barely had enough time to heave a shot that didn't even reach the rim. And Smith can be seen mouthing to James, "I thought we were up."

The game went into overtime and the Warriors won.

In the locker room, Smith claimed he knew the score was tied. But his coach, Tyronn Lue, told *Sports Illustrated,* "He thought it was over. He thought we were up one. It just happened too fast."

Roberto De Vicenzo, one of the greats of golf, won the 1967 British Open and had a chance to win the 1968 Masters. He pieced together a brilliant final round to shoot a 65 to tie the leader, Bob Goalby, and force an eighteen-hole playoff, scheduled to be played the next day.

But De Vicenzo's playing partner, Tommy Aaron, had wrongly marked down a score of par-four on the seventeenth hole for De Vicenzo when De Vicenzo had actually made a birdie-three. De Vicenzo signed the incorrect scorecard. The rules state that the higher written score signed by a golfer on his card must stand. This added a stroke and ended up costing De Vicenzo a shot at a second major, as Goalby won by a stroke and no playoff was needed.

"I play golf all over the world for thirty years, and now all I can think of is what a stupid I am to be wrong in this wonderful tournament," said Argentina's most successful golfer. "Never have I ever done such a thing."

In the 1993 NCAA championship basketball game, with nineteen seconds left and Michigan down 73-71 to North Carolina, Michigan's **Chris Webber** grabbed a rebound off a missed North Carolina free throw. Webber committed an obvious traveling violation as he headed up court, but the referee missed it. Webber dribbled coast to coast, then called a timeout when he was double-teamed in the corner with eleven seconds left.

There was only one problem—the Wolverines didn't have any timeouts left. That's a technical foul, giving UNC two free throws and possession. The Tar Heels won 75-71.

On Thanksgiving Day 1993, the Dallas Cowboys and the Miami Dolphins played on a field full of snow and slippery sleet. With fifteen seconds left in the game and the Cowboys leading 14-13, the Dolphins set up for a forty-one-yard field goal attempt.

Dallas' Jimmie Jones fully extended and got a hand on the football for a block. All Dallas had to do was let the ball roll to a stop, which would have resulted in a dead ball and Dallas gaining possession to run out the clock.

But the Cowboys' **Leon Lett** tracked down the ball and tried to pounce on it. It squirted away into the hands of a Dolphin on the one-yard line. That gave Miami another chance on a much shorter field goal, which they converted as time ran out for the 17-16 win.

We all make mistakes, mental or otherwise. Fortunately, ours aren't generally captured on camera for all the world to see.

This column first appeared in The Vacaville Reporter *on September 24, 2020.*

* * *

"Think Before Posting"

Back in July 2020, a firestorm erupted when DeSean Jackson of the Philadelphia Eagles re-posted a series of anti-Semitic messages. He made what appeared to be a sincere apology and took steps to patch things up with the Jewish community. In his apology, he said, "I didn't understand what this passage was saying" about one of those anti-Semitic posts. We will get into the specifics of what he posted later on.

I believe him. I have seen people re-post items on social media that I was horrified with, mainly because I knew the people well enough to know (or hope) that they didn't share those beliefs. Sometimes, I wonder if people even read what they pass along to their friends.

And I say that about Jackson even though I am Jewish. He made a ghastly mistake but has profusely apologized and promised to improve himself. I take that at face value and can forgive him for his statements.

What made matters worse was when former NBA player Stephen Jackson tried to defend DeSean Jackson. In a since-deleted Instagram video, Stephen Jackson said, "So I just read a statement that the Philadelphia Eagles posted regarding DeSean Jackson's comments. He was trying to educate himself and people and speak the truth. Right? He's speaking the truth. You know he doesn't hate nobody, but he's speaking the truth, the facts he knows, and trying to educate others."

Now that sure sounds like Stephen Jackson is defending DeSean Jackson's anti-Semitic comments as "the truth." But Stephen Jackson claimed he was misunderstood. He said he was speaking only about the fact that the Eagles did not cut Riley Cooper, a white Eagles receiver who was caught on video saying the n-word in 2013. Stephen Jackson said that DeSean Jackson was upset about that.

Said Stephen Jackson, "Y'all took the video the wrong way. I said he [DeSean Jackson] was right from a conversation we had before I got on *Live* about how they're handling him and how they handled Cooper when he said the n-word. They didn't handle them the same way, and that wasn't right. And that's what I was talking about."

But how do Stephen Jackson's statements that DeSean Jackson was trying to educate people make any sense if the two were having a private conversation? Even if we were to give Stephen Jackson the benefit of the doubt (he said he loves Jews), it would have been better if he stopped talking after that.

The next day, in a conversation with Fred Katz of *The Athletic,* when Katz was giving Stephen Jackson a chance to say that he was not claiming that Jewish people were trying to divide the black community, Jackson replied, "You know that for a fact? Do you know who the Rothschilds are? They own all the banks."

The claim about the Rothschild family has for centuries been the focus of anti-Semitic vitriol and conspiracy theories.

Stephen Jackson also posted this statement on Instagram: "Your race's pain doesn't hurt more than the next race's pain. Don't act like your hardships are more devastating than ours. And you wonder why we're fighting for equality."

One can only assume he is speaking about the Jewish race, given his previous comments. So he is accusing me and other Jewish people of discounting the sufferings of Black people in comparison to the sufferings of our race.

Wide receiver Marquise Goodwin, then an Eagle, left a comment on one of DeSean Jackson's posts. Goodwin said, "I wish people commented this much on a BLM topic." Goodwin later posted that "the Jewish community is lashing out at me" for that comment. He then posted this on Instagram: "I understand the Jewish community is mad at me for commenting on [Jackson's] page yesterday. I honestly don't see how I was being insensitive, disrespectful, or even supportive of his previous message. I never once said I agreed or disagreed with anything!"

I met Goodwin when he was a 49er, and he is a great guy, and I would not suspect him of anti-Semitism. And I understand what he is trying to say: that atrocities committed against the Black community are often overlooked.

But now let's look at those initial social media re-posts by DeSean Jackson. One was a quote attributed to Adolf Hitler (although Snopes has debunked the attribution), which said that white Jews "will blackmail America. [They] will extort America; their plan for world domination won't work if the Negroes know who they were." The quote also said that white Jewish people were secretly behind horrendous acts of violence against people of color, including lynching.

DeSean Jackson's re-posts also lauded Louis Farrakhan, the leader of the Nation of Islam. Farrakhan has made numerous anti-Semitic claims and comments, including about the Rothschilds. In a speech last year, Farrakhan said he was "here to separate the good Jews from the satanic Jews."

I think any race is entitled to define what is offensive to them. If Goodwin thought about how utterly offensive those re-posts by DeSean Jackson were, would he have tried to compare the degree to which Jewish people are upset with those comments to comments on a Black Lives Matter topic? I hope not. This is not a matter of comparing which groups have been most hated.

The sad part about all of this is that Blacks and Jews once literally walked arm-in-arm during the civil rights movement of the 1960s. But Farrakhan and his followers (and his re-posters) have helped drive a wedge between the Jewish and Black communities.

We cannot stop people like Farrakhan from denigrating minority groups. But we can be careful to read through everything we are considering re-posting before we hit the send button and it's too late.

Perhaps a bit of Jewish wisdom from the book of Proverbs in the Old Testament should guide us: "A gentle answer turns away wrath, but a harsh word stirs up anger." There are more than enough words of anger these days. Let's see if a gentler approach might help.

This column first appeared in The Vacaville Reporter *on July 9, 2020.*

***

"The Best Athletes are Students of the Game"

Wayne Gretzky once said, "A good hockey player plays where the puck is. A great hockey player plays where the puck is going to be." Great athletes are highly skilled. The best are also smart.

Oakland baseball fans will always live with the memory of shortstop Derek Jeter's "flip" play in Game 3 of the 2001 American League Division Series between the Yankees and

A's. With the Yanks leading 1-0 in the bottom of the seventh and Jeremy Giambi on first, Terrence Long drilled a Mike Mussina pitch down the right-field line. Shane Spencer retrieved it but made a wild throw over the heads of both cutoff men. Jeter came out of nowhere, running near the first-base foul line, grabbed the ball, and shoveled it backhand to catcher Jorge Posada, who tagged out Giambi, who chose not to slide.

Jeter downplayed the brilliant play, noting that he was just where he was supposed to be. It's a play that the Yankees ran in spring training. That's where the shortstop is told to be. So credit manager Joe Girardi for being smart as well.

Great athletes not only know where the ball or puck is going to be. They know where their teammates are going to be.

In the quarterfinal of the 2019 Women's World Cup match between France and the U.S., Alex Morgan made a beautiful lead pass for the U.S. down the right flank to Tobin Heath. Heath took the ball down to the end line. All eyes, including those of France's defenders, were on Sam Mewis, who was sprinting in the box toward the goal. Everyone anticipated Heath's crossing pass to go to her. But Heath delayed a bit, then sent her pass back behind Mewis, seemingly to no one. But in swooped Megan Rapinoe and blasted the ball into the net for a 2-0 U.S. lead.

"The most dangerous pass is a negative (backward) pass that is right between the penalty kick line and six-yard box," said Will C. Wood High (Vacaville, California) girls varsity soccer coach Andrea Daniels, who was in attendance at the game. "It's too far for a goalkeeper to come out and grab it, and usually a defender is sprinting toward their own goal, so it's hard to clear, and an offensive player is running towards goal, so it's an easier finish. I think she [Heath] just sent the pass to the right area, hoping someone would finish it."

Let's recall another stroke of genius—Arthur Ashe's unbelievable upset of Jimmy Connors in the 1975 Wimbledon final. Ashe was thirty-one. Connors, the reigning Wimbledon champ, was nine years younger and had won the 1974 Australian and U.S. Opens. Many thought he was invincible. After Ashe beat Tony Roche in the semifinals, he sat in the stands to watch Roscoe Tanner face Connors. Tanner had the fastest serve in tennis, but Connors sent back every serve faster and beat Tanner in straight sets. Ashe realized he could never outhit Connors. So he chipped, lobbed, and hit low to Connors' forehand volley, unlike Ashe's standard power game. It drove Connors crazy. Ashe won the first two sets 6-1. Connors fought back to take the third set, 7-5. Ashe won the last set 6-4 to secure the championship.

That was the tennis version of rope-a-dope, the blueprint Muhammad Ali employed to beat previously undefeated heavyweight champion George Foreman in the "Rumble in the Jungle" in Zaire in 1974. Employing a high-risk strategy, Ali leaned back on the ropes and allowed Foreman to come at him with everything he had. Ali absorbed many of the punches with his arms and body, but he also took some hard shots to the head. Ali repeatedly tied Foreman up and hung on him, further tiring him. He also taunted Foreman, whispering, "Is that all you got, George?" Foreman later admitted that the taunts dispirited him. He realized that was all he had. By the eighth round, Foreman was exhausted. Sensing the kill, Ali came out swinging and connected with at least three solid rights, the last one knocking Foreman down for the count.

In the 1973 NBA Eastern Semifinals between the New

York Knicks and the Baltimore Bullets, Baltimore's Phil Chenier guarded Walt Frazier. In a moment of frustration, with Frazier's back turned, Chenier intentionally delivered a hard punch to the back of Frazier's neck. Somehow, the refs missed it, but everybody watching that game on TV, including myself, stared at the set in disbelief. Did Chenier *really* do that? Why didn't Clyde (Frazier's nickname) turn around and clock him? As Bob Raissman of the *New York Daily News* described, "Frazier didn't blink an eye or look to return the blow. Clyde knew how to get even. He spent the rest of the night lighting up Chenier. It makes you wonder if Frazier would behave differently in this trash-talking, cheap-shot era of the NBA."

Let's credit some managers and coaches for smart and daring moves, too. Dick Williams was managing the A's against the Cincinnati Reds in the 1972 World Series. In Game 3, the Reds broke a scoreless tie with a run in the top of the eighth inning and threatened to score more in the frame. Cincinnati had runners on second and third with one out and the dangerous Johnny Bench coming to bat. The obvious strategy was to walk Bench and hope that Rollie Fingers could induce a ground ball from Tony Perez for a force at home or an inning-ending double play. But Williams never cared for the obvious. He had Fingers pitch to Bench. But when the count went to 3-2, Williams came out to the mound for a conference with Fingers and catcher Gene Tenace. He pointed to the on-deck circle and first base, seemingly wanting an intentional walk. But he told Tenace to set up behind the opposite batter's box as if he would receive ball four, then sneak back behind the plate. And he told Fingers to throw a slider for a strike. They did just that, the slider nipping the outside corner for a called strike three.

Then there was the Philly Special in Super Bowl LII. On fourth and goal, Eagles coach Doug Pederson decided to go for a touchdown instead of a field goal against the New England Patriots. Quarterback Nick Foles moved up behind his offensive line, and the ball was directly snapped to running back Corey Clement. Clement pitched the ball to Trey Burton, who passed to a wide-open Foles for the touchdown. Foles became the first player in Super Bowl history to catch and throw a touchdown, and the Eagles went on to win 41-33 and claim their first championship in 57 years.

It's great to be talented. It also helps to be smart.

This column first appeared in The Vacaville Reporter *on July 2, 2019.*

* * *

"Baseball's Smartest Plays"

Having previously written about baseball's dumbest plays, it seems only fair to highlight some of its smartest ones.

In April 2014, the Braves were on the road against the Mets. With Lucas Duda on first base for the Mets with two outs, Travis d'Arnaud hit a check-swing grounder to the second baseman. Freddie Freeman took the throw at first in a bang-bang play. The umpire called d'Arnaud out, but Freeman quickly fired the ball to third base to nab Duda for the fourth out. Why did Freeman bother? Because he realized that it would keep the Mets from challenging the play at first via replay review. A challenge would be moot because, even if successful, Duda would be the third out.

In July of this year, in a summer collegiate baseball

league, Ethan Surowiec of the Duluth Huskies, running to third base in the eighth inning of their contest against the La Crosse Loggers, fielded a ball before it could reach the shortstop. Why? Because the bases were loaded, there was one out, and it was a tailor-made double play ball.

The umpires ruled the play a "fielder's choice 6," which allowed for the bases to remain loaded. Surowiec was out. The runner on third base remained, while the runner on first base advanced to second base, and the batter went to first base. However, according to the Baseball Rules Academy, the umpires got the call wrong. Rule 6.01(a)(6) states that both Surowiec and the batter should have been ruled out. Here's the rule:

"If, in the judgment of the umpire, a baserunner willfully and deliberately interferes with a batted ball or a fielder in the act of fielding a batted ball with the obvious intent to break up a double play, the ball is dead. The umpire shall call the runner out for interference and also call out the batter-runner because of the action of his teammate. In no event may bases be run or runs scored because of such action by a runner." Okay, so maybe not the smartest play. But it sure fooled the umpires.

In Game 4 of the 2009 World Series against the Phillies, with two outs and nobody on in the top of the ninth and the game tied 4-4, the Yankees' Johnny Damon singled. With switch-hitting Mark Teixeira batting left, the Phillies shifted their infield defense so that third baseman Pedro Feliz would be taking the throw at second base if Damon tried to steal.

Damon did just that on Brad Lidge's first pitch. Damon executed a pop-up slide as Feliz took the throw. Damon was called safe and Feliz' momentum took him to the right side of second base. So Damon kept on running, correctly calculating that no one would cover third base. Feliz pursued in vain, and Damon had stolen two bases on one play. The Yankees scored three times in that inning to win the game and take a 3-1 Series lead. The Yanks went on to win the Fall Classic in six games.

In perhaps the greatest seventh game in modern World Series history, in 1991 the Braves and Twins were locked in a scoreless duel. In the top of the eighth, Atlanta's Lonnie Smith led off with a single. With Smith running, Terry Pendleton hit a deep drive to left-center that bounced off the wall. Smith should have scored easily but only made it to third base. Why? Because he apparently fell for a decoy by Minnesota shortstop Greg Gagne and second baseman Chuck Knoblauch.

The two middle infielders pantomimed a double play, Knoblauch pretending to field the ball and flip it to Gagne covering second. Smith, who had not glanced at home plate to track the ball, hesitated just past second base, which prevented him from scoring. Although Smith later claimed the Twins' infielders did not fool him and he was just waiting to make sure the ball wasn't caught, you can see him looking over at Knoblauch as he headed into second base. In any case, he never scored, nor did the Braves. Minnesota won the game, 1-0, in the tenth inning, on a pinch-hit single by Gene Larkin to take the Series.

Did you ever hear of a runner scoring on a foul pop to the first baseman? In 2016, Anthony Rizzo was on third base for the Cubs with less than two outs against the Colorado Rockies. Jorge Soler popped the ball up in foul territory between first and home. The pitcher and catcher drifted over toward the ball, which was caught by the first baseman.

Rizzo, who had tagged up, recognized that no one was covering the plate and sprinted home, scoring easily.

Rizzo was smart as a first baseman as well. In a May 2019 Cubs-Marlins game, the Marlins' Rosell Herrera led off the top of the tenth with a single. Attempting to advance Herrera to second base, Joe Berti popped his bunt high up in the air, making for what could have been an easy catch for Rizzo. Rizzo, realizing that Berti had slowed to a trot, let the ball drop, then picked it up, raced to first and stepped on the bag to get Berti out. All Herrera had to do was remain on first base, and once Rizzo touched the bag, he would have been safe. But Herrera became confused, attempted to advance to second, and was tagged out in a rundown. Double play.

The latest baserunning strategy, with two outs, runners on first and third or the bases loaded and a ground ball to the infield, is to have the runner on first go standing up as he steps on second base and continue past the bag. Why? Because a runner can reach second faster standing up than sliding. If he beats the throw, he then wanders well past second base. If the runner from third crosses the plate before the infielders can tag out the other runner, the run counts because the force play has been removed. Brilliant.

* * *

"Baseball's Best Trick Plays"

I have always felt that baseball is a thinking person's game. That's why I so enjoy a good trick play. Here are a few:

Before I retired, I covered high school sports for *The Reporter*, the newspaper of Vacaville, California. While covering a game between Vacaville High and Rodriguez High, Rodriguez pulled off a play I had never seen before: the double-suicide squeeze.

Vacaville led 7-4 heading into the top of the fifth inning. Danny Marino, who had relieved starter Kyle Bender, walked Jason Booker and hit Trentin Schmidt with a pitch to begin the frame. Kaden Wilde singled to load the bases and Booker scored on an infield error on a ground ball by Robert Searcy to make it 7-5 and keep the bags loaded. A passed ball scored Schmidt and put runners on second and third with no out.

Marino struck out the next hitter, bringing up senior designated hitter Colin Medeiros.

With both runners going, Medeiros laid down a bunt between home and the mound. Marino threw to first to get Medeiros, with Wilde scoring easily. But Searcy never stopped as he rounded third and headed home. First baseman Brewster Mott threw home but Searcy slid and beat the throw by an eyelash to give the Mustangs the 8-7 lead they would not relinquish.

In a 1982 College World Series game, Miami pulled off a great trick play against Wichita State. In a second-round matchup, the Hurricanes executed a gimmick that helped defeat the favored Shockers. Wichita State's Phil Stephenson, who had stolen 86 bases in 90 attempts, was on first base.

The Miami pitcher stepped off the rubber, wheeled around and pretended to throw hard over to first base. But he never released the ball. The first baseman pretended to lunge after the fake wild throw, and two Miami players rose to the steps of the dugout and pointed to where the fake throw supposedly went and yelled, "Ball! Ball!"

Stephenson, thinking the ball was bounding away past the first baseman, lit out for second base, whereupon the pitcher calmly threw to the second baseman, who tagged the bewildered Stephenson out before he even got to the base.

The same play has been used by several high school baseball teams, with the variation that the runner is on second base. The pitcher steps off the mound, pretends to throw hard to the second baseman covering, who pretends that a wild throw has gone past him. The center fielder races in as if to retrieve the ball, whereupon the runner takes off for third. The pitcher calmly throws to the third baseman, who tags the runner out.

A more basic trick play, and one that we used when I played high school baseball, is performed with a runner on second base. The shortstop comes from behind the runner who is taking a lead off second base and bluffs that he is going to cover second base, making sure the runner sees him. Then he retreats back to his position at shortstop, ahead of the runner, again so the runner can see him. The runner, now feeling safe, instinctively increases his lead off second base, whereupon the second baseman quickly runs over to cover second base. The pitcher simultaneously fires to second to pick off the runner.

You wouldn't think a Little League trick play would work in the major leagues, but it did on at least one occasion. The Brewers and Diamondbacks played in Arizona on September 14, 2024. In the top of the first, the Brewers had Garrett Mitchell on third and Willy Adames on first with two outs. With a 1-2 count on Jake Bauers, Adames lit out for second base. Diamondbacks catcher Adrian Del Castillo threw toward second base, but, in a designed play, pitcher

Brandon Pfaadt cut the throw off and fired to third baseman Eugenio Suárez, who tagged Mitchell off the base for the third out.

The Oakland A's took the first two games of the 1972 World Series from the favored Cincinnati Reds in Cincinnati. One of the Series' most memorable plays occurred in the eighth inning of the third game.

There was no score after six innings. The Reds struck in the seventh inning. Tony Perez led off with a single. Denis Menke sacrificed him to second, and Cesar Geronimo singled to center, scoring Perez to make it 1-0.

Left-hander Vida Blue came in to pitch the eighth inning against the Reds. Pete Rose lined out to first. Joe Morgan walked and moved to third on a Bobby Tolan single. A's Manager Dick Williams brought in Rollie Fingers to face Johnny Bench with runners at the corners and only one out.

Tolan stole second, which dictated an intentional pass to Bench, but Williams had Fingers pitch to Bench, with Perez on deck, rather than go for the potential inning-ending double play or the possible force out at home.

The count went full when Williams appeared to have a change of heart. He strolled to the mound and had a brief conference with Fingers and catcher Gene Tenace, signaling to them as if to give Bench ball four. Tenace went back behind home plate, stood tall, and signaled for ball four as he moved to the right.

Fingers went into his delivery, but Tenace jumped back behind the plate as Fingers was delivering the ball. Fingers fired a slider that caught Bench napping as it caught the outside corner for a called third strike.

It didn't matter; the A's never scored.

The hidden ball trick is perhaps the best known. Former

Red Sox second baseman Marty Barrett successfully pulled it off three times.

After covering first base on a sacrifice bunt, Barrett would keep the ball. The pitcher would pretend he had the ball and get ready to take the mound. The runner would take his lead off second base.

"Nobody was watching me," Barrett said. "So, I'd just reach over and tag him out."

* * *

"More Sneaky Baseball Plays"

I have written previously about some great trick plays at the major league, college and high school level. But I just learned of some new ones and was reminded of some old ones by my high school baseball teammates.

I extolled my Hackensack (New Jersey) High School baseball coach Dave Seddon, who recently passed away, in a previous column (see page 28). But now I am learning of some schemes he employed with teams after I graduated that he never used with our team.

Bob Meli, who was a sophomore when I was a senior in 1971, played varsity baseball at my high school in 1972 and 1973. He recently told me of one of Coach Seddon's trick plays. Bob explains:

"Seddon set up great pickoff moves at different bases with signals. When I played first base, with runners on first and second or the bases loaded, I played behind the runner rather than on the bag. I would signal to our third baseman, Carl Padovano, when I thought the runner on first was taking too big a lead. Carl would say something to the pitcher to alert him. When the pitcher went into his stretch, Carl would make a fist on his thigh. When he opened his hand, I would break for the bag and the pitcher would turn and throw to first. It worked great. Pitcher Tony Buono did it perfectly, as did Carl, and we picked off seven guys.

"We had a great pitcher who went on to play for the University of Pennsylvania who was very successful. But he would never throw over to first. He drove Carl and me crazy. We would have guys out by ten feet and he would turn and fake the throw. He was too good a pitcher to get angry with and he would be so apologetic. Great guy."

My guess is that the pitcher was afraid of throwing the ball away with runners on base.

With one of our pitchers, we didn't need a trick play. Rich Toscano was a great left-handed pitcher who was on the varsity for two years. As good as Rich was, the thing we remember best is his pickoff move. When I played shortstop, I marveled at how unaware the runners on first were that they had been picked off. They were charging to second base thinking they might have a successful steal, only to see me receive the throw from the first baseman and tag them out by fifteen feet.

If they stopped and retreated to first, Coach Seddon taught us a great rundown technique. As I slowly pursued the runner back to first (always run them back to the previous base, not forward to the next base), I would give a halfway downward arm fake once, then twice. The third time, I would give a full downward arm fake. Inevitably, the runner would turn and run right into me for the out.

Toscano's pickoff move is legendary. All-County shortstop Tom D'Arminio, who played four years of varsity ball, two of them with Toscano, described it this way:

"When Toscano pitched and Art Sarro (our All-County

catcher) caught, no one advanced to second. I don't know who taught Rich that move. Good guy, smart, and competitive. I just told [first baseman] John Russo that I would be covering second and to throw to the inside of the bag. I would be there. I don't know if John and Rich had a signal. A move like Rich's could fool a first baseman. Funny to see how many poor suckers fell for Rich's move. He never got called for a balk. Amazing."

Meli added, "That move was as natural as crossing the street for him. Sometimes certain guys just are gifted and able to do certain things in a sport because of their makeup or mindset, whatever, they have it and you never see it again. I never saw the move for fifteen years coaching or playing by anyone else. I am sure there are guys that have it, but few and far between."

What I remember most about Rich's move to first is that he was looking at home plate as he threw to first. He would raise his right leg straight up, and then avoid a balk by lowering his leg facing first base, but his whole body motion looked like he was throwing home until the last minute. Rich had the calm mental attitude necessary to pull it off. He was a soft-spoken, humble guy, but a real competitor. A great hitter also, he played first base when he wasn't on the mound.

Sarro and I had a signal when I played second base my senior year. If I saw the runner on second taking too big a lead, I would pat my glove on my left thigh a few times. Then Art would rifle the ball down to me on the next pitch. We ended a game that way against our arch rival, Wayne Valley, the first of the two times we played them. The game was on their field, and they were trailing 5-2 with a man on second base and two outs in the last inning. That was no time to be taking a big lead, but the runner did and I gave Art the signal. He fired the ball to me on the next pitch and we nailed the runner by ten feet. Game over.

We ended our season by beating Wayne Valley again, on our home field. They came into the game with a 14-3 record, and we were 15-2. So we had to win to clinch the league championship. No trick plays, but Sarro nailed their fastest runner on a throw to me at second when he tried to steal. And I executed a sacrifice bunt in the sixth inning which led to an insurance run. We won 4-1.

Small ball, trick plays, great execution—all make baseball a beautiful game.

***

"Use Your Baseball Brain"

In my column, "Lessons from Little League," I wrote that I love baseball because it is a thinking person's game.

Let me elaborate with some personal examples.

I grew up in Hackensack, New Jersey, where I played organized baseball from age eight on: Pee Wee League (ages 8-9), Little League (10-12), Babe Ruth League (13-15), and Connie Mack League (16-18).

I also played baseball in the school system, beginning in eighth grade on the junior high team. The team was made up of eighth and ninth graders. Our coach, Richard Buckelew, had a philosophy of playing only ninth graders. So I never played an inning that whole season. However, I learned to make myself useful as the first base coach.

During one game, I realized that I could see the opposing catcher's signs from the first-base coaching box. I soon figured out which fingers he put down for fastball and curve, which were the pitcher's only two pitches. I told Coach Buckelew, and he let the team know that if they wanted my help, they could look down the line at me in the coaching box and I would give them my signals (I forget what they were, but it wasn't banging trash cans) for a fastball or curve.

Our shortstop, Gene Roman, came to bat and I saw the catcher signal for a curveball. I signaled to Gene, and he clobbered the next pitch to deep right-center field for a home run, the key hit that helped us win the close game. The pitch seemed to come in harder than a curve, so I wondered if I had gotten the sign correctly. I asked Gene after the game, and he assured me that yes, it was a curve, just faster than the pitcher's usual curveball.

I advanced up the ranks of high school baseball, making the varsity my senior year. I tell that story in my column, "Listen to Your Coach," a tribute to my varsity coach Dave Seddon, who passed away recently. Among other things, Coach Seddon convinced me to change my stance prior to my senior year, which I was reluctant to do. But it made all the difference in my hitting once I took his suggestion.

In his last months before passing, Coach Seddon read my "Listen to Your Coach" column when his caretaker, Theresa Jones, a Hackensack High alum, found the column online. Here's what she wrote to me:

"Not only was he moved to tears by what you wrote, but he was so proud of you for your successful career as a sports writer. He told me what your stance looked like, the advice he gave you, and that you 'were a typical seventeen-year-old. He thought he knew everything because it had worked for him before, but after his initial resistance, he started to make the adjustments and he became a much better ballplayer. Matty was very smart; very analytical kind of kid. He was never gonna be a major leaguer, but he was a decent ball player. I loved working with kids like him. Give me one "coachable" kid, over ten naturally athletic kids who aren't, ANY day.'"

Another thing Coach Seddon taught me was to run down pop fly balls on your tiptoes, not on your heels. When you run on your heels, the ball looks like it is jumping around, making it difficult to catch. In a key game toward the end of the season against Teaneck High, when I was playing second base, the batter lofted a soft fly into right-center field with two outs and the runner (or runners, I can't remember) in motion, so a potential scoring threat. I realized that neither the center fielder nor the right fielder could reach the ball, so I sprinted back—on my tiptoes—and just as the ball was around the level of my knees, made a backhanded running catch to end the inning.

I was always an infielder—shortstop, second base, third base. When I was eighteen, I played third base for our Connie Mack League team. In addition to always being in ready fielding stance as the pitch came in, I always knew in advance what I was going to do with the ball if it was hit to me.

In one game, with men on first and second and less than two outs, I knew what I would do if a ground ball was hit to my left. Sure enough, here it came. I grabbed it, tagged the runner coming from second, then did a 360-degree spin and fired to first for the double play. When the same situation arose in another game, I had an alternate plan. Again, the ball was hit to my left. This time, I scooped it up, tagged the runner coming from second and still had time to fire to the second baseman for the force out on the runner from first. Double play.

Speaking of double plays, during the North Atlantic Regional Connie Mack tournament that summer (which we won and advanced to the World Series in Albuquerque, New Mexico), our ace lefthander Rich Toscano was on the mound. Rich had a great curveball which right-handed batters tended to beat into the ground toward third. In one of the games, with men on first and second and one out, I played parallel and close to the third base bag. Right on cue, the batter bounced one to me. I stepped on third and threw to first for the inning-ending double play. The identical situation arose in another game in the tournament—same positioning by me, same result.

Later in the tournament, when I was playing shortstop with a runner on second and less than two outs, he committed the cardinal sin of trying to advance to third on a ground ball hit in front of him. I scooped up the ball and fired to our third baseman, who tagged him out.

Not everyone is a baseball superstar. But we all have a brain. Use it!

* * *

"My 64 Years as a New York Mets Fan"

The New York Mets were created as an expansion team in 1962. I was nine years old, growing up in Hackensack, New Jersey, a suburb of New York City.

My dad, raised in Brooklyn, had been a Giants fan but later became a Dodgers fan, I think because of his admiration for Jackie Robinson. After the Dodgers and Giants departed New York City for the West Coast before the 1958 season, he was without a local National League team to root for.

So, like so many New Yorkers, he was thrilled when the Mets formed a team. The Mets cap is blue to recall the Dodgers and has the orange "NY" monogram to honor the Giants.

For their first two seasons, the Mets played in the Polo Grounds, where the New York Giants had played. My dad took me to a bunch of Mets games at the Polo Grounds.

Until 2024, when the Chicago White Sox lost 121 games, the Mets held the record for losses in a season in the Modern Era (since 1900). In 1962 they went 40-120 (they didn't bother to make up the two rainouts, as the Mets already had a stranglehold on last place).

The Mets first manager, Casey Stengel, memorably moaned, "Can't anyone here play this game?" Because the early Mets teams were so bad, anything we could find to cheer about was magnified one hundred fold.

On Memorial Day 1962, the Dodgers made their first visit to New York since playing in Ebbets Field to face the Mets in a doubleheader. A remarkable 55,704 attended, the largest crowd in the major leagues that season.

For the second game, my dad maneuvered us from well back in the stands on the third-base side to a couple of seats in the second deck right above home plate. As in the first game, the Mets lost, but we had a great view of an incredible play.

With Maury Wills on second and Jim Gilliam on first with no outs for the Dodgers, Willie Davis hit a liner that appeared destined to be a single to left field. But Mets short-stop Elio Chacon leaped skyward, pulled down the line drive in the web of his glove, and flipped to second base to nail Wills. Second baseman Charlie Neal fired to Gil Hodges at first, who appeared to stretch toward second too far and pull off the base. But the ball arrived before Gilliam, and the umpire gave the thumbs-up for the triple play. My dad said the ump had to overlook Hodges' questionable footwork with 55,000-plus fans in the stands rooting for the Mets.

We went to see the San Francisco Giants play the Mets at the Polo Grounds on "Willie Mays Night," May 3, 1963, with 49,4321 in attendance. I asked my dad, who had been a New York Giants fan from the days of Mel Ott, Bill Terry, and Carl Hubbell, who he would be rooting for. He said, "The Mets and Willie Mays."

With a lineup that included legendary former Dodger Duke Snider, the Mets faced off against the Cardinals on Friday night, June 7, 1963, in the Polo Grounds. Cardinals starter Ron Taylor carried a 2-0 lead into the bottom of the ninth, but the Mets managed to get runners on second (Ron Hunt) and third ("Hot Rod" Kanehl) with one out. As Snider strode to the plate, it looked like a redo of "Casey at the Bat."

The Duke did what Casey could not, jumping on a pitch from left-handed reliever Diomedes Olivo and smacking it into the upper deck in right field for a three-run walk-off homer and a 3-2 Mets victory. But when the ball struck the bat, all the fans in front of me—much taller than I—stood up, and I never saw Duke's shot land in the seats.

I can barely put into words the excitement of the 1969 season, when our perennial doormats defeated the Baltimore Orioles in the World Series, four games to one. As the last three games of the series were day games on weekdays, the best I could do was to listen on my transistor radio in the halls between my high school classes. So I didn't get to see center fielder Tommie Agee's spectacular catches in

Game 3 or Ron Swoboda's incredible grab in Game 4 until I watched the six o'clock news highlights.

The Mets were almost as miraculous in 1973. Going into a game against the Astros on July 11, the Mets were in last place with a 36-46 record in the National League East, twelve games behind the first-place Cubs. That's when reliever Tug McGraw inspired them in a clubhouse meeting with his now famous, "Ya gotta believe!" The Mets went 21-8 in their final games to finish 82-79 and win the division on the last day of the season in Chicago. They upset the Reds in the NL Championship Series and advanced to the Fall Classic against the Athletics, the defending champions.

My dad took me to the fifth game of that World Series at Shea Stadium. The Mets, behind Jerry Koosman, defeated Vida Blue, 2-0, for a 3-2 Series lead. But the A's won the last two games in Oakland to take the crown.

The Mets pulled off another miracle in Game 6 of the 1986 World Series (the Bill Buckner miscue game) and took Game 7. But by that time I had moved from New York to San Francisco, so the excitement of that season had to come through my TV rather than in person. Same for the Subway Series of 2000 and the 2015 Series against the Kansas City Royals, both losing efforts.

Now we have Francisco Lindor, Pete Alonso, and Juan Soto. It's harder to root for the Mets from three thousand miles away, but ya gotta believe. Let's go Mets!

* * *

"The Highs and Lows of a San Francisco Giants Fan"

N*ote: Still a lifelong New York Mets fan, when I moved from New York to San Francisco in 1980 I also became a Giants fan. When the two teams play each other, I lean toward the Mets.*

Ever since the San Francisco Giants won the World Series in 2010, 2012, and 2014, fans have been expecting another championship.

We're still waiting.

In 2018 the Giants hired Farhan Zaidi as president of baseball operations. A disciple of Oakland A's Billy Beane and "moneyball," Zaidi's analytics-driven approach worked in 2021 when the Giants won 107 games.

But the fans' trust in Zaidi eroded as the Giants went 81-81 in 2022 and then had two losing seasons. The Giants' management also soured on Zaidi, as they replaced him with Buster Posey, who played on all three of those World Series champions.

The fans let out a collective sigh of relief when Zaidi was let go. The writing was on the wall shortly before Zaidi was fired, when Posey, according to *The Athletic's* Andrew Baggerly, "personally dealt" with third baseman Matt Chapman to finalize a six-year, $151 million extension.

Zaidi's poor showing might have been more tolerable if the Giants had done a better job of developing players, but they are generally considered to have a bottom-third farm system. He also failed at acquiring enough good young players. Only one of Zaidi's first four first-round picks has reached the majors, and there are legitimate questions about the other three.

Too often the Giants ran out of depth, which frustrated many within the organization who had believed that Zaidi's greatest strength was building a forty-man roster. As Alex Pavlovic wrote, "Many of Zaidi's most controversial moves actually made a lot of sense on paper, but there was a coldness to them, and over time that added up. The most notable example came a couple of years ago, when the Giants agreed to terms with Carlos Correa without giving Brandon Crawford a heads-up that he might be changing positions."

So when the Giants hired Posey late last September, hope sprang among the Giants' faithful. With the future Hall of Famer leading, depending as much on his great baseball instincts as on analytics, fans hoped for a Giants resurgence.

In the off season, Posey made a bold free agent signing of Willy Adames for seven years and $182 million. Paired with Chapman, it would give the Giants a premier defensive left side of the infield. In 2024 Adames hit 32 homers for the Milwaukee Brewers and drove in 112 runs.

San Francisco also acquired future Hall of Famer Justin Verlander. Even at 42 years old, Verlander seemed like an excellent addition.

The Giants were expecting big things from Jung Hoo Lee, the South Korean center fielder who lost 2024 to injury.

For much of the first half of 2025, those hopes were fulfilled. The Giants stayed neck-and-neck with the Dodgers for first place. In the early months, the hitting was strong. The pitching improved as the season progressed, especially from the bullpen.

But before long, the wheels began to fall off. As of June 28, Adames is hitting .211 with 10 homers and just 37 RBIS. Lee has nosedived into a prolonged slump. The bullpen is in a tailspin. Chapman is out with an injury. Now both of his backups, Casey Schmitt and Christian Koss, are on the injured list.

The whole team is in a prolonged slump. Hitting with runners in scoring position has been abysmal. Verlander has pitched well, but has yet to win a game thanks to no run support. Robbie Ray, the outstanding southpaw with a record of 8-3 and a 2.75 ERA, has also been victimized by paltry offense.

Posey made another bold move in mid-June, acquiring Rafael Devers from the Red Sox in a blockbuster trade. Devers has contributed but has yet to pick up steam, especially in the power department.

As of June 28, the Giants are hitting .230 as a team, twenty-fifth out of the thirty major league teams. They rank twenty-fifth in home runs and twenty-fourth in OPS. They have lost twelve of their last seventeen games and fallen nine games behind the first-place Dodgers.

They keep finding new ways to lose. Their recent road trip started with a three-game series against the abysmal Chicago White Sox. They beat the Sox in the first game, 3-1, but in a portent of things to come, Brett Wisely was picked off first base. In game two, Wisely was on third and Koss on second with no outs and Devers at the plate. As Devers swung and missed to strike out, Wisely took a few steps toward home, trying to get a good jump if Devers hit a ground ball. The catcher threw a strike to the third baseman to nail him. Double play. They lost the game 1-0.

In the final game of the series, behind a strong six innings from Verlander, the Giants led 2-1 until the Sox scored four runs in the seventh. Then, in the top of the eighth, San Francisco loaded the bases with one out and their best hitter, Heliot Ramos at the plate. He grounded into a double play.

If the Giants weren't already feeling snake bit, the Diamondbacks delivered the *coup de grâce* the next day in Arizona. With the score 2-2 in the eighth, Koss hit a fly ball to deep left-center field. As the left fielder leapt for the ball, a fan leaned over the wall and caught it. It appeared on replay that the ball would have hit the top of the wall and bounced over for a home run. But the umps called it a ground-rule double. Devers struck out for the second out. Then Ramos was called out on strikes on a pitch that looked outside. Giants manager Bob Melvin had had enough and got himself tossed from the game for arguing that call. The Giants lost.

No one is blaming Posey for the Giants' struggles. He secured Chapman, Adames, and Devers, all with proven track records. Melvin is managing well. Unlike in the Zaidi years, the lineups have been stable. But, as Casey Stengel moaned about the New York Mets in their inaugural 1962 season, "Can't anybody here play this game?"

* * *

"When Fans Get it Wrong in Baseball All-Star Voting"

Baseball fans may hate me for this, but allowing them to pick the starters for the MLB All-Star team is unfair to the players.

The first All-Star Game was in 1933 at the White Sox' Comiskey Park. Chicago sportswriter Arch Ward brought it about, helping to revitalize a game that had been wounded by World War I, the Black Sox scandal, and then the Great Depression.

All-Star selections were made in part by the two managers and in part by the fans, who clipped ballots from the *Chicago Tribune* and mailed them in. From 1935 through

1946, the managers picked the entire All-Star rosters. In 1947 the fans regained some clout and were tasked with electing the eight starting position players, just as they are today.

But then came the 1957 vote. Cincinnati fans stuffed the ballot boxes and elected seven Reds to the starting lineup. Commissioner Ford Frick responded by pulling Gus Bell and Wally Post from the lineup and replacing them with Hank Aaron and Willie Mays. Then he took away the fans' voting privileges.

So managers, coaches, and players had exclusive control over the process until 1970. With interest in the All-Star game waning, commissioner Bowie Kuhn returned part of the voting to the paying customers.

In 2003, after some complaining that the All-Star managers were filling the bench and pitching staff with their own players, MLB gave players a larger say. And that's pretty much where we are today. Fans pick the starting lineup players. MLB players vote on five starting pitchers, three relievers, and eight reserves. Any remaining spots are filled by the Commissioner's Office to ensure that each roster reaches thirty-two players and that each team has at least one representative.

But allowing the fans to pick the starting nine (including the designated hitter) for each league continues to produce some inequities. I am not saying that fans are not knowledgeable. But they are understandably biased toward their hometown players. And with fans being allowed to cast five votes every twenty-four hours, it is inevitable that players in big-town markets such as Los Angeles and New York will receive a skewed percentage of the votes.

For example, this year the Dodgers' Teoscar Hernandez, although not named to the All-Star team, was an outfield finalist ahead of the Washington Nationals' James Wood. Wood is so feared by National League hurlers that on June 29 the Angels intentionally walked him four times.

As of July 7, Hernandez was hitting .257 with 14 home runs and 54 runs batted in. Wood was batting .288 with 23 homers and 67 RBIs. Yet Hernandez received more than a million more votes than Wood. In fact, eight of the Dodgers nine starters were finalists. Fortunately, the players selected Wood as a reserve. This makes a strong case for allowing the players to select the starters as well.

Atlanta Braves' Ronald Acuna, Jr. is a starting NL outfielder in the All-Star game ahead of Wood, yet Acuna has only played forty games this season. He has put up good numbers, but his high vote total is more a nod to his past four All-Star selections and his star status.

In the American League, the Minnesota Twins' Byron Buxton didn't even make it as a finalist, despite having better numbers than the Detroit Tigers' Javier Baez, who was selected as a starter. As of July 7, Baez was hitting .279 with 10 homers and 39 RBIs, while Buxton was batting .270 with 20 home runs and 53 RBIs. In fact, Mike Trout, hitting .233 with 14 home runs and 33 RBIs, made it as a finalist over Buxton. Again, fortunately, the players selected Buxton as a reserve. But he presents a strong case to be a starter.

Fans are sentimental. Baez is having a resurgence after a few disappointing years with the Tigers. And Trout, an eleven-time All-Star, is a perennial fan favorite.

When it comes to All-Star voting, how does a small market organization like the Tampa Bay Rays compete with the New York Yankees? The Ray's Jonathan Aranda has been the best first baseman statistically in the American League. Yet he was not one of the final two in the voting. That honor went to Vladimir Guerrero Jr. and the Yankees' Paul Goldschmidt.

As of July 7, Aranda was batting .319 with 10 homers and 48 RBIs. Goldschmidt was hitting .284 with 8 homers and 32 RBIs. The players were smart enough to vote Aranda on as a reserve ahead of Goldschmidt. But Aranda makes a strong case to be starting over fan favorite Guerrero Jr., who was hitting .277 with 12 home runs and 44 RBIs.

And how did Jackson Holliday of the Orioles make it as one of the two finalists for second base over the Rays' Brandon Lowe? It must be because of Baltimore's bigger market, because as of July 7 Lowe was batting .272 with 19 home runs and 50 RBIs, while Holliday was hitting .260 with 11 homers and 36 RBIs. Once again, the players noticed, as they picked Lowe over Holliday as a reserve.

The players are making better selections than the fans.

Being selected to the All-Star team is a great honor. Being selected as a starter is a greater honor. Should these honors be left for fans to decide? Players know other players best and are, for the most part, the most knowledgeable people about the game. They can analyze their peers' strengths and weaknesses.

The MVP and Cy Young awards are voted on by the Baseball Writers' Association of America. That is another option for All-Star selections.

However, I don't think MLB will ever eliminate fan voting. It would produce a huge uproar that would alienate the fans and negatively affect attendance and television ratings.

As Caleb Moody wrote for Just Baseball, "Fan voting certainly adds a unique personal aspect that undoubtedly keeps fans engaged, but it cannot be argued that it doesn't come without its frustrations."

***

"Go Fish!"

It's fun to watch baseball at any level.

I live in Martinez, California, a town of 38,000 about an hour north of San Francisco and the birthplace of Joe DiMaggio, whom I once interviewed (see page 199).

The Martinez Sturgeon, a team in the independent professional baseball Pecos League, have been here since 2019. Prior to the Sturgeon, we had a team called the Clippers (named for the Yankee Clipper, DiMaggio). The Clippers played one season in 2018 in the Pacific Association but folded after that year as their owner was indicted for a running a solar panel Ponzi scheme

The Sturgeon used to be the Mackerel. A fish by any other name . . .

I attended my first Sturgeon game the other night. I thoroughly enjoyed it. The Sturgeon play at Joe DiMaggio Field in Waterfront Park, near the marina. The team has a mascot, Sturgill the Sturgeon. (I happen to know the woman who was inside the costume), an announcer, streaming broadcast, raffle, refreshment stand, and great fans, many of whom don Sturgeon caps and jerseys. One of the fans had a cowbell, another a horn, and the locals love their Sturgeon.

My friend Pam is a Sturgeon host. That means she has taken two Sturgeons into her home for the summer, shortstop Tanner Graham of Fennimore, Wisconsin, and center fielder Mike Kelly of Philadelphia, Pennsylvania. For both, this is their first year on the team. As a host, Pam gets choice seats right behind home plate, and I was her guest.

The players are mostly college ballplayers who are looking to advance up the baseball ladder.

Some, like Kelly, have major league aspirations. Several players in the Pecos League have gone on to play in the majors.

Kelly plays a very smooth center field and is the fastest man on the team. A left-handed batter, he pushed a beautiful bunt down the third base line and beat it out for a hit. Then he stole second base.

The teams play a full nine innings, with major league rules, including the pitch clock. The Sturgeon faced off against the San Rafael Pacifics, who were in first place, just a half game ahead of the Sturgeon prior to the game.

The Pacifics carved out an early 3-0 lead against aptly named left-handed starter Elijah Pacheco-Martinez, and the Sturgeon were not having much success at the plate.

As at any level, good defense is the key to winning baseball. And the Pacifics' defense abandoned them, as they committed two costly errors. The Sturgeon took advantage, scoring two runs in the fifth inning, one in the sixth, and four in the seventh to take a 7-3 lead. They eventually won 8-4 to take over first place.

The key hit for the Sturgeon was a long line-drive double to center field by first baseman Andrew Curran, a bruiser who is batting .516 with 4 home runs in 64 at-bats this season.

Curran is less adept defensively. At one point a San Rafael batter bounced the ball between first and second base. Curran, who appeared to have a good chance of snagging it, didn't go after it, leaving his second baseman to scramble and lunge for it as the ball rolled into the outfield.

There were other mental errors. As the Sturgeon were

mounting a comeback, they had scored twice to cut the lead to 3-2 in the fifth inning. They had the bases loaded with one out. The batter hit a ground ball between third and shortstop. The third baseman ranged to his left, gloved the ball, tagged the runner from second who was trying to advance to third base, and fired to first base for the inning-ending double play.

The mental error was on the part of the runner on second. In that situation, he needed to stop before the third baseman could tag him, which would have prevented the double play.

The next inning, with the Sturgeon still down 3-2 with a runner on second base, the batter scorched a hard ground ball down the third base line, past the third baseman into left field. The runner scooted around third base, and, realizing there would be no play on him at home, slowed down and jogged the last thirty feet toward the plate. The problem was that he was unaware that the batter was trying to stretch his hit into a double. If the batter was tagged out at second base before the runner reached home plate, the run would not count. Fortunately, the batter slid in safely to second base, but just barely. Had he been out, it looked to me like the runner from second had not quite crossed home plate when the tag was made at second base, which would have cost the Sturgeon a run.

The other thing I noticed is that, as in the majors, a lot of these players hold the bat all the way down the end and are invested in launch angle, upper cutting their swing, trying to hit the ball out of the park, and, as a result, hitting a lot of lazy fly balls and pop-ups for outs. I still believe in level swings to make contact to put pressure on the defense. Oh well.

But overall, it was good baseball. I liked that the Martinez manager played some small ball, looking to advance the base runner with a bunt at one point. And there were a lot of stolen bases by both teams, a reflection in part that neither catcher had a major league arm. But even the speedy Kelly did get thrown out trying to steal second base.

As a traditionalist, I was also pleased to find that the Pecos League does not employ the designated hitter—the only professional league in the world that does not.

The enthusiasm of the fans is contagious. Many are regulars. And, as at major league stadiums, I found that hot dogs do indeed taste better at the ballpark.

Go fish!

* * *

"Why Baseball Is Still the Greatest Game"

I am in my seventies. I have seen a lot of major league baseball games in person and on TV. But I have never seen an ending to a game like the one between the Phillies and the Giants on Tuesday, July 8, 2025, at San Francisco's Oracle Park. I was there.

I live in the San Francisco Bay Area but don't get out to the ballpark very often. But my nephew had club level seats for this game through his company, and he, his brother, his dad, his uncle, my daughter, and I enjoyed the great view of the field from down the third base line.

I am a traditionalist when it comes to baseball. I'm a National League fan who has never liked the DH in the American League and groaned when the National League adopted it. I don't even like the pitch clock, though I have to admit it speeds up the game. I don't like that MLB has outlawed defensive shifts. And I hate the man on second base to start extra innings.

Having said all that, I found I can still thoroughly enjoy the game at the ballpark. There is nothing like being there and soaking up the atmosphere and sounds of the crowd, especially at beautiful Oracle Park.

Let me set the stage for this game. I grew up in New Jersey and have been a New York Mets fan since their inception in 1962. But in 1980 I moved to San Francisco and also became a Giants fan. So those are my two favorite teams. I am hard pressed to know who to root for when they face each other. I usually lean toward the Mets.

The Giants entered the game in second place, six games behind our mortal enemy, the Dodgers. The Mets were playing in Baltimore and were one game behind the Phillies, the Giants opponent that night. So if the Giants won and the Dodgers lost, San Francisco would cut LA's lead to five games. And if the Mets won, they would tie the Phillies for first place.

The game in Baltimore was already underway as we settled into our seats for the Phillies-Giants game. As I watched the scoreboard, I saw that the Orioles led 6-2 after seven innings. But then, as I followed along in the MLB app, Francisco Lindor and Pete Alonzo hit two-run homers in the eighth inning to tie the score. Then in the tenth, Juan Soto, who has hit .356 with 10 homers and 21 RBIs since June 6, singled in the go-ahead run in the tenth, and the Mets held off the Orioles in the bottom of the frame to win 7-6. And the Dodgers had lost.

So if the Giants could topple the Phils, the Mets would tie Philadelphia for first place and the Giants would gain a game on the Dodgers.

Things looked hopeful when left-handed batting Dominic Smith punched a single down the third base line to score Mike Yastrzemski and stake the Giants' All-Star pitcher Robbie Ray to a 1-0 lead. We hoped that one run by the offensively-challenged Giants might be enough for Ray, who is generally lights out.

But in the sixth, the Phils' Otto Kemp doubled with two outs to drive in a run and knock Ray out of the box. Spencer Bivens came on to get the third out and end the rally.

Then in the seventh, Kyle Schwarber, the Phil's ultimate strikeout, walk, or hit a homer guy, connected for his twenty-eighth round tripper, a two-run blast off Bivens over the right field wall into McCovey Cove to give the Phils a 3-1 lead.

As we headed to the ninth inning, the woman sitting behind us with her two young boys asked me if I thought the Giants could win, trying to give her boys hope. I told her that honestly, I doubted it. They had their chance in eighth inning when the top of the order got the first two men on, then went down one-two-three. So we would be depending on the bottom of the order in the ninth. She responded, "But there is a chance, right?" And my daughter said, "Yes, there is always a chance."

Facing a tough pitcher in hard-throwing right-hander Jordan Romano, Casey Schmitt led off with a double down the left field line. After Jung Hoo Lee popped out, Wilmer Flores lined a single up the middle that almost took Romano's head off, putting men on first and third.

Up came Patrick Bailey, a fine defensive catcher who was batting under .200 as he stepped to the plate. A switch hitter batting left, Bailey blasted the first pitch to deep right-center field. As the 40,000+ fans in the sellout crowd rose to their feet, it looked like the ball would carry over the high brick wall. Instead, the ball hit the very top of the wall and took a crazy carom back toward left field, rolling on and on along the warning track. Center fielder Brandon Marsh pursued it for a good fifty yards and then hit the cutoff man, who wheeled and threw wildly home to no avail. Bailey had easily circled the bases for a walk-off inside-the-park home run.

The 414-foot shot would have cleared the fences at every other major league ballpark,

"Off the bat, I just knew I got it well," Bailey said. "And then obviously, I saw it was towards Triples Alley. I was like, 'Oh, I've got to go. I've got to at least get to third here.' And then once I saw the bounce, I was like, 'All right, just don't fall over.'"

"You could play 100 more years here, and I don't think a ball hits right there on that spot," said Marsh.

As we celebrated, the woman behind me beamed, "I told you there was a chance!"

As Yogi Berra said, "It ain't over till it's over."

And that's why baseball is still the greatest game.

PART 6

Just for Fun

"Baseball Lingo 101"

When do you know you've been a baseball writer too long? It's when you're out for a walk with your wife, see ducks in a pond, and think, "Ducks on the Pond," which is baseball lingo. Here's what that saying means, together with several other of my favorite baseball metaphors.

Ducks on the Pond: Runners on second and third base, especially when the bases are loaded. The origin of the term for baseball is believed to have come from Arch McDonald, an announcer for the Washington Senators in the 1930s-1950s.

Baltimore Chop: A ball hit forcefully into the ground near home plate that produces a bounce high above a fielder's head. This gives the batter time to reach first base safely before the ball can be fielded. An essential element of Baltimore Orioles coach John McGraw's "inside baseball" strategy, the technique was popularized during the dead-ball era when teams could not rely on the home run.

Butcher Boy: A strategy where the hitter first shows he intends to bunt, pulls back the bat when the pitcher begins the delivery, and quickly swings at the pitch. Casey Stengel coined the term, inspired by the motion a boy in a butcher shop would use to cleave meat.

Bullpen: The area, generally located behind the outfield fence, in which relief pitchers warm up before entering the game. The origin of the term as used for baseball is unclear. Here are some theories: 1) It references the pen in which rodeo bulls were held before being released into the ring. 2) The term comes from nineteenth-century holding cells, which were often called bullpens—inspired by the bullish features of police officers. 3) It originated in the Polo Grounds, where relief pitchers warmed up near a stockade just behind the left-field fence. 4) Stengel suggested that managers came up with the term. Tired of listening to relievers "shoot the bull" in the dugout, the managers sent them off beyond the outfield fence where they wouldn't be a distraction.

Can of Corn: A high, easy-to-catch, fly ball hit to the outfield. The phrase is said to have originated in the nineteenth century. Clerks at grocery and general stores were looking for an easier way to reach canned goods—like corn—on high shelves, so they started using long, hooked sticks to pull them down. After dropping the cans toward them, they would catch them in their aprons—just like a fly ball.

Eephus: A slow, high-arcing lob pitch. The pitch first popped up in the nineteenth century but never entirely caught on. But Rip Sewell, a starter for the Pirates during the 1930s and 1940s, revived the pitch. After taking fourteen shotgun pellets into his right foot one winter, Sewell had to make profound alterations to his delivery. With his velocity diminished, he devised the lob pitch to keep hitters off balance. When he busted out his new pitch the next spring against the Tigers, Detroit outfielder Maurice Van Robys said. "Eephus ain't nothing, and that's a nothing pitch." No one knows what Van Robys meant by "eephus"—the best guess holds that "eephus" was really "efes," the Hebrew word for zero.

Mendoza Line: A batting average around .200, named after former major leaguer Mario Mendoza, who posted a .215 career average.

Pickle: When a baserunner gets caught between two bases and is besieged by infielders trying to tag him out, he's in a pickle. William Shakespeare used the phrase "in a pickle" in *The Tempest* to refer to someone drunk. When the term made its way to the States, the meaning shifted to signify that you're in trouble.

Texas League single: Outfielder Ollie Pickering is credited with giving baseball the term "Texas Leaguer," a pejorative slang for a weak pop fly that lands between an infielder and an outfielder for a base hit. According to the April 21, 1906, edition of *The Sporting Life*, John McCloskey, founder of the Texas League and then-manager of the Houston Mudcats, signed the twenty-two-year-old Pickering to play center field on the morning of May 21, 1892. That afternoon, Pickering strung together seven consecutive singles in one game, each a soft, looping fly ball that fell in no man's land between the first baseman and right fielder or the third baseman and left fielder.

Walk-off: A hit that wins the game for the home team in the last inning. Dennis Eckersley said that he originated the term, but, as he told the *Boston Globe*, "It was always a walk-off piece. Like something you would hang in an art gallery. The walk-off piece is a horrible piece of art." So the term was intended to describe a pitcher's dejected walk off the field after giving up a game-losing home run, but it soon grew into its own phenomenon.

Whammy: An evil influence or hex. It originated in the USA in the 1940s and is associated with various sports. The first reference to it in print appears to be in the *Syracuse Herald-Journal* in October 1939: "Nobody would have suspected that the baseball gods had put the whammy on Myers and Ernie when the ninth opened." Or, as Stengel said, "You put the whammy on him, but when he's [Sandy Koufax] pitching, the whammy tends to go on vacation."

This column first appeared in The Vacaville Reporter *on April 20, 2021.*

* * *

"Mascot Names That Need to Go"

I get the concern about mascots and team names that disparage others, and there are plenty of articles written and things said about those programs. But what about those names that are just plain ridiculous?

I understand the objections of Native Americans to specific team names. Dan Snyder, the owner of the Washington Commanders, tried to defend the former Redskin name as denoting "honor, respect and pride." On the other hand, Adrienne Keene, a citizen of the Cherokee Nation and faculty member at Brown University's American Studies and Ethnic Studies department, has this to say, "I would be honored and respected as a Native person if our treaties were honored, if our sovereignty was recognized, if our lands were taken back into Indigenous hands. Those are the type of things that honor me as a Native person, not a stereotypical image combined with a racial slur."

Any group of people can define what is disparaging to them, and we need to respect that. So, I get it. But some team names out there need to go, not because they necessarily disparage a particular group of people but because they are ridiculous. Here are ten.

The Jordan (Utah) High School Beetdiggers. The name was chosen due to the large areas surrounding the schools: sugar beet fields. Up until about 1950, at harvest time, classes were canceled during vacations of a week or two in October, which allowed students to assist with the harvest. That's a great explanation, but as an Athlon Sports blogger noted, "The nickname inspires fear. If you're a beet."

The Kimberly (Wis.) High School Papermakers. They play in Papermaker Stadium. Kimberly and the surrounding area are home to many paper mills, including Kimberly Clark. "With paper being such a large part of Wisconsin's history," wrote Steven Okonek for *On Focus,* "it is surprising that more schools do not take the Papermaker mascot." Not so surprising to me. Is that a name you want on your jersey when you go to battle in the football trenches?

Grafton/St. Thomas (ND) High School Spoilers. As that Athlon Sports blogger put it, "Isn't the nickname 'Spoilers' a concession that you suck and can only hope to spoil a good team's season?"

Cairo (Ga.) High School Syrupmakers. In 1986, ESPN named "Syrupmaker" the number one high school sports team nickname. I'm not sure if that selection was number one for weirdness or if ESPN was serious. During a driving rainstorm in the middle of a football game many years ago, workers at the local syrup plant brought over their raincoats labeled "Roddenbery's Syrup" to keep the players dry. Reflecting this heritage, the football team was named the Syrupmakers. The school mascot is a syrup pitcher.

Mount Clemons (Mich.) High School Battling Bathers. Named after the mineral baths that used to be in the area. Former NFL defensive lineman Wally Chambers is an alumnus. I wonder how much teasing he received from his Chicago Bears teammates when they learned his high school's nickname. Also, what is their mascot? A guy or girl in a bathing suit?

Watersmeet (Mich.) Nimrods. As Athlon Sports pointed out, "In the Bible, Nimrod was a mighty hunter. Nobody knows their Bible anymore. Today, a nimrod is merely a moron."

Orofino (Idaho) High School Maniacs. Orofino is the home of a mental hospital, State Hospital North. In 1993, the Idaho Alliance for the Mentally Ill wrote a letter to the school board requesting the mascot be abandoned because it stigmatizes and "perpetuates the old stereotype attached to the mentally ill." As it turns out, the name "maniacs" was first coined in 1927 after a feverish basketball game with neighboring Kamiah and had nothing to do with the hospital. The mascot logo depicts a yelling, jumping man with bushy black hair. The school board stated that the mascot "is not intended to depict a hospital patient enduring shock treatment as the alliance described." The board decided to keep the moniker.

Teutopolis (Ill.) Wooden Shoes. The wooden shoe has been around in this small town southeast of Chicago for over 150 years. Around 1860, George Dymann, an immigrant from Germany, came to the town and started making shoes out of wood. As Athlon Sports said of the team, "They're particularly loud on the basketball court. But slow."

Freeburg (Ill.) High School Midgets. This name was also contested, with the Little People of America urging the school district to change the nickname. The high school chose the mascot decades ago after a David-and-Goliath basketball game where Freeburg came out on top. The district elected to keep the name. "Once a Midget, always a Midget," Board Secretary Kim Towers said. "Our community is happy to be Midgets, and that's where it's at." In 2013, the *Huffington Post* labeled the Midget name as among the "most tasteless" in the nation.

Scottsdale (Ariz.) Community College Fighting Artichokes. Born during student unrest in the early 1970s, Artie the Artichoke was adopted as the school's mascot to express a difference of opinion concerning budget priorities. Originally intended to be a source of embarrassment, Artie has been embraced by students, athletes, staff, and the community as a beloved character. I would like to see them play the UC Santa Cruz Banana Slugs.

This column first appeared in The Vacaville Reporter *on June 12, 2021.*

* * *

"The Breakfast of Champions . . . and the Rest of Us"

As I sat eating my Raisin Bran the other morning (note to self: next time, get Kellogg's or Post, not the generic), my sports-starved mind strayed to the "Breakfast of Champions"—Wheaties. As a kid, I never believed I would become a champion athlete just by eating my Wheaties, but I used to enjoy looking at whoever was on the cover.

My breakfast reverie the other day led me to some Wheaties research. In 1921, a health clinician spilled wheat gruel on a hot stove and watched it transform into delicious wheat flakes. Washburn's Gold Medal Whole Wheat Flakes, introduced in 1924, soon became known as Wheaties. The product is a wheat-bran mixture.

Wheaties began its association with sports in 1927 through advertising on the southern wall of minor league baseball's Nicollet Park in Minneapolis, Minnesota. Wheaties sponsored the radio broadcasts of the Minneapolis Millers. A large billboard was provided in the park to introduce new slogans. The first slogan was "***Wheaties—the Breakfast of Champions***."

In the 1930s, Wheaties expanded its sponsorship of baseball broadcasting. In 1934, athletes began to be depicted on the side of Wheaties boxes, starting with Lou Gehrig. The 1930s and 1940s were Wheaties' heyday, as it expanded its testimonials to every sport imaginable, including circus and rodeo stars, jockeys, big-game hunters, automobile racers, speedboat racers, and parachutists.

The 1941 hit song "Joltin' Joe DiMaggio" mentions a case of Wheaties as a reward for a clutch hit by the Yankee

Clipper. Then, in the late 1950s, Wheaties began the first of several sponsorship deals with athletic legends who would appear on the iconic box and, for the first time, on the front. Olympic pole vaulter Bob Richards was the first Wheaties spokesperson, succeeded by Bruce Jenner, Mary Lou Retton, Walter Payton, Chris Evert, Michael Jordan, and Tiger Woods.

Since the debut of the front cover depiction of Richards, hundreds of athletes have been shown and promoted, including entire baseball, basketball, and football teams, while highlighting Olympic successes. Wheaties does not limit itself to current athletic stars, as special edition boxes have depicted baseball players from the early twentieth century and other athletes who were too early for Wheaties to cover, such as Jim Thorpe.

Around 1990, General Mills promoted "Picture Yourself on a Wheaties Box." For a fee, they would make a custom Wheaties box from one's photograph that was sealed in clear acrylic.

Back to athletes. Michael Jordan has the most individual appearances on a Wheaties Box—eighteen. And here are some Wheaties "firsts":

1934 – First woman depicted on a Wheaties box—aviator Elinor Smith

1935 – First woman athlete depicted on a Wheaties box—golfer and athlete Babe Didrikson Zaharias

1936 – First African-American athlete on a Wheaties box—Jesse Owens

1969 – First male golfer depicted on the front of a Wheaties box—Lee Trevino

1984 – First woman athlete depicted on the front of a Wheaties box—gymnast Mary Lou Retton

1986 – First NFL player depicted on the front of a Wheaties box – Walter Payton

1987 – First team depicted on a Wheaties box—1987 World Series Champion Minnesota Twins

1992 – First non-orange Wheaties box, colored red and black in honor of the Chicago Bulls

1997 – First automobile race driver depicted on the front of a Wheaties box—Dale Earnhardt

1999 – First professional wrestler depicted on the front of a Wheaties box—Stone Cold Steve Austin

2012 – Nine-year-old Samantha Gordon is the first female football player to be featured on a Wheaties box

2014 – First Mixed Martial Arts fighter depicted on the front of the Wheaties box—Anthony Pettis

2016 – First motocross racer to appear on Wheaties box—Ryan Dungey

To become a Wheaties expert, look for the ***Wheaties Breakfast of Champions Sports Trivia Game*** .

This column first appeared in The Vacaville Reporter *on May 16, 2020.*

* * *

"In Baseball, Any Day is April 1"

There's a group of people who are good at pranks and perform them not just on April Fools' Day but any old-time—baseball players.

Blaine Boyer, Atlanta Braves: "In the minor leagues in Scranton, we convinced one of our players that his hotel room was haunted and a ghost was trying to kill him, and he almost moved hotels before we told him. He packed his bags and was getting ready to move hotels. It was unbelievable. We were all down eating in the lobby, and I got the key from his roommate. I went upstairs and rearranged his room. He notices when things are different. When he was sleeping at night, we came running in. That was picture perfect."

Wes Helms, Florida Marlins: "In spring training when I was with the Phillies, they told Kyle Kendrick that he got traded to the Japanese league [for Takeru Kobayashi, a champion competitive hot dog eater]. They wrote an original contract with the general manager and had his jersey and everything made up in Japanese. They had his agent in on it, the media on it, and his mom in on it. He thought he was traded, and the look on his face—I mean, you can't—that's something I'll always remember. Everybody held their face for a good fifteen minutes."

Chad Billingsley, Los Angeles Dodgers: "Jason [Schmidt] switched his jersey with Clayton Kershaw, and he didn't know it, and he had to go out before the game and take pictures with fans and stuff. He had Schmidt's jersey on; he didn't know it. Schmidt wore his jersey out for the National Anthem, and they had it on the jumbo tron. That was funny."

Moe Drabowsky, eight teams in seventeen seasons (perfect for pranksters): Having played for the Kansas City A's, Drabowsky knew the intricacies of the stadium's bullpen phone system. He also knew the number for the home team's bullpen. So one day, when playing against the A's in Kansas City, while A's starter Jim Nash was pitching a dominant shutout, Drabowsky, seated in the opposing bullpen, summoned his gruffest manager voice, grabbed the bullpen phone and called the A's pen. *"Get Krausse up!"* he bellowed and slammed the phone down. "You should've seen them scramble, trying to get Lew Krausse warmed up in a hurry," Drabowsky said later.

Joe Carter, Toronto Blue Jays: Derek Bell was very proud of his Ford Explorer SUV, so it makes his dumbfounded expression all the more glorious when he saw his beloved car driven onto the field at the SkyDome while the public address announcer intoned *"one lucky fan will win Derek Bell's jeep."* Teammate Joe Carter orchestrated the whole thing.

Ken Griffey, Jr., Seattle Mariners: In 1995, during batting practice, when minor-league phenom Scott Davison was throwing, Seattle manager Lou Piniella bet Griffey a steak dinner he wouldn't hit a ball out of the batting cage. Griffey didn't know that Piniella had already ordered the pitcher not to throw the hitter anything near the strike zone. Piniella won the wager. Later that week, with half the Mariners lined up outside Piniella's office door, Griffey told him, "I bought you that steak." Piniella opened the door and came face to face with 1,200 pounds of beef. "I opened that door with a little trepidation," Piniella said, "but I didn't expect a cow." I've saved the best for last...

"Sidd Finch," New York Mets: Finch never existed. He is the subject of the notorious April Fools' Day hoax article "The Curious Case of Sidd Finch," written by George Plimpton and published in the April 1, 1985, edition of *Sports Illustrated*. His full name was Hayden Siddhartha "Sidd" Finch. According to Plimpton, Finch was raised in an English orphanage, learned yoga in Tibet, and could throw a fastball at 168 mph. His "yogic mastery of mind-body" was the secret to his pitching prowess. *SI* recruited Joe Berton, a junior high art teacher who stood 6-4 and wore a size fourteen shoe, to play Finch. The Mets gave him a uniform with No. 21 and a locker between George Foster and Darryl Strawberry. The story was accompanied by photos of Finch at spring training with Lenny Dykstra and Mets' pitching coach Mel Stottlemyre. The three major networks, *CBS, NBC, ABC,* and the local St. Petersburg, Florida, newspapers sent reporters to Al Lang Stadium for a press conference about Finch. Mets fans were thrilled to learn of their new phenom, and many fell for the prank, as did a New York sports page editor and two baseball general managers.

This column first appeared in The Vacaville Reporter *on March 28, 2020.*

* * *

"Let's Lighten Up"

It's never a problem finding lousy news in this world of ours. So, for a change of pace, let's focus on enjoyable and often ridiculous sports quotes.

Barry Zito: *"When you know, you know. You know?"*

Muhammad Ali: *"It's just a job. Grass grows, birds fly, and waves pound the sand. I beat people up."*

Yogi Berra: *"Baseball is 90 percent mental. The other half is physical."*

Bill Shankly: *"Some people believe football [soccer] is a matter of life and death. I'm very disappointed with that attitude. I can assure you it is much more important than that."*

Jerry Rice: *"I feel like I'm the best, but you're not going to get me to say that."*

Hank Aaron: *"It took me seventeen years to get 3,000 hits in baseball. I did it in one afternoon on the golf course."*

Jacques Plante: *"Goaltending is a normal job, sure. How would you like it in your job if a red light went on over your desk every time you made a small mistake and 15,000 people stood up and yelled at you?"*

Mario Andretti: *"If you have everything under control, you're not moving fast enough."*

Vitas Gerulaitis, upon beating Jimmy Connors after sixteen consecutive losses to him: *"And let that be a lesson to you. Nobody beats Vitas Gerulaitis seventeen times in a row."*

Tug McGraw on if he preferred grass or AstroTurf: *"I dunno. I never smoked any AstroTurf."*

Phil Rizzuto: *"I'm glad I don't play anymore. I could never learn all of those handshakes."*

Torrin Polk, University of Houston receiver, on John Jenkins, his coach: *"He treats us like men. He lets us wear earrings."*

George Rogers, New Orleans Saints running back, about the upcoming season: *"I want to rush for 1,000 or 1,500 yards, whichever comes first."*

Dizzy Dean after a 1-0 baseball game: *"The game was closer than the score indicated."*

Weldon Drew, former college basketball coach: *"We have a great bunch of outside shooters. Unfortunately, all our games are played indoors."*

Bill Belichick: *"I don't think anybody in this organization is not focused on the 49ers . . . I mean Chargers."*

Charles Barkley: *"These are my new shoes. They're good shoes. They won't make you rich like me. They won't make you rebound like me. They definitely won't make you handsome like me. They'll only make you have shoes like me. That's it."*

Pat Williams, former Orlando Magic General Manager: *"We can't win at home. We can't win on the road. As general manager, I can't figure out where else to play."*

Greg Norman: *"I owe a lot to my parents, especially my mother and father."*

Tito Fuentes, former MLB second baseman: *"They shouldn't throw at me. I'm the father of five or six kids."*

Gordie Howe: *"All hockey players are bilingual. They know English and profanity."*

President Gerald Ford: *"I know I am getting better at golf because I'm hitting fewer spectators."*

Garry Maddox after hitting a grand slam: *"As I remember it, the bases were loaded."*

Chad Ochocinco, former NFL wide receiver who changed his name to match his uniform number: *"I'm traveling to all 51 states to see who can stop 85."*

Terrell Owens: *"Don't say I don't get along with my teammates. I don't get along with some of the guys on the team."*

Jason Kidd: *"We're going to turn this team around 360 degrees."*

Ned Coletti, former Los Angeles Dodgers general manager, on scouting a prospective pitcher: *"He had good command, though. He didn't hit any cars or anything."*

Stephen Neal, former New England Patriots offensive lineman on Tom Brady's minor car accident: *"We can't protect him all the time."*

Brett Anderson, former Oakland A's pitcher, after slugger Manny Ramirez joined the team in spring training: *"Manny just asked if I was the video coordinator. Our relationship can only go up from here."*

Marshawn Lynch on Seahawks offensive line coach Tom Cable: *"Being from Oakland, all I knew about him is that he punched people. That's my kind of person."*

Steve Keim, former Arizona Cardinals general manager, on how the NFL assesses character in the Draft: *"If Hannibal Lecter ran a 4.3, we'd probably diagnose it as an eating disorder."*

Doc Rivers on welcoming back forward Blake Griffin to the Clippers after Griffin punched a team staffer and broke his hand: *"You forgive people. We built Nixon a library."*

Tony Gwynn: *"We know we're better than this, but we can't prove it."*
This column first appeared in The Vacaville Reporter *on September 2, 2020.*

* * *

"Bizarre Moments in Baseball History"

Joe Garagiola wrote a book, "Baseball is a Funny Game." But sometimes it's just plain crazy.

Most know that before Babe Ruth became a legendary hitter, he pitched. The southpaw, who threw for the Boston Red Sox from 1915–1919, posted an ERA of 2.16 and threw 29 2/3 consecutive scoreless World Series innings, a record which stood until 1961, when Whitey Ford compiled 33 2/3 goose eggs.

On June 23, 2017, Ruth got a World Series start against the Washington Senators. The first batter was Ray Morgan, who he walked on four straight pitches. Ruth was certain two of those pitches had been strikes and let umpire Brick Owens know.

Ruth told Owens, "Open your eyes and keep them open," at which point Owens threatened to eject him. Ruth replied, "You run me out and I will come in and bust you on the nose," which led Owens to give him the boot. The Bambino ran toward Owens and threw a left, which missed, but his next shot with his right nailed Owens in the left ear. Red Sox manager Jack Barry and several police officers removed the Sultan of Swat from the field.

Ernie Shore relieved Ruth, and Morgan was caught trying to steal second. Shore retired the next twenty-six batters, completing probably the weirdest no-hitter in baseball history.

In Game 7 of the 1925 World Series between the Pittsburgh Pirates and Washington Senators, the infield was unplayable due to rain. The inclement weather had already pushed the seventh game back a day, so the Forbes Field ground crew in Pittsburgh took drastic measures: they poured gasoline on the infield and set it on fire, then spread sawdust to dry the field. Smoke clouds filled the stands. The field was left scorched but playable. The Pirates defeated Walter Johnson to take the Series.

On August 4, 1983, the Yankees' Dave Winfield threw a warm-up ball in between innings that struck and killed a seagull. After the game ended, Winfield was taken to a police station and charged with cruelty to animals. Michael Sullivan of The Toronto Humane Society, helping police with the investigation, said, "We also accepted the bird from [police] and have submitted it to the University of Guelph for a full autopsy to give us a cause of death." The cause seemed obvious. Winfield was cleared of any intent to harm. As CBC's Vicki Russell quipped, "Never before has one bird caused such a flap. Late this afternoon, the Crown attorney said he'll ask the court next week to drop the criminal charges because he doesn't think Winfield flew afoul of the law."

When Winfield was invited six months later to speak at a charity event in Toronto, his family asked him, "Invited or extradited?"

In 2001, Randy Johnson let loose with a fastball right when a dove swooped into its path, resulting in an explosion of feathers. The pitch was ruled "no pitch" and Johnson at least was not charged with a crime.

In spring training in Tucson in 2005, swarms of bees invaded the field and forced a game between the Colorado Rockies and Arizona Diamondbacks to be called after five innings. The bees literally chased Rockies pitcher Darren Oliver from the mound. He kept trying to go back, but the bees would attack again. After a twenty-minute delay, he let reliever Allan Simpson complete the inning.

"I love this game," Oliver said, "but I like myself a little bit more."

Oliver theorized that the bees were attracted to the coconut oil in his hair gel. The Diamondbacks took the field in the sixth, but by then the bees had spread over the entire field. Shortstop Sergio Santos, who had just entered the game, was chased all the way into deep center field.

Arizona's Luis Gonzalez declared, "I think it was either their cologne or deodorant or something. They've got to switch it up."

Having now covered the birds and the bees, let's move on to gnats. In Game 2 of the 2007 ALDS between the Indians and the Yankees, Cleveland won an eleven-inning game amid an enormous swarm of bugs, probably a type of midge, a harmless gnat-like bug which Northern Ohioans call "Canadian Soldiers." While the Yankees complained that they had a hard time seeing what they were doing and were gagging on the clouds of bugs, Indians players shook off the midges and took them in stride, later saying they pretended not to be bothered because of the Yankees' protests. In 1946 a game between the Dodgers and Cubs was called in the fifth inning because of gnats.

Ten-Cent Beer Night was a disastrous promotion by the Cleveland Indians for a game against the Texas Rangers at Cleveland's Municipal Stadium on June 4, 1974. Beers went for ten cents, with a limit of six beers per purchase but no limit on the number of purchases made during the game. As the game proceeded, on-field incidents and massive alcohol consumption agitated the crowd, many of whom threw lit firecrackers, streaked (ran nude) across the playing field, and smoked marijuana. This culminated in a ninth-inning riot when fans rushed the field. Players protected themselves with their bats while retreating. The game, which was tied 5-5, was forfeited in favor of the Rangers.

Baseball teams frequently hand out souvenir balls with

team signatures when fans are walking out of the stadium, not in. That's probably because of what happened in Dodger Stadium on August 10, 1995. Hundreds of those balls wound up on the field. The onslaught got so bad that in the ninth inning, the umpires had to forfeit the game in favor of the St. Louis Cardinals.

Speaking of ill-fated promotions, let's not forget the Chicago White Sox' Disco Demolition Night on July 12, 1979, when customers who brought a disco album were admitted for 98 cents. All the albums were exploded between games of the doubleheader, resulting in mayhem. Fans raced onto the field, caused serious damage, and the second game was never played, the Sox forfeiting.

* * *

"Mind Your Spikes!"

From 2003-2005, Matthew Ceryes was a security guard at Pac Bell Park (now Oracle Park). He had a bird's-eye view of the inside goings-on at the home and visiting clubhouses.

Ceryes never let a Giant open the clubhouse door himself, which was a personal policy. Sometimes, the more exuberant of the team "exploded" the double doors outward on the way to the field. Guys were re-entering all the time, needing anything from a soda to a rubdown, and he didn't want the starting pitcher to go on the DL (called IL, now) because his right hand got blown up, reaching for the handle.

But there was a more insidious threat—spikes on concrete.

Pac Bell uses scarce waterfront and wastes nothing, leaving incomparable views. But it also caused unintended safety problems. One was corrected when foul territory bullpen bumps were moved out behind centerfield. The team also corrected the otherwise desirable problem of fans too close to the field with netted-in safety barriers.

Here's another. The underground clubhouses share perpendicular egress with the service tunnel to accommodate the aforementioned lack of real estate. This cold, narrow concrete artery simultaneously carries superstars and superloads of supplies. For safety, the Giants installed padded black floor runners to get players from the locker room, down the steps, and up to the field. These runners were the only thing keeping major league million-dollar ballplayers in metal spikes from serious injury.

Matthew Ceryes: "Noah Lowry was the first guy I saw slip. He was reaching out to someone when he left the runners and hit black ice, locking up his legs and hips and raising his arms halfway with a "*Whoa*!" He slid fourteen inches before coming to a precarious stop. Everyone had a smile, and he gingerly stiff-legged it back to safety. We developed a yell of '**MIND YOUR SPIKES**!' and weren't shy about using it. We never wanted to see our guys get hurt by something so mundane. I yelled it for visiting teams, as well. Twice, it wasn't enough.

"When L.A. came to town, everyone was on high alert. In July 2004, Giants outfielder Michael Tucker went after Dodgers starting pitcher Jeff Weaver only to challenge closer Eric Gagne the very next day. One day, Michael came screaming around the dugout corner below with at least four uniformed Giants in hot pursuit. He intended to sprint to the Dodgers' side of the stadium and give Mr. Weaver and Mr. Gagne the ol'-what-for. However, this line of attack had major problems. First, the service tunnel is a quarter-mile long. Secondly, two big guys in Giants' security gear are at the Dodgers' door. Finally, the ice-like concrete would bust him down hard the second he came off the pad.

"Those circumstances led to what happened next. Michael vaulted up the stairs three at a time, and the pursuing posse kept pace. It happened so fast that I threw up my hands in the universal stop sign, "**MIND YOUR SPIKES!**" just as the whole human, vertical dog pile reached our level. Incredibly, Michael's teammates collared him at the exact instant his metal-shorn shoes hit the pavement . . . just as he lost his feet, they had his arms. They lovingly had their teammate and talked him down off the cliff.

"Then there was the time Brett Tomko went down. He was alone in the Giants clubhouse in-game, the starting pitcher that day. He got caught going to the bathroom during a rare 1-2-3 inning against our guys that went maybe seven pitches. Late for his turn to throw, he came flying out the secret door trainers use, with his pants unbuttoned and unbelted. I was about to chuckle when I realized things weren't right. I never got to say the entire "MIND . . . " before Tomko's spikes hit the glass-like surface. Compounding the accident, Brett's hands were busy reassembling the lower half of his uniform. Unable to counterbalance, Brett's 6- 4 frame launched four feet into the air. He came down as hard as any man ever did from any fall anywhere."

Ceryes tried to reach him, but Tomko's pride and athleticism had him instantly back on his feet before he could help. Tomko waved off Ceryes and gingerly slid along until he reached the safety of the runners. There, he buckled his pants and pointed himself downstairs. He awkwardly straightened up and let out the smallest of groans. Two minutes later, Ceryes saw him pitching on the monitor.

He pitched normally that day and didn't show any ill effects again. Or did he? You be the judge. He was 73-58 as a major leaguer before the fall and 27-45 after.

Lesson: ***"Mind Your Spikes!"***

This column first appeared in The Vacaville Reporter *on August 31, 2020.*

***

"Baseball Board Games for the Bored"

Netflix will only take you so far.

If you are sick of streaming entertainment, let me suggest some other options, things people used to do when they were confined to the house for various reasons.

Where I grew up in northern New Jersey, the most common reasons were blizzards and the tail end of hurricanes that swept up the Atlantic Coast. We didn't have Netflix. We had a TV with a dial that numbered 2-to-13, and the only channels we got were the networks (2, 4 and 7) and local stations 5, 9, 11, and 13. Channel 9 had the "Million Dollar Movie" which played the same movie all day. My sister and I watched *The Loneliness of the Long Distance Runner* several times in a row.

But we also had board games. As a sports nut, my favorites were baseball board games.

The first I ever owned was Tudor's Electric Baseball, circa 1959. When you turned on the switch, the metal board vibrated under the runners, causing them to circle the bases.

Next was Cadaco's All-Star Baseball, which first appeared in 1941 and has been honored as one of the fifty most influential American board games of all time. Player discs were divided into sectors (likes slices of pie). Babe Ruth had a home run slice whose length at the outer edge was maybe a half-inch, while Bobby Richardson's home run sector was as thin as a pencil point. The "pie" was mathematically divided into doubles, triples, strikeouts, etc. to simulate the batter's statistics. The player disc was placed on a spinner which determined the outcome. Pitcher statistics were not incorporated.

That was left to 1961's Strat-O-Matic baseball, invented by Hal Richman. The game used dice to accurately parse the statistics of both pitchers and batters. Several major leaguers used to play Strat-O-Matic. When Lenny Dykstra hit a two-run, walk-off homer against the Astros in the bottom of the ninth to give the Mets a 6–5 victory in Game 3 of the 1986 National League Championship Series, he said that the last time he had done such a thing was when he played Strat-O-Matic against his brother.

Not only could you purchase the cards for every team each season, but Richman also made available old-timer teams, such as the 1927 New York Yankees with Ruth, Gehrig, and "Murderers' Row," or the 1948 Cleveland Indians with Bob Feller and, finally up from the Negro Leagues after the color barrier was broken, the legendary Satchel Paige.

One winter just after the New Year in the early 2000s, I phoned Strat-O-Matic in Glen Head, New York, to order their recently developed computer version of the game. The guy who answered was extremely helpful, explaining which version would work best with my computer and taking the time to go over other details with me. Toward the end of the conversation, he casually mentioned that he was Hal

Richman, pitching in because they were short-staffed after the holidays.

Pressman released a great game in 1962, Roger Maris Action Baseball, essentially a pinball game but designed for two players. One player launched a marble baseball from the pitcher's mound using a tiny spring, while the other operated a wooden bat on a spring to drive the marble on the board, which was populated with holes labeled single, double, out, double play, etc. The outcome was determined by the hole the marble fell into. There should have been more out holes, as games were usually of the 21-19, 17-14 variety. But it was still a lot of fun.

I made the mistake of trading my Cadaco All-Star Baseball Game with a friend for an impostor called Challenge the Yankees. It used the same model as Cadaco, with two teams, the then-current Yankees team and All-Stars from the rest of the Majors. I quickly tired of the game.

By the late 1980s, computer baseball games began to overtake the board games. One of the earliest (1987) was Earl Weaver Baseball, a simulation developed by Dan Daglow. The graphics were rudimentary, but the simulation of players' stats was quite accurate. I still have Earl Weaver Baseball II, which used the floppy disks that were actually floppy, the 5.25-inch versions.

Daglow developed this model to bring us the very popular Tony La Russa series of computer games. After rolling out version 3, Daglow replaced the twenty-eight teams' players and ballparks with the complete lineups of every big league team from 1871 to 1981 (12,000 players in all) and sixteen old ballparks. Ballparks included Seals Stadium, the Polo Grounds, and the original Yankee Stadium. He called it Old Time Baseball.

The stadiums were beautiful color renditions. The animations were very accurate in terms of body movements of the pitchers, batters, and fielders. But other than skin color, the players were generic and all wore number 11.

One could learn much history playing the game. One day I had the 1876 Chicago White Stockings host the 1941 New York Yankees. The White Stockings were the predecessor of the Chicago Cubs. Their primary starting pitcher was a guy named A.G. Spalding, who went 47-12 that season with a 1.75 ERA. He co-founded the sporting goods company that bears his name and helped organize the National League at its start. He also popularized the wearing of a baseball glove. Oh, and he beat the Yankees 4-3.

The video game market began to churn out arcade versions with much more realistic, 3-D graphics. Baseball simulation games became even more sophisticated. Diamond Mind Baseball so accurately represented what happens on the field that the Boston Red Sox started using the game as part of its data-driven approach to baseball in 2003.

Whatever your favorite game, it's always the perfect time to dust it off and roll it out, even when you are not confined to your home.

This column first appeared in The Vacaville Reporter *on March 24, 2020.*

* * *

"The Beauty of Computer-Simulated Baseball Games"

In 1961, Hal Richman, a Bucknell University mathematics student, began selling an early version of his baseball tabletop game, Strat-O-Matic, out of his basement. He lost money until 1963, when his decision to release a game containing one card for each player in Major League Baseball greatly increased sales.

In 1966 I turned thirteen and discovered Strat-O-Matic.

Strat-O-Matic's statistical research and development methods replicate ballplayers' abilities.

The set of cards that came with the game included several 1965 teams. I had the Dodgers (great pitching and not much offense) and the Giants (great hitting and not enough pitching). And I had the Minnesota Twins, so I could replay the World Series between the Dodgers and Twins. I was kind of a loner, and the beauty of Strat-O-Matic is that you can play by yourself, managing both teams.

My biggest thrill was adding to my collection some of the greatest teams in history—the 1927 and 1961 New York Yankees, the 1953 Brooklyn Dodgers, the 1954 New York Giants, and a bunch more.

Richman was inducted into the National Jewish Sports Hall of Fame in March 2011.

I can't count the hours of fun I had playing Strat-O-Matic as a youngster. I didn't play the game beyond my teenage years, and as a young adult lost the board game during a cross-country move.

Later in life I learned that Strat-O-Matic had developed a computer version. I phoned the company to order the game. The gentleman who answered told me all about the computer version and advised me on system requirements and other details. At one point, he identified himself as Hal Richman. I couldn't believe he was answering the phones himself. He explained that it was the New Year, and many of his employees were on a two-week break starting at Christmas.

I really enjoy the computer version, but I do miss the

cards and rolling the dice in the original board game version.

I bought my first computer in 1996, a Hewlett-Packard Pavilion desktop and discovered Stormfront Studios Old Time Baseball, an MS-DOS game released in 1995 by one of its chief developers, Don Daglow.

The game includes every team from 1871 to 1981, so it is a blast to play the 1927 Yankees against the 1961 Yankees, for example. You can choose either Mel Allen or Curt Gowdy as your announcer. The graphics are rudimentary, but the players' motions are realistic. Although one can play it as an arcade game, I find it more satisfying to play the game in managerial mode. I realize that graphics have come a long way since then with highly realistic-looking players and actions. But I am just looking for statistical realism and managerial freedom, and Old Time provides both. I play it on my Windows laptop using the DOSBox emulator.

The game also includes sixteen old time ballparks.

Although Old Time did not create new teams each year, a Canadian developer, Nick Keren, did so for several years, and, for a very decent price, I was able to add teams through 2001, until Nick discontinued that service.

When I was working as a sportswriter for *The Reporter*, the daily newspaper of Vacaville, California, I ran a contest. I asked readers to pick any team from 1871 to 2001, and I would conduct a double-elimination tournament. The last two teams standing were the 2001 Seattle Mariners, undefeated, nominated by my nephew, Stephen Petiti, and the 1975 Cincinnati Reds with one loss, nominated by reader John Erickson. The Reds beat the Mariners two in a row to take the title. I was afraid if Stephen won I might be accused of nepotism.

I also employed Old Time Baseball for the afterword of my book, *The God Squad: the Born-Again San Francisco Giants of 1978*. The God Squadders included pitchers Gary Lavelle, Bob Knepper, and Randy Moffitt, first baseman and pinch-hitter extraordinaire Mike Ivie, and outfielder Terry Whitfield. Here's what I wrote:

In 1889, Oscar Wilde wrote, "Life imitates Art far more than Art imitates Life."

But that was before computer simulation baseball games.

After completing this book, I was inspired to play one game between the 1978 Giants and the 1978 Dodgers on my favorite computer baseball game, Old Time Baseball by Stormfront Studios, published in 1995.

The lineups were those used most frequently by the two teams that year. The starting pitchers were Burt Hooton, who won nineteen games for the Dodgers and posted a 2.71 ERA in 1978, and Knepper for the Giants. The Giants were the home team and, just for fun, I played the game at Seals Stadium, the minor league park in San Francisco where the Giants played their first two seasons in 1958 and 1959.

I managed the Giants while the computer managed the Dodgers.

Knepper shut down the Dodgers for seven innings and took a 2–0 lead into the eighth. One of the Giants' runs was supplied by a homer from Whitfield. The Dodgers reached Knepper for two runs in the eighth, so I brought in righthander Moffitt, who yielded a hit, putting two runners on base with two outs and the score knotted at 2–2. With left-handed hitting Rick Monday coming to the plate, I brought in southpaw Lavelle, who induced a fly out to end the threat.

In the bottom of the eighth, the Giants got two runners aboard with two outs. Lavelle's spot was due up in the lineup, so I pinch hit Ivie for him.

If you read this book, you can guess what Ivie did.

That's right. He hit a three-run homer to give the Giants a 5–2 lead. John Curtis came on in relief of Lavelle for a 1-2-3 ninth inning to secure the victory for San Francisco.

Lavelle got the win in relief. Knepper recorded ten strikeouts.

Whatever you may think of the God Squadders, I think we can all agree on one thing—they could play some ball.

* * *

"Worst Baseball Team Ever?"

Many debate which team is the best in baseball history.

But how about the worst?

I conducted a computer simulation double-elimination tournament featuring the eight worst teams of the twentieth century. The "winner" is the team that loses two straight games, then loses in a "playoff" against the other team with two straight losses. Old Time Baseball is a computer game including every team from 1871 to 1981 and uses the model developed for Tony LaRussa Baseball. I added teams from 1982 through 1999.

In first day action, the 1962 New York Mets and the 1919 Philadelphia Athletics both lost:

1904 Washington Senators 9, 1962 New York Mets 6

The Mets got off to a great start in the battle for the worst team with a typically horrid performance at Griffith Stadium in Washington, D.C.

Their pitching staff had four members with seventeen-plus losses, including Al Jackson (8-20), who got the start.

It came down to who wanted this game less, and the Mets obliged, turning a one-run lead into a three run-deficit after Jackson gave up a grand-slam homer to Bill Coughlin in the bottom of the second.

New York tied it at 4-4 by the top of the third, only to give back three more in the bottom of the frame on an inside-the-park home run by Frank Huelsman. The Mets pulled within 8-6, aided by an error in the top of the sixth, but promptly coughed up the final run on a Huelsman RBI single in the bottom of the inning.

"The Mets have shown me more ways to lose than I even knew existed," said 70-year-old Mets manager Casey Stengel after the game.

1952 Pirates 1, 1919 Philadelphia Athletics 0

In an abysmal battle of attrition, the Pirates made their one run, batted in on a Pete Castigliano single in the bottom of the fifth, hold up for the victory. The Pirates had thirteen rookies on the squad and never managed a three-game winning streak the entire season.

Whether it was a pitching duel or anemic hitting, one must still credit Pittsburgh starter Murry Dickson with a complete-game two-hit shutout in which he struck out nine and walked two. A's "ace" Rollie Naylor, who compiled a 5-18 record on the season, fared almost as well, yielding just one run in eight innings and scattering eight hits, three of them by Castigliano.

In second day action, the Mets and A's both lost again, qualifying them to square off in the worst team final:

1935 Braves 10, 1962 Mets 6

Roger Craig was a lot more successful managing the pitching staff of the San Francisco Giants in later years than he was pitching as a Met. He went 10-24 in 1962 for the Amazins.

He didn't fare any better against the Braves, who jumped out to a 2-0 lead in the top of the first on RBI singles by Wally Berger and Pinkey Whitney. Boston made it 4-0 in the top of the third on a two-run inside-the-park home in the cavernous Polo Grounds by Buck Jordan. Mercifully, Craig was out of the game by the seventh, when Jordan creamed a three-run homer to right field for a 7-0 Braves lead.

The Mets clawed back with three runs in the bottom of the frame, one on a bases-loaded walk to Frank Thomas and two more on a single by Choo-Choo Coleman. But Les Mallon hit another inside-the-park home run for the Braves, good for three runs, in the top of the eighth. The Mets scored three in the bottom of the ninth, two on a homer by Felix Mantilla, but it was too little too late.

Fred Frankhouse got the win for the Braves with 6 2/3 innings of work, yielding three runs on eight hits.

With the loss, the Mets enter the double loser's bracket for a one-game playoff to determine the worst team of the 20th century.

"Don't cut my throat," said Mets manager Casey Stengel after the game. "I may want to do that later myself."

1909 Washington Senators 3, 1919 Philadelphia Athletics 2

The Athletics carved their way into the one-game playoff against the 1962 Mets with an uninspiring loss to the Phils.

Bill Burns got the win for Washington with eight innings of work, yielding seven hits and two runs, just one of them earned. Doc Riesling came on in the ninth for the save. Walt Kinney, who went 9-15 on the year but had a decent 3.64 ERA, pitched well, limiting the Senators to two runs on four hits while striking out seven in 6 2/3 innings of work.

Walter Anderson, in relief of Kinney, gave up the deciding run in the bottom of the eighth on a single by George Browne and a triple by Jim Delahanty.

Worst worst team: 1962 Mets
1919 Athletics 3, 1962 New York Mets 0

"There are three things you can do in a baseball game," said Mets manager Casey Stengel before the game. "You can win, or you can lose, or it can rain."

Unfortunately for the Mets, it didn't rain.

The Mets failed to score against starter Jing Johnson, who threw eight innings of two-hit ball, and Walter Anderson, who worked a hitless ninth for the save.

The Amazins wasted their biggest chance in the top of the sixth. With the bases loaded and one out, Marvelous Marv Throneberry and Choo-Choo Coleman, two iconic Mets, struck out in succession.

Jay Hook got the start and pitched a credible five innings, yielding three runs on eight hits.

The A's took a 1-0 lead in the bottom of the first on an RBI double by George Burns. They scored the next inning on a Fred Thomas RBI double and added their final run in the sixth on a run-scoring single by Burns.

Asked about his team's performance after the game, Stengel noted of the worst team of the twentieth century,

"Good pitching will always stop good hitting and vice-versa."

This column first appeared in three segments in The Vacaville Reporter *on April 28, May 1, and May 4, 2020.*

* * *

"'Baseball Mogul' is Baseball Computer Simulation Heaven"

Ever since the mid 1990s, I have been a fan of baseball computer simulation games. Not so much the arcade features, which I know have come a long way. I'm more into strategy and managing.

My all-time favorite has been Old Time Baseball by Stormfront Studios, the same company that developed Tony LaRussa Baseball. Old Time has all the teams from the beginning of baseball history through 1981 and some beautiful renditions of a number of the old ballparks. And you can choose between Mel Allen and Curt Gowdy as your announcer.

Recently my brother-in-law's brother (got that?) introduced me to Baseball Mogul. It is a very sophisticated simulation that lets you function as general manager of your team, including drafts, trades, contracts, etc. I'm not interested in being a mogul, just a manager. And that's an option.

Baseball Mogul includes the full rosters of all teams from 1901 to the present. You can pick any of those seasons, select your team, and play through the full 162-game schedule, plus playoffs and World Series. You can play each game in play-by-play mode as manager, or you can have the computer instantly give you the result of as many games as you like. But, since I like to manage each game individually, I'm not prepared to play 162 games that way with one team. What if my team doesn't make the playoffs? That would be just as frustrating as it has been rooting for the San Francisco Giants this year.

A beautiful feature of the game is the League Builder. You can make a league using any of the teams from baseball history. You are allowed up to thirty teams. I picked some of my favorites—the 1962 New York Mets, the 1969 Mets, the 1973 Mets, and the 1986 Mets. Do you detect a pattern? Yes, I have been a Mets fan since 1962 and saw them play in the Polo Grounds in 1962 and 1963 before they moved to Shea Stadium.

But don't worry. The other twenty-six teams are non-Met teams, including the 1924 Washington Senators with Walter Johnson, the Murderers' Row 1927 Yankees, the Mantle-Maris 1961 Yankees, the 1975 Big Red Machine, the 1971 Pittsburgh Pirates with Clemente, and the 1948 Cleveland Indians with Bob Feller and Satchel Paige.

The lineups are not pre-set, so I had to do a little research to find the most common lineup for each team, which you can then save. But you can modify that lineup before the game begins if you want.

One problem presented itself. Since the rosters are those in place on opening day, they do not include players who were traded to the team afterwards. This left a gaping hole in my 1962 New York Mets lineup, as Marv Throneberry, the quintessential original Met, was traded to the Mets from the Orioles on May 9, 1962. How can I have the 1962 Mets without Marvelous Marv?

Never fear. Baseball Mogul has a Facebook group. I shared my dilemma and within an hour heard back from a group member with a solution. You can create Marvelous Marv with a little effort, so I did. Similarly, Tim Foli was not on the opening day roster of the 1979 Pittsburgh Pirates and Vic Wertz was not on the opening day roster of the 1954 Cleveland Indians, so I created them. How can you not have Wertz on that Indians team when he is the guy that hit the ball over Willie Mays' head in the World Series that Willie ran down to the amazement of all?

One of my teams is the 1978 San Francisco Giants, about whom I wrote a book titled *The God Squad: The Born-Again San Francisco Giants of 1978*. I have become good friends with one of those God Squadders, pitcher Bob Knepper. I had Knepper lock horns with Jack Morris of the 1991 Twins. Knepper pitched a complete-game five-hit shutout, beating the Twins 4-0. When I gave him the news, he, like every pitcher, was more concerned about his hitting.

"Did I get any hits or steal any bases?" he asked. I had to break the news to him that he didn't. He replied, "Better check the box scores. I'm sure I went 2-for-4! One being a double off the right field fence!"

I just let him know that he pitched another complete game, a 5-2 win over the 1986 New York Mets. Both Mets runs were unearned. Mike Ivie, who was an incredible pinch hitter for the 1978 Giants, delivered a two-run, bases-loaded pinch-hit single in the eighth inning to break a 2-2 tie. Can't get much more realistic than that.

Sorry, Bob, you went 0-for-3 with two strikeouts. But you did draw a walk.

I've had some memorable matchups already, Jim Lonborg of the 1967 Boston Red Sox facing Bob Gibson of the 1967 St. Louis Cardinals, just like Game 7 of the World Series (Gibson won the computer game and the real one). Just for fun, I had the 1962 New York Mets go up against Sandy Koufax and the 1965 Los Angeles Dodgers. What a joke. Dodgers won 8-1, Koufax went all the way, and Maury Wills went 5-for-5 with five stolen bases. The Mets made three errors in one inning. As Mets manager Casey Stengel put it, "The Mets have shown me more ways to lose than I even knew existed."

I can play a game in one-pitch mode in about fifteen minutes. I can even manage both teams. The game comes preset with the man on second base in extra innings rule, the no-pitch intentional walk, and the requirement that a pitcher face at least three batters. Still a traditionalist who hates all those rules, I was overjoyed to discover that I can override them. There are ballpark sounds but no announcer, which I can live without.

Baseball Mogul didn't pay me to write this. But I can already tell this game is going to afford me hours of fun.

* * *

"Break Out Those Baseball Cards!"

In terms of baseball cards, 1965 was a great year for me. I was in sixth grade and spent a grand total of fifty cents on the Topps bubble gum cards. At five cents a pack, that was ten packs with five cards in each pack.

But I took those fifty cards and engaged in a form of legalized gambling for kids that spring and summer and multiplied my final total to about 650 cards. One method was a baseball version of the card game War, slightly revised. The cards of 1965 had different-colored bottoms as backgrounds for the player's name and position. Two kids would place their cards down one at a time, alternating turns until a card matched the previous card's color. The winner took the whole pile, which sometimes was pretty big.

Another way to win cards was to literally throw them down on the sidewalk. If your card landed on your opponent's card, you picked up both. If your card didn't touch your opponent's card, he (I knew no girls in 1965 who collected baseball cards) would get a chance to throw down a card and touch one of the two cards, and this could continue for a while if you both had bad aim. Whoever finally touched one of the other cards with his card would win the whole pile.

Unfortunately, none of those 1965 cards were rare, and they certainly weren't in mint condition after we got through flipping them on the sidewalk or plunking them down in a pile.

But if you've got some shoeboxes full of old baseball cards in your attic and basement, get them out. For one thing, they are fun to look at for nostalgia's sake. For another, maybe you'll find one that will be a real winner, monetarily speaking.

Hopefully, they're in great shape, as a card's condition means everything for its value. PSA (Professional Sports Authenticator) is the world's most trusted third-party sports card grading and authentication company. They grade on a 1-10 scale; "1" denotes a card in "Poor" condition, while "10," the most sought-after grade, is considered "Gem Mint."

Here are the ten most expensive baseball cards ever sold, courtesy of blogger Sheng Peng:

1909 T206 Honus Wagner
Price: $3.12 million

There are only about fifty known copies of the T206 Wagner, the undisputed "Mona Lisa" of baseball cards. Wagner himself is the reason for the card's rarity. Apparently, the Pittsburgh Pirates star barred the American Tobacco Company from continuing production of the card—either because he didn't want children to buy cigarettes to acquire his card or because he wanted to get paid more for his likeness.

1952 Topps Mickey Mantle
Price: $2.88 million

Topps has dominated the baseball card scene for the past seven decades, issuing a set in every year since 1951. And the 1952 Topps Mantle is the crown jewel of modern baseball cards.

1951 Bowman Mickey Mantle
Price: $750,000

The 1952 Topps Mantle may be the crown jewel of modern baseball cards, but it's not the slugger's rookie card. That distinction belongs to the 1951 Bowman Mantle.

1916 Sporting News Babe Ruth
Price: $717,000

There may be no rookie card more important than the 1916 Sporting News Ruth. Unlike the T-206 Wagner, which was strictly a promotional tool for American Tobacco Company, the 1916 Ruth was "a collectible business card" with a blank back which enabled businesses to add their own advertising to the back. There were as many as sixteen businesses advertised, but *The Sporting News* reverse is the most coveted.

1963 Topps Pete Rose
Price: $717,000

Despite his lifetime ban from baseball for gambling, Rose cards remain as popular as ever. As of August 2018, there have been 3,711 rookie cards of "The Hit King" graded by PSA, and only this one has been graded as "Gem Mint."

1909 T206 Eddie Plank
Price: $700,000

Like the T206 Wagner, the exact reason for the T206 Plank's scarcity has been lost to time. Was it a broken printing plate? Did Plank, who was stridently anti-tobacco, object to being used to promote the American Tobacco Company? Or did the future Hall of Fame pitcher simply not like how much he was being paid for his likeness? Whatever the reason, there are only about seventy-five T206 Planks in existence.

1909 American Caramel E90-1 Joe Jackson
Price: $667,149

Like Rose, "Shoeless" Joe Jackson is the symbol of the disgraced American sports hero, just as famous for a career-ending gambling scandal, the 1919 Black Sox World Series, as he was for his prodigious hitting exploits. Along with cigarettes, baseball cards were also included as premiums with candy in the early twentieth century.

1909 T206 Sherry Magee (Error)
Price: $660,000

Sherry Magee led the National League in RBIs four times, but that's not why his PSA 8 T206 card sold for $660,000 in September 2018. It's because Magee's name was initially spelled "Magie" before being corrected. The card is considered the most celebrated "error" in baseball card history.

1968 Topps Nolan Ryan
Price: $612,359

While this Ryan rookie card is relatively plentiful (as of August 2018, PSA had graded 8,279 copies) only one of this fireballer's debut issue has been graded a PSA 10. Ryan, who holds the all-time record for strikeouts, figures to hold his popularity in the baseball card world for years to come.

1910 T210 Old Mill Joe Jackson
Price: $600,000

It's been over one-hundred years since the Black Sox scandal and more than thirty-five years since *Field of Dreams*, but the public continues to be fascinated by "Shoeless Joe."

This column first appeared in The Vacaville Reporter *on May 19, 2020.*

***

"Keeping Stickball Alive"

During the twentieth century, impoverished and lower-middle-class kids living in cramped apartments in northeast cities like New York, Philadelphia, and Boston made the streets their playground. The quintessential game was stickball.

Stickball developed in the late eighteenth century from such English games as old cat, rounders, and town ball. Stickball also relates to a game played in southern England and colonial Boston in North America called stoolball.

The modern game is played, especially in New York City, on the street, where fixtures such as fire hydrants or parked cars serve as bases. These fixtures also provide targets off of which to carom the ball, generally the high-bounce pink Spalding ball, known as the Spaldeen. Manhole covers serve as home plate, and the length of hits is measured in terms of sewers. Kids who could hit the ball two or three "sewers" down the block became neighborhood legends.

In back alleys and side streets—more confined spaces—singles, doubles and triples were determined by where the ball landed. Belting a Spaldeen on a building roof was either a home run or an out, depending on preset verbal rules.

The bat is a broomstick or mop handle. Players often wrap adhesive or electrical tape around one end of the stick for a better grip.

On the street, the ball is generally pitched on one bounce to the batter. A variant is fungo, where batters toss the ball in the air to themselves and hit it on the way down or on the bounce.

In the 1950s, Willie Mays, the New York Giants superstar,

used to play stickball on the streets of Harlem with the neighborhood kids. Mays said the ritual helped him to hit curveballs, as experienced stickball pitchers could make the ball curve after the bounce, and the rough surface of the asphalt also produced some unexpected twists to the pitches. When Mays made contact he whacked the ball so hard that it went for three or four sewers—three or four city blocks.

Not everyone was a stickball fan. For some residents, shattered windows and traffic interruptions went too far. Building superintendents and police driving by confiscated balls and broke sticks. They often dropped the brooms down sewer holes, ending the game.

Italians, Puerto Ricans, Irish, African Americans, and Jewish kids had their own teams. Usually, they risked street fights if they wandered onto each others' turfs, but when a stickball match was scheduled there was a free pass. But as soon as the game ended, the visiting team had minutes to clear out or the gathering would turn violent.

Once city car traffic increased, stickball found a home in school yards and open lots.

In my hometown of Hackensack, New Jersey, a suburb of New York City, we played a variant of stickball on our high school handball courts. When a court was not in use, which was most of the time, we either drew a strike zone with chalk or used adhesive tape to form a strike zone against the wall. It was one-on-one stickball. If you hit a ground ball and the pitcher fielded it cleanly, you were out. If he bobbled it, it was a single. If the grounder went past him, it was a single. We had various markers. If you hit the ball on the fly beyond the marker, it was a double, triple, or home run. We had a three-foot high fence at the end of the asphalt (which encompassed handball and basketball courts). A fly ball over that fence was a home run.

I would pretend I was a certain major league team and bat lefty or righty (I'm a natural righty) depending which big leaguer in the lineup I was impersonating. I couldn't hit very well from the left side, but it was fun to try. I had pretty good control as a pitcher and could throw a pretty good fastball, which served me well enough, even though I didn't have a good breaking ball in my arsenal.

We also played this version of stickball on weekends in the parking lot of a bank, when the bank was closed.

Stickball had pretty much died out on the streets of New York by the 1980s. As *Sports History Weekly* noted, "The 1980s ushered in video games and cable TV, resulting in youngsters spending more of their leisure time indoors. Overprotective parents also turned sports into organized and sanitized activities, controlling everything from playdates to transportation."

But the game is still alive on Stickball Boulevard in the South Bronx. In 1985, Newman Avenue was officially renamed after the street game that for generations had been part of New York City's social fabric.

The New York Emperors Stickball League (NYESL), founded in 1985 by Frank Sanchez and Frank Calderon, keeps the tradition alive. Over the years, the NYESL has grown from two teams to upwards of sixteen teams in league season play, which starts in early April and continues each Sunday through August.

"The Mecca of stickball is in the South Bronx", says Jennifer Lippold, former President of the NYESL. "It's where you go for bragging rights."

Hall of Fame pitcher CC Sabathia is one of several baseball

stars who have shown up on a Sunday at Stickball Boulevard to help raise interest in the game. There are also stickball leagues in California and Florida, though I haven't encountered one here in Martinez, CA, birthplace of Joe DiMaggio, an hour north of San Francisco.

I am tempted to find a nice broom handle, wind electrical tape around one end, order some Spaldeen balls, and find someone to play stickball with. But I'm in my seventies and don't know if my arm will hold up pitching to that strike zone on the wall of some local schoolyard.

But maybe I can pass on the tradition to my grandkids.

* * *

"Wiffle Ball"

Looking for a fun backyard game for the summer? Look no further than the great pastime of Wiffle ball.

I was pleased to learn that the history of Wiffle ball began in the year of my birth, 1953. From a very young age and up until my teenage years, I played Wiffle ball in my backyard or on the sandlots of my suburban town in northern New Jersey. It was also great on vacations, as you could set up for a game of Wiffle ball wherever you went, even on the beach.

The beauty of the game was that the ball doesn't travel very far, which was ideal for backyards and enclosed areas. When our boys were young, they enjoyed playing Wiffle ball in our rather small backyard. They could be home run hitters by smashing the ball over our not-too-distant fences (a lot of trips for me to the neighbor's yard).

It was practical considerations that led David N. Mullany

of Fairfield, Connecticut, to design the Wiffle ball for his twelve-year-old son, David, to use in their backyard. The younger David and his friends had begun to play a game in the Mullany yard with a perforated plastic golf ball and a broomstick handle. They had given up on baseball and softball because they couldn't find enough players, there was no field available, and they had broken too many backyard windows.

Young David tried to throw curves and sliders with the tiny golf ball, but he told his dad it was killing his arm. His father had been a semi-pro pitcher and knew that throwing curveballs was harmful to young arms. So he got some ball-shaped plastic parts from a nearby factory and, on his kitchen table, cut various designs into them and sent his son out to test them.

The design with eight oblong perforations on one half of the ball worked the best. Young David and his friends could throw curveballs, sliders, screwballs, sinkers and rise balls. That led to a lot of strikeouts, which the kids called "whiffs." Hence the name Wiffle ball was adopted.

Not long after that summer, Mullany produced and sold the first Wiffle perforated plastic balls. The game caught on fast and now the balls are available across the U.S. and in many countries around the world.

The Wiffle Ball is about the same size as a regulation baseball, but is hollow, lightweight, of resilient plastic, and no more than 1/8 inch (3 mm) thick. The ball manufactured today is nearly identical to the original ball.

The rules are based on those that young David and his pals used in the backyard.

The field is laid out with foul lines and markers for single, double, triple and home-run areas. The recommended size of the playing field is a minimum dimension of twenty feet wide (approximately eight paces) at the home run markers by roughly seventy-five feet long (about thirty paces) from home plate to each home run marker on the foul lines.

Single markers are placed approximately twenty-four feet from home plate on the foul line. Double markers are placed approximately twenty feet in back of the single markers on the foul line. Triple markers are placed on foul lines about twenty feet back of the double markers.

You can play the game with only two players, but you can comfortably include up to five players per team—pitcher, catcher and a fielder in each of the hit areas—single, double and triple. There is no base running.

A batter can make an out in three ways: 1) He or she swings at a pitched ball and does not foul tip the third strike. A foul tip caught by the catcher does not count as an out with two strikes. 2) The batter hits a fly ball that is caught in fair or foul territory. 3) The batter hits a ground ball that is caught while the ball is still in motion in the single area.

If, for example, the batter lines a ball that lands in the air in the double area, it counts as a double even if the fielder retrieves the ball while it is still rolling. The fielder must catch the ball in the air. The same applies in the triple area. Fielders cannot go beyond the triple area to attempt to catch a home run.

Bunting is not allowed and the batter cannot obtain a base on balls.

Wiffle Ball is one of the safest sports around, so the Wiffle Ball company was shocked when in 2011, the State of New York proclaimed that Wiffle ball, kickball, freeze tag, and dodgeball were "unsafe" and a "significant risk of injury" for children. The state declared that any summer camp program that included two or more such activities would be subject to government regulation.

Wiffle ball executives originally thought the order was a joke, and the story became a frequent source of ridicule and amusement. People from across the nation successfully pressured the New York legislature to remove Wiffle ball and other tame entries from the list of high-risk activities.

After the reversal, State Senator Patricia Ritchie of Watertown, New York, said, "At a time when our nation's No. 1 health concern is childhood obesity, I am very happy to see that someone in state government saw we should not be adding new burdensome regulations by classifying tag, Red Rover and Wiffle ball as dangerous activities. I am glad New York's children can continue to steal the bacon and play flag football and enjoy other traditional rites of summer."

When our nation's No. 1 health concern became the coronavirus, I was happy to see that the game of Wiffle ball, invented over seventy years ago, was still a safe backyard sport that can be enjoyed by all.

This column first appeared in The Vacaville Reporter *on July 13, 2020.*

***

"Mushball!"

I hadn't had this much fun in ages.

Did you ever hear of mushball? Also known as Chicago ball, it is played like softball but with a ball that is sixteen inches in circumference. The circumference of a regulation softball is twelve inches. Also, the more you hit the mushball, the softer it gets, so players don't generally wear gloves.

The earliest known softball game of any kind was played at the Farragut Boat Club in Chicago on Thanksgiving Day 1887. The sixteen-inch softball was eventually adopted in Chicago, apparently because it did not travel as far as the twelve-inch ball. This allowed for play on smaller playgrounds or even indoors, accommodating for the Chicago landscape and cold winter climate. Another advantage of the mushball was that it allowed everyone to play barehanded, and gloves were a rare luxury, as the Great Depression hit Chicago particularly hard.

Up until two years ago, I had been playing softball with my church team, but at age seventy I hung up the spikes. My daughter recently moved to our town of Martinez, California. She used to play softball in high school and we were looking for a fun baseball activity we could do together, as we had bonded around baseball, attending a San Francisco Giants game every year around her birthday since she was four years old.

So when I heard about mushball, I bought a couple of balls and tried to drum up interest at my church for an informal game of mushball on alternate Saturdays this summer. The first two dates we only had two or three others show up, so we just took batting practice. But on the most recent Saturday we had a total of eight.

As a kid, we learned to play baseball games with that few. So I felt like a youngster again as I explained the rules to the mushball participants. We counted off by twos to form two teams. Each team would pitch to itself, leaving four fielders. All of the players batted right-handed, so you had to hit to the left of second base. Any ball hit to the right of second is a foul ball. With four fielders, each team had a third baseman, shortstop, left fielder and center fielder. If the ball was hit on the ground, the infielder had to throw it to the pitcher before the batter reached first base, resulting in an out. If there had been a left-handed batter, we would have reversed the rules. Any ball hit to the left of second base would be a foul. The fielders would be first baseman, second baseman, right fielder and center fielder. Since in this setup the defensive team would have a first baseman, ground ball outs would be recorded by throwing to the first baseman rather than the pitcher.

We had all ages at the game. Graham, a senior gentleman around my age who hails from England, grew up with cricket and had never before played baseball. He caught on quickly, taking my tips in batting practice. He played three innings, but pulled a muscle as he ran to third base on a base hit and had to withdraw. I asked him today if he wants to play again in a couple of weeks, and he replied, "The only thing stupider than doing something you shouldn't do in the first place is doing it again." So no Graham next game.

The other players ranged in age from eleven to seventy-two (me) and everything in between. A couple of the players were really good catching line drives and pop ups with their hands. Only my daughter and I used gloves. The eleven-year-old and his older brother got bored catching with their hands and decided to catch fly balls in their baseball caps.

My daughter played an excellent third base. She was always a good fielder but had been a first baseman in high school and had never played third before.

When pitching to his own team, the eleven-year-old didn't seem to understand the concept that one is supposed to play defense as pitcher to get your own team out. He showed a distinct disinterest in fielding balls hit near him or in receiving throws from the infielders after they caught ground balls. I, on the other hand, when pitching to my own team, caught a number of balls hit right back at me. I will have to educate him on mushball etiquette next time.

We were trailing 6-1, but our youth pastor, who runs like the wind, hit a couple of line drive home runs in the gap in left-center field, and we tied the game 6-6. We decided to play one more inning. We were the home team. The visitors clubbed the ball around in the top of the frame and scored four runs. We failed to score in the home half.

But nobody was too concerned about the score. We played five innings. We had started batting practice a little bit after noon, but my daughter and I were amazed when we realized we had finished the game by 1:15 p.m. So mushball goes pretty fast. No commercials between innings, no replay review, no throwing over to first base to hold the runner on, no timeouts, no bringing in a relief pitcher from the bullpen.

It is difficult to hit the ball too far, which worked out perfectly within the dimensions of the back lawn of our church. So if you have a smaller space that is not ideal for baseball or softball, give mushball a try. Our ball didn't get too mushy yet, but I can feel it softening. By the end of the summer, it should be even harder to hit far and easier to field with our bare hands. You can purchase a mushball on Amazon. I bought two because, like when I was a kid, it's inevitable that one will land on a roof or go down a sewer.

* * *

"Vintage 'Base Ball' Players Enjoy the Game as Played in 1864"

It's a beautiful day for base ball. No, that's not a typo. That's how the game was spelled until around 1902-03, according to Matt "Brandywine" Stone, founder and director of Central Valley Vintage Base Ball, which has four teams, including the Aetna Base Ball Club of Dixon, California.

Stone doesn't call it a league because it focuses more on history, education, culture, and community. He prefers the term "association." But the fifteen men who came out for Saturday's open scrimmage at Northwest Park in Dixon had a blast. The association includes three other clubs: the Oleta Vintage Base Ball Club of Davisville, the Sacramento Vintage Base Ball Club, and the Athletic Base Ball Club of Woodland.

Rick "Crash" Rohrback, the president of the Aetna team, said newspaper accounts reveal there was an Aetna Baseball Club in the mid-1870s. The club in Davis then was the Oleta Baseball Club, a rival to Aetna. Stone learned that a game was played on the Jerome Davis ranch in 1857 before Davis or Davisville even existed.

The games are played according to 1864 rules. Stone chose that specific year for a couple of reasons. First, before 1864, the umpires only called strikes, not balls. So a "striker" could be at bat for twenty or thirty pitches, and the game could drag on. Secondly, the "bound" rule had disappeared by 1865. That rule said that a ball fielded on one bounce was an out.

Rohrback noted that the bound rule makes the game

more inclusive. Players did not use gloves back then, so nobody uses them in the association's games. The very young and very old (he says they've had players from ages eight to eighty) are less intimidated fielding the ball because they can let it bounce once.

Stone called the ball used in 1864 the lemon-peel ball. It contains an ounce or so of India rubber wound with cotton or wool thread and wrapped in one piece of leather cut into the shape of a star, folded up on itself, and stitched.

The clubs only use one ball per game (they cost twenty dollars each). Rohrback noted that the ball is hard at the beginning of the game (they play nine innings) but has been bashed around so much that it is much softer by the end. So smart outfielders play shallower as the game progresses because the ball will not travel as far.

When the clubs played vintage teams from 1845-57 outside their association, they switched to a dark ball, which Stone called a quartered ball. It is made from four pieces of leather, contains no rubber, and is what he termed a "dead ball." In 1864 the typical bat was the wedge bat. It had no defined handle or barrel, a flat top, and was made from ash, maple, or hickory.

Saturday's scrimmage included some team members and some newcomers. Pitching is underhand from forty-five feet, and bases are ninety feet apart, so it is a mix of softball and baseball. The pitcher may not wind up and must have both feet on the ground during delivery, so getting enough leverage to throw the ball very fast is difficult.

But Stone noted that there wasn't a pitcher vs. batter mentality back in the day. "The idea behind 1864 baseball is to put the ball in play, to let everybody participate," he said. "And it still is. That's what we're trying to do with this program."

The Aetna club's roster is almost full, but Stone said the other three clubs desperately need more players. Although only men turned out to play in Saturday's scrimmage, all the clubs welcome women players. Rohrback said there is evidence that women played in the 1860s, although on all women's teams.

Dixon resident Chris "Pops" Thaiss joined the Aetna squad last summer after seeing a photo in *The Dixon Tribune* of some players with an invitation to come out to Northwest Park.

Now, about those nicknames. All the Aetna players have one. "*Crash*" is a California Highway Patrol officer specializing in analyzing car crashes as part of his office work. Stone is "*Brandywine*" because he first got interested in vintage baseball in 2014 via the Brandywine Vintage Base Ball Club of Westchester, Pennsylvania. When he moved to Davis and founded Central Valley Vintage Base Ball, he kept telling his fellow players about Brandywine—the beauty of the Brandywine Valley, the history of the Revolutionary War Battle of Brandywine Creek, and the base ball club there. So the players dubbed him "*Brandywine.*" "*Pops*" is so-named for a simple reason—his age. Chris "Express" Taylor works for Federal Express.

A self-described "history nut," Stone had never played baseball. But he was intrigued when he heard about the 1864 Base Ball Club of Brandywine. He played with them, even though he knew nothing about the game. He loved it. When he moved to Davis, he wanted to establish 1864 baseball here. His is now the only 1864 base ball association west of Denver.

Rohrback was more of a baseball nut. His father-in-law, Tom Andres, makes wooden bats. Stone happened to contact Andres by email about the bats, and when Rohrback heard about it, he "hijacked" his father-in-law's email, as he put it, reached out to Stone, and is now hooked on vintage base ball.

Thaiss said he is "a baseball guy going way back" who coached baseball for fifteen years. But he also loves history. He lived in Virginia for a time and developed a strong interest in Civil War history.

Stone started Central Valley Vintage Base Ball in late 2017. In 2018 he started developing the clubs and recruiting players. His association now has officers and a board of directors. Noah Plueger-Peters, the president of the Oleta Vintage Baseball Club, is also communications director of Central Valley Vintage Base Ball.

Stone has obtained a grant from California Humanities, the Schwemm Family Foundation, and the Yolo County Historical Society. This enables him to buy uniforms for all players and to reserve the fields for games so that players do not have to pay any dues.

This column first appeared in The Vacaville Reporter *on February 18, 2019.*

* * *

"'British Baseball' on the Playing Fields of Cornell"

You may remember the book *Paper Lion* (1966) by George Plimpton and the movie of the same name (1968). At age thirty-six, the author joined the training camp of the 1963 Detroit Lions on the premise of trying out to be the team's third-string quarterback. The coaches were aware of the deception, but the players were not until they saw Plimpton did not know how to take the snap from center. But Plimpton convinced the coach to let him take the first five snaps in an intra-squad scrimmage. Plimpton managed to lose yardage on each play.

One day, I found myself just as out of my depth as Plimpton. In my case it was on a cricket field.

But first let's talk cricket.

Most Americans think of cricket as an inferior brand of baseball designed for elderly Englishmen with short pants and knobby knees. Yet it requires the same amount of strength, coordination, quick thinking, and concentration as its American counterpart and is just as popular in England and most of her former colonies.

The baseball/cricket analogy was driven home in a *Sports Illustrated* article by English novelist John Fowles.

"All Americans need understand," Fowles wrote, "is that whatever the obvious superficial differences between the two modern games, they are both about precisely the same things: pitching and batting, catching and fielding, running and tagging bases."

In summer 1974, between my junior and senior years at Cornell University, I wrote about the Cornell Cricket Club, which was founded in 1903. I talked with Paul Salamanowicz, a Cornell junior who joined the club as a freshman. He was the only American on the club, which was made up mostly of students and professors raised in countries where cricket was as popular as baseball is in America.

Salamanowicz's mother is English, and his great grandfather was a cricketer in England at the turn of the century. At age fourteen, Paul came across some books on cricket and wrote about them to his grandfather in England. A few weeks later he received a cricket bat and some cricket balls from his grandfather.

"I felt like a Stone Age man coming under a strange influence," Salamanowicz reflected. "I didn't know exactly what to do with the things. I just started tinkering around with them in the backyard. My father wasn't too happy about it. He always wanted me to be a baseball player."

Clive Holmes, assistant professor of English history at Cornell, talked about the day he discovered the club in August 1969, a few months after arriving from England:

"My wife, Pat, and I had just come up from New York City to get settled at Cornell. It was very hot, and we were feeling kind of homesick, so we took a walk and happened to pass by Hoy Field. I looked out on the grass and I couldn't believe what I saw. 'My God, Pat! They're playing cricket!' I shouted."

Here's how the game is played:

In the center of the cricket field is a sixty-six-foot-long strip of smooth flat turf called the pitch. There are two bases, or wickets, one at each end of the pitch. The batsman stands at one wicket while the bowler faces him from the other. The bowler—a misleading term since the bowler throws overhand—generally makes the ball land a few feet in front of the batsman, who must hit the ball on a bounce with his paddle-like bat. He may hit it in any direction, since there is a 360-degree fair zone. But a pop fly is just as fatal in cricket as in baseball—an easy out.

Two players from the batting team, the batsman and nonstriker, stand in front of either wicket holding bats, while the bowler bowls the ball toward the batsman's wicket from the opposite end of the pitch. The batsman's goal is to hit the ball and then switch places with the nonstriker, with the batting team scoring one run for each of these exchanges.

The hard leather-covered cricket ball is slightly smaller than a baseball and slightly heavier. Although required to keep their arm straight from shoulder to wrist, the best cricket bowlers can hurl the ball at speeds approaching one-hundred miles per hour. The catcher or wicket keeper is provided with padded gloves, but the ten other fielders must use their bare hands.

If the ball knocks over the wicket, the batter is bowled, or out. The pitch is centered within a large oval boundary chalked on the grass. A cricket home run, called a "six" and good for six runs, is a blast that clears this boundary, usually 420-480 feet away, on the fly.

The batsman stays on the field until he is either bowled out (the ball knocks over the wicket), a fielder catches the ball in the air, or the fielder hits a wicket with the ball before a batter can cross the crease line in front of the wicket. A good batsman will remain on the field for a long time, scoring many runs.

One Sunday that summer, I traveled with the Cornell Cricket Club to a match in a nearby city to help me write my article. When we arrived, the Cornellians were short one player. Guess who they asked to play?

I felt just like George Plimpton, a fish out of water. But I was a pretty good baseball player, so when I stepped up to the wicket for my turn, I thought I could clobber that little cricket ball.

The very first pitch bounced in front of me, but as I got ready to swing, the ball changed direction (evidently the bowler had put some spin on it.) I took a mighty cut but just weakly popped the ball up to a waiting fielder. My turn was over.

There was no joy in Mudville. Mighty Matty had struck out.

A version of this column first appeared in the Ithaca New Times *on July 28, 1974.*

ABOOKS

ALIVE Book Publishing and ALIVE Publishing Group
are imprints of Advanced Publishing LLC,
3200 A Danville Blvd., Suite 204, Alamo, California 94507

Telephone: 925.837.7303
alivebookpublishing.com

www.ingramcontent.com/pod-product-compliance
Lightning Source LLC
LaVergne TN
LVHW041054080826
845145LV00007B/1575

* 9 7 8 1 6 3 1 3 2 2 8 0 8 *